# CULTURAL THEORY IN EVERYDAY PRACTICE

To Nymphea Agnes Bussell (1909–2007)
The Little General

OXFORD

# CULTURAL THEORY IN EVERYDAY PRACTICE

nicole **anderson**
& katrina **schlunke**

# OXFORD
## UNIVERSITY PRESS

253 Normanby Road, South Melbourne, Victoria 3205, Australia

Oxford University Press is a department of the University of Oxford.
It furthers the Universityís objective of excellence in research,
scholarship, and education by publishing worldwide in

Oxford  New York

Auckland  Cape Town  Dar es Salaam  Hong Kong  Karachi
Kuala Lumpur  Madrid  Melbourne  Mexico City  Nairobi
New Delhi  Shanghai  Taipei  Toronto

With offices in

Argentina  Austria  Brazil  Chile  Czech Republic  France  Greece
Guatemala  Hungary  Italy  Japan  Poland  Portugal  Singapore
South Korea  Switzerland  Thailand  Turkey  Ukraine  Vietnam

OXFORD is a trademark of Oxford University Press
in the UK and in certain other countries

National Library of Australia Cataloguing-in-Publication data

Anderson, Nicole.
Cultural theory in everyday practice / Nicole Anderson,
Katrina Schlunke.

9780195562453 (pbk.)

Includes index.
Bibliography.

Culture—Study and teaching.
Schlunke, Katrina.

306.07

Edited by Venetia Somerset
Cover and text design by Jo Groud
Typeset by Jo Groud
Proofread and indexed by Pete Cruttenden
Printed in Australia by Ligare book Printers Pty Ltd

# contents.

# contributors.

**nicole anderson** teaches in the Department of Critical and Cultural Studies at Macquarie University, Sydney, Australia. She is one of the founding editors of the international journal *Derrida Today* (Edinburgh University Press). She is author of a forthcoming book, *Derrida and an Ethics of Practice: Ethics Under Erasure*. She has published in the areas of bodies and technologies, visual culture (including film theory), deconstruction and Derrida studies, ethics and biopolitics.

**ruth barcan** teaches in the Department of Gender and Cultural Studies at the University of Sydney. Her research interests include feminist and other approaches to the body. She is the author of *Nudity: A Cultural Anatomy* (Berg, 2004), the co-editor with Ian Buchanan of *Imagining Australian Space: Cultural Studies and Spatial Inquiry* (UWA Press 1999) and one of the editors of *Planet Diana: Cultural Studies and Global Mourning* (UWS 1997). Her current research projects are on alternative therapies, including a book for Berg Publishers provisionally titled *The Body in Alternative Therapies: Cultural Practice and the Boundaries of the Senses*.

**anne cranny-francis** is Professor in Critical and Cultural Studies at Macquarie University, Sydney, Australia. Her most recent books are *MultiMedia: Texts and Contexts* (Sage 2005) on the semiotics of multimedia, and *Gender Studies: Terms and Debates* (Palgrave 2003). Her current research focuses on the relationship between embodied being and technologies (material, social, cultural) and includes studies of touch and of sound.

**vicki crowley** is currently the Director of Research in the School of Communication at the University of South Australia where she lectures in Cultural Studies. She has particular research interests in the cultural politics of the body and postcolonialism.

**jean duruz** is a Senior Lecturer in Cultural Studies in the School of Communication at the University of South Australia. Her research focuses on cultures of food and place within the everyday of global cities, and on ethnography. Current projects involve ethnographies of Ethiopian food businesses in suburban Adelaide, markets as cosmopolitan spaces in cities of South-east Asia and 'ethnic' neighbourhoods in New York City and Singapore. Publications from Jean Duruz's research appear in such journals as *Cultural Geographies*, *Space and Culture* and *Environment and Planning D,* and in edited collections such as Cheung and Tan's *Food and Foodways in Asia.*

**brett farmer** is a Lecturer in the Department of English at Chulalongkorn University, Thailand. He is the author of *Spectacular Passions: Cinema, Fantasy, Gay Male Spectatorships* (Duke University Press 2000) and numerous chapters and articles in the fields of cultural, media and sexuality studies.

**tara forrest** lectures in Cultural Studies at the University of Technology, Sydney. She is the author of *The Politics of Imagination: Benjamin Kracauer, Kluge* (2007) and the editor of a special issue of *Cultural Studies Review* on the topic of 'History Experiments' (2008).

**bob hodge** is a Professor in the Centre of Cultural Research at the University of Western Sydney and is widely published in the areas of social semiotics, cultural theory, postmodern studies, Australian studies, postcolonial studies and Latin American studies. His latest books are *The Multicultural Hypertext of Postmodern Mexico*, (with Gabriela Coronado) and *Borderwork in Multicultural Australia* (with John O'Carroll). Forthcoming in 2009 is *The Larrikin Principle: Advances in Organisational Studies* (with Gabriela Corronado, Fernanda Duarte and Greg Teale).

**nick mansfield** is Associate Professor in Critical and Cultural Studies at Macquarie University in Sydney. His books include *Masochism: The Art of Power*, and *Subjectivity: Theories of the Self From Freud to Haraway. Theorizing War: From Hobbes to Zizek* is forthcoming from Palgrave MacMillan. He is also one of the founding editors of the international journal *Derrida Today*.

**fran martin** lectures in Cultural Studies at the University of Melbourne. She is author of *Backward Glances: Contemporary Chinese Cultures and the Female Homoerotic Imaginary* (Duke UP forthcoming) and *Situating Sexualities: Queer Representation in Taiwanese Fiction, Film and Public Culture* (Hong Kong UP 2003); editor of *Interpreting Everyday Culture* (Arnold 2003); co-editor, with Peter Jackson, Mark McLelland and Audrey Yue, of *AsiaPacifiQueer: Rethinking Genders and Sexualities* (Illinois University Press, forthcoming 2008); and co-editor with Larissa Heinrich of *Embodied Modernities: Corporeality, Representation and Chinese Cultures* (University of Hawaii Press 2006). She also edited and translated *Angelwings: Contemporary Queer Fiction from Taiwan* (University of Hawaii Press 2003).

**stephen muecke** is Professor of Cultural Studies at the University of Technology, Sydney. A recent book is *Joe in the Andamans and Other Fictocritical Stories* (Local Consumption Publications, 2008).

**fiona nicoll** lectures in Cultural Studies at the University of Queensland. Her first book, *From Diggers to Drag Queens: Configurations of Australian National Identity*, was published in 2001. Her subsequent research within Cultural Studies incorporates critical race and whiteness studies and Indigenous sovereignties, queer theory and intersections of gendered and racialised drag performance. She was a founding member and former vice-president of the Australian Critical Race and Whiteness Studies Association and is currently working on a book examining cultural histories, practices, identities and policies related to gambling in Australia, Canada and the USA, *Governing Bandits: A Cultural History of Gambling in Australia: 1988–2008*.

**greg noble** is Associate Professor in Cultural Studies in the Centre for Cultural Research and the School of Humanities and Languages at the University of Western Sydney, Australia. His research interests include youth, ethnicity and identity; material culture and technology; and consumption, subjectivity and embodied practice. He has published widely on various topics and is co-author of *Cultures of Schooling* (Falmer 1990), *Kebabs, Kids, Cops and Crime: Youth, Ethnicity and Crime* (Pluto 2000), *Bin Laden in the Suburbs: Criminalising the Arab Other* (Institute of Criminology 2004) and *Lines in the Sand: the Cronulla Riots and the Limits of Australian Multiculturalism* (Institute of Criminology 2008).

**goldie osuri** lectures at the Department of Critical and Cultural Studies, Macquarie University. Her current research projects include work on transnational cultural formations that contribute to representations of national identities.

**joseph pugliese** is Associate Professor of Cultural Studies at Macquarie University, Sydney. His research areas include race and ethnicity, cultural theory, migration and diaspora, visual culture, embodiment and technology, terrorism and racial profiling, and cultural studies of law. His work has been published in international books and journals, including *Boundary 2, Studi Culturali, Law and Critique, Revue Internationale de Sémiotique Juridique, Social Identities, Borderlands* and *Studi Emigrazione*. He is currently researching the inscription of race in new and emergent technologies such as biometrics.

**katrina schlunke** is a Senior Lecturer in the area of Cultural Studies and Writing, is a co-editor of the *Cultural Studies Review* and is currently working on a research project looking at Captain Cook and natural histories. She is the author of *Bluff Rock: Autobiography of a Massacre* (2005).

**linnell secomb** teaches in the Department of Sociology, Criminology and Cultural Studies at the University of Greenwich and has also taught in philosophy and gender studies in a number of Australian universities. Her research areas include social philosophy, gender theory, politics and ethics. She has recently completed a book titled *Philosophy and Love: From Plato to Popular Culture*, co-published by Edinburgh and Indiana University Presses. She is currently working on two further projects: on cultural representations of terrorism and on friendship, politics and the problem of community.

**elizabeth stephens** is a Research Fellow in the Centre for the History of European Discourses at the University of Queensland. She has published widely in the areas of queer theory, gender studies and poststructuralist theory. She is currently completing two monographs: *Anatomy as Spectacle: Public Exhibitions of the Body from the Nineteenth Century to the Present* (forthcoming with Liverpool University Press) and *Queer Writing: Homoeroticism in Jean Genet's Fiction* (forthcoming with Palgrave Macmillan).

**nikki sullivan** is Associate Professor of Critical and Cultural Studies, and Director of the Somatechnics Research Centre at Macquarie University. She is the author of *Tattooed Bodies: Subjectivity, Textuality, Ethics and Pleasure* (Praeger 2001) and *A Critical Introduction to Queer Theory* (Edinburgh University Press 2003), and has published widely on a variety of body modification practices.

**theo van leeuwen** is Dean of the Faculty of Humanities and Social Sciences at the University of Technology, Sydney. He has published widely in the areas of critical discourse analysis, multimodality and visual semiotics. His books include *Reading Images: The Grammar of Visual Design* (with Gunther Kress), *Speech, Music, Sound; Multimodal Discourse: The Modes and Media of Contemporary Communication* (with Gunther Kress), *Handbook of Visual Analysis* (with Carey Jewitt) and *Introducing Social Semiotics*. His new book *Global Media Discourse* (with David Machin) appeared in 2007. He is a founding editor of the journal *Visual Communication*.

**audrey yue** is a Lecturer in Cultural Studies at the University of Melbourne. She is co-editor of *Mobile Cultures: New Media in Queer Asia* (Duke University Press 2003) and *AsiaPacifiQueer: Rethinking Gender and Sexuality* (University of Illinois Press 2008). Her current research includes queer Asian migrations in Australia and cultural policy in Singapore. She is the co-recipient of the 2008 Barbara Falk Award for Excellence in Teaching at the University of Melbourne.

# acknowledgments.

This book began with pleasure. It was the remembered pleasures of seeing, for a moment, when we grasped and were touched by a theory, how knowledge worked and the laughing excitement that that produced. And it was the desire to pass some of that along, or to at least provide the material from which students could create their own moments of pleasure. It was in the corporeal pleasure of the theory that we knew so clearly the practice of it.

We were also a bit cross. We seemed to be living in an academic moment when the value of 'doing' (practising) theory was being belittled by some, as if it were something that could be taken up and put down on an academic whim, when it was such a vital and sustaining force. We also noticed our students disconnecting themselves from the idea of theory because they were exposed to the idea from a few that there was theory and then all the fun stuff. This was not what we remembered and it was not what we intended to teach or write.

When we began discussing with contributors 'theory in practice and practice in theory' we were delighted with the ease with which the idea was understood and the need for the book acknowledged. Our contributors make the book with their diversity of approaches and topics, their writings that are themselves examples of practice as theory and theory as practice and their scholarly imaginations. We thank them also for their adherence to deadlines, their diplomatic negotiations of requested changes, their charming courtesy and their collegial friendship. In this community of Cultural Studies scholars we became excited once more about the work that is being done and the work that will be done. Thank you Ruth Barcan, Anne Cranny-Francis, Vicki Crowley, Jean Duruz, Brett Farmer, Tara Forrest, Bob Hodge, Nick Mansfield, Fran Martin, Stephen Muecke, Fiona Nicoll, Greg Noble, Goldie Osuri, Joseph Pugliese, Linnell Secomb, Elizabeth Stephens, Nikki Sullivan, Theo van Leeuwen and Audrey Yue.

The idea of theory as a new way of thinking about history or politics or feminism or philosophy was passed onto us by a range of teachers-friends and we would particularly like to thank Ruth Barcan, Lennard J. Davis, the late Greg Denning, Jane Hobson, Liz Jacka, Lesley Johnson, Sara Knox, Jenna Mead, Philip Mead, Nick Mansfield, Julie Marcus, Catherine Mills, Stephen Muecke, Greg Noble, Joseph Pugliese, Penny Rossiter, Linnell Secomb, Susan Stryker, Elizabeth Stephens, Nikki Sullivan and Carolyn Williams. We would also like to thank our current and previous postgraduate students who constantly challenge and support us.

For their generous willingness to read drafts, comment and encourage the writing we would like to thank Anne Cranny-Francis, Bob Hodge and Jean Duruz. And a very special thanks to Nikki Sullivan for teaching us about gender and sexuality, and body modification. And to Kelly Greene, photographer and graphic artist *extraordinaire*. When discussing the aim of the book with Kelly, her description of Cultural Theory in visual terms was amazing and inspiring. We would also like to thank our colleagues for their support amid numerous demands on everyone's time. The first part of the introduction of this book, written by Nicole Anderson, was based on a talk Nicole gave at a symposium called 'Re-framing Art: The Conditions of Theory'. For the invitation to speak about theory at this symposium many thanks go to the organiser, Blair French, executive director of Artspace: Visual Arts Centre, Sydney.

For her willingness to pitch and develop this project we would like to thank our first editor at OUP, Lucy McLoughlin, and for taking over the project upon Lucy's departure to the UK we would like to thank Karen Hildebrandt, who has been a calm and reassuring force. For her willingness to care about more than our commas we would also like to thank our tireless copyeditor, Venetia Somerset, for making this a better book.

Our partners, family and friends have been wonderful all of the time. Much love and thanks to our partners Pete Evans and Susan Brock. And in no particular order, to our ever-evolving family and friends: Danni Anderson, Jane Phillips, Oscar Phillips-Anderson, Jacq-Jacq Reilly, Andrew Reilly, Paddy Reilly, John Anderson, Ann Hull, Ruth Ritchie, Jhonnie Blampied, Clare Anderson, Sheila Evans, Chris Armstrong, Jan Idle, Pip Nicholson, Jan Schlunke, Catherine Robinson, Tara Forrest, Virginia Watson, Lyn Hughes, Fiona Nicoll, Sarah Gardner, Stephen Muecke, Pru Black, Diana Caine, the Film Gals, the Ping Pong Players and so many others who helped sustain this work directly and indirectly.

Finally we would like to acknowledge each other! The task of co-editing requires the sometimes abrupt, sometimes continuous slide in and out of one another's lives as the space to write is hacked out of existing schedules in well-planned hours and unscheduled slabs. We enjoyed it!

*Nicole Anderson & Katrina Schlunke*

# introduction.

## 1. theory ←——→ practice.

AUTHOR: nicole anderson

This book is organised around the premise that theory is practice and practice, theory. What this means is that both theory and practice (in)form each other, and that the separation between the two is not so clear-cut. One of the aims of the book, then, is to demonstrate the ways in which theory and practice slide into each other. This is not to suggest, however, that there is simply one theory or one practice. Because the other aim of this book is to show the myriad theories and practices and their combinations. At first sight it may not appear that these are the aims, given that there are seven parts, each devoted to a particular theory. But on closer reading, what we hope reveals itself is the way in which even the parts and the chapters within them blur with each other. For example, Cultural Studies practitioners use various theories, so a chapter that is within, say, the Postmodernism part could easily fit into the Bodies and Embodiment part, and so on. Having claimed that theory and practice (in)form each other, we want to begin a discussion of what is commonly meant by 'theory' and then what is commonly meant by 'practice'. Hang on! But by proceeding with a discussion of theory first and practice second, are we not also perpetuating a divide between theory and practice, one that we attempt to blur performatively throughout the book? Yes. But if everything were blurred, if there were no separation between terms, the book would fall into meaninglessness: a form of endless textual freeplay. So we think separation or divisions (differings and deferrals) between words, language, bodies, texts, things, objects and so on are necessary. Terms can only be blurred if there is division or separation in the first place. Drawing attention to these divisions is also a means of bringing to the fore the way they operate discursively within culture and society. So before the rest of the book plays with the boundaries/ separations/divisions between theor(ies) and practice(s), we would like to begin by maintaining the separation in order to define the necessary questions: what is theory? And what is practice?

## theor(ies).

In order to come up with a definition, we may begin by turning to a dictionary. The Oxford English Dictionary tells us that theory is:

**4a)** A scheme or system of ideas or statements held as an explanation or account of a group of facts or phenomena; a hypothesis that has been confirmed or established by observation or experiment, and is propounded or accepted as accounting for the known facts; a statement of what are held to be the general laws, principles, or causes of something known or observed. **4b)** an art or technical subject which consists in the knowledge or statement of the facts on which it depends, or of its principles or methods, as distinguished from the *practice* of it. **4c)**. A systematic statement of the general principles or laws of some branch of mathematics; a set of theorems forming a connected system: as *the theory of equations, of functions, of numbers, of probabilities*. **5.** In the abstract (without article): Systematic conception or statement of the principles of something; abstract knowledge, or the formulation of it: often used as implying more or less unsupported hypothesis ...: distinguished from or opposed to *practice* (cf. 4b). **in theory** (formerly **in the theory**): according to theory, theoretically (opp. to *in practice* or *in fact*).

But this is confusing. Is theory a hypothesis or is it abstract knowledge, and what is the difference? Turning to a thesaurus, we find that theory is synonymous with hypothesis, knowledge, supposition, postulation, speculation, theorem and so on. And synonymous with knowledge are the terms enlightened, learned, educated, informed, ascertained, known, and so on. If theory is knowledge, and knowledge is synonymous with the educated, does this mean that only those who are educated are knowledgeable? Or can you only practise theory if you are educated? Is theory simply 'highbrow' and practised by an elite small number of people? We will return to this point shortly.

Meanwhile, what the synonyms make obvious is that the word theory is slippery: there is no single definition. The problem is made acute when we start to think of how varying disciplines define theory. In fact there are more theories than there are disciplines: from transcendental, humanist to empirical; ethnographic to scientific; structuralist, poststructuralist to postmodern; there are ethical and moral theories; theories of language and linguistics; of embodiment; psychoanalysis; philosophy; economics; there are film, literature and art theories, not to mention critical theories and cultural theories. All of which define themselves in different ways through their differing methodologies, as you will see by the parts in this book. And within disciplines there are also varying definitions. For instance, within the humanities, theory is defined as either 'the art of making or understanding or *judging* the world around us in a way that we did not see previously' (Booth 2003: 2); or as 'the undermining of complacent presuppositions' (Galison 2003: 381); or it's 'a methodological *self-consciousness* about critical practice' (Chandler 2003: 317); or finally, it's a way of '*interpreting* the world anew' (Harooturian 2003: 398).

Despite the varying definitions and applications, what becomes obvious is that they are all imbricated with not only differing methodologies, but also consequently with differing ideological and political positions (some transcendentally based, others empirically, and yet others immanently). It is precisely because theories are political that they compete as truth-claims about the world: claims that may be, ultimately, incommensurable (meaning incapable of being measured, judged, interpreted or considered comparatively). If there is any apparent commensurability it is due to the political, ethical and historical norm of an era and is therefore *contingent*. To put it another way, theories are contingent because we can never step outside history or language to know if their foundations are truly 'transcendental' (and by this we mean that which is universal across or throughout time and place). Therefore, theories are contingent because they are situated within a particular historical and political context. In this sense theory can also be defined as an **embodied** mediation, which we will discuss in more detail further on. Given this, we can probably safely conclude that there can be no single unified definition of theory or theory itself. This is despite the fact that, in the history of Western philosophy, attempts at a unified theory in the form of grand narratives have been, and continue to be, sought. And this unified theory in the form of grand narratives is discussed in the Introduction to Part 3, Postmodernism.

It seems, then, that any attempt to define theory in any absolute way can only lead to an infinite regress (that is, a theory of theory requires a theory and so on ad infinitum). Does this mean we should not do theory? Does it mean that theory isn't useful and that we should abandon all attempts and leave it to academics to fight it out among themselves about which theory makes the best truth-claim about the world? Is theory simply 'highbrow' and only for the educated? While there are varying definitions and practices of theory, what we can say is that whether or not we are educated, high school or university students, plumbers, accountants, housewives or academics, all of us are always already implicated in the production of knowledge. And knowledge, and the production of it, is always already mediated and therefore theorised in one way or another. So what does it mean to say that knowledge is mediated?

Any experience and perception of the world is always already mediated by languages such as words, numbers, images and sound and bodies, but also by socio-cultural habits, beliefs and knowledges. Let us give you a hypothetical example. Say, for instance, that my partner comes home with a puppy. I am not going to go out and buy it a cot, or a dummy, as I would a human baby. Instead I am going to buy it dog food and some chew toys. What in effect I am doing is interacting with the puppy based on my knowledge that it is just that, a dog, a puppy. But in interacting with it as a puppy, I don't make a list about how to do that, or a list about how dogs are dogs, because my knowledge is based on what I 'know' about 'dog-ness' in general. And I 'know' about dog-ness because it has been passed on to me by socio-cultural knowledge. In another culture that knowledge about dogs might be different: it might involve seeing the gift of a dog as something one should, and would be rude not to, eat. What we are attempting to demonstrate here is that we do not have any ideas, feelings, behaviours or experiences that are not unmediated. And we could define experience as the affect/effect of the relation between knowing and '**being**' in the world.

The relation between knowing and being means that even the most banal assertion, opinion or statement is an affect of a range of ideas and practices that come together over time. This relation between knowing and being is what the French **phenomenologist Maurice Merleau-Ponty** calls 'bodily knowing'. In other words, we learn knowledges, like not picking our noses in public, through **mimesis**, that is, in and through bodily comportment (through becoming human). What all this means is that theory (as that which mediates and at the same time produces knowledge of the world) is also embodied. Thought or thinking, then, does not exist apart from or separated from bodies. (This is a 'theory' outlined in more depth in the Introduction to Part 1, Bodies and Embodiment.) Therefore, to mediate is to create, construct and to embody the world in which we live. To be human is to mediate, and to mediate is to theorise. That is, in mediating the world we are at the same time theorising about the world. And in theorising particular realities, we are also constructing them.

Of course, there are 'theories' about what constitutes or counts as mediation. For example, as I discuss in the Introduction to Part 2, Poststructuralism, a humanist position would try to establish a separation between experience, that is, the relation between knowing and being, and mediation; so that mediation reflects a single true reality. Another theory, a poststructuralist one, might argue that experience and mediation cannot be separated and that they (in)form each other, implying that there is never one experience and never one true reality (a transcendental signified) underlying mediation. There are theories that fall between the two. And even if we agree that to mediate is to theorise, we can still argue that the term be understood in either an idealist or transcendental, or a materialist theoretical paradigm.

So where does this all lead us? We have ascertained that there is more than one theory competing for truth-claims about the world. We have also ascertained that despite the various definitions and applications of theory, experience (the relation between knowledge and being) is always mediated, thus we always already mediate the world: there is no knowledge, perception or experience that is unmediated, and so to mediate is to theorise about the world around us (why it works the way it does, why it makes us feel, think, behave in certain ways, etc.). So the question now becomes, not what *is* theory, but what *kind* of theory? And *how* explicit, overt or rigorous is the theory going to be? And *which* theory is best (for the objects and cultural phenomena/experiences we are conceptualising)? Is there a distinction between theory and practice? And most politically and ethically important, what are the consequences of the theor(ies) by which one lives?

Answering any of these questions presupposes that there *is* a use to theory. In our economic rationalist society there is, as Terry Eagleton has put it, a 'conviction that anything which is not useful, which has no immediate cash-value, is a form of sinful self-indulgence … Even our thoughts must be rigorously instrumental … Unless thinking is directly tied to doing it is worthless' (Eagleton 2003: 86–7). And unfortunately, theory in the humanities has had a bad rap, marked in the press and by politicians, and by some academics even, as serving no use, no cash-value outcome. There are at least two reasons for the importance of theory (and we use this word 'theory' to suggest multiple theories, not one unified theory). First, theories of whatever form and in whatever discipline produce 'critical self-reflection', especially when they are juxtaposed or compared with each other. This is because comparison enables one to evaluate, analyse and discriminate between worldviews and applications, and in doing so creates an awareness, a comprehension, a recognition of how and why we experience the world and others the way we do. It brings to the fore that our experiences are embodied and mediated through gender, race and class, and that therefore there are myriad experiences and realities, not just one. In producing critical self-reflection, theory also enables us to consider the material effects of particular forms of knowledge/theory and political practice.

At this point you may object and state that what is being perpetuated in this discussion of critical self-reflection is the idea that some forms of mediated experience are better than others, and that learning to be critically self-reflective means applying theory through the use of rational skills. It is, you may be thinking, a form of 'high theory', where the privileging of rationality or reason (theoretical analysis) creates a hierarchy between reason and general assertions, opinions or statements on the one hand, and knowledge as embodied on the other. In this way, an autonomous rational subject is privileged over other possible subjects. Granted, but what should we do? Deny theory altogether? The problem with denying theory, saying it is of no use, or that it just perpetuates a rationalistic discourse that is privileged over other forms of mediation, is, ironically, to theorise. It is to make a judgment, an interpretation, to form a hypothesis (that is, a theory) about the use of theory.

In the humanities there have been many who have claimed that because they think that theory is of no use, theory is dead. But those making this claim have to acknowledge that there is theory, precisely because to make this claim is to theorise. If they don't acknowledge this, then the onus is on them to show that there is anything outside theory: and to do so would be to theorise! And since experience, or the relation between knowledge and being, is mediated, this is going to be a difficult task. Now, as we have suggested, the onus is also on those making this claim to define what they mean by 'high' theory. And as we have seen, this will lead to an infinite regress, precisely because it entails opposing 'theory' to something else: non-theory or medium or low theory, and/or theory and practice, theory and life, and so on, which is not necessarily the most productive of responses to the homogenising tendencies of the knowledge industry. The other problem with this hierarchy is that it not only places rational value judgments on what theory is best to use (high or low theory, etc.), but that this value judgment inevitably disavows difference (the different ways in which we mediate and understand the world).

Despite this hierarchy and the problems it inevitably entails, this does not mean that rationality (which produces theories) is of no value, or that we should not theorise (because right now we are theorising and using cognitive and rational skills to do so). Theory, even as it entails rationality, is of value because, as we mentioned earlier, it produces critical self-reflection, which enables us to consider the material effects of particular forms of knowledge/theory and political practice. But this brings us to the second reason why theory is important. Critical self-reflection produces, at least potentially, responsibility. Responsibility means recognising our complicity in rational discourses, but it also means acknowledging that 'recognition' (critical reflection) is not simply cognitive, but also, at the same time, tacitly embodied knowledge and bodily response. In acknowledging this we take responsibility for the fact that we are (all of us) imbricated in the theoretical. And acknowledging this is not to deny theory, or to say it has no use; it is to think about the benefits of theories. One of the benefits is that it is precisely because various theories produce differing interpretations and experiences of the world that dialogue can be opened. And dialogue is responsibility, because dialogue produces responsibility as a 'sharing' that does not close down debate, which would result in a denial of difference and of the uniqueness of context, but instead moves towards democracy. What this book attempts is to open dialogue by presenting various theories and their approaches and applying them to various texts, events and practices. One of the aims is to produce a movement between the various theories, exposing their contingency, revealing how they are similar or different to each other and thus opening a dialogue between the theories themselves. The book is divided into seven parts revolving around a particular theory or theoretical approach to thinking about the world around us and everyday practice (and this will be discussed in more detail in the section below). And while it could be seen that making these divisions between theories simply reiterates a theory/practice divide—or more aptly a theory/theory divide—part of the reasoning for creating these parts is to demonstrate, in and through the essays that make up each one (since each essay in fact uses a number of theoretical approaches), that the boundaries between theories and between theory and practice are never pure and stable but continually blur into one another. Without recognising that there are divisions (no matter how arbitrary and contingent), this blurring of theoretical approaches perhaps would not be so obvious. In other words, the juxtaposition of theories through these divisions invites comparisons, which contribute to critical self-reflection. Furthermore, without the divides in the first place there would be nothing to blur, and the notion of interdisciplinarity, and theoretical pastiche (so evident in Cultural Studies) would not exist.

# practice(s).

What we hope this discussion of theor(ies) has revealed is that the distinction between theory (of whatever type) and practice is not only a constructed one, but that practice is always in and of itself theoretical. What do we mean by this? And, what does it mean to practise something? To practise something is to *do* something. It is an activity that is done either once or habitually, like reading a book, watching a film, cooking, putting on clothes, housework, walking, listening to music or driving a car. While we may only see a particular film once, the act of going to watch a film and sitting in a theatre from the start to the end of a film is a social-cultural practice, with particular rules. There are two levels of practice operating here. First, there is the actual activity of watching a film (whether once or for the second time it doesn't matter). Second, there is the embodied knowledge of *how* to watch a film, which is a general knowledge of how to go about doing that particular practice (generally you are not supposed to talk through a film, rattling of plastic can be considered offensive, you generally sit and watch the film in the dark, sometimes you have popcorn or chocolate).

Another example: feelings or emotions are a form of practice because they are a learnt and habitual activity (that is, response) to particular behaviours or actions. Going swimming might make you happy, being criticised might make you depressed, angry or sad. And we learn what behaviours, actions or things make us happy, sad, angry. Finally, 'practice' can also be defined as institutional practices: medicine (the practice of medicine, of healing people), the practice of education, the practice of government, and so on. In this sense there is always a set of discourses that helps to maintain and perpetuate or create the rules and the socio-cultural embodied knowledge that are associated with certain practices.

So practice is an activity and our everyday lives are made up of these practices, which produce or make meaning. What we mean by this is that a practice is meaning-making when it generates a range of meanings for consumers or viewers or readers. So to take a walk would for some readers produce meaning in that the practice can be read (or analysed). Taking a walk (depending on context) could be analysed or read as someone needing exercise and fresh air or needing a break from conversation with family and friends, or someone who is angry and needs to walk it off. Now, the fact that meaning is made or can be produced by practices suggests that all practices are not only interpretable, but in being interpretable are mediated. And as we mentioned earlier, because thought or thinking does not exist apart from or separated from bodies, and because all practices produce or make meaning, all practices are theorised in various ways. The fact that we can analyse or interpret a practice as meaning a particular thing in a particular context means that we theorise about *why* practices produce certain meanings and not others. Given this, it might be more useful to say that there is no practice without theory, no theory without practice. Or more aptly, practice *is* theory, and theory *is* practice. What would a practice be that could not be analysed or interpreted and thus made meaningful? Would it exist? So, again as we mentioned earlier, if practice is theory and vice versa, then the real questions become: *what* kind of theory? And *how* explicit, overt or rigorous is the theory going to be? And *which* theory is best (for the objects and cultural phenomena/experiences we are conceptualising)? For example, we could theorise someone leaving his or her home to go for a walk as someone needing or wanting some exercise. To speculate or interpret in this way is to theorise. But we can go further. We could decide to interpret the practice of 'walking' in general by applying a particular type of theory, and making the application of this theory explicit and rigorous. For example, we could produce a reading of the cultural practice of walking by applying a deconstructive theoretical approach (using the work of Derrida, for instance). In this way we could then introduce a little rigour into our initial interpretation or analysis by suggesting that the notion of walking is socially and culturally perceived as a *good* activity (because it helps lower obesity rates that have risen in Western culture in the past decade) as *opposed* to 'sitting' and watching TV or playing computer games, which are perceived and believed by some to be *bad* activities. On this basis we could theorise that Western culture, at least in this era, privileges exercise over and above sedentary practices, so that what is constructed (as deconstruction teaches) is a binary opposition where exercise is opposed to and privileged over sedentary practices. This means that the values attached to exercise and thus certain types of bodies—fit, healthy, slim—also become privileged, while obese, sedentary or unhealthy bodies are marginalised and discriminated against. Often in Cultural Studies a combination of theories is used to understand the 'meaning' of a practice (or text). For example, to become even more rigorous, we may add to deconstructive theory some theories of globalisation. For instance, not only can we examine the way in which the binary opposition between exercise and sedentary lifestyles forms a hierarchy where exercise is privileged over sedentary practices, and thus privileges and values those bodies that exercise over those that don't, but in turn, by applying some theories of globalisation, we could argue that only bodies that are situated within a certain class structure (middle- to upper-class) can in fact afford the time to take exercise (working-class people are too busy working longer hours). We could then use theories of race, and gender, and embodiment to push this analysis even further if we wanted.

The point of this example is to show at a basic level how various theories help us to understand and create the meanings we attach to cultural-social practices. And this, in turn, helps us to rethink the ways in which our particular cultural practices represent us and produce us as particular (classed, raced, gendered, sexualised) individuals (or **subjects**). By rigorously applying or using theor(ies) to think through why and how a practice is enacted and perpetuated in Western culture, we can construct ourselves as politically and ethically aware (critically reflective), and therefore potentially able to effect change.

# what is cultural studies?

What is evident from this discussion of practice is that Cultural Studies is interdisciplinary. In tertiary education a discipline is a traditional field of study (English literature, anthropology, philosophy, biology) with its own rules and discourses and methodologies for studying a particular practice. For instance, the discipline of English literature studies literature from a particular perspective, which involves a style or method of reading and interpretation: it might, for example, apply theories of metaphor and language to help reveal the meanings within a book. While theories of metaphor and language may change over time, often the field is defined by an obvious or dominating approach or method that distinguishes it from other disciplines. Generally speaking, you would not find the discipline of English literature using anthropological theories and empirical approaches. You may on occasion find this, but then this practice would not, perhaps, be defined as a disciplinary but rather an interdisciplinary approach. To be interdisciplinary, then, means to apply or combine methodologies and theories from two or more disciplines, in order to think about and understand a 'practice' differently. In other words, by viewing a practice from various disciplinary perspectives, what can be produced is critical reflection about that practice's role and value in a culture and society.

Cultural Studies is interdisciplinary in precisely this way, and there are a couple of reasons for this: generally, for Cultural Studies practitioners, teachers and researchers, there is not one true or right interpretation of a particular practice, and thus never one true reality. Across Cultural Studies departments, the types of practices examined and the types of theories are diverse, and also the level of rigour employed to examine practices. However, while Cultural Studies is interdisciplinary in this way, what is common to most Cultural Studies analysis of practice is the notion of representation. Traditionally representation means that things like the arts (painting, photography, television, film, etc.) function to depict, portray and symbolise aspects of the 'real' world. In Cultural Studies this use of the term representation has been contested, and in fact there are theories (such as postmodern or poststructuralist, or textual theories) which argue that to represent something is not to represent some ultimate truth about reality, but rather in representing someone, something, the world, we are simultaneously creating or shaping that reality, or the world we are attempting to present. So the clothing we wear, the cars we drive, the music we listen to, for instance, are all forms of representing to others not only our individual desire and tastes, but our cultural and social positioning. In other words, on an individual level, every day we represent ourselves through our clothing, the books we read, the food we eat, and as a culture we represent ourselves to other cultures and to ourselves through film, documentaries, books published, political speeches, technology, media and multimedia, architecture, government policy on immigration, work laws, refugees, war, economic policies: for instance, the way in which the USA represented itself in and through government policy on the Middle East has been argued to have led to the 9/11 terrorist attack. In a nutshell, we can say that Cultural Studies is *the study of the ways we represent ourselves to each other*. To put it a different way, we adopt various theories to study how we represent ourselves in and through our practices, and this is what makes Cultural Studies diverse and interdisciplinary.

Given all of this, this book is not an attempt to absolutely define what Cultural Studies or cultural theory *is* (it is constantly evolving and changing); rather it is concerned with providing various Cultural Studies theoretical perspectives on the world and everyday life, and thus to provide a range of essays that articulate what Cultural theories *do* (or more aptly, the theoretical *doings* in Cultural Studies). So, in juxtaposing various theories, and in revealing the symbiotic relationship between theory and practice, the book aims to foster critical self-reflection as well as dynamic creative directions and perspectives in thinking about the world and everyday life and practice.

# 2. style(s): theory, performance and creative production.
AUTHOR: katrina schlunke

## moving in and out of theory and practice.

Theory *in* practice isn't always pretty. And it often isn't comfortable. But it can be exciting and work like a thunderbolt of connection between you and the world, and in particular between you and others. Perhaps you got up this morning and had a shower? If you live in a water-poor country like Australia you have already stepped into the most fraught environmental politics of the moment. If you have any history of watching western films you may shiver with some recall of the shower scene from *Psycho*. And if you operate within Western traditions of hygiene you will believe yourself to be making yourself clean and participating in a common, shared practice that is so banal, so everyday, that to question how we came to consider showers ordinary is to engage in a pointless trivial exercise. But this moment of ordinariness, this moment of 'common sense', is perhaps where we experience power in its greatest intensity. That is, when power produces unquestionable practices in which masses of people participate readily and with true hearts. What to do? Cultural Studies gives us three basic steps. First, what are the exact conditions and style of your shower-taking? Describe it in detail; include the sensations of heat, running water, your own embodied experience. Note the material environment: the quality of the tiles, the brand of soap, the hour, the music, the complaints from other bathroom users about the length of time you're taking. Leave nothing out, including how you might feel about writing out this detail about such an event that is often understood as a private one. There must be enough complexity in your description for you to use it as a case study, as a particular performance within a particular context for you to draw comparisons or make connections with others' experience. The act of writing this in itself begins a process of making the familiar strange and the strange familiar. Second, who has written about domestic rituals, histories of hygiene, made films featuring showers or used particular images in advertising or water-saving campaigns? How does your description 'fit' with their accounts? How does your experience jar with or contradict theirs? Third, what will explain the connections and/or absence of connection between the accounts? How does your pleasure in the shower mean that the *Psycho* scene works in a particular way? How has a shared idea of cleanliness arisen so that water-saving campaigns can ask for shorter showers but not advocate having a shower only once a week? How can the contradictions of wanting to be understood as superclean and a good environmental citizen be resolved? Are such campaigns doing the right thing in emphasising time rather than rethinking whether showers need to be private given the history of communal bathing?

This third step can be a thunderbolt experience. You may just realise what a really good water campaign could look like: you could help save the planet. Or you might now step into the shower uncomfortably aware of the gendered order of body cleanliness—no more easy daydreaming in the shower. Or something else entirely could happen. There are no guarantees when we connect our thinking to other thinking. There are no guarantees about what a change in our practice might produce. But what we would hope from this book is that you will continuously connect thinking and doing. The critical practice described above should lead to a creative re-theorisation and a creative inventing of new practices. Observe, connect, create.

The first example began with your body and your practice, but an equally accessible position is when we are pulled into events outside our immediate experience when we read a headline, participate in a web forum or get caught up in a YouTube controversy. Think of catching sight of a headline on a billboard, or on a small screen in a lift or as a news flash banner across your personal computer that says: Four Americans killed by car bomb in Iraq. In our information-rich environment we will quickly, via Google and other sources, find out where, when and why. Eventually you may discover the names and positions of those killed. But information alone will not help you to understand how this event came to be worthy of international coverage, why you were drawn to read it or what the story hides as it appears to tell all. As a viewer you have already participated in this event (consciously or not) and so your position as an actor within the event does not disappear, but this time you may begin with existing and established connections. That is, in an effort to understand the event of that headline you will start with a set of knowledges like **Orientalism** or ethnographies of audience or globalisation and television—and work through that practised thinking to reinterpret what is on your screen being 'read' (seen, heard, experienced) by you. By doing that you will have created another understanding and capacity to make different kinds of stories, or the same kind of news stories in a knowing way.

# conclusion.

While *Cultural Theory in Everyday Practice* does offer an explication of the theories that Cultural Studies employs, it also brings together theory and practice in a unique way. It does this through a range of essays by various cultural practitioners and scholars with varying styles and theories. In this way the book offers concrete, but varied, examples of ways in which theories engage with practices. By offering more than one example in each theoretical part, the book reveals that there are not only many theories and many practices to which theory can be applied, but also many styles of writing; many styles of thinking about and articulating cultural practices and everyday life. *Cultural Theory in Everyday Practice* offers 'performative' examples of how theory is utilised in an analysis of cultural practice and everyday life. In presenting essays that apply theory to various cultural practices, the book aims to provide readers with concrete examples of how to go about writing and thinking theory in relation to everyday life *and* vice versa. This book has been divided into parts that offer different points of connection as well as a practical body of theory to work with. The divisions between the parts should be imagined as flexible, contingent and porous. They are there to signal the key focus of the work that is contained in them. But you will soon find that, like a pack of cards, these chapters can be reshuffled to make an order to fit things that happen to you in a world that will never be categorised quite so easily. Let's go back to the shower for a moment. That single experience, that moment of theor(ies)/practice(s) would move between ideas of embodiment, sex and sexuality and ideas of self and others. Your engagement with this book should not only be about reading it but about conducting some experiments, making up some new texts so that your new knowledges can be seen in new forms of practice(s)/theor(ies). Good luck.

# 1

# bodies and embodiment.

# the stories so far.

AUTHOR: nicole **anderson**

## the mind/body opposition.

The French philosopher **Jacques Derrida** argues that **Plato** inaugurated binary oppositions (Derrida 1981; Harvey 1983: 124), which have constructed Western ways of thinking and perceiving the world and 'reality'. Examples of binary oppositions include male/female, nature/culture, inside/outside, speech/ writing, white/black. Derrida tells us that these oppositions are never neutral or universal; rather they are hierarchical, in that one term in an opposition is always privileged over the other in a particular culture, or in a certain historical era. For instance, male is generally privileged over female, speech over writing, and so on. Furthermore, each term depends on the other for its meaning, no matter which term in the opposition is privileged. For example, take the binary opposition inside/outside: there would be no concept of an 'inside' without reference to and understanding of the 'outside', and equally no understanding of the outside without a concept of the inside. Despite this, binary oppositions are governed by an either/or distinction, which operate to organise and classify events, objects and relationships, and the way human beings think.

One such binary inaugurated by Plato was the mind/body opposition. The result was that in the history of Western thought the mind, in one way or another, has been privileged over the body. In the *Meno*, Plato constructs this opposition in and through his discussion of the soul. He tells us that the soul is different from the body and thus it does not depend on the body, which acts simply as a vessel for its existence. In other words, the soul can exist without the body, or the soul is that which exists in a disembodied state.

While this kind of binary thinking about the soul/body has persisted since the Greeks, it culminated in the thought of French philosopher **René Descartes** in the 17th century. Descartes opposes the 'mind' (the 'thinking thing' or 'self-consciousness') to the body. That is, he argues that the thinking thing is separate from the body in which the thinking thing arises. In summary, in his famous *Meditations on First Philosophy*, Descartes postulates the following:

1   He rejects the 'senses', and thus the body in which those senses arise, as unreliable for ascertaining the 'truth' or knowledge of reality (the world around us) and God. What Descartes is looking for is the foundation of metaphysics. Metaphysics can be defined as that which grounds the questions of God, Being, reality, morality, truth, etc., in absolute and fundamental principles. So he claims that the senses cannot give us a means for determining the foundations (absolute principles) of metaphysics.

2   For Descartes the only way we can be certain about metaphysical foundations is through the 'mind' (which he defines as the thinking thing, which in turn involves rational and self-conscious thought). He believes that the 'mind' is the only way to produce certainty and dispel scepticism. But how does the 'mind' produce certainty and become the basis for metaphysical foundations? Descartes requires that we suspend judgment about anything that can be doubted (which is nearly everything). We are also asked to suspend judgment, or doubt the *way in which* we come to know the world: through our memories, our senses, and so on. Once we have realised that all of these things can be doubted and that our memory and senses (and at times our reason) are unreliable, what can we be certain of? Descartes claims that the only certain point, the only thing that can never be doubted, is the fact that the 'I' can think. In other words, I can think, or be aware, that I am thinking. (In thinking what becomes certain is that there is something, and not nothing, because I am 'aware' that I am thinking, and doubting.) All doubt in fact arises from this thing that thinks. This has been famously summed up in the phrase *cogito ergo sum* (I think, therefore I am).

3   Having established that the one true certainty is the thinking thing (*res cogitans*), and that this thinking thing is the means for determining metaphysical foundations, Descartes then privileges the mind over the body, and consequently gives preference to rational cognition over the senses derived from matter. Descartes defines matter as 'extended substance', which is characterised by the length, breadth, depth, size, shape and forms of observable phenomena. Interestingly, he considers matter (and thus the body) as involving nothing more than 'extended substance'. As we will see shortly, this is important because it subsequently influenced the idea of the body as simply a biological phenomenon that does not influence or contribute to the

mind. In his last book *Passions of the Soul*, Descartes argues that intellectual pursuits (reason or thinking) belong to the mind, and physiological and chemical impulses to the body. However, he concedes that sensations and emotions involve both mind and body, and thus in these areas at least the two are intermingled. Yet despite this concession, what has had the greatest and enduring influence into the 21st century is this belief in the mind/body dualism: an opposition that privileges the mind.

# the subject, the body and biological determinism.

The mind/body opposition instantiated by the Greeks and perpetuated during the **Enlightenment** period by Descartes also led to the **humanist** version of the **subject**. The Enlightenment began in the 17th century and culminated in the 18th-century movement in Western philosophy that claimed rationality as the basis of all knowledge. The humanist notion of the subject was part of this movement, and developed out of Descartes' 'thinking thing'. As Vincent Descombes (1991: 121–2) puts it, the humanist version of the subject has developed from the argument that 'one thinking thing' cannot be distinguished 'from another thinking thing' unless those thinking things have identities. In other words, it is the ability for self-determination, characterised by free decision-making, rationality and autonomy, that not only defines the humanist subject in general but also produces individual identity. Our identity is not connected to our bodies; rather, identity is situated in the mind. And given that identity is located in the mind, and the mind is that which exists apart from the body and is therefore not located in a particular place or time, then for this particular brand of humanism there is an essential identity that exists outside or beyond any historical, cultural and social context. Consequently, during this time, and continuing today, the body came to be seen not only as a vessel that holds the mind, but simply a chemical and physiological network of chemical attributes and impulses. And it is because of this view that the body has come to be constructed in negative terms, while the mind occupies a privileged position in the social imaginary (Sullivan 2005: 3–4). This view of the body as simply a network of chemical impulses has led to a position called 'biological determinism'.

If one hypothetically takes as true Descartes' notion that the mind is separate from the body, it should follow that all 'minds' would therefore be equal (and universal) because the body is inconsequential and therefore notions of gender and race would mean little and have no political consequence. The irony is that it is precisely this view of the body as biological that has produced further binary oppositions that have deep political and ethical consequences. That is, the biological determinist position states that a person and his or her capacities and roles are determined by his or her biology. Or to put it another way, biological determinism assigns roles and values to the function of particular bodies (Sulllivan 2005: 4–5). For example, because a woman's body functions in particular ways, like giving birth to children, a role is given to female biology. Historically, the role assigned to women (albeit middle-class white women in modern Western societies), and based on the idea that they are 'biologically' equipped to raise children, is generally the role of home-maker. (And of course this role would depend on class and race, because for many working-class and ethnic families the roles of women vary, for example where both men and women have to work to feed their families.) What's more, this role is in turn assigned a 'value': the belief that women are nurturers and carers, rather than hunter-gatherer professionals (which is associated with males) (Rubin 1975). By contrast, women's bodies have been perceived (in modern society) as inferior to the ideal male body (conceived as strong, hard, tough, enduring, as that of a hunter-gatherer), because women's bodies have been aligned with the general historical construction of the female body as fleshy, subject to carnal appetites and desires that need to be constantly controlled by law and morality. So this biological determinist position has arisen from the mind/body opposition, leading to the further opposition between male and female, where the male and the male body has been, in the history of the West, privileged over the female and the female body. Implied here is yet another opposition between sex and gender (Deutscher 1998; Sullivan 2005). But rather than discuss this distinction, because it is discussed in detail in 'The Stories so Far' in Part 4, let us turn to an exploration of the political implications of, and problems with, the biological determinist position.

There are at least three problems with this position. First, it fails to take account of the way in which values are culturally constructed, and in doing so perpetuates sexual, gender, race and class discrimination, marginalisation and inequality. Moreover, assigning 'values' to bodies involves making moral judgments about those bodies. For example, in the history of the West 'black' bodies are considered inferior to white bodies and are thus assigned particular roles; in the past one of these roles was slavery. And in all Western democratic countries it was only in the 20th century that women (of any colour and class) were given the right to vote, since their bodies were for childbearing only, and the idea that a woman could think and have opinions was undervalued. The irony here is that this biological determinist position inadvertently reveals how our bodies inform **subjectivity** and our **identity** (that is, our identity is often based on, and develops out of, our assigned roles, or the roles we happen to construct for ourselves; this is called 'identity politics'). This is ironic given that biological determinism arose out of the mind/body dualism in which the body is simply seen as a network of physiological and chemical impulses. We will come back to this connection between bodies and subjectivity shortly. In the meantime the question we need to ask is where exactly do these values come from?

There are two dominant and opposed positions on this question: a social construction and a biological position. The social construction position, fostered mainly by various poststructuralist and feminist philosophers, developed in response to the biological determinist position and the negative political implications it has for bodies in the world. This position argues that the body, and subjectivity, are the product of politico-cultural systems. **Gayle Rubin**, for instance, points out that we only understand the notion of biology though particular cultural points of view, and that therefore 'we never encounter the body unmediated by the meanings that cultures give to it' (Rubin 1984: 276–7). In other words, as **Michel Foucault** also argues, we can only think (speak and write) in certain specific discourses and not others. In the same way, the body is the product of our particular cultural discourses, habits and values. That is, we read bodies according to the values and language surrounding bodies at a particular period in history. These moral and social values have been constructed by legal and educational institutions. The problem here is that the social construction position is in danger of privileging culture over biology, fostering and perpetuating an opposition. Meanwhile, one recent biological position states that our morals and values are selected by evolution: 'On the one hand we have selfish tendencies, which have obvious adaptive benefits, especially when we are in a competitive environment. On the other, we have altruistic tendencies selected to encourage us to cooperate with others, thus benefiting all' (*Cosmos* 2007, Issue 17: 53). What is being suggested is that morality (and thus human nature) is hard-wired along these selfish/altruistic lines, although there is no empirical evidence of this. And while the obvious implication is that there is no 'single morality, and no single human nature' (*Cosmos* 2007, Issue 17: 53) and that we can therefore determine the type of morality we want to adhere to, there is in this position a subtle and insidious danger. In suggesting that our biology (via evolutionary selection) determines our culture(s), the danger is that it implies that despite the varying cultural values that change across time and place, there is really only one essential 'human' culture based on the tension between selfish and cooperative selection. One problem with this is that it leads to the potential for homogenisation by denying the differences between cultures, which then raises various unanswerable questions: for instance, does homogenising culture lessen wars between cultures? Or does fostering difference between cultures—religious, ethnic, economic, cultural, social, political, etc.—lead to war? Another problem is that this biological position denies the way in which culture also shapes genes and thus evolution (more on this below). In other words, this position falls into an essential notion of human nature, and thus subjectivity; one that can never be changed because it is fixed by biology.

This discussion is part of the first problem with biological determinism: its failure to take account of the way in which values are culturally constructed. But related to this is a second problem, and that is its failure to take account of the way in which the body is affected by others and the environment around us, and the way our subjectivities are informed by, and form, the body. In fact there are other biological theories that take a different tack to the position outlined above, by arguing that culture can change our genes. For example, scientist Professor Christopher Wills of the University of California argues that 'there are also plausible ways in which culture itself could be driving natural selection'. In other words, he says that 'there has been, and still is, positive feedback between our culture and our genes that led to the rapid evolution of the most characteristic human attribute, the mind' (*New Scientist*, 11 March 2006: 32). In other words, our biology, our genes, are also shaped by culture. So the old notion that we have the cultures we do solely as a result of our biology and genes has recently been questioned by some forms of science. This questioning also undermines the common assumption that the mind is separate from the body. In fact, what it suggests is that the mind is part of the body: our bodies and minds are always shaped by our cultural and social environments, and that these cultural and social environments shape the way our bodies look and behave, which in turn shape our minds and vice versa. While this may be a new discussion going on in evolutionary science, the acknowledgment of the cultural construction of the body is not new for the humanities, or indeed for Cultural Studies. In fact this notion has been called 'embodiment', and the next section will outline some theories of embodiment.

Finally, the third problem with biological determinism has been outlined by **Judith Butler** in her book *Gender Trouble*. In relation to the biological determinist notions about gender and the body, she argues that the biological opposition between male and female homogenises the notion of 'woman', so that the differences between women (class, race, ethnic, sexual, political) are 'decontextualised' or cut off from their cultural and social 'specificities' or situations. Critiquing this homogenisation of women into one category (as if differences between women did not exist), Butler asks: 'Is the constitution of the category of women as a coherent and stable subject an unwitting regulation and reification of gender relations? ... To what extent does the category of women achieve stability and coherence only in the context of the heterosexual matrix?' (Butler 1999: 32). This question is taken up in Vicki Crowley's chapter on gender.

# theories of embodiment.

The mind/body opposition has perpetuated the idea that the mind, and thus subjectivity, is separate, in fact completely detached, from the body. On this view, the body has no influence on subjectivity and identity. The notion of embodiment challenges this mind/body dualism.

Let it be noted though that there is no single theory of embodiment. Rather, there are various embodiment theories: from philosophical to feminist to postmodernist, and so on. In what follows the focus will be on the theories of embodiment put forth by **Maurice Merleau-Ponty** (1908–61) and **Michel Foucault** (1926–84). The reason for focusing on Merleau-Ponty is because he is considered (along with **Marcel Mauss**) one of the early 20th century's most significant proponents of the notion of embodiment, not least because of his thorough and resolute pursuit of the topic in large volumes such as *Phenomenology of Perception* and *The Visible and the Invisible,* but also because of his influence on a later generation of philosophers (late 20th and early 21st century) such as **Pierre Bourdieu** and **Jean-Luc Nancy**, and feminists such as **Luce Irigaray**, **Hélèn Cixous**, Judith Butler, **Moira Gatens** and **Elizabeth Grosz** (the notion of embodiment for many feminists has advanced feminist theory by enabling a rethinking of the sex/gender distinction. This is addressed in Part 4, 'Sex and Sexuality', and it is why feminist notions of embodiment—of which there are many—are not the focus of Part 1).

## 1. Merleau-Ponty

For Merleau-Ponty the mind is not separated from the body (from matter or space), and therefore it is not separated from others or the world (as the humanist notion of the subject, outlined earlier, would have it). That is, the mind does not exist as a separate phenomenon within a body that acts simply as a vessel. Rather, the mind and body are entwined and they (in)form each other, and as a result we are 'embodied' beings. But what exactly does it mean to be embodied (to have our minds and bodies entwined)? The answer to this can be elucidated through Merleau-Ponty's notion of 'perception', which is the heart of his theory of embodiment.

Traditionally, to perceive means to observe and to be aware of the world outside the body. In some traditional philosophy, being aware of the world is to let that world impact on the passive mind: one that receives and processes information. For Merleau-Ponty, however, because the mind is not distinct from the body, and in turn, because the body inhabits the world and is not separate from it, perception (consciousness/awareness) is incarnated. What this means is that perception is a *lived experience*. Perception, then, is not simply a mind thinking or reflecting *on* the world (as if the world exists apart from the mind). Rather, we perceive information through our bodies, which create meaning through sensuous experience. Or to put it another way, perception does not simply receive information which it then gives meaning to; instead perception is already produced by preconceived understandings, meanings and knowledges of the world, as well as by social practices, so that 'there is no meaning which is not embodied, nor any matter that is not meaningful' (Crossley 1994: 14). In a nutshell, there is no thinking without the body. Thinking (the mind or consciousness or perception) is incarnate. The implication of this is that perception, unlike Descartes' notion of 'mind', is not universal, autonomous and separated from the objects of the world, but rather that the line between inside (consciousness, mind, perception) and outside (the world of objects and other people) is blurred. As Merleau-Ponty argues, 'inside and outside are inseparable. The world is wholly inside and I am wholly outside myself' (Merleau-Ponty 2002: 407). In fact, for Merleau-Ponty mind and body, perception and matter, constantly inform and change each other. But as Elizabeth Grosz makes clear, this does not mean that Merleau-Ponty valorises the body over the mind and thus reinstitutes another binary opposition; neither does it mean that in blurring the distinction between mind and body he affirms 'their unity and oneness in some kind of global or local holism (which always entails some kind of reductionism)' (Grosz 1994: 93). Rather, for Merleau-Ponty 'perception is ... mid-way between mind and body and requires the functioning of both' (Grosz 1994: 94).

## 2. Foucault

The reason for the following discussion of Foucault's notion of embodiment, one that has been informed by both **Friedrich Nietzsche** and Marcel Mauss, is because his work has been taken up by numerous Cultural Studies scholars, so much so that the impact of Foucault's work is endemic in the field. Furthermore, the three chapters in Part 1 in one way or another utilise and refer to Foucault's work in order to understand contemporary body practices.

As outlined in 'The Stories So Far' in Part 2, Foucault's **genealogical** analysis of the ways 'power' and 'knowledge' in culture and society emerge and operate in and through 'discourse' has also shaped his notion of embodiment (Foucault uses the term 'discourse' to refer to social knowledge, what he calls 'bodies of knowledge', which are scholarly disciplines: science, medicine, philosophy, psychiatry, and institutional disciplines: schools, hospitals, prisons, law courts). That is, for Foucault genealogy is the attempt to reveal the contradictory and non-linear aspects of historical events in order to show the influence power has on subjects and bodies. Like Merleau-Ponty, Foucault in his book *Madness and Civilisation: A History of Insanity in the Age of Reason* (1973) critiques Descartes' mind/body binary opposition and suggests that the subject (that is, 'mind') is an effect of power in the body. In other words, Foucault suggests that the notion that there is a soul or mind that exists apart from the body is not so much an illusion; rather the notion or perception is a result of the operations of power/knowledge. This is very similar to Merleau-Ponty's notion that perception is produced by preconceived understandings, meanings and knowledges of the world, as well as by social practices. In *Discipline and Punish* (1991), Foucault argues:

> It would be wrong to say that the soul is an illusion, or an ideological effect. On the contrary. It exists, it has a reality, it is produced permanently around, on, within the body by the functioning of a power ... This real, noncorporal soul is not a substantive; it is the element in which are articulated the effects of a certain type of power and the reference of a certain type of knowledge. (Foucault 1991: 29)

It is in *Discipline and Punish* that Foucault explores through history—in the ancient and visible examples of techniques of punishment such as public torture and execution through to the Christian confessional—how sovereign and disciplinary power produces techniques for constraining and controlling human beings, in order to bring them into accord with institutional and social norms. As Elizabeth Grosz rightly claims, Foucault's 'history of punishment can ... be seen as a variable series of technologies of the body. He shows how transformations in conceptions of subjectivity or self are a consequence of changing investments of power in the body' (Grosz 1994: 151).

Moving from an exploration of the history of techniques of bodily control, in his later work (*The History of Sexuality*) Foucault directly connects bodies of knowledge (discourse) to the operations of power on the individual body in modern society through the example of sexuality. For Foucault, power has direct access to the body at an individual level through forms of 'self-government' or 'self-surveillance'. As Ruth Barcan points out in Chapter 1, 'social control has ... come to take place less by visible external force [public torture, for instance] than via internalised self-surveillance'. That is, Foucault demonstrates the way in which power and knowledge in modern society are carried out by individuals on themselves. In modern society self-surveillance is a modern disciplinary technique that regulates bodies, and the mode of this confession and surveillance takes the form of divulging information (the modern confessional) to others about 'who' we are. Or it takes the form of the surveillance of our own appearance (fashion) and practices (such as yoga or dancing). And this modern surveillance is a means by which to create 'normal' bodies. Bodies of knowledge, then, produce normalising forms of bodily behaviour (sexuality) and understandings, in and through self-surveillance. Again, as Grosz argues, 'the deployment of sexuality, as one of the finer and more successful threads that bind knowledge-power to bodies, is not the promise of liberation but a way of tying individuals and groups ever more firmly to the biopolitical control of bodies' (Grosz 1994: 155). What better way to control bodies than to get those bodies to control, constitute and normalise themselves through the power of self-surveillance (Foucault 1980: 104). This form of self-surveillance power is what Foucault called **biopower**.

# cultural studies and embodiment ... where to next?

The implications of Merleau-Ponty and Foucault's theories of embodiment for notions of subjectivity have been quite profound, and have set the scene for a whole range of contemporary discussions on embodiment across several disciplines and theories from feminist to postmodernist. These contemporary discussions are reflected in, and have been taken up by, Cultural Studies in various ways. In general, notions of embodiment have enabled Cultural Studies scholars to think through not only how subjectivity and the body inform each other, but how the classed, gendered and raced body in its particular cultural-social situation constitutes subjectivity. Thus, what are explored in Cultural Studies are the unstable boundaries between the cultural (external) environment, the body and subjectivity (identity). The danger with this turn to exploring and celebrating the body is to inadvertently reverse the mind/body opposition, where the body becomes privileged and/or an object of fetishism. This fetishism can arise when bodily experience becomes the focus without thought of how that experience is mediated. Generally, however, this has been avoided by the work of Cultural Studies scholars, who draw on theories of embodiment (whether it be Merleau-Ponty's 'incarnated perception', Foucault's 'biopower', or any number of feminist theories of embodiment, such as Judith Butler's 'performative bodies' or Elizabeth Grosz's 'corporeal feminism') to analyse, evaluate and explore everyday contexts, texts, events and practices in order to unravel various current political and ethical consequences. For example, each of the three chapters in Part 1 applies a different theory to a particular text, event or practice: Ruth Barcan's Chapter 1 discusses the issue of theory and the application of theory. When discussing alternative therapies and the way it has been, or hasn't been, taken up in Cultural Studies, she astutely argues that a focus on body practices reveals the sociological and cultural effects of those practices. Barcan's chapter deftly outlines the way in which Michel Foucault's work, in particular his notion of biopower, can be used to think about how alternative therapies in contemporary society might be congruent with surveillance medicine, consumer culture and modern psychology, with the result of situating 'individual practices of body therapy within larger questions of the meaning of both health and illness in late modernity'.

Likewise, Vicki Crowley in Chapter 2 uses Foucault's work to explain the body as 'a site of power'. However, Crowley draws more on the work of Judith Butler, who was influenced by Foucault's notion of power. As discussed in 'The Stories So Far' in Part 4, Butler's notion of embodiment can be defined as bodily practices that are performed every day in the form of repeated acts. For example, gender is a performative effect that arises from repeated acts. These acts then 'congeal over time to produce the appearance of a substance, of a natural sort of being'. There is no 'natural' body/gender and thus there is no essential identity; rather they are constantly (re)constructed. Crowley outlines this theory, applying it to the example of 'intersex'. In particular, Crowley explores the 'stage *performance*' of Shorona (a person with an intersex body: neither male nor female) in the stage show *Gurlesque*, which makes social and political commentary on women's sexualities and bodies. Applying Butler's notion of performance to the stage performance, Crowley reveals the way in which not just staged bodies but everyday 'normal' bodies are also social and political constructions. This enables Crowley to question the binary opposition between male and female, thus bringing to light how our constructed bodies are normalised by a regulatory regime of power.

Finally, in Chapter 3, Anne Cranny-Francis argues that when analysing texts the sense of touch 'is rarely considered'. She argues that using 'sensory (rather than just verbal or visual) analysis enables us to explore the meanings created by our embodied responses to these texts'. Drawing on contemporary theories on touch and the senses, she analyses the work of the famous sculptor Ron Mueck, who uses contemporary materials such as resin and fibreglass to reproduce the human figures with the visual appearance of real skin (with hairs, moles, freckles, calluses, rough patches). The point of this analysis is to demonstrate how we experience the world and create meaning, not just through the visual and verbal but through touch, and thus through bodily positioning.

# THINKING WITH THIS SECTION
when reading the three chapters in this section think about the following:

- o    How does each chapter apply theory to the particular event, text or practice they are discussing? How does Barcan apply Foucault's notion of 'biopower' to alternative therapies? How does Crowley apply both Foucault's and Butler's notion of body performance to the stage performance of Shorona, who has an intersex body? How does Anne Cranny-Francis apply theories of touch to sculpture?
- o    While Barcan, Crowley and Cranny-Francis discuss and use various theories of the body, they apply these theories in different ways. In other words, the application itself is a methodology, an approach to apply to theory and practice. There is, therefore, more than one theory operating within each chapter. Reflect on the mode of application each uses. For instance, Barcan does two things simultaneously. First, her application of Foucault involves a form of critical theory (that is, a form of problematising and self-reflection) about the everyday practice of alternative therapies, and what that means for our identities, 'allowing us to ask *why* certain kinds of bodily experience might be valued by particular kinds of person or in particular social contexts'. So the 'application' of Foucault's work is a method of critical theory. Second, she turns this application (this form of self-reflection and problematisation) onto Foucault, thus revealing the limitations of Foucault's own theory. Again, Crowley's application of Foucault and Butler's theories to intersex bodies is a form of critical self-reflection that makes us as readers aware of how bodies are constrained by normative gender roles (heterosexual male and female roles). And Anne Cranny-Francis applies current theories on touch in order to produce a textual analysis (in particular, an analysis of generic conventions and reader/audience responses) of Ron Meuck's resin sculptures. That is, Cranny-Francis uses Mueck's work to reveal the way cultural meanings around notions of bodily touch are represented.

Now reflect and evaluate on your bodily and gender experiences:

o   What kinds of bodily experiences do you value? What kinds of bodies does Western
    society value and perpetuate?

o   In what ways are we positioned in society by our gender? How are you positioned
    into performing in certain ways or feeling certain things? Or to put it another way,
    as a man or woman, how are you expected to act in certain roles? For example,
    think back through some interactions that you have had with others in the last
    few days: you might recollect an interaction that you had with a colleague, a
    friend, a student, family member, stranger, doctor. Pick one interaction and try
    and identify how your gender was reaffirmed and/or played an important part of
    the interaction. Did you notice how you were positioned, or expected to behave
    in terms of your gender? Turn to the author's chapters and find a paragraph or
    passage where you think this application of theory to understand a particular
    practice occurs. Discuss and compare your example with others.

Now reflect on the mind/body split discussed above:

o   How does the mind/body split foster a belief in an essentialist subjectivity or
    identity?

o   Can you think of everyday practices or situations where the mind/body split
    is continually reinforced? What are they? For example, by disconnecting the
    relationship between mind and body, a humanist autonomy, where the individual
    is seen as separate and distinct from the world around them and from others, is
    perpetuated and enforced. In this way, the mind/body split and the essentialism
    it fosters fail to account for the way the body, and thus identity, is affected by
    others around us. We can see the mind/body split operating in our language,
    our discourses, our institutions and our ethics and values. The mind/body split is
    carried out in and through essentialising discourses. For example, think about how
    star signs (Sagittarius, Leo, Virgo, etc.) or the Chinese zodiac (snake, goat, dragon,
    etc.) might perpetuate essentialism.

# CHAPTER ONE

# alternative therapies as disciplinary practices: the uses and limitations of a foucauldian approach.

AUTHOR: ruth barcan

## INTRODUCTION

In a powerful conclusion to the preface to his book *Governing the Soul*, Nikolas Rose cites a comment from the great German writer Johann Wolfgang von Goethe: 'I too believe that humanity will win in the long run. I am only afraid that at the same time the world will have turned into one huge hospital where everyone is everybody else's humane nurse' (Rose 1999: xxv). *Governing the Soul* is an analysis and critique of the modern therapeutic drive, inspired by—and often beautifully echoing—the work of **Michel Foucault**. It is an exemplary critical reading of the psychological disciplines, the kind of careful critical work that typifies the best of Cultural Studies, and that demonstrates the usefulness of a Foucauldian perspective as an analytical tool.[1]

My current long-term research project is on New Age/alternative therapy practices in modern Australia. For a Cultural Studies writer interested in such practices, it makes obvious sense to turn to Foucault and to the critical lineage his work on biopolitics and discipline has engendered. This chapter outlines the 'obvious' applicability of a Foucauldian approach to alternative therapies, drawing primarily on *Discipline & Punish* (1979a) and *The History of Sexuality,* vol. 1 (1979b) as well as on Foucauldian-inspired work like that of Rose and the sociologist David Armstrong. A Foucauldian approach potentially gives rise to a reading of alternative therapies as part of what Armstrong (1995: 398–9) calls 'surveillance medicine'—a medical regime in which the distinction between health and illness has become blurred, and everyday life increasingly medicalised. The rise of alternative therapies represents a new type of surveillance, where the vigilance of external bodies is supplemented to greater or lesser degree by *self*-monitoring, *self*-'management', *self*-surveillance. From such a perspective, alternative therapies would figure as exemplary instances of disciplinary practices. They represent not so much the imposition of external social control as the transformation of health into a set of daily, internalised, often pleasurable body practices bound up in personal identity work.

Foucault's work aims to chart how particular orderings of the body, and especially sexuality, are produced in different historical contexts. Rather than considering the body as a potential ground of being, as in the **phenomenological tradition**, he is concerned to see how a particular **episteme** (Foucault's term for the largely unconscious **epistemological** paradigm of an era) produces particular kinds of subjects and bodies. In other words, he sees the body 'as an effect of **discursive** power' (Turner 1992: 52). As a historian, albeit an unconventional one, his focus is on what is distinctive about the *modern* ordering of the body. How did we moderns come to be who we are today? he asks, a question that forms part of his long-term project to write what he called 'an **ontology** of the present, an ontology of ourselves' (Foucault 1986: 96). Foucault's work relativises and historicises our understanding of the body. Although he has been accused of a certain romantic nostalgia for the 'untrammelled, uncivilized, prediscursive body' (Turner 1992: 54), he himself claimed that his work was animated precisely by a rejection of the kind of nostalgia that imagines bodies, sexuality and subjects as 'some ineffable humanity' (Rose 1999: viii) corrupted by the social order and that longs for 'a form of power innocent of all coercion, discipline and normalisation' (Foucault 1980: 117). For Foucault, power does not 'crush subjectivity'; it 'actually fabricate[s] subjects—human men, women and children' (Rose 1999: viii). As he puts it: 'it is not that the beautiful totality of the individual is amputated, repressed, altered by our social order, it is rather that the individual is carefully fabricated in it, according to a whole technique of forces and bodies' (Foucault 1979a: 217).

Perhaps the two key Foucauldian concepts of use to a study of alternative therapies are that of **biopower** (and related concepts like discipline) and the confessional. A useful starting point is Foucault's dramatic contrast, in *Discipline and Punish* and *The History of Sexuality*, between ancient and modern modes of power. In ancient societies, he claims, power took the form of the right to take life, whereas in modernity it is increasingly 'power over life' (Foucault 1979b:

139). The spectacular opening to *Discipline and Punish*, where Foucault contrasts the gruesome public execution of a murderer with the bureaucratic regimes of a modern (19th-century) prison, is used to illustrate this fundamental shift in both the reach of state power and its mechanisms. He contrasts the public spectacle of the monarch's power with the much more hidden, bureaucratic and seemingly humane or edifying workings of modern disciplinary power. Social control has, he argues, come to take place less by visible external force than via internalised self-surveillance—'the government of the self by the self' (Foucault, quoted in Bernauer & Mahon 1994: 119).[2] Every society has modes by which people come to know and govern themselves, but these modes differ from society to society. In the modern disciplinary society, we ourselves are frequently part of the mechanism of power, having largely internalised external power into subtle and powerful forms of *self*-regulation, *self*-surveillance. 'Our society is not one of spectacle', Foucault writes, 'but of surveillance' (Foucault 1979a: 217). Foucault isolates two aspects of this modern power over life, which he considers to be its 'twin poles': the disciplining of the body and the regulation of populations. Both of these are forms of what he terms 'biopower' (Foucault 1979b: 139).

One of the core modalities by which (self-)surveillance occurs is via a technique (or a 'technology') that he calls the confessional: a concept he derives from its literal sense as the Christian practice of confession before a priest. In modern times, he argues, this religious ritual is a relatively minor form of power, but its basic mechanism has spread throughout modern society, in the form of a vast array of truth-telling practices before socially constituted 'authorities' (doctors, teachers, therapists, judges). In some circumstances a confession is forcibly extracted, as in the legal system, where it may be 'driven from its hiding place in the soul, or extracted from the body' (Foucault 1979b: 59). More often, however, it is freely given. We have become, he says, 'a singularly confessing society' (Foucault 1979b: 59). Ritual confessions of the truth of ourselves have the function of actually *constituting* ourselves as beings with inner depths in need of explanation, declaration, expiation or liberation. Paradoxically, though, these seemingly liberating confessions are part of the webs by which we are tied in as members of the modern state. We are, in Nikolas Rose's (1996: 17) beautiful formulation, not so much 'free' as *obliged* to be free. Biopower and its various mechanisms are thus not simply repressive—a means whereby governments and other powers regulate their societies—but also productive, in the sense that disciplinary techniques make us who we are. The inherent ambiguity of these techniques is evident in Foucault's characterisation of them as 'centr[ing] on the body as a machine: its disciplining, the optimization of its capabilities, the extortion of its forces, the parallel increase of its usefulness and its docility, its integration into systems of efficient and economic controls' (Foucault 1979b: 139). Modern human subjectivity is, then, inherently paradoxical: we are disciplined into being free. Foucault deliberately calls into play the doubleness of terms like 'subject' and 'subjection' to describe this process: we are simultaneously made into people and/as we are subjected to power.

# alternative therapies as disciplinary practices.

Given the establishment of this conceptual apparatus in the contemporary humanities, it is by now a fairly straightforward matter to produce a Foucauldian reading of alternative therapies. They are, after all, a prime example of investing in depth (searching for the inner self through working on the outer body); of disciplinary techniques (the weekly yoga class, the meditation practice, the regular massage); and of a widespread uptake and internalisation of an injunction to manage one's own health, which not incidentally serves the efficient economic management of populations.

The Foucauldian perspective thus situates individual practices of body therapy within larger questions of the meaning of both health and illness in late modernity. David Armstrong argues that in modern biomedicine (his exemplary instance of surveillance medicine), no longer is illness coterminous with the physical symptoms reported by a patient—part of a logic in which health and illness are 'distinct clinical categories' (Armstrong 1995: 395). Rather, it is dispersed and distributed more nebulously. If this is true of biomedicine, it is even more so of alternative medicine, in which illness is widely understood as part of the much broader category of 'dis-ease', whose 'symptoms' include everything from physical illness to relationship breakdown to business failure or spiritual malaise. In its extreme New Age formulation, all disease is one ('all disease comes from a state of unforgiveness' [Hay 1987: 14]) and all life problems are symptoms of the same disease ('When people come to me with a problem, I don't care what it is— poor health, lack of money, unfulfilling relationships, or stifled creativity—there is only one thing I ever work on, and that is LOVING THE SELF' [Hay 1987: 14]). It is hard to imagine a more manifest example of what Armstrong (1995: 395) calls the 'problematisation of the normal'. We are *all* 'precariously normal' (1995: 396); we are *all* patients (1995: 397).

Alternative therapies are part of a larger set of formations (spiritual, psychological, consumerist and medical) in which the conception and experience of **subjectivity** itself are distinctively modern. Foucault's work provides a way of connecting discourses (ideas, beliefs, **ideologies**, ways of thinking and speaking) and institutions (church, state, legal system) to the creation of actual subjects and bodies, for 'the body is the historical outcome of formations of power/ knowledge which actually produce different orders of body' (Turner 1992: 94). It can illuminate the workings of four interwoven kinds of production: of discourse; of forms of knowledge and expertise; of new forms of subjectivity; and of bodies. Alternative therapies can be examined from each of these perspectives.

The question of discourse has proved the most obvious starting point for Cultural Studies. I have argued elsewhere (Barcan & Johnston 2005) that Cultural

Studies has displayed a surprising reluctance to engage with alternative therapies, despite the fact that they are exemplary instances of popular body practices with, moreover, significant implications for gender. The few Cultural Studies analyses that have emerged engage with alternative therapies primarily as discursive phenomena, via readings of New Age or alternative texts. Rosalind Coward (1989) and Jackie Stacey (1997), for example, have produced highly critical discursive analyses of the language and concept bank of alternative medicine, in particular the discourses of nature, holism and authenticity.[3]

We could also use Foucault's work to explore the new kinds of subjects produced by this discourse, not only the new raft of authorities with special expertise over body and soul (from the yoga teacher to the masseur), but also the patient-client-consumer-spiritual questor assumed and produced by these practices. Here I am thinking of alternative therapies as modes of confessional practice. Just as the Christian confessional constituted the self as 'a **hermeneutical** reality, an obscure text requiring permanent decipherment' (Bernauer & Mahon 1994: 146), so many alternative therapies are interwoven with or underpinned by ideas of the self as 'a hidden treasure trove to discover and explore' (Shumsky 1996: 30). In the spiritual paradigm underpinning alternative medicine, life is a journey of self-discovery, since 'all the answers lie inside of you, deep within your own heart of hearts' (Shumsky 1996: 31). Foucault's work alerts us to a central paradox around the idea of the quest for our 'true' self and the 'free' communication of its inner secrets: that this quest in turn imposes its own constraints on our liberty. Practitioners and clients of alternative therapies alike would be horrified that a critical theory with an interest in human freedom should think of their practice as a form of bondage, but for a Foucauldian, seemingly voluntary confessions, no matter how compassionate the setting—such as the truths produced by and for the client of alternative therapies—are the benign cousins of those 'wrung from a person by violence or threat' (Foucault 1979b: 59). The Foucauldian paradigm warns us not that their benevolence is a 'cover' for some deeper conspiracy (that would be to subscribe to a **Marxist** notion of ideology that Foucault [1980: 118] explicitly rejects), but that their very benevolence is captivating. We are the willing agents of our own enmeshment, and we are thus bound into the state as useful, efficient, 'docile' bodies.

Such a perspective would, against the grain of a standard social analysis, see alternative medicine as an extension rather than a critique or rejection of biomedicine. It is a new and even more insidious form of biopower, since it is pleasurable and seemingly freely chosen. The state's project of the active prolongation of life, via the management of bodies, has been taken on (and paid for!) by the individual, who now becomes the responsible 'manager' of his/her own health. This project involves not the repression but the active production of bodies. Self-knowledge, enhanced health, responsibility, the prolongation of life—all these might seem laudable goals, but when understood as bound up in historically contingent conceptions of individual self-mastery, they appear rather less benign, as in Rose's condemnation of the 'ethical paucity of the contemporary obligation to fulfil ourselves through the mundane achievements of our everyday lives, and to evaluate all aspects of our lives in terms of the extent to which they do or do not contribute to such an inexorable trajectory of self-improvements and lifestyle maximisation' (Rose 1999: xxiv).

This is certainly a good way to understand how alternative therapies are both medical and pop-consumer practices. They are a form of surveillance medicine that is also bound up in the individualism, hedonism and narcissism of consumer culture, whose insistence on a healthy, youthful and ideally beautiful body gives rise to a range of what Mike Featherstone (1991: 182) calls 'body maintenance' techniques, of which the massage, the yoga class and the iridology reading could be read as just some examples. Read this way, alternative therapies emerge as part of the 'appeal to the rationality of self-preservation' (Featherstone 1991: 183) and the hedonistic consumerist injunction to look good and stay 'young'. Featherstone sees these consumerist imperatives as part of a culture of narcissism that points to a 'new relationship between body and self', one with significant stress on 'appearance, display and the management of impressions' (1991: 187).

This section has suggested that alternative therapies can plausibly and usefully be read as a consumerist extension of surveillance medicine, in which medical surveillance has increasingly become part of a project of individual self-formation, often connected to the pursuit of 'lifestyles'. Later on, I will argue that this is a limited reading of the phenomenon, but first I want to elaborate a little more on what this approach enables us to understand.

# the value of a Foucauldian approach.

Clearly, such a counter-intuitive and **denaturalising** analytical lens has much to offer. The Foucauldian approach allows us to get *behind* beliefs that people might hold. As Foucault repeatedly insists, this is less about ideology—about how people are duped—than about how certain beliefs, ideas, priorities, values and assumptions come actually to *function* as true in a given historical context. This is what is meant by the common assertion that Foucault sees power as productive rather than repressive. This 'productive' process may be as insidious, if no doubt less brutal, than older 'repressive' forms of power.

With Foucault, we can see some of the complexities of power: how subjection and subjectification are inseparable, how interior and exterior worlds are interwoven. A Foucauldian approach allows one to critically examine the costs of contemporary forms of subjectification and the 'obligation' to be free (Rose 1996: 17). Late-modern freedom, says Rose (1999: 231), presupposes and produces an autonomous choosing self whose health and happiness are understood as the outcome of individual choices made as part of a universal quest to make a meaningful life for oneself. For a Foucauldian, such a freedom is at best equivocal:

> We have been freed from the arbitrary prescriptions of religious and political authorities, thus allowing a range of different answers to the question of how we should live. But we have been bound into relationship with new authorities, which are more profoundly subjectifying because they appear to emanate from our individual desires to fulfil ourselves in everyday lives, to craft our personalities, to discover who we really are. Through these transformations we have 'invented ourselves' with all the ambiguous costs and benefits that this invention has entailed. (Rose 1996: 17)

Our individual lives, our regular body practices, our hopes and fantasies connect, then, to a bigger social picture. The use of alternative therapies is not just a matter of individual lifestyle 'choices' or even of social trends, but is connected to much bigger orderings of power-knowledge and much more abstract conceptions of selfhood itself. Through the Foucauldian lens, we can see how the biggest of big pictures (the modern episteme) connects with the micro-activities of everyday life (for example, the weekly yoga class). We can see that governance and self-governance are related, and that the relationship between the two operates differently in different historical periods. In the case of alternative therapies, we can see how particular health practices connect up to the governmental regulation of health and of populations, as well as to other aspects of the social formation, such as consumerism.

The Foucauldian paradigm, then, is an invitation to see how interior worlds and social worlds are organised and how these different orders of existence are interlinked. In the case of alternative therapies, it allows us to ask whether individual and social wellbeing are really best assured by teaching people that their life should be a never-ending quest for psychological wholeness and/or physical health and/or spiritual awareness. From this perspective, such a quest is not only doomed to failure (for, it would be argued, psychological wholeness, spiritual awareness and so on exist as illusory ideals) but it is also at best a waste of human time, money, creativity and hope—energies that could, some might argue, be better spent on more political ways of improving the human lot. At worst, this quest is a harnessing of human potential in the service of state power, an example of 'the meticulous, concrete training of useful forces' (Foucault 1979a: 217).

I write as both a fan and a regular user of alternative therapies. So how can I reconcile my admiration for the Foucauldian approach with my regular and pleasurable use of these therapies? Well, in one sense, the Foucauldian paradigm never splits pleasure and power in the first place—indeed the pleasurability of these practices, freely chosen, would be precisely the point. But do I consider my occasional relaxation massage, for example, to be an example of 'the optimization of [my body's] capabilities, the extortion of its forces, the parallel increase of its usefulness and its docility' (Foucault 1979b: 139)? Well, yes, in so far as it keeps me going: keeping me able to meet the multiple demands placed on me as an academic, mother, partner, family member and dutiful citizen. This chapter, for example, has been powered by orange, sandalwood and lavender oils, chamomile tea, a CD of Westernised yoga chants and a yoga nidra relaxation tape. So how do I meet the more serious charge: that these practices are not just about simultaneously securing and obscuring my docility, but that they are part of an ethically impoverished contemporary mandate to 'fulfil myself'? Let me avoid this difficult question by turning the spotlight back onto the Foucauldian paradigm itself, at least until I can think of an answer.

# limitations of the Foucauldian approach.

Foucault's analysis of the role of self-surveillance in the construction of modern selves and bodies, and the role of knowledge, expertise, institutions and authority in this process, is an outstanding contribution to the understanding of contemporary society. Once one has learnt to see the world through this lens it is hard to imagine ever 'unlearning' it. This is by no means always a pleasant thought, at least if one wants to remain relaxed and comfortable. As Rose argues:

> Foucault's own work shows that we can question our present certainties—about what we know, who we are, and how we should act—by confronting them with their histories: this experience can prove more unsettling and provocative than either the exposure of empirical errors or the formulation of conceptual critiques. (Rose 1999: x)

This type of critical enterprise is avowedly political: foregrounding the values that underpin it, often in contrast to analytical modes that pretend to be objective or value-neutral.

The project of unsettling, denaturalising and problematising commonsensical, **hegemonic** or taken-for-granted ways of seeing the world is a hallmark of many types of contemporary critical theory. It allows us to see how certain things came to be as they are (the infamous 'history of the present' [Foucault 1979a: 31]), to ponder the question of whether they might have been otherwise, and to speculate about how they might yet be changed. Some forms of critical theory (such as feminism, or critical race theory) have a stronger commitment to this latter question than others. For Foucault, who held no belief in revolution, the question lies outside his aims; his work is not a defined political program so much as a warning that 'everything is dangerous, [and that] we always have something to do' (Foucault 1983: 231–2). But the 'moral disgust' (Turner 1992: 21) that arguably underpins his analyses of processes of normalisation implies a longing for, if not a belief in, some better way of ordering knowledge, bodies and in particular sexuality. This is, perhaps, what Bryan Turner (1992: 54) means when he accuses Foucault of a certain romanticism, despite Foucault's overt and repeated repudiation of narratives of liberation.

Foucault's conception of power means that he cannot but reject a revolutionary politics and rhetoric, but repeated warnings that 'everything is dangerous' are ultimately not intellectually or politically nourishing or sustainable for a discipline that claims to be in the business of cultural change. Something more precise and useful than a rhetorical flourish ('we always have something to do') is required if not of Foucault himself, then of any discipline that incorporates his approaches to such an extent that they start to resemble a 'method'. Inevitably and legitimately, readers might begin to hope that the end or goal of this criticism might be something other than to repeatedly show that things might have been different and that we have to be careful.

There is nothing new in getting impatient with certain programmatic and romantic tendencies in Cultural Studies. **Meaghan Morris** (1990: 22) famously argued many years ago that in Cultural Studies politics was all too often reduced to a restrictive 'proliferation of ... restatements' with a banally redemptive conclusion (1990: 26). Eight years later, Tony Bennett (1998: 25) critiqued what he saw as a residual romanticism in Cultural Studies, arguing that the discipline is 'concerned more with cultivating a certain ethical style and demeanour than with the pursuit of any practicable courses of action with specific political or policy goals in view'.[4] More recently still, **Eve Sedgwick** (2003: 124) has compellingly argued against another form of critical reflex, arguing that the hermeneutics of suspicion that underpins contemporary theory has become a 'habitual practic[e]' to the detriment of other ways and styles of analysis. Suspicion, she argues, has become 'a mandatory injunction rather than a possibility among other possibilities' (Sedgwick 2003: 125), to the point where to theorise out of anything *other* than what she calls a 'paranoid critical stance' has come to seem 'naïve, pious, or complaisant' (2003: 126). What she calls paranoid reading strategies are a vital part of the 'ecology of knowing' (2003: 145), but they are just one strategy. Their unquestioned use may, she claims, 'unintentionally impoverish the gene pool of literary-critical perspectives and skills' (2003: 144). As Sedgwick's critique suggests, the critical enterprise can be a double-edged sword. On the one hand, it allows you to get *behind* social truths. On the other hand, this very process, when repeated over and again, can become a habit of mind that not only doesn't suggest solutions to the problems it raises, but may unintentionally block other ways of thinking.

I agree with Bryan Turner's (1992) contention that a Foucauldian perspective needs to be supplemented or corrected by some way of considering the lived body.

In the case of alternative therapies, it seems especially important, since they are bodily practices that frequently claim to be undoing or remaking conventional mind/body relations and to open up new forms of bodily experience. While the Foucauldian approach allows us to see the complexities of power, the role of body maintenance practices in late-modern identity work, and their connection to various ideologies (for example, of freedom, of individualism, of authenticity), it doesn't give much insight into these body practices as **embodied** experiences. As Turner argues, it doesn't allow one to understand much about the lived body. Indeed, while it puts the body at the centre of things, the Foucauldian approach is paradoxically quite disembodied. In Foucault's work, as in other forms of contemporary theory, such as that of feminist **Judith Butler**, 'the body is an effect of discourses' (Turner 1992: 94).

To understand the lived body we need to turn, if not to the phenomenological tradition, at least to perspectives informed and inspired by an interest in the real detail of what bodies feel like in particular contexts and/or in the physiological workings of the body. Foucault was generally hostile to phenomenology, seeing it as an obstructive philosophy because it posited a universal, ahistorical idea of the subject as its starting point rather than investigating how particular types of subjects are produced (Foucault 1980: 117). While this may be true, an interest in the actual *workings* (bodily and mental) of contemporary users of alternative therapies does not have to be based on an ahistorical notion of 'the' body or 'the' subject. Rather, it could allow us to consider the question of *why* these therapies are so popular in terms that engage more deeply with the physiology and materiality of the body as well as in sociocultural terms. Such a phenomenologically inspired method allows us to explore not just how these practices are understood, but what actually *happens* to those who engage in them. Moreover, as I have said, a contemporary phenomenology need not be ahistorical but can actually introduce a critical social perspective into this enquiry, allowing us to ask *why* certain kinds of bodily experience might be valued by particular kinds of person or in particular social contexts, and what kinds of person these practices might in turn help to produce.

A commitment to social critique does not preclude an interest in physiology or in bodily experience. A more embodied method would also allow us to consider the question of the physiological effects of body practices. In recent years, Elizabeth Wilson (2004), Anna Gibbs (2002) and Elspeth Probyn (2005), among others, have argued powerfully for the necessity of engaging with the body, not just as an effect of discourse or even as a social metaphor but as a physiological reality. Take the case of the so-called 'subtle' model of the body, on which many alternative therapies are based, and which is quite different from that underpinning orthodox medicine. This is a model that sees the body as a layered energetic system comprising multiple bodies (known popularly as auras).[5] Like any body model, the aura model can be analysed as a metaphor and thereby linked to contemporary social and cultural circumstances. This type of critical work can be powerful and fascinatingly counter-intuitive. But it doesn't answer the question of whether a particular model of the body, or a particular 'medical cosmology', is actually a *better fit*, physiologically, than another. Instead, the relentless attention to the historical and cultural contingency of a particular idea of the body implies the contingency of *any* idea of the body. While models of the body are unquestionably social, this does not mean that *any* model of the body is as physiologically tenable, useful or accurate as another. Few would dare to argue explicitly that this is the case, of course, but the inattention to questions of physiology in much contemporary cultural criticism tacitly hints that it may (as well) be.

Much of what I have been saying is more a question of the *uptake* of Foucault into the Cultural Studies context, which has its own interests, patterns, assumptions, biases and exclusions. Both the emphases of the earlier Foucault and the interests (and exclusions) of Cultural Studies tend to encourage a reading of alternative therapies as practices of self-making; and the self that is made is assumed to be the autonomous individual of modernity. I have not yet seen, for example, any cultural study of alternative therapies that takes them seriously as spiritual practices or as practices that could open up possibilities for new models and experiences of the body and subjectivity (Barcan & Johnston 2005). Such a study might discover that despite the repeated images of inner authenticity (true self, quest for self-knowledge, and so on), there is also significant cross-fertilisation with spiritual traditions in which the self is imagined as diffuse, radically **intercorporeal** and potentially indistinguishable from other selves, since we are ultimately all 'one'. Viewed this way, alternative therapies look less like simple enactments of modern individualism than sites of discursive struggle between several models and experiences of selfhood and corporeality. And rather than assuming that all therapies buy into the confessional modality and aim at producing truths of the self, a more engaged study would discover that many therapies are actively *anti*-interpretive, either seeing the production of psychological truths as rationalist prevarication or else seeing narratives of the self as therapeutic tools to be used strategically rather than as eternal truth-statements. In that context, the government of the self by the self might not just be the internalisation of external control in the service of personal fulfilment. And while the humanism underpinning most alternative therapies means that this is never going to be a project of selfhood that sits very comfortably in the Cultural Studies paradigm, it is nonetheless worth considering that this reformulated self might look a little less like the modern confessing subject than at first appears.

In conclusion, the concept of a modern disciplinary regime analysed in *Discipline and Punish* and *The History of Sexuality* Vol. 1 allows us to see how alternative therapies might be congruent with surveillance medicine, modern psychology and some aspects of consumer culture. But, as I have argued, the disciplinary blind spot of Cultural Studies, and the particular modes in which

Cultural Studies has been interested in using Foucault, suggest only a limited set of contexts in which they may be read: as a form of 'work of the self on the self' (Veyne 1993: 7) that is complicit with the contemporary psychological investment in the idea of an inner self that needs expression and sometimes liberation and/ or with the body maintenance logic of consumer culture. To my mind, this constitutes a restricted reading emanating out of a disciplinary reluctance to take spiritual practices seriously. In the case of alternative therapies, this reluctance means that Cultural Studies has hitherto not been able to take account of either the histories or the conceptual import of the expanded model of the body (its multiplicity, its radical intercorporeality and its image of interfusion with a wider cosmos) that is part and parcel of the spiritual lineage. Instead, Cultural Studies' own lack of interest—indeed, its *embarrassment* (Frow 1998: 207)—with things spiritual, alongside Foucault's own earlier focus on the clinic, may lead us either to ignore the spectacularly important new popular formation of New Age and alternative therapies altogether or to assume that these practices are best (or only) to be understood as part of the 'psy matrix' so astutely analysed by Nikolas Rose and/or of consumer logic. While they are undoubtedly both of these things, they are also undoubtedly more (or other).

But what of the tricky ethical question I so deftly sidestepped earlier? Does a commitment to the practices of alternative medicine necessarily entail buying into the ideologies of self-mastery and self-fulfilment so roundly critiqued by Rose? Perhaps, but as Cressida Heyes (2007) argues, if we take Foucault seriously and agree that power operates in and through the body, then perhaps it takes bodily practices to help us *undo* that power. This idea seems to me both intellectually exciting—a way out of a critical impasse—and true to the liberationist philosophies that underpin many of these practices. At this point in my own thinking, I tussle still with the place of Foucauldian critique in understanding my fascination for these alternative therapies. But the light shone on them by the Foucauldian paradigm certainly allows me, as an engaged researcher, to challenge my interviewees with such questions, to see if bridges can be built between the complexity, subtlety and richness of the bodily experiences themselves, and the New Age discourses through which they are so thinly described, and to wrestle with, if not reconcile, paradigmatic differences.

## key readings

Gabriel, Yiannis, and Tim Lang 1995. *The Unmanageable Consumer: Contemporary Consumption and its Fragmentation.* London: Sage.

Miles, Steven 1998. *Consumerism as a Way of Life.* London: Sage.

Nava, Mica 1992. *Changing Cultures: Feminism, Youth and Consumerism.* London: Sage.

## notes

[1]  The word 'tool' implies that Foucault's histories can be adapted to form a 'method'. The question of whether archaeology and genealogy should be considered 'methods' or 'approaches' is too big a topic to canvass here. I consider that a number of Foucauldian concepts have been so widely taken up in Cultural Studies and elsewhere as to be legitimately considered conceptual tools. For a discussion of the question of Foucauldian 'method' see Rose (1999, pp. xi–xii).

[2]  The quotation comes from Foucault's essay 'Subjectivité et vérité', as do similar formulations like 'the mastery of the self by the self or knowledge of the self by the self' [ *des rapports de maîtrise de soi sur soi ou de connaissance de soi par soi* ] (1989, p. 134).

[3]  In a similar vein, Heidi Marie Rimke (2000) has produced a highly critical Foucauldian reading of the self-help genre.

[4]  I share his concern at the romanticism, but balk at his solution—a Cultural Studies that is, to take up Bennett's lexicon, more 'prosaic', 'limited', 'practical', 'pragmatic' and 'applied'.

[5]  Space does not permit me to elaborate on this model here, but for a fuller explanation see Johnston (2007) and Johnston & Barcan (2006).

# body, gender, *gurlesque*, intersex.

AUTHOR: vicki crowley

## INTRODUCTION

In the serious play of questions and answers, in the work of reciprocal elucidation, the rights of each person are in some sense immanent in the discussion.

Michel Foucault (1984: 381)

The grace of the body offering itself is always possible.

Jean-Luc Nancy (1993: 195)

## ubiquity and anomaly.

Everywhere we are surrounded by the visual and aural noise of the body: it is ubiquitous. Yet a decade ago the preface to Australian historians Long, Gothard and Brash's edited collection *Forging Identities* (1997) began with Phyllis Mack's

pithy statement, 'The body is hot' (1997: ix). The editors of the book were
bringing the then vigorous and resurgent cultural interest of the body into the
theoretical and analytical frameworks of history. Their claim came at a time of
intense attention in feminist theory, feminist philosophy, **queer**, **postcolonial**
and cultural theory energised by concepts in the titles of such books as *Thinking
Bodies* (MacCannell & Zakarin 1994), *Volatile Bodies* (Grosz 1994), *Imaginary Bodies*
(Gatens 1996), *Uncontrollable Bodies* (Sappington & Stallings 1994), *Sexy Bodies*
(Grosz & Probyn 1995), 'mundane bodies' (Fiske 1992) and *Bodies That Matter*
(Butler 1993). It was time, as Elspeth Probyn (1993) termed it, to attempt thinking
and 'theorising through the body'. This cluster of bodily considerations named
through the above concepts provides us with a delicious array of approaches
to the body. It suggests that bodies are labelled and categorised and that the
labelling and categorisation of bodies deserves attention and scrutiny. Bodies
figure in our worlds in the realm of object and subject. As we know from studies
of **representation**, **ideology** and **semiotics**, the body can become an object
that is stripped of its selfhood. It can be and is the object of law and regulation
through institutions such as schools, health services and marriage. Global and
national politics intervene and nations decide which and whose bodies are seen
as legitimate and will be, for instance, accepted into a nation's refugee program.
There are bodies that count as being in some way significant. Some bodies are
understood as powerful and noteworthy.

Still others, like those we pass routinely on the streets or those cocooned in
cars motoring to this or that place, are unremarkable and remain unnoticed in
our everyday worlds unless they draw attention to themselves through decoration
or action that shifts them from their state of anonymity and ordinariness to a
body that becomes manifestly evident and under scrutiny. These shifts to noticing
and noting might be generous and pleasurable or they might be accompanied
by annoyance and judgment, anger or inconvenience. We experience the world
through our bodies: bodies that we take for granted and bodies that are taken for
granted.

We are all bodies, and our body transports us through our day and night. It
is how we experience our worlds. It mediates our engagements and it mediates
our estrangements. It may be unproblematic, at times problematic and at other
times deeply problematic. For some it may always be problematic, not because
of its intrinsic comportment (because at a base level we are all cells and liquids),
but because particular bodies have come to be thought of and acted on as if they
command sanction, deserve monitoring and require disciplining. The body, as the
subheading suggests, is always and simultaneously ubiquitous and anomalous; it
is everywhere, containing 'webs of affect' (Gopinath 2005: 60) that are specific
as well as incoherent. The body is endlessly multifarious, acting and reacting,
immersed in strategies of control and performing tactics of resistance. **Michel**

**Foucault** (1973, 1978, 1991) tells us that bodies have been the site of myriad **discourses**, interventions and practice. The body is a site of power, meaning that it is acted upon by legal, educational, social institutions and capable of acting upon others.

The body trail I am establishing interweaves the commonsense and familiar, the somewhat critical and the relatively uncritical and suggests the presence of desire and pleasure. It hints at the deadly serious and names the body as a site of uneven political intervention and commentary. The interweaving mirrors a sense of vertigo in which, from time to time, we may experience our bodies and the bodies of others, especially as we are bombarded with many competing ways to think about or through the body. There are a few things in here that are critical to consider: bodies exist in contexts, that is, they are never outside narrative or discourse, both of which are shaped in time and space. Many may find themselves immersed in questions of the 'mobile cultures': bodies that do not inhabit place and space in singular ways but engage in the 'I' world of MP3s and pods, blogs, high-speed internet, *Second Life* and SMS mobilisations or gatherings. Still other bodies remain sequestered in zones of stricture and enforced conformity.

Across all of this the body remains deeply fraught. It continues to be controversial and subject to constraints and practices. What I am interested in conveying here is a plethora of tensions that exist within and across a sense that the body is so ordinary as to go relatively unnoticed. Yet the body is never just so: it is always noteworthy, and as Foucault so powerfully demonstrates in his three volumes of *The History of Sexuality* (1978, 1985, 1986), acts of silencing, and discourses of repression, which take bodies and sexuality as their object, have the effect of bringing them into greater view and into endless discussion. For Foucault, oppressive measures are productive, and within this endless discussion resides the dispersal of power through which acts of resistance emerge.

Having traced some broad lines of thinking about the body as theory and as flesh immersed in circuits of power, I want to move the focus of this chapter to a small example of popular culture (albeit 'alternative' popular culture). The example comes from a live performance that took place in a Sydney club. The performance was filmed and although its audience is likely quite small, it now circulates the globe, sits in some university libraries and has captured the attention of many audiences at international **queer** screen festivals. The example I draw on is when Shorona se Mbessakwini performed what has become the short documentary film *Intersex Exposition: Full Monty* (2002). The documentary and performance present a moment in time where cinema viewer, club audience and reader can glimpse and sense that body meets theory, theory meets practice, and observe where theory helps us to think into and through what we might ordinarily take for granted, even when we think we inhabit a world in which the strictures of sex, gender and sexuality are less rigid.

# intersex@*Gurlesque*, interrupting gender.

*Gurlesque* is a lesbian strip show that describes itself as '[a]n exciting bumper to bumper, bump and grind show' that is 'a cross between old time burlesque and a future filled with sexual freedom' (www.gurlesque.com). It began in 2000, promising as its promo says to put 'the "skin" *into Erskineville*', which is an inner-city suburb of Sydney (www.gurlesque.com/whats/whatson.htm). *Gurlesque* has been hugely successful and has travelled its shows to festivals around Australia, attracting large audiences, and it has been invited to tour European Gay Pride. The idea behind *Gurlesque*, designed by the hosts Sex and Glita (shortened versions of their stage names, Sex Intents and Glita Supernova), is to provide 'a space that allows women to explore and interpret the essence of striptease'. Added to this is the intent to practise and perform comedy and drag as well as the 'seriously sexy'. At its home base (that is, when it is not travelling theatre) *Gurlesque* is also designed and crafted for participation in which 'all women can get up on stage … express themselves … confront fears and insecurities … challenge taboos, both sexual, social and those to do with the physical body, to explode myths about body structures and what a **patriarchal** society dictates is sexy or attractive' (www.gurlesque.com/about/about.html).

Gurlesque exists in the realms of traditional burlesque known for rowdiness and varying degrees of bawdiness and participated in as an interstitial space of the carnival where norms of all sorts are transgressed. Historically, burlesque was often staged across and in critique of class divides, with skits and jokes lampooning the hypocrisy and manners of the ruling classes. Burlesque is thus associated with a form of social and political commentary. *Gurlesque* positions their political commentary in relation to women's sexuality and women's bodies. While established as a lesbian strip club, the show has by no means exclusively lesbian performers or a lesbian-only audience. Like traditional burlesque it is comprised of several acts that are vibrant, witty, polished and culminate in a grand finale. Unlike traditional burlesque it provides the opportunity for women to perform. For the most part these performances have been along the lines of striptease, drag, satire and slapstick. Women's bodies are performed as a celebration of what they are in all their various shapes and sizes, be they athletic, balletic, with or without rhythm, humour, or professional acting and performance ability. *Gurlesque* travels to cabaret and arts festivals performing a circus of flesh, inviting audiences to immerse themselves in the irony of the 'forbidden' and repressed.

Into this arena, in *Gurlesque*'s second year, came Shorona se Mbessakwini, whose arrival on stage was greeted with anticipatory whistles, calling out and much encouraging applause. Shorona came onto the stage dressed in very ordinary street clothes: zippered pants and a buttoned top. Holding a microphone to her mouth with one hand, Shorona slowly removed her clothes. She spoke of fear at exposing 'her' (as she described it at the time) body. With no music or sound accompaniment, standing in the one spot and barely moving, Shorona described her experience of intersex. Historically, intersex was known as hermaphrodism and referred to bodies that have both female and male reproductive organs and secondary sexual characteristics. The term intersex has replaced hermaphrodite but continues to classify a body as simultaneously belonging to two different sex classifications. In contemporary medical and political discourse intersex is generally a term that describes a variety of conditions in which a person is born with a reproductive or sexual anatomy that doesn't seem to fit the typical biological and medical definitions of female or male. This might mean, for example, that a person may be born with a micro penis and also have a vagina, or a person's genitalia may appear to be female on the outside and contain typically male anatomy on the inside. Intersex thus refers to a person with non-visible or visibly mixed genitalia. The term also refers to those born with an extra chromosome, being XXY rather than XY (male) or XX (female).

Sometimes one's intersex anatomy is realised at puberty or in adult life through infertility or when, for instance, a surgery is performed for another ailment and reveals that an apparently male body also contains a vagina and uterus. It is also possible to live and die without ever knowing that one's body conformation is intersex. Complicating this still further is that the meaning of intersex varies. It isn't a discrete category, and Western medicine has an extensive range of terms for the variation in human physiology associated with divergence from the male and female sex binary.

Intersex is lived and experienced within an array of medical, social, cultural, legal and psychological histories of intervention and treatments.

Against this background and as noted already, Shorona performed her experience of intersex. She performed it by pointing to scarring and medical interventions that were conducted on her body without her consent, carried out by doctors, authorised by parents buoyed and encouraged by medicos to intervene as early as possible to reshape a child's body to 'conform' to female. The audience anticipating titillation were soon subdued and then listened intently in a quietness that would rarely, if ever, occur in a venue of this kind.

Shorona presented 'her'-self, 'her' body, 'her' intersex, and spoke through, with, of and to 'her'-self with her audience.

She refers to her body with the intimacy and knowing that comes with a life deeply engaged with a body that is put into question: the same body that knows no other way of being and that is all that a body can be. Shorona refers to, and touches, her body in ways that draw the audience into questioning the notion of self-touch, and a self-touch mediated by the medical and parental gaze; a body touched and handled by doctors, nurses and surgeons and moved to and fro in a world most profoundly structured by gender and sex insisted upon via the most forbidding, brutal and inhospitable sex-gender determinations. Just like many, many intersex bodies, as baby, as child and as adolescent, Shorona's body has been subjected to surgical, pharmaceutical, psychological, social and cultural interventions without her consent.

Shorona stood before her audience, a group of people that formed part of what she describes as her routine everyday worlds of identification and dis-identification (Munoz 1999). Up to this point her community, apart from those closest to her, knew her as a lesbian, but lesbian presupposed by sex framed within the dichotomy of male or female although aligned, perhaps, with a more fluid gendering than conventional femininities. For Shorona this lesbian 'knowing' presumed a body allied to the specificities of the sex binary, male *or* female. It did not presume a body that knew itself in far more complex ways, which in Shorona's case involved a bodily understanding that could never know itself in terms of the polar opposites of masculinity and femininity that are ascribed singularly to male or female bodies, despite the intentions of doctors and societies' desire for bodies that conform and are neatly aligned to what we know narrowly as female or male.

Shorona's performance and the reflections on it suggest to audience and readers that sex and gender are not static and perhaps, as Edward Mussawir (2007: 54) writes, 'There are not gendered individuals in an ungendered world, but rather different genderings of the world'. Shorona's performance at *Gurlesque* was partly choreographed and partly left to emerge and respond according to the moment. In her performance at *Gurlesque*, Shorona's body is, in her terms, a living and lived canvas comprised of an intricate weaving of cultural, gender and sexual politics, arrangements and rearrangements that belie the taken-for-granted sex and gender binary as static and singular. An audience familiar with sex and gender performance found itself to be in the presence of a deep challenge to cultural and subcultural thinking and practices, to become even more aware of the constraining power and authority of the binaries male/female, sex/gender.

# sites of performance: heteronormed gender and intersex.

As the introduction to this chapter indicates, the body has been the site of much academic attention. It has been considered within all disciplinary practices, each having their particular set of perspectives and parameters. Without overstating the case it is possible to say that Cultural Studies approaches to the body have drawn on a broad range of perspectives and traditions that mix such disparate elements as ethnography with literary, screen and market analysis. There have been periods in the early years of British Cultural Studies where the body was understood through class, race and gender relations in relatively unproblematic ways: especially where questions of identity and difference pertained to aggregated forms of political oppression. Increasingly, however, the turn to culture meant that the body became diversely configured through practices of representation and the visual arts, with cinematic, literary, gender, postcolonial and queer considerations being brought to the complex play of uneven interrelationships. Gender theory is one of the most significant theoretical interventions in recent times, opening the body to politics in ways that account for much more than gender understood as a homogeneous element of the mantra of race, class and gender (Mercer 1994).

The work of **Judith Butler** (1993, 1997a,b, 1999, 2002, 2004c) has had an immense impact on contemporary gender and cultural theory in relation to the body, particularly through the case she has made about the indivisibility of sex and gender, arguing that neither are natural phenomena, but rather each is constituted through discourse and hailed into being through each other. Butler contends that we cannot know gender without sex and that each is necessary to the constitution of the other. Following on from the work of Adrienne Rich (1980/1994) and **Gayle Rubin** (1984), she also placed this understanding of sex and gender within the structure of heterosexual **hegemony**.

The notion of hegemony was developed by Antonio Gramsci and referred to power structures in which individuals and groups are understood in ideological terms. For Gramsci hegemony is about the inculcation of the populace into dominant and prevailing ideas which seem to be so 'natural' and 'normal' that they are taken for granted and circulate in mostly unquestioned ways. The point at which ideas are taken for granted is when we can describe them as being hegemonic. Important to the concept of hegemony, however, is that the inculcation does not occur through force. It occurs through the influence of those in the position to have their ideas circulated and cemented. Hegemony is thus about power.

When we take up the concept of heterosexual hegemony we are engaged with thinking about power, ubiquity and the 'naturalness' of heterosexuality. Butler questions this and sees heterosexuality as a normative structure, a kind of default position against which all sexualities and gender identifications are measured. Her work questions assumptions about heterosexuality as being universal and as the rightful way in which human beings conduct or should conduct their sexual lives and live their bodies. Butler argues that heterosexuality forms a matrix through which all sexuality is understood. At this point the focus on the effects of gender as always and already being heterosexual raises the question of **heteronormativity**, the social and cultural imprimaturs that pressure us to conform to a heterosexual ideal, and a norm of heterosexuality. For Butler, heterosexual hegemony and heteronormativity are forms of violence because they exclude and preclude other forms of sexuality and other forms of bodily practice. In her work to **denaturalise** the hegemonic position of heterosexual sex and gender, Butler exhorted feminist and gender theory to question sex and gender typologies, to examine the function of heterosexuality and disentangle the presumed coherence of sex and gender, sex and sexuality, male and female, especially as they are understood in relation to bodies and power.

Over the past decade we have seen an expansion of how we understand and accommodate **embodiment**. Masculinities and femininities are seen to encompass much broader gender norms than previously and the new place, for instance, of the 'metrosexual' seems secure whether or not the term endures. To be an urban and urbane man now embraces many activities traditionally associated with femininities, such as the use of cosmetics, magazine reading, and attention paid to grooming, fashion, interior design and food. Television programs such as *Queer Eye for the Straight Guy*, gay men in the *Big Brother* house, *The Secret Life of Us*, *Sex and the City* and *Desperate Housewives* expand the perceived possibilities of gender and sexualities. They test out and display the conceptual parameters of fictive possibility. The borders of sexual propriety may no longer seem so clear cut and the borders between gay and straight may not seem so apparent, visibly problematic or, at least, to matter as much as they have in the past. Two big questions remain: up to which point are these seemingly loosened or refreshed modes of bodily possibility a fundamental shift towards freedom of expression, changes to repressive legal regulations, medical beliefs and practices or removing discrimination? To what extent do they remain underpinned by regulation of masculinities as discrete and opposite to femininities, heterosexuality as discrete and opposite to homosexuality? From here we need to ask: where do we draw the boundaries between fictional portrayals and what is acceptable in lived practices of everyday embodiment? Still further, what are the limits of how we understand sex and gender and what do these limits mean to the everyday? On whose bodies do they most impact? Why do we continue to insist on impossibly singular bodies, genders and sexuality?

# conclusion: the grace of the body.

The body in all its various incarnations is never far from centre stage. It is a site of pleasure and pain, a site of turmoil and affective disequilibrium. We live within our body and among bodies that are presented as ordered and chaotic, controllable and uncontrollable; on the one hand as if the exceptional body is ordinary, and on the other as if there exists the exceptional body that remains unspeakable and out of sight.

The body provides a rich site to which we can bring the wide array of Cultural Studies practices and recent and historical strands of thought. It is an abundant cultural site in which we can take time to think about the ways we consume bodies through visual and aural media and mediums; wired and wireless connections of the cyberworld and play-stations; the arts of contemporary stylisations in goth, emo or green, and through our sense of affective community (who we are and to whom we have forms of affiliation). We can reflect on what we take for granted about our corporeal engagements, the extent to which the visual body tells us much or little, how cinematic representations and narrative forms shape our ability and capacity to engage in one of the most fundamental elements of human life, our bodies, and to consider what it is we are able to recognise, to perhaps think anew as we strive to move across the almost infinite worlds to which we now have multiple forms of access. Yet these infinite options and possibilities continue to be constrained. Being alert to constraints, unravelling the formations and their new trajectories are important practices as we strive to engage with bodies and the everyday, and ask of ourselves and perhaps others: what is and is not so everyday? And just whose everyday are we talking about?

The philosopher Giorgio Agamben (2002: 13) writes: 'Some want to understand too much and too quickly; they have explanations for everything. Others refuse to understand; they only offer cheap mystifications'. 'The only way forward lies', he argues, 'in investigating the space between these two options'. In this space is the ordinary life, infinitely harder to grasp than the exceptional. It brings into question the 'I', 'we' and 'them' that underpin our sense of bodies and embodiment. It may be useful to pause and consider the working parameters of the ordinary and the extraordinary in the everyday. The extraordinary is not, for instance, the asylum seeker or intersex *per se*; rather it is how we act upon them, acts that without question rest on what is taken for granted, positions of power (or powerlessness) and the presumed need for intervention. It may be worthwhile, therefore, and without disavowal, to listen for and to the ordinary that is denied through everyday thinking, our practices and our being in binarised worlds. Perhaps it is much more than mere words that will enable us to form a future that embraces the body as thinking, volatile, imaginary, uncontrollable, sexy, mundane and clearly, 'bodies that matter'.

## key readings

Berlant, Lauren, and Michael Warner 1998. 'Sex in Public.' *Critical Inquiry* 24(2): 547–66.

Dreger, Alice Domurat 1999. *Intersex in the Age of Ethics*, Hagerstown: University Publishing Group.

Halberstam, Judith 1998. *Female Masculinity*, Durham, N.C. and London: Duke University Press.

## acknowledgments

With very special thanks to Cassandra Loeser and Katrina Jaworski for inspiring thinking, teaching and enduring friendship. To Chris, Eli, Michael, Lexton, David, David and the sparkling John, in the hope that we might live in worlds in which it is possible for everyone to be all we are.

# touching skin: embodiment and the senses in the work of ron mueck.

AUTHOR: anne cranny-francis

## INTRODUCTION

This chapter demonstrates one of the new directions in Cultural Studies, which is the study of the senses, sometimes called the 'sensorial turn'. As David Howes notes, sensory studies questions the verbal focus of older models of analysis and the visual focus of some more recent models, arguing that neither acknowledges the complexity of our engagement with the world, which includes all of the senses. As well, he argues, both the verbal and the visual model of analysis assume that our experience is consistent and coherent—that we see and feel and think about things and events and people in a coherent and consistent way—and yet our experience is far more 'dynamic, relational ... and conflicted' (Howes 2006: 115). In other words, our different senses and the understandings of the world they generate may be in conflict or may interrelate in a variety of ways, which means that we can simultaneously hold contradictory views of and ideas about things and events and people, and the ideas and arguments associated with them. It also means that we need to explore the ways in which our senses are engaged by the cultural practices (for example, texts of all kinds) that we encounter every day so that we understand how they affect how we feel and think. And note that I am interrelating thinking and feeling here, because the model of human subjectivity with which I am working is **embodied**; that is, it understands human **subjectivity** not as an intellectual construct, but as a complex interrelation of all human capacities including the sensory and the intellectual. So that understanding how our senses are involved in the meanings we make, and in the meanings we generate from other things and people and interactions, is crucial to knowing ourselves and our world.

The chapter deals with the sense of touch, which is rarely considered when we analyse texts—though we are used to exploring what a text might say, how it looks, and even how it sounds. I'm going to start by reflecting on one of the fundamental Western myths of touch, the story of King Midas, and what it might tell us about the nature of human subjectivity. I then discuss the work of contemporary sculptor Ron Mueck, whose hyper-real sculpture not only appeals particularly to the sense of touch, but also uses that appeal to direct our attention to the sensory nature of human embodiment, subjectivity and being.

# the myth of King Midas.

Once upon a time there was a king named Midas. One evening he found a man called Silenius, drunk and disoriented in his garden. Kindly, he took him in and looked after him until he was able to go on his way. Silenius was foster father and former teacher of the god Dionysius, who was very impressed by Midas' generosity and so offered him any gift he desired. Midas' choice was that anything he touched should turn to gold. Dionysius urged Midas to reconsider, but Midas persisted and so Dionysius assented: Midas was granted this gift. Midas was delighted and immediately broke a branch from a tree, watching as the wood and leaves turned to fine gold. However, Midas' joy did not last long because when he sat down to eat, the food in his mouth turned to gold and was inedible; the wine in his cup turned to gold as he tried to drink it. And when his daughter hugged him to comfort him, she too was transformed into gold.

Grieving for his beloved child, and starving, Midas begged Dionysius to take back his 'gift'. Dionysius sent Midas to bathe in the River Pactolus where the waters washed his powers away—and ever after that river was known for the gold deposits washed up by its waters.

# reading the myth.

The Midas myth is usually read as a warning against greed; Midas' fault is his desire for material wealth, which blinds him to the other treasures of life: the embodied pleasures of food and drink and the love of others, such as his daughter. The problem with Midas' wish, in this reading, is that he asked that everything he touched *should be turned to gold*. However, the story can be read slightly differently. Along with Dionysius we can see the problem as being that *everything Midas touched* would turn to gold. So the meaning embedded in the myth, which gives it its power, is that touch is pervasive. Midas could not confine his golden touch to some things and not others; *everything* he touched turned to gold. We cannot limit and control touch by strength of will because we are always already touching.

Implicit in this myth is recognition of the fundamental nature of embodiment: that we are embodied beings, physically impinging on, related to, connected into, the world—not disembodied will-driven minds. What distinguishes our being-in-the-world (Heidegger 1993) is not our voluntary, will-driven acting on the world (as Midas assumed), but this connectedness—our constant (being in) touch (which Midas failed to recognise). So we are, at all times, touching and being touched. Even as we walk down the street, we touch the air around us, and are touched by it—and so perceive it as wet or dry, hot or cold. That bodily touch is the basis of our sense perceptions; it is what grounds the information we gather—perceptually and conceptually—about the world. And it is an embodied deconstruction of the Cartesian dictum 'I think, therefore I am', which is commonly read as signifying the primacy of rationality and of mind (over body). If instead we understand embodiment as the fundamental condition of being and of knowledge formation, then we must reverse the terms: I am embodied, therefore I think. Further, if that embodiment is understood as a connectedness that is experienced as touch, then we might reword this as: I am embodied, therefore I touch, therefore I think.

The value of this formulation is that it works against not only the hierarchisation of mind and body, but also their separation. In other words, against the notion of the mind as a rational machine trapped in a decaying, physical body—a disembodied mind that could be downloaded into a chemical vat or digital database—it argues, along with Bruno Latour (2003), that the mind is a brain, a fully organic entity; another organ of the sensing body that is the essence or basis of being. We think as and what we think because we are embodied as we are, and touch the world, and are touched by it, as we do.

It's not surprising, therefore, that Midas was granted the gift of touch by Dionysius, the god of wine. As the god of celebration Dionysius knows that being is about more than the ability to think. Rather, it is a fully embodied, fully connected being-in-the-world—as the consumption, and overconsumption, of wine makes clear. The Dionysian consumption of wine is about good time in company, about celebration and being with others—the connectedness of being. About being *in touch* with others.

So rethinking the Midas story leads us to an understanding of how touch is critical to an understanding of embodied human subjectivity. To explore this further I want to turn now to a set of contemporary texts: the work of sculptor Ron Mueck, known for his hyper-real depictions of human beings. Mueck's work raises a centuries-long debate about the relationship between sculpture and painting that hinges on the sense of touch, and I use this debate as a way to explore the specific appeal and power of Mueck's work, and how it operates as an exploration of human subjectivity, particularly through its evocation of the sense of touch.

# sculpture and touch.

The relationship between touch and sculpture has a long cultural history. As Andrea Bolland explains in an article on the work of Bernini, sculpture was distinguished from the arts of painting and poetry 'by its ability to give pleasure and to grant certain knowledge through the sense of touch' (Bolland 2000: 318). Bolland relates this to early classical accounts of sculpture, such as Ovid's account in *Metamorphoses* of the sculptor Pygmalion who falls in love with his beautiful statue:

> Often he lifts his hands to the work to try whether it be flesh or ivory. He kisses it and thinks his kisses are returned. He speaks to it, grasps it and seems to feel his fingers sink into the limbs when he touches them and thus he fears lest he leave marks of bruises on them. (Ovid quoted in Bolland 2000: 318)

In Ovid's account Pygmalion makes a bed for his statue so that it/she is comfortable, a kind act for which Venus rewards him by bringing the statue to life:

> a miracle that is certified, but also apparently accomplished, through touch. (Ovid 10.282–6, quoted in Bolland 2000: 318)
>
> Again he kissed her, and with his hands also he touched her breast. The ivory grew soft to his touch and, its hardness vanishing, gave and yielded beneath his fingers, as Hymettian wax grows soft under the sun and, moulded by the thumb is easily shaped to many forms. (Bolland 2000: 318)

This account is worth quoting at some length because it reveals, as Bolland notes, the number of different ways that touch is deployed to explain sculpture's pleasure and power: the touch of the sculptor, which is both creative and erotic, and the touch of the sculpture itself (hard or soft). Ovid's *Pygmalion* story also acknowledges the role of vision in sculpture, which, in the classical account, is related specifically to its mimetic power. Touch is the means by which the viewer confirms that this lifelike reproduction is not, in fact, alive: it is ivory, or marble, or stone or wood (Bolland 2000: 321).

Other early accounts, however, argue for a tactile mimesis. Sixteenth-century sculptor Nicolo Tribolo claimed that a blind man would recognise a sculpture of a man by touch as it has the form of a man, but would find a painting a faulty representation because it is a flat surface: hence sculpture is the superior art-form. Others argue the opposite case: that the power of painting is that it can suggest a three-dimensional shape even though it is a flat surface, which is demonstrated when viewers try to touch the represented object (Bolland 2000: 321). So touch is still critical, but here as validation of visual mimesis.

This classical history of sculpture establishes touch as a key factor in its composition, status and power. More recent analyses rely less on its mimetic function and refer rather to the sculpture's definition of space. For example, Robert Hopkins refers to Suzanne Langer's description of sculpture in *Feeling and Form* (1953) as 'the image of kinetic volume in sensory space' (Langer 1953: 92), and concludes:

> [W]e see the space around a sculpture as structured by the potential for movement and the action of the represented object. Thus while painting preserves a sharp division, within our experience, between the world represented and the world of the representation; sculpture precisely erodes this division, so that the world in which the representation sits is seen as organized by the kinetic potential of the object represented—be it man, beast, or something altogether more abstract. (Hopkins 2004: 166)

For Hopkins, sculpture 'connect[s] with a hypersensory aspect of experience': 'sculpture is neither visual, nor tactile, but a complex mixture of the sensory, as standardly conceived, with our awareness of our own bodies, and their possible interactions with the world' (2004: 166).

Hopkins' definition refers to the proprioceptive (haptic) sense by which we perceive our position in the world around us. We engage a kind of internalised touch sense when we position ourselves in relation to the world, which includes our creation of the spaces and volumes through which we move. In Langer's and Hopkins' formulations, sculpture provokes the viewer not necessarily through a **mimetic representation** of ourselves or our world, but by stimulating our awareness of sensory experience. And for Hopkins that specifically includes our embodied connection to the world around us.

# the sculpture of Ron Mueck.

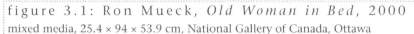

figure 3.1: Ron Mueck, *Old Woman in Bed*, 2000
mixed media, 25.4 × 94 × 53.9 cm, National Gallery of Canada, Ottawa

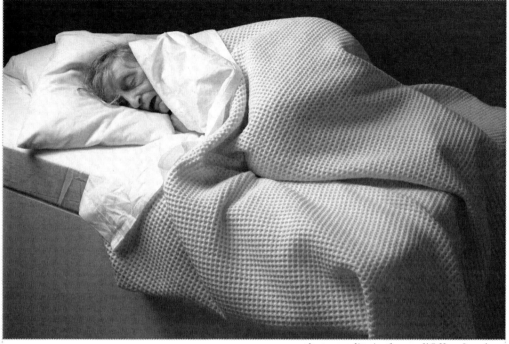

photo credit: Anthony d'Offay, London

Susanna Greeves (2003: 30) identifies touch as a major characteristic of Ron Mueck's work: 'Touch, the sense which Mueck's rendering of warm, heavy, flesh or fine, downy hair most arouses, has been deemed unreliable, dangerous or even morally questionable'.

Yet one action forbidden to the viewer of Mueck's sculpture is touch, as his work is (relatively) fragile, unlike marble or bronze statuary, for example, which can be freely touched by viewers, and which is sometimes created with that interactive touch as part of its meaning and being. Tribolo's test for sculpture could not be applied to Mueck's work, even though one of its most striking features is the **mimetic realism** that Tribolo claims as the superior quality of sculpture. Mueck uses contemporary materials—fibreglass and resins—to construct his hyper-real figures, and these materials are not amenable to public handling. When Greeves writes that Mueck's work arouses touch, then, she is not inciting readers literally to touch his work—as did much classical writing, not least the foundational story of Pygmalion. Instead she notes that the work makes the viewer *desire* that touch ('arouses'), which begs the questions, why and how does it do this?

One of the most striking features of Mueck's work is its *apparent* verisimilitude, and I will shortly discuss the use of the qualifier. Mueck's sculptures reproduce the visual appearance of skin with astounding accuracy—its grain and translucency. Mueck reinforces this by adding the appearance of skin pigmentation (moles, freckles, uneven patches), thickening (calluses, roughness) and hair (synthetic [usually] or animal [horsehair], depending on the size of the piece), inserted laboriously strand by strand into its own hole. Some of the figures are clothed or partially clothed; many are naked. And some sculptures also include non-figural elements—clothing, blankets, a boat (*Man in a Boat*, 2002), a stool (*Angel*, 1997), a chair (*Wild Man*, 2005)—all rendered with the same verisimilitude as the figures with which they are associated. So their mimetic quality is not only in the shape of the work, as it is with statues of marble or bronze, but also in its visual surface.

figure 3.2: Ron Mueck, *Angel*, 1997
mixed media, 110 × 87 × 81 cm, Saatchi Gallery, London

photo credit: Anthony d'Offay, London

One impulse to touch the work seems to come from this painstaking surface realism. Visitors to the work report an urge to touch the skin of the pieces, to check whether it is as soft and 'natural' as it appears to be. An art teacher told me that a student of his, viewing Mueck's *Old Woman in Bed* (2000/2002), said in hushed tones, 'I saw her blink!' The astonishing thing about the student's response is that *Old Woman in Bed* is a tiny work, only 24 × 94.5 × 56 cm. The reason for my use of the qualifier 'apparent' to describe the verisimiltude of Mueck's work is his play with scale. Mueck's work is almost never lifesize.

figure 3.3: Ron Mueck, *Two Women*, 2005–06
mixed media, 85 × 48 × 38 cm

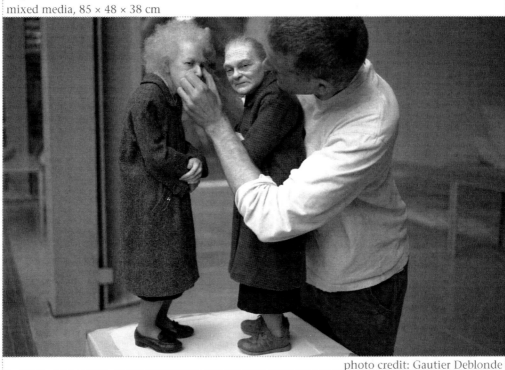

photo credit: Gautier Deblonde

Most pieces are either much larger (*Boy*, 1999, a crouching figure, is a massive 490 × 490 × 240 cm) or much smaller (*Baby*, 2000 is 26 × 12.1 × 5.3 cm) than life. So the viewer is confronted with a contradiction—work that is astonishingly or disturbingly realistic on the surface, but impossibly sized to be real. *Wild Man* (2005) is another example of this non-realist scale: a seated figure of a naked man, with the dimensions 285 × 162 × 108 cm.

The urge to touch the works to confirm their reality is related to, though not quite the same as, the touch impulse in the classical stories. In the Pygmalion story, for example, the touch of the sculptor turned lover confirms the reality of his creation (eventually literally, when the statue comes to life). With Mueck's statues the impulse seems to be related to a need to confirm that the works are *not* real, despite the evidence of the eyes—or, at least, one part of that evidence. The visual evidence is in conflict: realist surface, non-realist size. In this, his work serves as a confrontation to/with the age of spectacle, ironically confirming that the viewer cannot always believe what she/he seems to see. Unable to touch the work, viewers confirm that Mueck's figures are statuary, not people, based on the evidence of not only the distanced and relatively disengaged (and, in his case, problematised) sense of vision, but also the fully engaged proprioceptive, olfactory and aural senses. We know these are statues, even though their surface is convincingly 'human' because they are not lifesize *and* because they do not move, they do not smell, they do not make any noise. So engaging with Mueck's work effectively deconstructs the classical binary between painting and sculpture, vision and touch, and by implication between distanced, abstracted experience (mind) and sensorially engaged experience (body). In Hopkins' terms (quoted earlier) engaging with Mueck's work is a '**hypersensory**' experience, making us aware of our own embodiment and of our connectedness with the world around us.

figure 3.4: Ron Mueck, *Wild Man*, 2005
mixed media, 285 × 162 × 108 cm

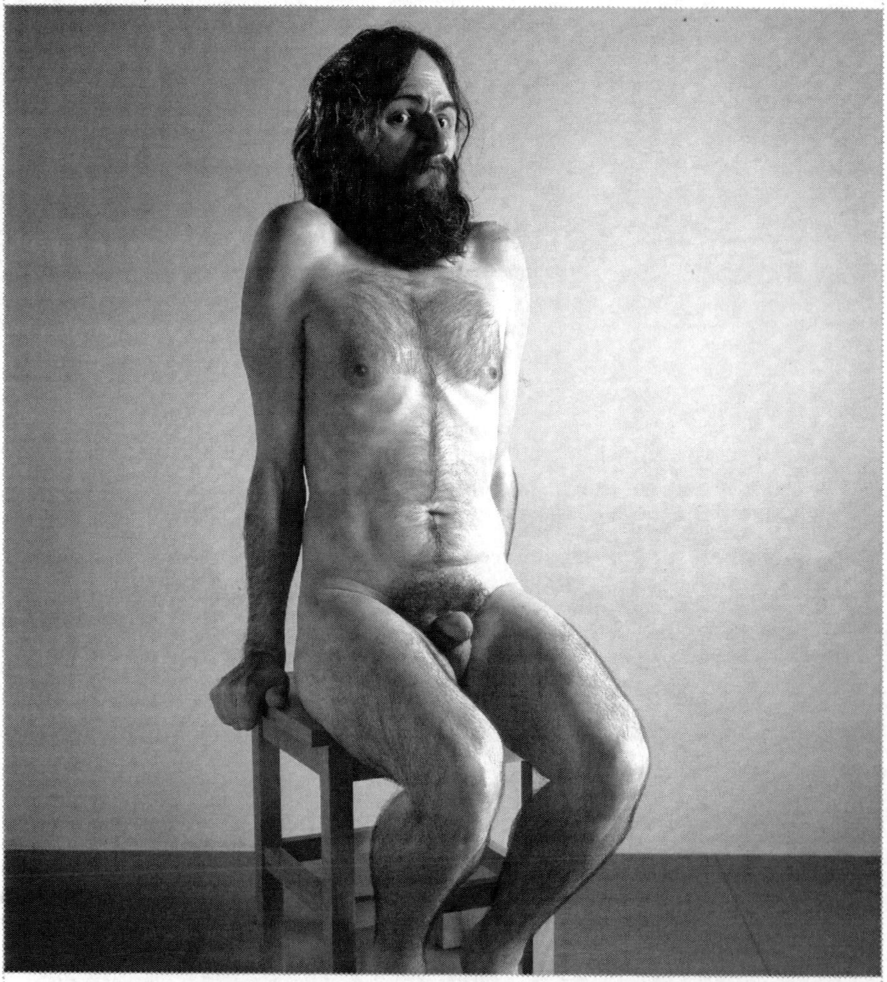

credit and photo: Anthony d'Offay, London

Mueck's work also addresses the classical distrust of touch as 'unreliable, dangerous or even morally questionable' that Greeves describes in her catalogue essay (Greeves 2003). As noted earlier, touch is virtually the only sense that Mueck's work cannot directly engage; it creates the desire to touch while making an actual touch impossible, which serves to heighten the viewer's awareness of this sense. However, this is not the deceptive touch of classical thought, with its implicit distrust of sensory engagement, but rather a validating or authenticating touch that thereby confirms knowledge as positioned, embodied and engaged, not as distanced, abstract and disembodied. So while (or because) we cannot touch Mueck's work, we are reminded of our embodied propensity to use touch to explore our world—not in order to subject it to our carnal appetites and so, consequently, to corrupt our judgment, but rather to position ourselves in the world and as part of the world, creating an ethical basis on which to make judgments.

The other haptic sense associated with sculpture is proprioception—not touch as surface-to-surface contact, but as bodily positioning. That is, we experience the world not simply as a set of objects but as a set of potentials and spaces created by the interaction between people and objects in the world, our embodied selves, and the social and cultural values, practices and expectations that determine their interactions. As noted earlier, for Langer and Hopkins sculpture is a manifestation in space and time of this complex practice of embodied being. So, when we experience a work such as Mueck's *Wild Man*, we not only see a representation of a very large naked man sitting on a proportionally large chair; we sense, proprioceptively, the volumes he would occupy if he stood up from his chair and walked away from (or towards) us.

Mueck encourages this interaction with the figure by his oppositional presentation of the man. Though monumental sculpture is conventionally associated with 'power and status, spiritual or temporal, and so also with propaganda' (Greeves 2003: 39), Mueck's huge Wild Man looks apprehensive, even frightened. He grips the seat of his chair, arms tensed and shoulders raised in a self-defensive posture. Culturally, he is a contradiction. His physical size and white, masculine body should suggest power and control—and that possibility remains. Yet his posture suggests that it is he, not the viewer, who feels intimidated. This contradiction can create a momentary disorientation for the viewer, habituated to reading naked male figures as threatening or intimidating. Of course, the art gallery context also frames the interaction so that, at some level, the viewer also 'knows' that this figure will not get up and walk; that this naked man is not Spenser's Wild Man of the Forest or a more rapacious contemporary figure. Nevertheless, the Wild Man does occupy more than the space of the sculpture; viewers approach the figure in quite specific ways, according to their own proprioceptive comfort. For example, few viewers choose to stand front-on to the figure, looking between his legs (which are tensely straight, not splayed) at his genitals. This generates a volume around the front of the figure that is less occupied than other spaces in the room—the 'kinetic volume' of Langer's description; a volume generated culturally by the sculpture that is not the same as the space it physically occupies. This is another sense in which the viewer is touched by the work and again it demonstrates the sensory continuity of the viewer and her/his world, which is culturally determined and not a simple matter of material contingency.

Ron Mueck's work is particularly interesting in its evocation of touch, not least because it is untouchable. As contemporary sculpture it engages with both the history of its own art-form and with contemporary embodied viewers, negotiating both to generate its own specific meanings about the art of sculpture and about the nature of contemporary being—and it does this largely through its arousal of the sense of touch.

# the final touch.

As noted earlier, Ron Mueck's sculptures provoke in viewers a desire to touch the work. For some viewers it is because of the contradictory meanings generated by their visual appearance (hyper-real, yet too big or too small); for others, it is to use touch to determine whether the sculptured flesh is as 'human'—soft, warm—as it visually appears to be. (And for some it is to check whether the part of the human figure sometimes not visible—in a bed or under clothing—is as realistic as the visible parts.) Further, as noted with the *Wild Man* sculpture, Mueck's work engages an aspect of touch, proprioception, that is specifically to do with our positioning in the world.

David Howes (2006: 115) writes that the problem with many corporeal models of being is that they treat bodies as 'physical wholes', rather than as 'bundles of interconnected experiences and properties'. By showing how our eyes can give us contradictory messages and that we (want to) use the sense of touch to resolve those contradictions, Ron Mueck's work demonstrates both the role of our senses in generating our experience and knowledge of the world and that they are interconnected, not homogeneous. Further, in showing that our experience of the world is constituted by this set of interrelated experiences, Mueck's work evokes the fundamental nature of human being—as embodied and sensorially engaged. Visitors to his work leave the gallery more aware than ever of the fragility, cultural specificity, social overdetermination, multiplicity and complexity of our (sensory) being.

## key readings

Greeves, Susanna 2003. 'Ron Mueck—a Redefinition of Realism.' In Heiner Bastian (ed.), *Ron Mueck*, Ostfildern-Ruit: Hatje Cantz, 26–40.

Hopkins, Robert 2004. 'Painting, Sculpture, Sight, and Touch.' *British Journal of Aesthetics* 44(2): 149–66.

Howes, David 2006. 'Charting the Sensorial Revolution.' *Senses and Society* 1(1): 113–28.

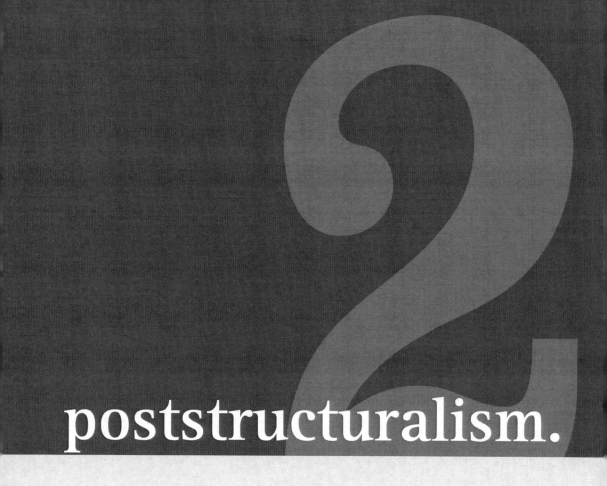

# 2

# poststructuralism.

# the stories so far.

AUTHOR: nicole **anderson**

## Prelude.

Poststructuralism cannot be understood as a singular and homogeneous 'theory'. Indeed, some aspects of poststructuralist thought, like some aspects of postmodern thought, critique any notion of a unified theory existing as distinct from practice or from the contexts and sites in which both theories and practices take place. In other words, depending on the discipline in which one is situated, the emphasis on its origins and historical context will be different. This means that some disciplines might use a particular theorist to lend credence to a form of postmodernism, while that same theorist will be associated, in another context and in another (or even in the same) discipline, as purely poststructuralist. This begs the question: is poststructuralism the same as postmodernism? This is a question that has caused much debate. Some argue that they are different names given to the same theory, and consequently the two terms have been, and are often, conflated. A variation of this position suggests that while poststructuralism is not postmodernism *per se*, it is nonetheless one manifestation of postmodernism, because they have a significant perspective in common: a scepticism about universal truth, reality and objectivity. Still others argue that poststructuralism has a different history from postmodernism: the latter developed in relation to, or as a break from, or as a rejection of modernism; while the former developed out of, or as a break from the structuralist movement initiated by **Ferdinand de Saussure** and theories of language (semiotics and linguistics). Whichever way you want to look at it, the process of defining poststructuralism, like postmodern theory, is contentious. However, while I acknowledge that postmodernism and poststructuralism do share some common theoretical ground, conflating the two overlooks their significant and nuanced historical and theoretical differences. Given this, and despite the deep problems associated with either separating or conflating the two terms, the aim of this introduction is to provide a brief genealogical background to the formation of the term, as well as situating the chapters within this section in relation to 'poststructuralism' as a theory. To do this means taking a brief step back in time to the 1950s: the heyday of structuralism, out of which poststructuralism arose.

# structuralism.

With the publication of Ferdinand de Saussure's (1857–1913) *Course in General Linguistics* in 1916, the traditional historical and rationalist approaches to language and meaning were turned upside down. This traditional approach assumes that there is an intrinsic connection between a thing (in the world) and a word (in language). That is, words are not just names for things and objects (which is what they also are), but words also 'name', or 'stand in directly' for (represent), what is absent. To put it another way, a concept or an object in the material world pre-exists the 'word' and is simply labelled by it. Saussure's own term for this notion was 'nomenclaturism'. In other words, the fallacy of the traditional position lies in their view that the signified, be it an object in the material world or a concept, pre-exists the 'word' (or signifier). The consequences of this view are the following: take the word or label 'house', which *represents* four walls, doors, windows and a roof. I can use this word to refer to a particular house (that is absent from vision) or to all houses generally. This may seem obvious and true, but what this position assumes is that a word (or language) captures or represents accurately and purely the one, true and permanent and essential meaning of the thing/object. Thus there is an essential nature to objects in the world, and as a result there is one reality unchanging through time and space, eternal and existing independently of us: reality is always already constructed without input from human beings, and language simply labels that reality.

Saussure challenged this traditional position. The implications of this challenge were profound at the time and were taken up, particularly in the 1960s, by a variety of philosophers and theorists in a movement that challenged the traditional notions of language and meaning. This movement came to be known later as 'structuralism'. Saussure challenges this traditional notion of language by arguing that this traditional approach to the study of linguistics, which had always been historical (diachronic), needed to be supplemented by a proper 'science' of language (his 'semiology'), which could only be synchronic. By synchronic Saussure means the entire abstract system of language (*la langue*) at a given moment in time, free from its historical determinations or the unsystematic chaos of actual use (*la parole*). Saussure believed that language (*la langue*), so defined, was a system or structure where all the elements, rules and words are available to every user of the language (Saussure 1991). For Saussure, users combine elements (words, grammar, sentences, etc.) of the system in constructing spoken or written texts, within the rules of the structure. For example, 'b' in 'bat' can be replaced by 'c' to become 'cat'. So the words (bat or cat) only have value because of their *relation* to other possible choices of words or letters in that structure: a meaning of a word is determined by its difference from other words. For instance, while 'b' in bat can be substituted for a 'c' to form cat, bat and cat have meaning and value because they are different from each other: the meaning of 'cat' is that it is not 'hat', not 'dog', and so on. So words have intrinsic value *only* within a structure. Words become meaningless outside that structure. But what exactly is this 'structure'? For Saussure, language is formed in and through a structure of differences: what Saussure calls the 'differential relation'. Therefore, 'difference' *per se* is the structure.

For Saussure, since the structure of language is based on its *differential relation*, language is *arbitrary*. The implication of this is that because the connection between word and thing is based on differences within a structure or system there can be no unified, true, universal, unchanging, eternal reality to which a word in language refers. Language is arbitrary and thus contingent precisely because it is constructed by its users (language does not exist apart from its users). For Saussure (1991: 3), 'the structure of language is a social product of our language faculty … it is also a body of necessary conventions adopted by society to enable members of society to use their language faculty'. This is in fact a radical departure from the traditional language position; a departure that is developed and utilised by poststructuralists.

Saussure demonstrates the arbitrariness of language in his discussion of the 'sign'. A 'sign' is made up of two elements: the signifier (the sensory/mental impression of the word: what we see or hear) and the signified (a general abstract concept associated with that sensory/mental impression). Meaning is produced by the relationship between the signifier and the signified. Let's use the example of the word 'dog'. When we hear or see the word 'dog' we get a sensory/mental impression of a dog: we either see marks on a page or hear sounds. This is called the *signifier*. At the same time, the signifier invokes an abstract concept of a dog. This abstract concept is *not* an image of a particular dog, rather the signifier 'dog' invokes a general or abstract notion of a dog: a domesticated furry canine animal with four legs and a tail that comes in many shapes and sizes, and is considered to be 'man's [sic] best friend'. This is called the *signified*. And when the sign 'dog' invokes an image of a particular dog or type of dog (whether we know this dog or not) in the world, this is called the referent (Thwaites, Davis & Mules 1995: 31).

Now, just because a word or sign 'dog' refers to the general concept of dog, or even an image or object of a dog in the world, this does not mean that this word/ sign 'dog' can only ever refer to 'a domesticated furry canine animal with four legs and a tail'. As any dictionary will tell you, it may also refer to a mechanical device for gripping, or to an unpleasant human, or to an unattractive female. What this means is that signs or words have several meanings, not just one, and that these can be changed: dog could refer to something altogether different; for instance, it could refer to a type of plant. It is these notions of the differential relation and arbitrariness of language that poststructuralism took up and developed in the late 1960s and 1970s.

# poststructuralism.

Poststructuralism came to be associated with thinkers such as **Jacques Derrida**, **Michel Foucault**, the later **Roland Barthes**, **Jacques Lacan**, **Julia Kristeva**, **Luce Irigaray**, **Pierre Bourdieu**, **Louis Althusser**, among others. The works of these thinkers are varied and take different approaches. For instance, Kristeva and Irigaray used, but also moved beyond, structuralism to provide a platform from which to discuss feminism; Bourdieu to develop social and class structures; for Althusser, **Marxist** and political philosophy; for Lacan, psychoanalysis; for Barthes, 'textual analysis'; for Foucault, relations of power and knowledge; for Derrida, **deconstruction** and **différance**, and so on (deconstruction and différance are defined below). In a nutshell, the scholarship on this topic (for example, Storey, Agger, Culler, Lechte, Sarup, Sturrock, Hawthorn and Weedon) defines poststructuralism as a theory that accepts the *differential* and *arbitrary* relation of language that Saussure put forth, but develops the implications of this for a wide variety of issues; from subjectivity, textuality, power, feminism and political theory to society and culture (including issues of race, gender and sexuality).

Accepting Saussure's argument that there is no intrinsic connection between word and thing, because language is based on differences, and that there can be no true, universal, unchanging reality to which a word refers, poststructuralism goes further, arguing that reality (the world) is constructed in and through the language we use. The 'real' world has no value or meaning independent of us; rather the way we view or perceive the world is a consequence of the language structure into which we have been born. Furthermore, poststructuralism uses Saussure's notion of the *differential relation* to reveal the instability that pervades all human relations, language and communication, and its political consequences for culture and society. Of course, to summarise or define poststructuralism 'in a nutshell' involves a form of reduction: a homogenising of various philosophers' approaches and argumentative subtlety. In an attempt to counteract this, I have decided to concentrate on two famous poststructuralists: Michel Foucault and Jacques Derrida. Exploring their differences and similarities will help give a sense of the diversity of poststructuralism as a body of thought. I have chosen these two because, first, they have both had significant impact on the discipline of Cultural Studies, and in fact it has been argued by a number of Cultural Studies theorists that 'post-structuralism is virtually synonymous with the work of Jacques Derrida' (Storey 1993: 86) and Michel Foucault (Hawthorn 1992: 137). And second because the chapters that follow draw specifically on these two philosophers.

## Foucault's power/knowledge

French philosopher Michel Foucault (1926–84) was professor of the 'history of systems of thought' at the Collège de France from 1970 until his death in 1984. Foucault, like Derrida, believed that Saussure's notion of the 'structure' of language betrayed or contradicted his notion of differential relations, because Saussure fails to see that 'structure' becomes an extra-systemic entity, or a meta-structure. It is an entity that inevitably homogenises or simply structures the differences in language as nothing more than a comparison/contrast relation between elements, rather than something absolutely '**other**'. Moving beyond Saussure, Foucault in his books *The Order of Things* and *The Archaeology of Knowledge* forms a genealogical analysis of the ways 'power' and 'knowledge' in culture and society emerge and operate in and through 'discourse'. And genealogy here does not mean a search for origins or an understanding of time (and the past) as a linear development through history. Rather, Foucault's genealogy attempts to reveal the contradictory and non-linear aspects of historical events in order to show the influence power has had on subjects and bodies. In this way, Foucault rethinks and challenges the traditional notions of '**discourse**', 'power' and 'knowledge' as they had been previously articulated by Saussurian and structural linguistics, **Marxist** philosophy and the history of ideas, respectively. His nexus between discourse, power and knowledge is the means by which he explores the ways people become both enabled and constrained to think in particular ways. But what does Foucault mean by these individual terms and their relation to each other?

Discourse for Foucault is not 'text' (as the term is sometimes traditionally used in semiotics or linguistics); it is not simply a means of grammar (as in **speech-act theory**) or a form of formal communication or social interaction. Instead, Foucault uses the term 'discourse' to refer to social knowledge: what he calls 'bodies of knowledge'. Bodies of knowledge are scholarly (science, medicine, philosophy, psychiatry) and institutional (schools, hospitals, prisons, law courts) disciplines. Bodies of knowledge always already produce practices of social and cultural control and regulations and modes of thought (McHoul & Grace 1993: 26; Storey 1993: 92). And language use is (in)formed in and through bodies of knowledge (discourse), which is, in turn, the way power operates. This is what Foucault calls the 'discursive formation' of thought, by which we can only think (speak and write) in certain specific discourses and not others, in any historical era, thus constraining our thought within those historical limits. For example, in the 16th century, 'thinking' about how to continue a person's life by giving them a heart transplant was impossible, precisely because of the way in which 'bodies of knowledge' operated in relation to socio-cultural assumptions, presuppositions and practices (both technological and religious/political) about healing and medicine at the time. But these discourses also enabled the possibility of changing cultural assumptions and practices, thus moving beyond constraints in thinking, which is why Foucault argues that Saussure's structure of language should not be thought of as an extra-systemic entity because it is always being displaced by the local and unique events in any given era.

So, institutions produce, and are produced by, bodies of knowledge (discourse), which provide ways of thinking about, and acting in relation to, the world. But what has this to do with power? In the words of Foucault:

> [I]n any society, there are manifold relations of power which permeate, characterise and constitute the social body, and these relations of power cannot themselves be established, consolidated nor implemented without the production, accumulation, circulation and functioning of a discourse. (Foucault 1980: 93)

What Foucault is arguing here is that conflicting discourses and discursive formations create 'manifold' forms of power, which operate by circulating through the social body as an 'economy' of production. Relations of power do not *only* operate vertically (ie: top down), where one individual or institution, class or gender dominates another and thus dictates prohibitions and rules, etc. Rather, power is polymorphous: power is everywhere (vertically, horizontally, diagonally). Again Foucault argues:

> Relations of power are not in a position of exteriority with respect to other types of relationships (economic processes, knowledge relationships, sexual relations), but are immanent in the latter; ... relations of power are not in superstructural positions, with merely a role of prohibition or accompaniment; they have a directly productive role, wherever they come into effect. (1990: 94)

As Foucault (1991: 194) suggests here, power does not simply censor, repress, exclude. Power is, at the same time, 'productive', because it produces reality, which is therefore always open to change.

Moving from an exploration (in *Discipline and Punish*) of the way in which power—through bodies of knowledge—produces disciplinary techniques for constraining and controlling human beings, in order to bring them into accord with institutional and social norms, Foucault in his later work (*The History of Sexuality*) directly connects bodies of knowledge (discourse) to the operations of power on the individual body in modern society. For Foucault, power has direct access to the body at an individual level through forms of 'self-government' or 'self-surveillance'. That is, power and knowledge in modern society are carried out by individuals on themselves. Bodies of knowledge produce certain forms of bodily behaviour and understandings, which create self-surveillance: a form of power which operates to extract time and labour from bodies and to produce and constitute social norms (1980: 104).

## Derrida's deconstruction

Derrida was a French philosopher whose work is controversial but also enormously influential around the world and across various disciplines. He published over forty books and 250 articles, essays and interviews. His work is significant for the way in which he employed various strategies and tactics to challenge and undermine traditional concepts, especially in philosophy and **metaphysics** (the primary principles and causes of things). Two of these strategies and tactics involve, first, disrupting or displacing binary oppositions that construct the way we think and, second, undermining traditional notions of communication and language. Derrida employs these tactics in order to contaminate the boundaries between philosophy and other disciplines, and to destabilise political, social, cultural and individual conceptions of identity and subjectivity. These strategies and tactics have become synonymous with the term 'deconstruction', a term first coined by Derrida in his book *Of Grammatology*. The term is built on German philosopher **Martin Heidegger's** word *destruktion* (Ger.), which he used to challenge metaphysics. However, Derrida considered *destruktion* to be too negative because it implied annihilation and demolition, and Derrida does not want to demolish metaphysics, but to reveal and disrupt its assumptions, so instead he reformulates *destruktion* into 'deconstruction'.

For Derrida deconstruction is a double movement: it is a disordering and disruption and also a rearranging of systems of thought (including language and philosophy). To rearrange is not to destroy or replace one system with another but to reveal how systems of metaphysical thought constantly undermine themselves and transgress their cultural, social and historical boundaries and limits and reveal themselves to be contextual and contingent.

In other words, Derrida does not want to demolish metaphysics, but to reveal and disrupt its assumptions. One of the assumptions of metaphysics is its belief and search for foundations or origins, and Derrida labels this search 'logocentrism', derived from the Greek word meaning speech, logic, reason, the word of God. A number of methods are used in Western metaphysics to found this 'origin', but Derrida famously focuses on '**binary oppositions**', which he argues were inaugurated by Plato (Derrida 1981; Harvey 1983: 124). Binary oppositions are constituted in and through metaphysics, and construct ways of thinking and perceiving the world. However, Derrida demonstrates that these oppositions are never neutral or universal; rather, they are hierarchical, meaning that one term in an opposition is always privileged over the other by particular cultures or in certain historical eras. Furthermore, each term depends on the other for its meaning, no matter which term in the opposition is privileged. For example, take the binary opposition black/white: there would be no concept of black without reference to and understanding of white. So binary oppositions are governed by an either/or distinction, which operates to organise and classify events, objects and relationships and the way human beings think.

Derrida outlines how deconstruction displaces oppositions in his essay 'Signature Event Context':

> [A]n opposition of metaphysical concepts (for example, speech/writing, presence/absence, etc.) is never the face-to-face of two terms, but a hierarchy and an order of subordination. Deconstruction cannot limit itself or proceed immediately to a neutralization: it must, by means of a double gesture, a double science, a double writing, practice an *overturning* of the classical opposition *and* a general *displacement* of the system. It is only on this condition that deconstruction will provide itself the means with which to *intervene* in the field of oppositions that it criticizes, which is also a field of nondiscursive forces. (Derrida 1986: 329)

This 'overturning' or 'displacement', then, is not a destruction of conceptual oppositions. It doesn't simply mean pulling something apart, such as a book or poem. More subtly, the deconstruction of oppositions reveals that there is a limit or boundary between the two terms in an opposition and, at the same time, that each term always already 'haunts' or informs the other and vice versa. This haunting is a consequence of what Derrida calls *différance*, which Derrida develops out of Saussure's theory of the arbitrary and differential relation of signs. And for this reason it is worth outlining this notion, not least because it is one of the strategies and tactics, mentioned earlier, for undermining traditional notions about communication and language.

*Différance*, based on semiology, replaces the 'e' of difference with an 'a' and thus 'incorporates two significations' (Derrida 1973: 129) of the word *différer* (difference, with an 'e'). The first signification, 'to defer' (deferral), suggests that différer (difference) encapsulates 'both spacing/temporalizing', which involves an operation of delay and detour (1973: 136). By following Saussure's '*arbitrariness of signs*' Derrida (1973: 139) demonstrates how this spacing/temporalising works in relation to signs and writing. That is, the sign always already 'represents' or stands in for or replaces what is absent (the word 'cat' replaces the object cat, for instance). So for Derrida, this replacement, or representation, is the sign as 'detour', or the sign as the deferral of the thing or object it is representing. The second signification of difference (*différer*), is 'to differ', which encapsulates Saussure's '*differential character* of signs' (1973: 139). To 'differ' refers to the sense of otherness, 'of not being identical'. The signifier (sensory/mental impression of the word 'cat') is not identical to the signified (the concept cat). That is, 'to differ' is a moment of differentiation that 'produces different things' (Derrida 1982: 9).

It is because the word 'difference' (with an 'e') cannot simultaneously refer to the two different meanings of 'to differ' and 'to defer', that Derrida uses the term *différance* (with an 'a'). *Différance*, then, captures the multivalence of meaning, and thus reveals how a differing and deferring movement in language and thought haunts and blurs the boundary between the terms in binary oppositions (such as sensible/intelligible, presence/absence, identity/other, nature/culture, intuitions/signification, male/female, black/white, and so on indefinitely) (Derrida 1982: 9).

*Différance* thus challenges a logocentric metaphysics that relies for its foundation on oppositions *per se*.

# cultural studies and poststructuralism … where to next?

Derrida's work in general, along with his notion of deconstruction, is employed in Cultural Studies as a tactic for reading political, ethical, social and cultural texts. Just like poststructuralists who were informed by but eventually moved beyond or developed certain assumptions latent in structuralism, so too do contemporary cultural theorists continue to develop the political and ethical implications of Derrida's work for everyday life, contemporary issues and practices. For instance, Nick Mansfield in Chapter 4 uses Derrida's work (in particular Derrida's discussion of **Emmanuel Levinas** and **Carl Schmitt**) to deconstruct the binary opposition between war and peace, friend and enemy, in our contemporary era. In this way Mansfield demonstrates how Derrida's deconstruction can 'provide a way of understanding the complexities and fluidities of historical events, outside the dogmatic and bigoted simplicities that we are often invited to endorse by cunning politicians and a passive media'. Nicole Anderson's Chapter 5 uses the work of Derrida to 'read' the recent consensual cannibalism of Armin Miewes and Bernd Brandes. One of the aims of Anderson's chapter is to use this cannibalism case to reveal the way in which traditional ethics is based on binary oppositions that construct behaviour and decisions along yes/no, right/wrong, good/bad choices only. In doing so, Anderson attempts to deconstruct the **humanist** ethical responses and discourses that surround and contribute to dominant thinking on this case of consensual cannibalism, as well as to make possible a different ethical 'response' not only to consensual cannibalism, but also to the various events and situations in our everyday lives.

Likewise, Foucault's work has enormous influence on Cultural Studies as a discipline, and provides cultural theorists with the tools with which to analyse contemporary cultural practices. In Chapter 6, Nikki Sullivan uses Foucault's notion of **power/knowledge** to outline the ways in which tattooing is perceived and received in contemporary Western society. Like the traditional view of language, she argues that the body is commonly understood as a 'sign' that refers to the essential identity or soul of the subject (the one true, unchanging reality). The implication of this traditional way of reading bodies is to posit that the soul/self exists outside society and culture: for example, tattoos are read by psychological or crime 'experts' as marks of deviance, psychological disturbance, and so on; while those with tattoos commonly view tattoos as a means by which to 'non-verbally communicate something about his or her inner-self to others'.

Drawing on Foucault's work, Sullivan argues against these traditional readings. She suggests that 'the soul/self is an effect of systems of "power/knowledge" rather than something that exists prior to, and/or outside, systems of power/ knowledge'. Given this, the aim of Sullivan's chapter is to reveal 'the ways in which we understand and experience tattooing', as well as telling 'us much about the stories that make us who we are'.

# THINKING WITH PART 2

o   Reflect on the binary opposition 'nature/culture'. It could be argued that 'nature' is the privileged term in the opposition. Why? One argument would be that in the context of global warming in the 21st century, nature is perceived by those governments that *are* pursuing the Kyoto Protocol as in need of preservation or protection from industrialisation or from societies and cultures that emit greenhouse gas (cars, fridges, factories, etc.) Because of this, in our current political climate, 'nature' is given more *value* than societies that do not want to join the Kyoto Protocol. Therefore, the implicit moral judgment of these societies is perpetuated by labelling them in negative terms, for example as selfish or irresponsible, whereas nature is morally prejudiced as 'good' because nature provides aesthetic pleasure or gives us medicinal cures. Or it could be argued that 'culture' is the privileged position. For example, from a humanist position it could be argued that culture is what separates the human from the animal, what enables creativity, sociality, language and community and what has enabled enlightened progress.

Here are some binary oppositions: man/woman, reason/emotion, conditional/ unconditional, subjective/objective, science/humanities, anglo/ethnic (white/ black), youth/age, good/evil.

o   *Identify* the privileged term/word in all of these oppositions listed above, and then

o   Choose one of the oppositions and *explain*, in no more than half a page, *why* you think this term is privileged. Remember there is no right or wrong answer. What might be some of the value judgments or moral or political prejudices surrounding the opposition?

o   Reflect upon the ways in which the line between the two terms in a binary opposition is blurred or arbitrary. For example, one term in an opposition (such as nature) always depends upon or refers to its other term, which is constructed as its opposite (such as culture). Reflect upon how this is an arbitrary construction by identifying some other words or concepts that each term in an opposition refers to. For example, nature does not simply refer to culture, but to other words or concepts that are also perceived as opposites, such as 'technology' or 'representation' (art for instance). More complex still, the word 'nature' evokes other terms that are not so much opposites but are synonymous, such as pleasure, purity, beauty, natural medicines etc. Likewise, culture refers to other words or concepts that are also perceived as opposites, such as biology or gender. Again culture also refers to words or concepts that are synonymous, such as art, music, national identities, dance, etc.

- ○ What does this say about the stability of binary oppositions? What does this say about the notion of the signified? (That is, signifieds are also signifiers that slip and slide into one another.)

- ○ What might be the ethical and political consequences of these binary oppositions? And what might be the implications of these oppositions being blurred? Think about how these oppositions operate on a daily basis in your life. Can you think of examples where binary oppositions work for or against some people in some situations?

- ○ How do each of the chapters in this section apply theory to expose the political and ethical implications binary oppositions have on particular practices (war, cannibalism, tattooing)?

# no peace without war, no war without peace: deconstructing war.

AUTHOR: nick mansfield

## INTRODUCTION

No term has been more controversial in recent cultural criticism than **'deconstruction'**. Deconstruction has been celebrated and vilified, mystified and ridiculed like no other term in academic circles: even lambasted as the end of 'Western civilisation' as we know it. The term has also passed into common speech: to describe the way you might approach an argument, what you might do with scaffolding when you're finished with it, and even as the name for a style of denim!

The word 'deconstruction' first appeared as the translation of German philosopher **Martin Heidegger's** (1889–1976) term *'Destruktion'*. Its widespread use, however, is identified with the Algerian-French philosopher Jacques Derrida (1930–2004), who rose to prominence in the French philosophical scene in the 1960s and in the English-speaking world a decade later. Derrida's work was first taken up by literary critics and so it was in English and literary studies that deconstruction first really developed as a technique. One of the initial ideas associated with deconstruction was that the meaning of a particular linguistic sign always involved some uncertainty. A sign might be *present* to a reader or viewer in the sense that it is part of their literal material experience of the world. They can see or hear a word on the page or a spoken word. Yet, at the same time, the *meaning* of the word—what that word is supposed to communicate—is always *absent*: it cannot be part of the immediate experience of the reader or viewer. That's why it has to be represented or mediated to us. It must emerge through a material sign of one kind or another. The material sign, therefore, is something present that indicates something that is absent: it is, in other words, the absent made present. The consequence of this is that what we experience in the world is only ever a 'trace' of the meaning the words are supposed to be communicating. We pursue this trace, but it always means there will be no certainty that we will arrive at the 'absent' thing we imagine we are connecting with when we experience the sign. The meaning cannot be made present and cannot attain even the unstable material certainty of a mark on a page, or a sound in the air. So the meaning of any text will be uncertain, even indeterminate. We experience this uncertainty every day in classrooms, domestic arguments and legal courts and parliaments when the meaning of a text is debated, and fiercely different interpretations of even the simplest language can lead to violent disagreement.

In literary interpretation, this first wave of deconstruction led to a fairly repetitive style of critical writing: critics merely showed that in every text there was an uncertainty and irresolution hanging over the processes from which meaning was inferred. If this was to be true of every sign, it would of necessity be true of every text. After that, what more could be said? Derrida tried to separate himself from this approach to literary study, which he saw as a dead end. However, this view of deconstruction—that it sees everything as meaningless—remains widespread. The key problem here was that it presented deconstruction as simply a philosophy of language and textuality. In fact, Derridean philosophy proposes this deconstructive view of language as merely one example of a much more general phenomenon. Deconstruction is not a philosophy of language. Rather, it is a response to the **metaphysical** traditions in Western philosophy that have manifested themselves through a logic of **binary opposition**.

Binary oppositions define things in terms of opposing pairs. These can be highly abstract, such as 'ideal versus material'. They can be highly literal: 'up/down', 'in/out'. They can be somewhere in between: 'male/female', 'us/them'. Derrida argued that these pairings were not mutually exclusive opposites, but that they determined and required one another. He demonstrated this by what he called the logic of supplementarity, which works like this. Normally we would consider some simple thing or identity to be self-contained and self-sufficient. For example, take the concept 'masculinity'. Normally we would define masculinity in terms of its own fixed attributes: masculinity is connected with the male body, which has a penis, or XY chromosomes. Masculinity also has more abstract attributes: on the positive side we like to think it's associated with bravery and a desire to protect. On the negative side, it's commonly associated with violence and gratuitous competitiveness. Whether any of these particular things is true or not doesn't matter: the point is we believe that something like masculinity is defined in terms of what it *is*. Femininity, on the other hand, has its own list of attributes that give it content and identity.

The problem Derrida points out with this is that if there were only masculine things in the world, there would be no need for us to have the term 'masculinity'. Everything would be masculine and the category would not have any use. In other words, the only reason we need a category 'masculinity' is because of the feminine. Something different from the masculine exists, causing us to need to have definitions of both of them. This sounds obvious, but the consequence is that neither masculinity nor femininity is to be defined in terms of itself, of what it is, but each requires the other in order to make any sense. Masculinity is a term that really only comes to mean things because of its difference from femininity. Masculinity, therefore, is not a self-contained thing defined according to its own enduring nature and content. It is that thing that is not-feminine.

Derrida's term 'the supplement' is used to summarise what the consequences of this are: masculinity is supposed to be a self-contained thing defined by what is *inside* it (masculine attributes). However, masculinity can only be a meaningful term because of what is supposedly *outside* it. It is supposed to be a fully self-contained and self-same thing, but in fact what defines it is not inside but outside. It is not defined by what it is, but by what is *supplementary* to it. This supplement complicates things because it is *both* outside it—as what it is not—and inside it—defining what it is. In the end, the difference between outside and inside becomes meaningless: the outside is inside; the inside only means anything because of the outside, and so on.

What this means is that femininity is part of the definition of masculinity. Femininity can never be resolutely separated from masculinity. This goes for all binary oppositions, especially those that have a strong moral, political or cultural meaning: us versus them, the national versus the foreigner, the familiar versus the strange, and so on. Each of the first terms only has meaning in relation to the other, or, to be more accurate, through the other. Therefore, it is impossible to clearly separate one side of the pair from the other. The familiar can only make sense in relation to the strange. Thus the strange is always part of the logic of the familiar. Politics commonly works by insisting that these differences are real, unambiguous and eternal. Yet to deconstruct these oppositions shows that the dividing line imagined to separate one group from another is artificial. It has to be installed within a complex that is far more unclear and fluid.

The aim of this chapter is to look at these issues in relation to a binary opposition that is usually seen as incontestable: the opposition between war and peace. Common sense would seem to insist that war and peace are radically different things and it would be disastrous for mankind, and deeply immoral, to allow them to be confused. There are two broad problems with this way of thinking: one historical, the other theoretical.

Historically, the difference between war and peace is constantly breaking down. Let us take two examples. First, it has become common parlance to describe things that were once viewed as social or political issues as wars. Poverty, crime and the illicit drug economy are now all dealt with not by politics, administration, healthcare or even policing, but by war. Our initial response to this would be to say that this use of the term 'war' is simply metaphorical. However, there has been a slippage between metaphor and fact, so that what was originally simply *labellled* as a war starts to take on the *attributes* of warfare: police forces, for example, have become increasingly militarised in terms of the weapons and tactics they use, and even the uniforms they wear. Most police forces in the Western world have at least a paramilitary unit, such as a SWAT team, developed in imitation of military special operations units. The announcement, almost immediately after September 11, 2001, that the response was to be 'war on terror', meant that other approaches—diplomacy, policing and so on—were excluded. Once you announce something is a war, you put yourself under pressure to act in a warlike manner, by invading another country for example, as the USA did in relation to Afghanistan in 2001 and Iraq in 2003. In short, there has been a confusion between war, which is supposed to arise only at the frontiers between societies and nations, and social issues, which are supposed to be dealt with by policy and negotiation.

The second way in which warfare and peace have become confused historically is in the way in which Western countries are now unwilling to accept warfare if it has consequences. These consequences might be the death of co-citizens, something now increasingly intolerable. Similarly, societies no longer accept that the normal cycle of social or economic life should be disrupted for warfare. In his book *The New Western Way of War*, Martin Shaw writes of recent wars: 'The key understanding ... was that warfighting must be carried on simultaneously with "normal" economics, politics and social life in the West. It was imperative it did not impact negatively on these' (Shaw 2005: 73). In earlier eras, societies often changed the patterns of government, economics and social policies in order to gear their societies to warfare. This no longer seems to be the case. Governments are desperate to make sure that the normal fabric of social life is undisturbed by whatever wars a society is fighting. This is not the complete separation of war from society, as much as a way in which the two can become fundamentally compatible and consistent: the practice of war and the profits of peace should be allowed to work together. In short, then, war and peace have become confused in the way they are practised.

Theoretically, the issue is similarly complex. War is a theoretical issue for a number of reasons. First, because war is a legal as well as an historical matter.

Declarations of war have significant consequences for nations, combatants and peoples, so the actual legal definition of war is a serious and complex matter. In more abstract philosophy, however, war has long been evoked as a fundamental issue to do with the very way in which human societies constitute themselves. Most influentially, the English political theorist **Thomas Hobbes** (1588–1679) defined war as the natural state of humanity, and the thing that the constitution of society is supposed to guard us against. Most theoretical and philosophical thought about war refers to this argument in one way or another, implicitly or explicitly, either confirming, adapting or refuting it. Whatever the response, it is clear that the modern understanding of what human social life is pivots on a clear appraisal of the relationship between violence and social life in general, and between war and peace.

How does deconstruction deal with this complex issue of the relationship between war and peace? I would like to address this question by a reading of two contributions Derrida has made to the philosophical treatment of warfare. The first is a commentary on the theme of hospitality in the work of Lithuanian-French philosopher **Emmanuel Levinas** (1905–95). The second is part of Derrida's critique of the work of German jurist and legal philosopher **Carl Schmitt** (1888–1985).

Hobbes had argued that human beings live in nature in a state of uncontrollable antagonism towards one another, and the only way this violence can be controlled is by the creation of a sovereign authority capable of arrogating the right to violence to itself, and thus eliminating violence from society at large. Hobbes imagined a perhaps mythical event where humans granted this power to a sovereign authority figure and, as a consequence, political authority was the result of a consensual act wherein power was willingly conceded by humanity in general. Peace, according to this argument, is the work of human culture, an interruption or exclusion of our natural violence. Other later philosophers like **Immanuel Kant** (1724–1804) echoed Hobbes' view of peace as an artificial and sophisticated act of civilisation, in which the aim of society and political structures is always to control violence. Even in the work of a writer as vastly different from Kant and Hobbes as **Sigmund Freud** (1856–1939), violence is something primitive and archaic that interrupts the surface civility of advanced and ordered social life.

Levinas' view is the inverse of Hobbes'. Levinas' central philosophical idea was that the individual human subject comes into the world not as something autonomous and self-motivating, but in response to something or someone that always precedes it. In Levinas' own work, this idea was a profoundly religious one and the '**Other**' who calls the self into existence is at least comparable to God. Other writers, however, have taken a much more social interpretation of this idea, arguing that what precedes and calls us into being is other people within the social world. This could take the general form of our being in and responsibility to other people in general, or it could be something more individual: the fact that our existence is a response to the longing, anticipation and love for us of our parents, which called us to them even before our conception. There is also a more abstract philosophical view: that the Otherness to which we respond is the simple fact that whatever exists precedes us, and will always *exceed* us as well, by being always larger and prior to us, and too much for us to simply accommodate within our consciousness.

The consequence of Levinas' idea is that within our individual subjectivity there is always an openness to the otherness that precedes us. This openness means that whatever we do is a *response*, and thus an act of *responsibility*. We live in a world where certainty is more valued than speculation, where fixity and identity count for more than fluidity and ambiguity. This results in our social obligation to have a fixed sense of who we are, to have a personal identity that is stable, consistent and rational. Yet, according to Levinas, these fixities float on the surface of an instability that is a direct consequence of the fact that the most primary aspect of our being is our openness to that which is outside us, the Other to whom our very existence is always a response. Within our apparent assured self-identity is a trace of the Other outside and prior to us.

This way of thinking leads to an interesting rethinking of the relationship between war and peace. War, for Levinas, is not our natural state that social institutions must exclude. It is, in fact, the reverse. War is a clash that happens within the ferment of identities and values that define the social world. Our primary state is one of openness to the Other, our own offering to the Other as an act of responsibility and mutual welcoming. Peace then is our primal state, of which war is an interruption. This is the direct inverse of the Hobbesian/ Kantian idea.

Derrida discusses these issues in a few pages in his book on Levinas, *Adieu— To Emmanuel Levinas*. Derrida was profoundly influenced by Levinas' work, but never took this to mean that it was beyond rigorous scrutiny. Indeed, he believed that only such scrutiny showed real respect for the work of other thinkers. In this particular argument he starts by raising doubt that war and peace are indeed simple opposites, to be viewed as mutually exclusive and separate from one another. Nor is he satisfied by the idea that war simply precedes peace, or vice versa. Levinas had argued that prior to all human action and identity was an initial openness to the Other. Every human act that follows on from this will always be *after* that preliminary openness and thus somehow *junior* to it. Indeed, according to Levinas, every act, no matter how violent it might be, bears within it some trace of openness to the other. Levinas even famously argued that it is impossible to murder the Other, because even as you kill someone, you cannot fully extinguish the openness that constituted you in the first place. This would mean that even the most violent act bears within it some residual trace of responsibility.

In terms of war, this means that every act of war is at some level residually peaceful, despite itself. No hostility can be so pure and complete that it does not at some point exclude peace totally and completely. At first, this seems to be peace's ultimate victory: no war can defeat peace because peace is so deeply installed in human interaction that it is impossible to absolutely erase it. Derrida, however, is troubled by the argument that war is always residually peaceful. The consequence of this would be to undermine the drive to destroy or surpass war as a form of human interaction, because war is in part always peace anyway. To Derrida, the ethics of this argument are deeply problematic.

In terms of deconstruction, the consequences are twofold. First, it is acknowledged that the frontier between war and peace is not a simple dividing line where two totally alien concepts set themselves rigorously apart from one another. War and peace interpenetrate and overlap, just as we have seen with the supplementary logic of masculinity and femininity outlined above: war and peace include one another, because they can make no sense without some reference to one another. This means that war and peace will always bear within one another some trace or part of their opposite, no matter which point of view you adopt, the Hobbesian or the Levinasian. The second consequence is that this relationship never settles into a situation with which we can be happy. The relationship between the two will always be unfixed and deeply problematic. War will always bear a trace of peace and vice versa, and this is the political complexity with which we must deal. In political terms, this idea should not surprise us. Where wars are fought in the name of peace, democracy, liberation and human rights, it seems clear that the relationship between war and peace even in its most brutally literal and material reality is unstable and problematic.

The second binary opposition relevant to war that Derrida deconstructs is the one between friend and enemy in the book *Politics of Friendship*. Carl Schmitt had argued influentially in his *Concept of the Political* that politics was the process by which a human group like a nation gained its identity and solidarity by identifying an enemy. It was, therefore, the real and determined possibility of war (Derrida 1997: 84) that constituted a political group. The important thing about the enemies that groups constructed for themselves was that they were public. In fact the choice of an enemy defined what the public actually was, according to Schmitt. It brought the 'public' into being. Therefore, the relationship of enmity you feel for your nation's enemies has nothing to do with your personal feelings about them, nor does it even have anything to do with any aspect of their nature, such as their ethnicity, history or identity. It is possible to identify your enemy as a member of a particular group but that is not why they are your enemy. A group simply needs to have enemies in order to reach the threshold of politics.

Theoretically, therefore, since you have no personal feeling about your enemy, your enemy could also be your personal friend. Mostly, we would explain this paradox by saying that the person your society chooses as your enemy is to do with your *public* identity, while your personal liking for them is *private*. The problem with this argument is that Schmitt has already said that the public only comes into being *after* the enemy has been identified. Up to that point, the difference between public and private wouldn't make any sense. So there's a contradiction. Your private friend cannot be absolutely distinguished from your public enemy before the criteria by which you could do this are defined. The announcement of your public enemy cuts across your friendship, contradicting and undermining it.

So, Derrida argues, according to Schmitt's logic someone can be both your friend and your enemy at the same time. What complicates this even further is that Schmitt argues that this whole concept of politics is not one that he is inventing, but one that he is merely deriving from European political history. It is therefore something that he defines as essential to the European tradition. If your enemy is outside this tradition—interestingly and crucially for our era, the example Schmitt gives is the Islamic world—then they are not only the enemy of your group (while, remember, they could be your friend), but the enemy of politics, perhaps even the enemy of the friend/enemy distinction altogether. In short, they could be your friend-enemy-enemy, or your enemy-friend-enemy, or any number of other combinations!

The consequence of this is that the distinction between friend and enemy on which politics supposedly depends could be contradicted by other levels of friendship and enmity. The distinction then operates in contradiction and break-down. Potentially then, friendship and enmity are always in a state of confusion, despite the fact that it is this distinction that is supposed to allow politics to make sense in the first place. The consequences of this deconstruction of Schmitt's logic is that it reveals that, as with war and peace, the distinction between friend and enemy is always forced. The example of Islam is telling, because the history of relations between the Islamic and the Christian world is always talked about as if it is an encounter between strangers, despite the complex and often intimate entanglement of these two cultures throughout their history: from their cohabitation in the Iberian peninsula through their shared inheritance of the Ancient Greek philosophical legacy, to confrontation in the era of European **colonialism** to the deep involvement of the West in the politics and resources of the Middle East. In other words, historical reality bears out the fact that the distinctions we draw between friendship and enmity betray very complex and deep entanglements that political leaders have to deny in order to make their contrived enemies look alien and unknowable.

The historical parallels we have been able to draw with the consequences of deconstruction show that the latter is not some abstract, obscure and elegant intellectual game. It can provide a way of understanding the complexities and fluidities of historical events, outside the dogmatic and bigoted simplicities that we are often invited to endorse by cunning politicians and a passive media. Deconstruction gets beyond the simple assumptions and unquestioning acceptances that political institutions often encourage us to adopt. It is in dealing with these complexities and uncertainties that the often ambiguous and difficult issues with which we are confronted can be properly addressed. In simplicity lies quick and easy, but false and inevitably costly, solutions.

key readings

Caputo, J.D. (ed.) 1993. *Deconstruction in a Nutshell*. New York: Fordham University Press.

Derrida, Jacques 2005. *Rogues: Two Essays on Reason*, trans. Pascale-Anne Brault and Michael Naas. Stanford University Press.

Royle, Nicholas 2003. *Jacques Derrida*. London: Routledge.

# CHAPTER FIVE

# eating the other: deconstructing the 'ethics' of cannibalism.

AUTHOR: nicole anderson

## INTRODUCTION

As reported by the BBC news, in 2001 Armin Meiwes (a computer service technician from Kassel, Germany) was arrested for the cannibalism of Bernd Brandes (an engineer from Berlin). The court ruled that as cannibalism was not a recognised offence under German law, and because this particular cannibalism was consensual, Meiwes could not be tried for murder. Instead, it constituted 'illegal euthanasia' (euthanasia being, under strict control, legal in Germany), for which the appropriate charge was manslaughter. On these grounds, in 2003, Meiwes was convicted, contentiously, of manslaughter and sentenced to eight years and six months. However, the prosecution requested a retrial, arguing that the case constituted 'murder for sexual gratification' because, after having sex with Brandes, Meiwes videotaped the killing and eating of Brandes, preceded by Brandes' consent (Meiwes stabbed Brandes to death then tenderised his flesh on meat hooks in the basement of his home. He then filleted the body, froze the parts and over several weeks thawed, cooked and ate them). For these reasons, and for fear that his lust for flesh would not stop with *consenting* adults, the prosecution argued that Meiwes was not fit to be released into society. Consequently, in a Frankfurt court on 9 May 2006, Meiwes was reconvicted of murder and given life in prison.

When I first read this case, what immediately came to mind was Jacques Derrida's interview 'Eating Well: or the Calculation of the Subject', where he suggests that we, symbolically, always already cannibalise the 'other' (other people, animals, things). By this he means that we cannibalise in and through varying forms of appropriation, ownership, desiring, repetition, mimicking of the other. For example, we adopt as our own another's style, mannerisms, desires, tastes, attitudes, habits, beliefs, politics, and so on. Derrida puts it this way: symbolic cannibalism of the other is the appropriation, the taking in of the other 'whether it's a matter of words or of things, of sentences, of daily bread or wine, the tongue, the lips, or the breast of the other' (Derrida 1991: 113). In suggesting that we always already cannibalise the other, Derrida deconstructs what it means to be an 'ethical subject'. In order to prepare for this discussion of Derrida's **deconstruction**, I want first to give a brief outline of what Derrida, in his interview, means by the terms 'subject' and 'ethical'.

Since the **humanist** tradition 'the subject' has been conceived as an 'I' or 'self' that is autonomous. To be autonomous means that each individual has an 'essential' personality and identity (inherent qualities that exist beyond historical, cultural and social *context*). To be autonomous also means having the freedom to make decisions without reference to this context, and by means of a rational calculability (hence the subtitle of Derrida's interview). And rationality requires the ability (uniquely human, on this view) to categorise, calculate and objectivise (classify) the environment and other people. It also means believing that we make decisions independently of emotions as well as the **body-politic**, by which I mean the society and political state or culture in which the subject lives. So decisions are believed to be calculable, and made in relation to laws, rules and objective facts. To be autonomous, then, is to be rational, and to be rational is to be a 'human subject'. Now, we make 'ethical decisions' based on this rational calculability. And this rational calculability in our decision-making is procured by 'setting down a set of universal principles for regulating behaviour' (Diprose 1994: 18). What is more, these universal principles set up **normative** standards for judging and deciding which human actions can be called right or wrong. As a result, individual identity, or the 'subject', is formed in and through this standardised normative ethics (hence the humanist notion of an 'ethical subject').

It is precisely these humanist-**metaphysical** notions of the subject and ethics that Derrida deconstructs in his interview. To deconstruct, as Derrida explains, is to 'practice an *overturning* of the classical opposition *and* a general displacement of the system' (Derrida 1986: 329). The 'classical oppositions' Derrida refers to here are the **binary oppositions** on which our Western philosophical-metaphysical traditions have been founded: they permeate our language and therefore construct our rationalist modes of thinking, as well as inform our politics, ethics, and so on. Examples of binary oppositions include male/female, white/black, reason/emotions, good/bad, mind/body, etc. But these binaries are never equal, or simply neutral, terms. Rather, they are always already hierarchical (male is higher on the hierarchical scale than female, which is lower on the scale and thus underprivileged or marginalised. So male is privileged over female, white is privileged over black, good over bad, mind over body, reason over emotion, and so on). Consequently, binary oppositions perpetuate and continually reinforce political and **ideological** views of the world.

In deconstructing binary oppositions, Derrida does not simply reverse the opposition, privileging the previous marginalised term, and thus creating a new hierarchical opposition (as if it were that easy). What he does in this overturning is to 'displace them': to defamiliarise or **denaturalise** their construction. In and through this displacement what Derrida reveals is the ideological, political, cultural and ethical operations of these binary oppositions. Specifically, in his interview 'Eating Well', Derrida deconstructs the 'ethical subject' so as to reveal and displace the ways in which traditional ethics construct the subject's decisions along binary oppositional choices only: either yes or no, right or wrong, good or bad. In the first half of the chapter, then, my first aim will be to offer critical insights on the ways in which the notion of the humanist ethical subject is perpetuated in and through the dominant thinking and discourses that surround this particular case of 'consensual cannibalism'. The second aim will be to use this case, and the humanist ethical responses to it, as a lens through which to explore Derrida's notions of 'symbolic cannibalism' and 'eating well' in order to reveal the ways in which Derrida's deconstruction of the humanist ethical subject might make possible a different ethical 'response' not only to consensual cannibalism, but also to the various events and situations in our everyday lives.

# consensual cannibalism: some humanist ethical responses.

After researching this case of consensual cannibalism, and after reading dozens of newspaper articles, internet discussions and interviews with Meiwes' and Brandes' relatives and friends, I have come to the conclusion that there are two dominant ethical responses to the case. The first response argues that it is unethical to prohibit consensual cannibalism since this would constitute a violation of the rights of human subjects to make their own decisions about their bodies. This position is humanist because it assumes that the subject is independent of others and that the subject 'comes prior to relations with others' (Diprose 1994: 102).

That is, what the subject does to his or her body has no bearing on the bodies of others or on the 'body-politic'. In other words, the subject is autonomous. However, to take the position that we are, as subjects, not connected to others is problematic, not least because it perpetuates **René Descartes'** notion of the *ego cogito*, which posits that a 'thinking thing' is separate from the body in which the thinking thing arises. And to posit this is to deny the way in which we think and learn through the body. That is, thinking, learning conventions, discourses and techniques are habitually reproduced in and through the body (this is called **embodiment**). So to deny the way in which we are embodied is to deny how individual identities and bodily habits are (in)formed by others, and by culture and society.

The other, more dominant, humanist response argues that consensual cannibalism is unethical because it is harmful, obviously to the one being cannibalised, but also to the body-politic in general, because eating another human is a transgression of a cultural taboo and thus attacks the ideals, values, ethics and beliefs of the body-politic. Because this position suggests that the body-politic is affected by this transgression, then unlike the first position, it does not posit that an individual body has no bearing on the bodies of others, or that the individual body exists in isolation (autonomous). Yet despite this, this second position still argues, somewhat contradictorily, that consent to cannibalism cannot be rational: to desire to be eaten is by definition 'irrational', because at the heart of the 'rational subject' is the opposite desire: 'self-preservation'. Thus, in this context at least, the individual does not have the right to determine what she/he does with her/his body. This is because in order for one to exert one's 'individual human rights' one has to be a subject, and in order to be a subject one has to be rational. Therefore, Brandes cannot consent to be eaten, because he is not rational and therefore he is not a subject (and by implication, not human).

However, in relation to Meiwes, who was deemed rational (after undergoing psychological tests), those who hold this position also argue that if the decision to eat another is made rationally, then the person making this decision (in this case, Meiwes) can only be morally sick or evil, and thus a danger to the body-politic. And as **Michel Foucault** argues, the reason why exponents of this position think that to make the 'rational' decision to eat another human is morally sick or evil is because such an act transgresses ethical, medical and legal notions of what constitutes 'human nature' and hence, bodily and psychological norms (Foucault 1997: 51–2). Meiwes and Brandes, then, not only transgress but also disrupt the bodily and ethical norm, and in consequence the body-politic marginalises them as abnormal.

Furthermore, because Brandes cannot consent, precisely because he is irrational, and because Meiwes is morally evil, this second position **discursively constructs** an opposition between Meiwes as 'active' and Brandes as 'passive' participants in the relationship. Meiwes is perceived as 'active' because he is constructed and described as a 'hunter' due to his 'search' on the internet for someone to cannibalise (this is how Meiwes and Brandes found each other). While Brandes does consent, this desire to be eaten is deemed irrational because it is the opposite desire of the rational subject, that of self-preservation. In this sense Brandes is constituted as 'passive' because he is not rational enough to consent (that is, make a reasoned decision about his life). He is therefore perceived as vulnerable, and thus constructed as 'victim'. Furthermore, because Brandes is not considered to be rational, he is not considered a subject (because in humanist discourse a subject is defined and constituted by rationality). Implicitly, then, Brandes is positioned as an 'animal', existing outside or marginalised from the body-politic. (He was also described as an animal by those commenting on the case in newspapers and internet sites.)

What both these humanist ethical positions have in common is the presumption that humans are 'subjects' and thus rational, and that rationality goes hand in hand with ethics. That is, these positions either argue that humans are 'rational' enough to make 'ethical decisions' about their bodies (individual human rights), or that in consenting to being eaten one *cannot* be 'rational'. Despite their differences, both positions make 'rationality' the basis for the subject's capacity to act ethically: autonomy and rationality form the cornerstone of a humanist ethics.

This notion of the humanist subject as autonomous and rational not only produces a binary opposition between mind and body, rationality and irrationality, etc., but also implies that 'embodied differences between subjects are inconsequential' (Diprose 1994: 18). However, the consequences of not acknowledging embodied differences (such as gendered, classed, racial or cultural-social differences) is that we deny the differences that context fosters and in so doing we attempt to reduce the **other** (another person) to the same (to something that corresponds with, or is like, me, my ego; to identify the other as like me is to disregard or reduce their differences). This attempted reduction, then, entails sacrificing the difference of the other in order to preserve the social and ethical norms of the body-politic (and the individual's identity and role or place—that is, membership—within it).

This sacrifice is further reinforced by the institutional (legal, educational, political) regulation of behaviours and thus bodies, which in turn marginalises bodies that do not conform. This entails a distinction between bodies considered normal (that is, bodies that conform to social and cultural conventions that are instituted by juridical regulations) and bodies that do not conform, which are pathologised in various ways and finally marginalised, either willingly or not. I am not suggesting that we simply abandon, or can abandon, rules and laws. Rather, I want to focus on the cost of this sacrifice of the other so as to preserve a notion and belief in the humanist subject, which is materialised in and through the body.

The problem, then, with the humanist positions or responses to the issue of consensual cannibalism that I have outlined is that in privileging the notion of the subject as rational the position denies the singular context of every event, and thus brings about 'closure': a reduction of the difference of the other. (And by context I mean not only the socio-cultural context, but the context of the singular relation between subject and other.) But also, the polarised responses so characteristic of humanist ethical positions *perhaps* limits the subjects' and the body-politic's potential for responding differently to an issue like consensual cannibalism. I would argue, then, that one of the problems with a humanist ethical position is that there is little room for difference generated by, and encountered in, the ethical dilemmas and conflicts arising from the subject's relation to others. For example, the aspect of consent in this cannibalism case is finally ignored and thus any singular ethical relation between Brandes and Meiwes is denied and marginalised as abnormal. (I will touch on this further in the last section of this chapter.)

In what follows, I want to suggest that this 'closure', this humanist reduction and sacrificing of the other in order to stabilise normative behaviours, bodies and identity, is itself a cannibalistic gesture. This raises the question: how do we, indeed can we, ethically respond to this issue of consensual cannibalism, in fact to anything in general, without being cannibalistic?

# eating well: deconstructing humanist ethical responses.

It is precisely a humanist ethics of the subject (which I have argued is operating in the dominant responses to this case of consensual cannibalism) that Derrida deconstructs in his interview 'Eating Well: or the Calculation of the Subject'. What I touched on in the previous section is that these humanist responses to the case of consensual cannibalism constitute and maintain a binary opposition between human and animal. And as animals are generally considered 'other' to humans, the position also reinforces the opposition between human and other (in general). Now, Derrida is not interested in eliminating this opposition (if that were possible), nor does he suggest that we can simply abandon the notion of the subject. Instead, Derrida unpacks the presumptions underlying this opposition in order to dislocate or disrupt (rather than eliminate) the humanist ethical subject. According to Derrida, one of the main presumptions behind this opposition is that the human, and not the animal, is defined as a 'subject', who in turn is characterised as rational (a principle of calculability) and is 'subjected to the law in its very autonomy, to ethical and juridical law, to political law or power' and thereby has the 'power to ask questions' (Derrida 1991: 99, 100). As I mentioned earlier, the humanist position argues that it is only because the subject is rational, autonomous and so on that ethical questions can be posed.

Derrida not only throws into question the opposition constructed between human (subject) and animal (other), but also the corresponding opposition between the ethical maxim 'Thou shalt not kill' another human, and the idea that it is legally and morally permissible to kill and eat animals (cannot kill humans/can kill animals). For Derrida, what is enabled by these oppositions is the construction of 'distance' between human and animals (and thus subject and other more generally), which works to justify the status of the subject as different from the animal, and thus, in turn, justifies killing and eating animals.

What is interesting in the light of this is not only the humanist responses to Brandes (rendering him 'animal' by arguing that he is not a subject, because rational subjects do not consent to being eaten), but also the myriad questions this raises. For example, because Brandes has been constituted as animal, shouldn't it be permissible to eat him? And, if the distinction between human and animal is not fixed, and if the boundary between the 'who' and the 'what' is ambiguous, then eating an 'animal' may be cannibalistic, and if this is so is this not perhaps more problematic than eating another human with their consent? Asking these questions is to start to deconstruct the distinction between human and animal, and/or it means having to redefine what constitutes an animal and a human. Blurring the distinction between animal and human reveals the ambiguity latent in the notion of the humanist subject (as simply rational). According to Derrida (1991: 108), the subject renders the animal distant enough to be edible, and in doing so the subject is able to maintain its autonomy and its essential identity. But in eating the animal we not only distance it, but we acknowledge that we sacrifice this other, and it is here, as Derrida argues, that the distinction between human and animal becomes problematic. He demonstrates this in his interview by shifting between the *literal* eating or ingesting of the animal and the *symbolic* ingesting or eating of the other as human (a symbolic representation of cannibalism) (Guyer 1995: 68). Through this shifting between *literal* eating of the animal and the *symbolic* eating of the human, Derrida explores the shifting boundary or limit or distinction between the eating of animals and the eating of humans, and in doing so reveals the ambiguity, the difference (**différance**) at the heart of subjectivity (difference being something that is never simply ego, or identity, but rather an 'otherness' that is elusive, unknowable and undefinable).

What this deconstruction of the human/animal opposition also highlights is that there is not simply a unified, essential identity; rather, if there is any identity at all it is because it is based on what is different within and to itself: it is based on a relationship with others. This is why Derrida (1991: 100) argues that while rationality, autonomy and so on are real, the autonomous subject, in the humanist sense, is a fable. I imagine the humanist response to this paradox would be to argue that while Brandes is marginalised as 'animal' in one sense he remains 'human' precisely because he has the *potential* to be restored to rationality and thus subjectivity.

For Derrida, then, the literal eating of the animal becomes a metaphor of eating the human, in order to demonstrate that we always already, symbolically, cannibalise the other (as human). As I mentioned earlier, this symbolic cannibalisation of the other is the appropriation, the taking in of the other, but it is also a reduction of the other to the same in the most negative sense (because it denies the difference, the 'otherness' of the other person). How does the fact that we already symbolically cannibalise the other suggest we should respond to this literal case of consensual cannibalism: can we do so without being cannibalistic? Any attempt to answer this question with a yes or no would itself be cannibalistic, because an answer is always at risk of offering a prescription, and thus potentially delineating response into yes/no, either/or oppositions characteristic of the humanist ethics of the subject. Rather than answering the questions, Derrida poses an entirely different question, one that does not close down ethical response but opens it to dialogue and to the possibility of perhaps being able to think and respond ethically in another way. The question is not 'should one eat or not eat, eat this and not that, the living or nonliving, man or animal, but since one must eat in any case ... *how* for goodness sake should one *eat well* (*bien manger*)?' (Derrida 1991: 115). That is, if we always already (symbolically) cannibalise the other, then how do we do this responsibly? Applying Derrida's notions of 'symbolic cannibalism' and 'eating well' to this real and literal case of consensual cannibalism, the question becomes not *only* one of whether or not it is right or wrong to practise consensual cannibalism (and I say *only* because one can never stop making decisions or get beyond the subject and the humanist logic this entails, politically as well as ethically; that is, we cannot not cannibalise the other). Rather, the question also becomes how do we take *responsibility* for an issue such as this one? And is this literal case one of 'eating well'? To answer this, let's look at what responsibility (which does not simply repeat a humanist ethics) means for Derrida.

As I pointed out earlier in this chapter, the humanist position suggests that one cannot make ethical decisions if one is not rational and autonomous. Yet for Derrida (1991: 115) that 'one must eat well does not mean ... taking in and grasping itself, but learning and giving to eat ... One never eats entirely on one's own.' What Derrida is arguing here is that ethics, and thus responsibility, does not exist in isolation from others, but that responsibility is defined as a sharing that invokes both hostility and hospitality; a 'respect for the other at the very moment when, in experience (I am speaking here of metonymical 'eating', as well as the very concept of experience) one must begin to identify with the other who is to be assimilated, interiorized, understood ideally' (1991: 115). What this means for the real case of consensual cannibalism will be discussed in the following section.

# a dialogue: symbolic and real cannibalism.

In ascribing one meaning to Brandes (that he is not a subject because he is irrational) and to Meiwes (that he is a murderer) and thus marginalising their actions as ethically and bodily abnormal, we silence them; we ignore the context and reduce their ethically singular relationship and its singular ethical meanings and context to a universal prescriptive ethics. Does this mean that we should not make legal, ethical and moral judgments and decisions about this case? And if prescriptive decisions have to be made, what does this say about the effectiveness of Derrida's notion of 'eating well'? And how does the 'real' case shed light on Derrida's interview, if at all? To address these questions I want to start by quoting Derrida from 'Force of Law' on a notion touched on briefly in 'Eating Well':

> [F]or a decision to be just and responsible, it must, in its proper moment if there
> is one, be both regulated and without regulation: it must conserve the law and
> also destroy it or suspend it enough to have to reinvent it in each case, rejustify it
> … Each case is other, each decision is different and requires an absolutely unique
> interpretation, which no existing, coded rule can or ought to guarantee absolutely.
> (Derrida 1992: 23)

In this passage Derrida suggests, first, that we always have to make legally and ethically prescriptive decisions. And a lawful decision requires that Meiwes is either a murderer or he is not, he is either insane or evil or he is not, and so on. As we have seen in my explication of 'Eating Well', and in the passage from 'Force of Law', for Derrida it is not a question of whether or not we make decisions, but that every case, every other, every decision is contextual and requires interpretation. Second, it is precisely in the fact that 'each case is other', and thus produces differing interpretations and a plurality of ethical meanings, that dialogue is opened. Dialogue not only produces 'responsibility' as 'sharing' (that is, eating the other), but also suspends the law and reveals the ambiguity in every decision made and enforced by law. I would argue that what this enables is a refusal to close down or deny difference, even when the very (humanist) structure of decisions and judgments inherently attempts to do so. There is a negotiation, a dialogue, then, between the law (and thus the norm and the body-politic) and the context of every situation and event that requires interpretation, and thus never entirely ingests the fixed meaning that prescriptive decision creates. This form of ethical negotiation I have, elsewhere, coined 'ethics under erasure'. What this dialogue enables is not only a refusal to close down difference, but also a more nuanced thinking about the factors and context of events in general and in this case of consensual cannibalism in particular.

On the one hand, the critical intervention that Derrida's interview 'Eating Well' brings to the real consensual cannibalism case is that it gives us tools to think about the effects of the humanist responses to such an event and how these responses are a form of (symbolic) cannibalism. Thus, while we (individually and as a body-politic) cannot simply step outside this type of humanist thinking, Derrida's interview enables dialogue. On the other hand, the critical intervention that the consensual cannibalism case brings to Derrida's interview is that it reveals that this 'dialogue', this negotiation, between the law and the context of every event or case, is not simply the privilege of those who read Derrida's work, but that the paradox of symbolic cannibalism constitutes every event. For example, while a judge might determine the ultimate decision about Meiwes' sentence, it is the jury that has to take into account the plurality of meanings that this case generates. It is the court jury (as well as the larger jury, the body-politic, of which we are all members) that engages in dialogue, which produces further and endless negotiation, interpretation and reinvention: something that this particularly unusual consensual cannibalism case highlights.

## key readings

Derrida, Jacques 1991. '"Eating Well", or the Calculation of the Subject: An Interview with Jacques Derrida.' In E. Cadava, P. Connor & J.-L. Nancy (eds) *Who Comes After the Subject?* New York and London: Routledge.

Derrida, Jacques 1992. 'Force of Law: The "Mystical Foundation" of Authority.' In D. Cornell, M. Rosenfeld and D.G. Carlson (eds) *Deconstruction and the Possibility of Justice.* New York and London: Routledge.

Guyer, Sara 1995. 'Albeit Eating: Towards an Ethics of Cannibalism.' *Angelaki* 2(1): 63–81.

# CHAPTER SIX

# tattooing: the bio-political inscription of bodies and selves.

AUTHOR: nikki sullivan

## INTRODUCTION

In an interesting account of tattooed bodies and the subjects who allegedly inhabit them, psychologist and 'dermal diagnostician' Gerald Grumet elaborates a detailed set of considerations which, he claims, psychologists should bring to bear on the bodies of their tattooed patients. What is interesting about Grumet's article is that it shows, perhaps inadvertently, that '[i]n the process of this moral and somatic surveillance [that is, dermal diagnosis], the soul of the deviant is both exteriorized to the body's surface and annexed to its various recesses where only men of science can peer' (Terry & Urla 1995: 11). This practice of reading the body (as text)—a practice not confined to psychiatry, but so common and so naturalised as to be almost invisible—is generally presumed to provide the canny reader with access to the soul, the core self, of the tattooed subject. However, taking **Judith Butler**'s account of the ways in which bodies come to matter and/or selves are materialised, one could argue, as I will in due course, that dermal diagnosis—the reading of the marked skin as the external expression of an inner, core-self—in fact produces the subject it claims to simply dis-cover. In other words, the soul/self is what **Michel Foucault** would call a 'truth effect' of systems of **power/knowledge** rather than something that exists prior to it and/or outside such systems. As Foucault sees it, the soul is 'the effect and instrument of a political anatomy ... the prison of the body' (Foucault 1979: 30), rather than, as commonly understood, the metaphysical aspect of the self that inhabits and/or is trapped by the body that is its fleshly shell.

> It would be wrong to say that the soul is an illusion, or an ideological effect. On the contrary, it exists, it has a reality, it is produced permanently around, on, within the body by the functioning of a [disciplinary] power ... This real, non corporal [sic] soul is not a substance; it is the element in which are articulated the effects of a certain type of power and the reference of a certain type of knowledge, the machinery by which power relations give rise to a possible corpus of knowledge, and knowledge extends and reinforces the effects of this power. (Foucault 1979: 29)

This claim, as I will go on to show, provides a means of critically engaging with the assumption that the soul or the internal self can be read on the open page of the tattooed skin. Perhaps more important still, it provides a means by which we might critique the dominant model of the (humanist) subject. What we find in Foucault's work, in particular *Discipline and Punish* and the first two volumes of *The History of Sexuality*, is a **genealogical** analysis of the ways in which systems of power/knowledge construct determinate types of bodies and their alleged 'souls' or interior selves. According to Foucault, through processes of enculturation bodies are discursively produced in and through procedures which mark, through a plethora of social mechanisms and practices that range from violent constraint to less obviously coercive means such as beautification, education, and the codification and partitioning of time, space and movement—tattooing, I want to suggest, literalises this process of inscription. Despite commonly held conceptions of body art, tattooing could be said to illustrate the Foucauldian claim that 'the body' is neither a biological entity nor a pre-social *tabula rasa* upon which culture torturously writes its repressive mandates, or individuals materialise the selves they desire to become. Indeed, my poststructuralist analysis of tattooing will be used to mobilise the following ideas as outlined by **Elizabeth Grosz**:

> The subject is marked as a series of (potential) messages from/of the (social) Other, and the symbolic order. Its flesh is transformed into a *body*, organised and hierarchized according to the requirements of a particular social and family nexus. The body becomes a text and is fictionalized and positioned within those myths that form a culture's social narratives and self-representations. (Grosz 1990: 65–6)

In their various critiques of the liberal **humanist** notion of the **subject** as an autonomous, pre-cultural being who inhabits a body that she/he owns and can manipulate at will, poststructuralist theorists have developed the notion of

**(inter)corporeality**, of **embodiment** as the materialisation of complex and competing **ontologies** particular to a given time and place. In this chapter I will draw on this work in order to critique the assumption that tattoos provide access to the truth of the subject(s) they adorn, and to argue instead that the ways in which we understand and experience tattooing can be said to tell us much about the stories (or dominant ontologies) that circulate in our culture and that make us who we are.

## mainstream accounts of tattooed bodies and subjects.

Tattooing is an increasingly popular practice that is commonly understood, at least in the West, as a means by which the individual expresses him or herself, non-verbally communicates something about his or her inner self to others. For example, Carla says, 'I ... have a blue iris ... that symbolises ... a sense of spirituality that's ... directed towards feminism. Feminism is a very important motivating force in my life' (*Skin and Ink* 1994: 63). Here, the tattoo is presumed to signify an affiliation with and commitment to a particular political movement and the idea(l)s with which it is associated: it provides a medium for articulating both interiority and community membership or belonging. Further, in so far as the tattoo tells of the individual's identification with counter-hegemonic discourses, practices, and lifestyles—in this case, feminism—it is often regarded as a performative act of symbolic rebellion. This is, of course, not surprising given that historically tattooing (in the West) has been largely associated with stigmatised groups such as bikers, criminals, gang members, prostitutes, sideshow 'freaks', and so on. Tattooing was, for much of the 20th century, 'firmly established as a definedly deviant practice in the public mind' (Sanders 1989: 18). While things may have changed somewhat, tattooing is still largely regarded as an antisocial practice. Interestingly, this (negative) view of tattooing has been embraced by many who practise it and who experience their tattooed bodies as 'a symbolic poke-in-the-eye' (1989: 19) aimed at mainstream culture and morality. Indeed, in most celebratory and/or reclamatory accounts of this particular modificatory practice, tattooing as a mode of self-expression and/or self-(trans)formation is conceived as both political and liberatory. Daniel Wojcik, author of *Punk and Neo-Tribal Body Art*, claims that 'the body is a site of symbolic resistance, a source of personal empowerment, and the basis for the creation of a sense of self-identity. By ... altering their bodies in symbolically powerful ways, both punks and neo-tribalists may proclaim their discontent [and] challenge dominant ideologies' (Wojcik 1995: 36).

Similarly, Juno and Vale (1989: 5), the editors of the landmark text *Modern Primitives*, argue that in contemporary Western culture 'our minds are colonized by images' that repress individuality, and as a result we feel powerless, unsure about our 'basic identities'. Tattooing and other forms of 'non-mainstream' body modification, they claim, exemplifies the individual's ability to produce change by 'freeing up a creative part of themselves, of their essence' by reclaiming the body as the one thing that the individual still has power over. Such resistance or reclamation is often portrayed in feminist terms in writings by women. For example, Karen describes her experience of her dragon tattoo in the following (relatively commonplace) terms:

> I came out of an abusive childhood. I was sexually abused by an uncle ... So, the dragon [tattoo] was my way of reclaiming my body, claiming my breasts. ... [H]aving a dragon put on my breast was a way of saying 'this is mine'. It was an evolution of that whole process of keeping myself safe and keeping myself whole. (cited in Pitts 2003: 58–9)

This voluntarist reinscribing of the body(-self) is often simultaneously understood and experienced as a rewriting of dominant notions of femininity, female sexuality and feminine beauty ideals, and the forms of socio-sexual relations to which they give rise. As Margot Mifflin puts it, 'tattoos serve as ... visual passkeys to the psyches of women who are rewriting accepted notions of feminine beauty and self-expression' (Mifflin 1997: 9). In other words, tattooed bodies, unlike the bodies of those who have undergone 'mainstream' procedures (most particularly those associated with cosmetic surgery), allegedly 'write back to the larger culture', 'subvert[ing] proscribed physicality' (rather than reproducing gendered beauty norms) and 'broad[ening] our sense of body aesthetics with monster beauty' (Braunberger 2000: 19). Such sentiments can also be found in Leslie Asako Gladsjo's 1991 documentary *Stigmata: The Transfigured Body*, in which post-punk author Kathy Acker states that women who get cosmetic surgery 'are just looking to come as close as possible to norms they have internalized', whereas women who get tattooed, pierced, cut or branded 'are actively searching for who to be and it has to do with *their own* pleasure, *their own* feeling of identity ... they're not obeying the normal society ... it's very different' (Gladsjo 1991).

As one might expect, the inscription of resistance on the skin is often read as cause for concern rather than celebration by those for whom deviance is conceived as detrimental to the wellbeing of both the individual and the social body. Consequently, in much criminological and psychological writing, tattooing is regarded as a sign of unhealthy risk behaviour, of a 'problem' in need of a cure, and, as I said earlier, this negative view of tattooing has a long history in the West. In 1908, for example, Adolf Loos (1908: 100) stated that '[t]hose who are tattooed but are not imprisoned are latent criminals ... If a tattooed person dies at liberty, it is only that he died a few years before he committed a murder'. While it may no longer be the case that a small butterfly discreetly placed on an ankle is commonly thought to signify murderous intent, tattooing, in particular in its more extreme forms, continues to provoke discomfort in many people, including those with institutionalised authority, a point I will return to later. This is because in contemporary Western culture tattoos are almost always read as the external expression of an inner essence: they are conceived as an indicator of an individual's character. (In other socio-historical contexts tattoos have been conceived in significantly different ways. For further elaboration of this point, see Sullivan 2001.) So let's consider some fairly standard examples of this.

In 1963 psychiatrists Yamamoto et al. described '[t]he tattooed man' as 'show[ing] definite personality deviations from his contemporaries … [as] more likely to be immature and impulsive, to be psychopathic, to aspire to be more "masculine" than his fellow patients, to have a criminal record, and to be something of a liability to society' (Yamamoto et al. 1963: 367), and this characterisation is still prevalent today: just think, for example, of the stereotypical figure of the tattooed person in popular television shows, in particular those associated with crime. More problematic still is the fact that this conception of the tattooed subject shapes much contemporary research on tattooing, leading psychologists and criminologists to repeatedly ask questions such as, 'Is there a link between body modification and substance abuse in adolescents?' (Brooks et al. 2003). The assumption that drives such research (that is, there *is* in fact a link between body modification and substance abuse in adolescents) and the imperative to prove the assumption correct functions to render research on tattooing less amenable to even imagining other kinds of questions, that is, questions that do not rely on and reiterate what Luce Irigaray (1985: 174) refers to as the 'same old stories [that] reproduce the same old histories'. The dominant Western conception of tattooing as somehow inherently problematic or pathological also blinds researchers such as Brooks et al. to the fact that the information provided by the young people interviewed might also be informed by commonly held conceptions of tattooing. So, for example, the researchers fail to consider what social factors may lead tattooed adolescents to conceive themselves 'as more adventurous, creative, artistic, individualistic, and risky' (Brooks et al. 2003: 47) than their non-tattooed peers, to explore what the investment might be (particularly for adolescents) in conceiving oneself in these sorts of terms.

# (re)inscription.

One of the most detailed examples of the imperative to classify, know and thus control the (body of the) tattooed other, and the (alleged) risks associated with it, is Gerald Grumet's (1983) account of 'dermal diagnosis'. In its meticulous categorisation of tattoos this article clearly highlights the impossibility of talking about tattooing in the abstract, that is, making claims about tattooing that ignore the significance of different kinds of tattoos, their design, size, number, quality and placement, as well as the context in which they are read. Grumet's thesis is predicated on two long-held interrelated assumptions shared, as I've suggested, by those for whom tattooing is a positive form of political resistance: first, that 'the human flesh has proven itself a suitable canvas on which to portray psychologically relevant themes' (Grumet 1983: 482); and second, 'that tattoos are a form of non-verbal communication that can often be deciphered' (1983: 489). Such assumptions inform and are supported by the fact that Grumet has, in and through the complex process of dermal diagnosis, (allegedly) come to know the truth about tattooed bodies and the subjects who inhabit them. While Grumet's thesis is, in my opinion, far from convincing, his work is nevertheless important, first because it makes explicit the assumptions that inform almost all contemporary accounts of tattooed bodies (both pro and anti), and second because it exemplifies a trend towards increasingly sophisticated modes of what Foucault refers to as 'governmentality': in this case, classificatory methods for rendering transparent the body, the subjectivity, of the **other**, and, in turn, the nature of 'man'—'procedures of individualization' (Foucault 1980a: 59) that in fact produce the 'individuals' they claim to simply describe. In other words, rather than seeing subjects as innately autonomous and individual, and the body of the subject as a true expression of his or her interior essence, Foucault argues that, on the contrary, we are the embodied product of historically and culturally specific ways of knowing, seeing and being, of, in his terms, power/knowledge. In a piece entitled 'Power/Knowledge' he writes:

> The individual is not to be conceived as a sort of elementary nucleus, a primitive atom, a multiple and inert material on which power comes to fasten or against which it happens to strike, and in so doing subdues or crushes individuals. In fact, it is already one of the prime effects of power that certain bodies, certain gestures, certain discourses, certain desires, come to be identified and constituted as individuals ... The individual is an effect of power. (Foucault 1980b: 98)

The complex ways in which 'the individual' is discursively constructed are nowhere clearer than in Grumet's account of dermal diagnosis as a clinical method. Grumet argues that the number, sequence, location, quality and content of tattoos all provide clues to the subject's character, and 'the evolution of [his/ her] character development' (Grumet 1983: 490). Further, the subject's emotional reaction to his/her tattoo(s), as 'earlier efforts to galvanize an identity and consequently symbolize the self' (1983: 489), serves, according to Grumet, as an indication of current self-esteem: embarrassment, for example, is read as indicative of the subject's subsequent psychological maturation and current capacity to communicate in less 'deviant' ways. In order to illustrate this claim Grumet discusses a person whose knuckles are adorned with 'jailhouse' letters spelling H-A-T-E. As Grumet sees it, the location, quality, content and mode of acquisition of this particular tattoo tells of a delinquent past and an antisocial temperament, a proposition with which many would unquestioningly agree. However, the subject concerned informs Grumet that for him, the letters H-A-T-E now signify 'happiness all through eternity'. This leads Grumet to concede that 'the [alleged] objective meaning of the tattoo does not [always] coincide with the private meaning for its bearer' (1983: 490–1). But despite this acknowledgment, Grumet nevertheless fails to recognise, or at least to articulate, the ways in which this disjunction undermines his understanding of the tattooed individual and, more fundamentally, the model of subjectivity and of signification on which his understanding is founded. Before I go on to explain what I mean by this I want to summarise the points I have made thus far about the dominant model of tattooing (and the ontological assumptions that inform it).

In both pro and anti accounts of tattooing, tattoos are most often read ideographically, that is, as pictures or graphics which tell an unambiguous story of the individual's innate self. On the one hand, for proponents of subcultural practice tattooing as 'a political act and sign of dissent' (Curry 1993: 82) is, to put it simply, a positive statement. For example, in an interview in *Body Play and Modern Primitives Quarterly*, Idexa, who describes herself as a 'radical primitive she/boy', states: 'I am part of this culture but I don't believe in it. My body modifications are a way to say that' (Body Play... 1993: 11). For criminologists such as Cesare Lombroso, on the other hand, tattoos tell of the subject's pathological need for attention and atavistic propensity to crime, whereas for feminist Sheila Jeffreys, tattoos are corporeal confessions of the subject's internalisation and perpetuation of the intrinsic violence of patriarchal relations and structures (Jeffreys 1994: 21). While these accounts vary somewhat, particularly in their polarised evaluation of tattooing (as either 'good' or 'bad'), they nevertheless share an understanding of the body as a canvas on which psychological themes are portrayed. In other words, each is founded on a number of assumptions particular to liberal humanism. These include a depth model of the subject which assumes a distinction and, at the same time, a causal connection between interiority and exteriority (mind and body, or self and body, or subject and object); the notion of an autonomous subject whose relations with others and with a world are secondary; and an expression-reception model of communication whereby the intentional expression of a sign designating the thought of an innate I is simply cognitively perceived by another as a sign of the truth of the subject.

I want to challenge this model of the body-subject by drawing on insights developed by a number of poststructuralist theorists, and in doing so to offer an alternative approach to the subject in/of tattooing. Let me begin by returning to Grumet's discussion of the H-A-T-E tattoo. The disjunction that Grumet identifies between what he refers to as the 'objective meaning of the tattoo' and the 'private meaning for its bearer' (Grumet 1983: 490–1) is interesting for a number of reasons. First, it clearly shows that tattoos neither contain nor represent a fixed referential reality, or, to put it another way, the relation between signifier and signified is arbitrary and unstable. It also demonstrates that the tattoo is not simply reducible to a symbolic representation of the truth of the subject, but rather is inseparable from the subject and can be understood as a process (rather than an object) in and through which the ambiguous and open-ended character of identity and of meaning is constantly (re)negotiated through relations with others and with a world. Further, the disjunction between the 'objective meaning of the tattoo' and the 'private meaning for its bearer' points to a problem inherent in the process of interpretation and evaluation that informs not only medical discourse, but social relations more generally. As poststructuralist theorists have convincingly shown, there is no such thing as objective or innate meaning: the tattooed body, like all texts, will generate different meanings depending on a range of factors including the embodied history of the subject who interprets, the relationship between him/her and the tattooed person, the other ways in which the tattooed body is marked (for example, in terms of gender, race, class, etc.), the context in which such an encounter takes place, and so on.

The obvious clash of opinion between Grumet and the guy with the tattooed knuckles—a disjunction that mirrors the difference of opinion between those who celebrate tattooing and those who pathologise it—is worth paying attention to, then, because it also tells us something about the misguidedness of voluntarist attempts to simply (re)inscribe a practice or an identity (in this case the subject in/of tattooing) in ways that ignore, or are at odds with, its discursive history. Let me explain what I mean by this. In so far as tattooing has historically been denigrated in the mainstream imaginary, at least in the West—it has, as I said, been associated with pathology: crime, mental instability, the 'social underbelly', 'perverse' sexuality, the use of 'needles', and so on—then attempting to simply reverse the paradigm and argue that in fact tattooing is a positive form of rational self-transformation or self-invention ignores the fact that some knowledges (in particular those associated with medicine or science) are imbued with a level of authority not accorded to others. In fact, what celebratory accounts of tattooing all too often fail to recognise is the very real material effects produced by psychological accounts of tattooing, that is, the fact that the latter inscribe 'non-mainstream' body modifiers as 'discredited persons' (Pitts 1999: 300), self-mutilators who are driven by irrational and uncontrollable psychological impulses. What this means is that not only is the personhood of the tattooed/'self-mutilated' individual discredited, but so too are his/her claims and the 'subjugated knowledges'—that is, 'knowledges that have been disqualified as nonconceptual ... as insufficiently elaborated ... naïve knowledges, hierarchically inferior knowledges, knowledges that are below the required level of erudition or scientificity' (Foucault 2004: 7)—with which non-mainstream conceptions of body modification are associated. As a result, claims of agency such as those made by Wojcik, Juno and Vale, Curry, and so on, are easily invalidated (though they are never entirely silenced) in so far as they are regarded by those opposed to tattooing as attempts to rationalise and thus disavow aberrant behaviour and the psychopathology to which it is wedded. Moreover, the form such **counter-cultural** resistance takes—that is, individualised body projects—is symptomatic of (and unquestioningly reproduces) a very specific epistemology (liberal individualism) in which the body is (re)inscribed as the (com)modified stuff of (individual) self-actualisation. And as Victoria Pitts (2003: 34) reminds us, 'self-invention is an *ideology* that informs body projects as much as it is a practice that constitutes them'. Body projects do not, she continues, quoting Elizabeth Grosz, '"invent" the self as a matter of personal choice'. Body projects may appear to be productions of the self, but they are historically located in time and place and provide messages that 'can be "read" only within a [specific] system of organization and meaning' (Pitts 2003: 34).

In conclusion, then, rather than expressing the truth of the tattooed subject, signifying his/her resistance as counter-culturalists would have it, or deviancy as criminologists and psychologists have suggested, tattooing tells of the complex, contradictory and shifting ways in which meaning, identity and difference are continuously (re)negotiated at the level of the flesh, of the (inter)corporeal. Indeed, a critical analysis of tattooing in contemporary Western culture can 'show how deployments of power are directly connected to the body—to bodies, functions ... sensations and pleasures' (Foucault 1980a: 151–2); it can enable the articulation of what Foucault refers to as a 'history of bodies' (1980a: 152), of the ways in which bodies come to matter. Via the notion of illustrative bodies that I've developed throughout this chapter, rather than simply arguing that one or other of the positions I outlined earlier is right and the other wrong, I have tried to suggest that the way around the impasse is to begin to seek out alternative models of subjectivity, of mind, body and the relations between them, of textuality, and of social relations and systems of power/knowledge.

## key readings

Atkinson, Michael 2003. 'The Civilizing Resistance: Straightedge Tattooing.' *Deviant Behaviour: An Interdisciplinary Journal* 24: 197–220.
Pitts, Victoria 2003. *In the Flesh: The Cultural Politics of Body Modification*. New York: Palgrave Macmillan.
Sullivan, Nikki 2001. *Tattooed Bodies: Subjectivity, Textuality, Ethics and Pleasure*. Westport, Conn.: Praeger.

## notes

[1] It is interesting that rather than destabilising dominant ontologies, much counter-cultural work on body modification by women simply reverses commonly held assumptions about proper and improper bodies and bodily practices. For a critique of this tendency see Sullivan (2006).

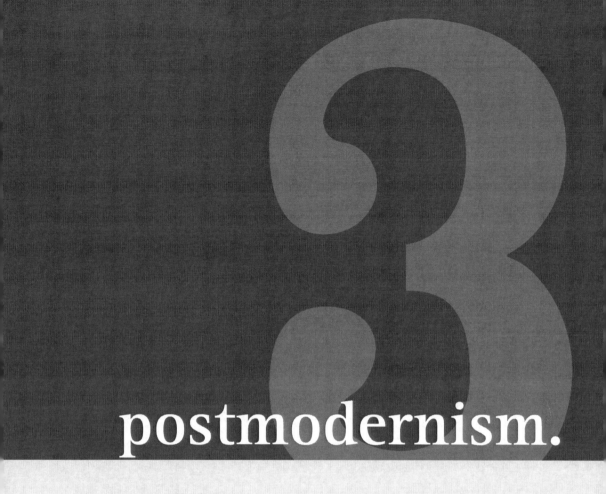

# postmodernism.

# the stories so far.
AUTHOR: nicole **anderson**

## prelude.

Thomas Docherty (1993: xiii) warns that the term postmodernism 'has often been used with a great deal of imprecision' and that it also 'would be [a] futile and pointless exercise to offer any single definition of the term itself', and Andreas Huyssen (1988: 58–9) argues that 'the amorphous and politically volatile nature of postmodernism makes the phenomenon itself remarkably elusive, and the definition of its boundaries exceedingly difficult, if not per se impossible'. Or as Ihab Hassan (1985: 121) clearly states, 'Like other categorical terms ... postmodernism suffers from a certain *semantic* instability. That is, no clear consensus about its meaning exists among scholars'. These scholars were commenting on the uncertainty of defining postmodernism from within its heyday in the late 20th century, but is this still the case in the early 21st century? Is postmodernism, from this vantage point, still undefinable? And would this mean that postmodernism has passed, occurring only in limited time in the 20th century?

In the late 20th century, in one form or other, postmodernism(s) extended its reach into 'nearly' every cultural field in both practical and theoretical ways: from architecture (e.g. Charles Jencks and Venturi), literature (e.g. Thomas Pynchon, John Ashberry), art (e.g. represented in 'neo-geo' and the 'proto-sublime'), film (e.g. *Terminator*, *L.A. Confidential*), music (e.g. Cage, Varese) and photography (e.g. Goldstein and Largo) to psychoanalysis (e.g. Felix Guattari), philosophy (e.g. Deleuze, Lyotard, Baudrillard), sociology (e.g. Fredric Jameson), theology (e.g.

Mark C. Taylor), politics (e.g. Ernesto Laclau), geography (e.g. David Harvey, Edward Soja), and so on. Having been taken up by various disciplines meant also that postmodernism has been defined, understood and applied in myriad forms. For example, in *The Evil Demon of Images* and *Simulations* **Jean Baudrillard** defines postmodernism as an era of hyper-reality and simulation. Frederick Jameson in *The Cultural Logic of Late Capitalism* argues that postmodernism, as the cultural foundation of late capitalism, finds expression in practices of artistic and literary pastiche and nostalgia, while in *The Postmodern Condition: A Report on Knowledge* Jean-François Lyotard claims that postmodernism is an 'attitude', characterised as the questioning of legitimating metanarratives.

It is precisely because postmodernism has been taken up across various disciplines, and thus applied in differing ways, that it is arguably *still* extremely hard, as well as problematic, to define. And it is also for this reason misleading to argue that there is *one* form of 'postmodernism' or postmodernist theory, because as we have just seen, there are many versions and descriptions of postmodernism, and therefore no single theory. However, it could be argued that from the perspective of distance, and removed from the heyday of postmodernism we can now, in the 21st century, if not define postmodernism *per se* then at least begin to survey the scholarship on postmodernism at the time in order to understand how various postmodernisms developed and became so diverse in application.

Postmodernism is predominantly believed to have developed out of or in reaction to **modernism** (both as an artistic movement and as a period after the Enlightenment: see the Glossapedia for a more detailed definition), and this reaction is evident in not only cultural production (literature, art, etc.) but also in a cultural attitude: what Jameson calls 'cultural logic'. Postmodernism is believed to have also pushed the limits of poststructuralism's focus on the 'arbitrary and differential relation of the sign', leading to the rejection of totalising and universalising systems and embracing the idea that the structure of thought, language, subjectivity and the world in general is defined by 'difference'.

# modernism/postmodernism: what's the 'difference'?

As I outlined in 'The Stories So Far' in Part 2, postmodernism developed out of, or in response to, modernism, while poststructuralist theory developed out of, and as a break from, structuralism. These categories are never clear-cut; they are contingent and therefore simply help provide a map of knowledge about particular subjects. For example, not only is there scholarly debate about whether or not poststructuralism and postmodernism can be conflated, but there is also debate about whether or not postmodernism developed as a result of a clear break from, or simply a more radical continuation of, modernism. It is this latter issue I want to focus on, and this will entail beginning by outlining some characteristics of modernism, with a particular focus on Lyotard's and Jameson's positions on postmodernism.

The beginnings of modernism have been traced to the mid-19th century and it is said to have waned in the mid-20th century (around the 1950s). The movement was characterised by the rejection of traditional styles and theories through new styles and techniques. In literature and the arts, one of the issues was to convey the alienated nature of human identity. This alienation was thought to be a result of the industrialisation of society. Importantly, the traditional idea that our identities, and therefore 'characters' in literature or art, are represented as knowable to him/herself and others was exposed as myth rather than a true reality by modernist intellectuals, artists, writers (Virginia Woolf, Proust), philosophers (Friedrich Nietzsche) and psychoanalysts (Sigmund Freud). For modernists, in general, the self or subject was never what it represented to others; one had to probe beneath the surface to reveal the truth and unity of identity. The techniques used in literature to reveal the identity of human beings included experimentation with stream of consciousness, multiple point of view, narrative interruption and fragmentary structure: all of which was attempted in the hope of revealing the truth of reality and **representation**. This modernist position is represented by authors such as T.S. Eliot, Ezra Pound, D.H. Lawrence, James Joyce, Franz Kafka, Virginia Woolf and Marcel Proust.

Another characteristic of modernism was to question the notion of 'reality'. As Hawthorn (1992) suggests, modernism reacted not so much against the 19th-century notion that literature and art should represent reality (the world outside literature), but against the conventions of what came to be associated with 'representing' that reality, such as style and technique. This meant that many writers and artists attempted a new style, one that made the reader self-reflective about what they were reading. That is, they were, through various devices, made conscious that they were reading a novel, or viewing an artwork (Hawthorn 1992: 108).

So, the defining aspects of modernism are, first, the belief in multiple perspectives (a relativism) to show that we can only ever know the world from our unique and singular perspectives, and second, a belief in surface and deep reality (where we represent our identities so that things and people are never what they are made out to be, because there is always something else beneath the surface representation). Yet despite the belief in multiple perspectives and surface realities, modernism still believed in a unifying underlying reality, albeit at times an unknowable one (Harvey 1989: 30). It is in this way that modernism carries forward the belief in the 18th-century Enlightenment ideals: **humanism**, the march towards progress, and the belief in underlying and unifying grand theories or structures. It is this belief in an underlying unified reality or structure that is rejected by postmodern philosophers and writers. For example, French philosopher **Jean-François Lyotard**, considered one of the main proponents of postmodernism due to the publication of his now (in)famous book *The Postmodern Condition: A Report on Knowledge,* became disillusioned with what he considered to be the totalitarian thought of **Marxism** and modernism (to which Marxism belonged) (Lyotard 1984: xxiv) because they attempted to answer and solve humanity's problems through universalising and totalising theories. Lyotard called this attempt at universalisation and totality the belief in 'grand narratives' or 'metanarratives', which have underpinned our political, cultural and religious ideas, institutions and practices.

For Lyotard, the belief in metanarrative is supported by humanist beliefs in the 'emancipation of humanity (Progress of Spirit)' and the 'march to freedom'. The former is the modernist (and Enlightenment) belief that reason and autonomy, which resides in 'man' (not woman), will result in universal *consensus* and enable the 'Progress of Spirit'. That is, universal consensus and totalising structures and theories will enable *progress* through the stages of conflict and resolution in history (to use a Marxist analogy) to the ultimate final goal of peace, justice and enlightenment. And by 'consensus' Lyotard means the belief that it is possible to 'come to agreement on which rules … are universally valid' (Lyotard 1984: 65). The 'March to Freedom' is tied to the 'Progress of Spirit', in that modernism believes that through reason, justice, consensus and social innovation, humanity will march closer to this ultimate goal.

But according to Lyotard the problem with metanarrative is that it is an illusion and that belief in this illusion is dangerous. Metanarrative is an illusion for two related reasons. First, because quite clearly the emancipation of humanity towards peace and enlightenment through reason has failed: the two world wars, the continuing terrors and conflicts of the 20th century (and now the 21st century) attest to the fact that humanity has been unable to arrive at consensus, and humanity is not rational and objective when it comes to trying to achieve one single ideal or goal for itself. In this way, Lyotard is critiquing modernism and the Enlightenment and their humanistic values and the ideals they perpetuate: 'The nineteenth and twentieth centuries have given us as much terror as we can take. We have paid a high enough price for the nostalgia of the whole and of the one' (Lyotard 1984: 81).

Second, the belief in metanarrative is an illusion because consensus and universalisation is *always already* deferred by the little narrative; by the 'heteromorphous nature of language' (1984: 66). What Lyotard means by this is that language is always changing and differing across and within cultures and historical eras. Consequently, Lyotard reveals that 'for all speakers to come to agreement on which rules or metaprescriptions are universally valid' for social and institutional systems is impossible. This is because if language is heteromorphous, then those rules are simply a game; a game that is not universal but contingent and thus 'subject to heterogeneous sets of pragmatic rules' (1984: 65). Lyotard argues, then, that there is no universalising language game (totalising system) because we do not necessarily establish stable language combinations, and the properties of the ones we do establish are not necessarily communicable. Thus the society of the future falls less within the province of a Newtonian anthropology (such as structuralism or systems theory) than a pragmatics of language particles. There are many different language games [little narratives]—a heterogeneity of elements. They only give rise to institutions in patches—local determinism. (Lyotard 1984: xxiv)

Thus, to believe in metanarratives is dangerous because by trying to universalise and totalise political, cultural and religious ideas, institutions and practices, modernity, at best, inadvertently homogenises individual and cultural *differences*, and at worse enables the agendas of the most powerful groups in societies to thrive at the expense of others: in the 20th century, at least, these 'others' have included women, the poor, ethnic minorities (those without white skin) and sexualities that do not conform to the heterosexual norm.

Furthermore, when Lyotard claims that language is 'heteromorphous', he meant differing not only across and within cultures, but at the level of grammar as well. That is, the structure of language is constituted by *difference*. It is this notion that has enabled postmodernism to be conflated with poststructuralism. Let me explain this further: poststructuralism accepts the structuralist **Ferdinand de Saussure**'s argument that there is no intrinsic connection between sign (word) and referent (thing), because language is based on differences (*differential relation*), and that there can be no true, universal, unchanging reality to which a word refers (because language is *arbitrary*); but poststructuralism goes further, arguing that reality (the world) is constructed in and through the language we use. The 'real' world has no value or meaning independent of us, rather the way we view or perceive the world is a consequence of the language structure into which we have been born. As Niall Lucy puts it:

[S]tructuralist thinking is part and parcel of postmodern literary theory. The very idea that difference is embedded in the sign, for instance, or that texts are encoded with particular meanings and values arising from sets of rules that correspond to the grammar of a language, cannot be dissociated from postmodern theories of simulation and heterogeneity. (Lucy 1997: 95)

If we think about poststructuralism's adoption of Saussure's *differential and arbitrary relation* of language, and his notion that there can be no universal reality to which a word refers, in relation to postmodernism's abandonment of the modernist idea that there is an underlying depth to people and things that points to an ultimate reality, we can see why the terms poststructuralism and postmodernism are often conflated to mean the same thing (although I argue in the 'The Stories So Far' in Part 2 that there are significant differences). Taking up the poststructuralist idea that reality (the world) is constructed in and through the language we use, postmodernism, unlike poststructuralism more generally, is sceptical of, and thus abandons, the notion that there is universal truth, reality and objectivity. Indeed, poststructuralism does not argue that there is *no* truth or reality as some extreme forms of postmodernism suggest, but that reality, truth and objectivity are constructed in and through language and therefore are contextual.

Given all of this, Lyotard defines postmodernism as 'incredulity towards metanarratives' (Lyotard 1984: xxiv): an incredulity that has developed in the second half of the 20th century in response to the burgeoning of technology, particularly in communications and electronic industries, and the political and social conflicts that followed the two world wars. This incredulous response has been called a 'crisis' by Lyotard because, unlike the era of modernism, it is characterised by a scepticism towards, and abandonment of, rationality, absolute truth, progress, objectivity, universal principles and dichotomous logic. While little narratives have and always will exist and enable difference, Lyotard's manifesto is that we should not leave the revealing and unfolding of difference and heterogeneity to chance; rather we should continually 'wage war on totality' and '*activate* the differences' (Lyotard 1984: 82; italics mine). The implications of Lyotard's claim is to suggest not only that there is no universal position and therefore no transcendental and universal truth, but that consequently all stories and perspectives of the world, all the knowledges and practices, and all subjectivities and identities, are contingent and contextual (and it is in this way that Lyotard has been considered by some a poststructuralist as well as a postmodernist). That is, all positions and viewpoints and identities are a result of the particular class, sexual, gender, racial and historical situations or contexts into which we are born or by which we are situated. It is these differences that Lyotard asks us to activate, rather than attempting to realise universal and absolute knowledge.

Lyotard's call for activating 'difference' is considered either a negative or positive aspect of postmodernism. On the negative side, critiques of postmodernism interpret the war on totality and the activating of difference as an embracing of relativism, indeterminism and therefore nihilism, leading to the death of the **autonomous subject**. With the destruction of the autonomous subject political action becomes ineffectual. This critique of postmodernism is also a result of the way in which postmodernism as it has been philosophically outlined by Lyotard and others has been taken up and practised in literature, art, architecture, music, and so on. For example, what characterises postmodern literature is what has been called *fabulation* and *surfiction*. (Writers considered postmodernist include Thomas Pynchon, Samuel Beckett, William Burroughs and John Ashberry (Hawthorn 1992: 111).) This means that there is a celebration of textuality: a delight in the surface rather than the depth, or to put it another way, the celebration of the surface in and through various writing techniques (pastiche, puns, intertextuality, and so on) is used as a way to demonstrate that reality (depth) is a construction, or that reality is textuality. Or as Niall Lucy in his book *Postmodern Literary Theory* describes it, 'postmodernism celebrates a certain kind of text that makes a game out of searching for the truth' (Lucy

1997: 15). The notion of reality 'is itself an effect of textual operations, such that reality is never anything more than a textual projection: it is something that texts allude to, point at, grope for and search after but which they can never be identical with' (1997: 14). Thus, the subject as constructed in and through language is nothing more than 'pastiche', as Jameson calls it, of endless play, textual styles and surfaces with no depth. This celebration of surface or textuality, and the world's increasing fragmentation via commercialisation and technology, its 'incredulity towards metanarratives' (Lyotard 1984: xxiv) and thus its abandonment of the belief in a unified underlying reality (Harvey 1989: 45) is what mostly distinguishes postmodernism from modernism.

Yet, as Lyotard (1984: 79) argues, the postmodern 'is undoubtedly a part of the modern'. For example, in relation to literature, the modernist techniques of stream of consciousness, multiple point of view, narrative interruption and fragmentary structure have been taken up and pushed to the extreme, so that the realist position, and what Lyotard calls the 'modern aesthetics ... of the sublime, though a nostalgic one' (1984: 81) becomes abandoned in favour of playful self-reference and textual freeplay (an intertextuality), to the point, some have argued, of solipsism. This extreme appropriation of modernist techniques is characterised as postmodernism (Lyotard 1984; Jameson 1991; Hawthorn 1992), and it is why Lyotard has argued that postmodernism is not a clear break; 'it is undoubtedly a part of the modern' (1984: 79) and thus a continuous development.

Unlike Lyotard, the American Marxist **Fredric Jameson** believes that postmodernism is a periodising concept. In other words, this incredulity is, for Jameson, the cultural logic or the human condition of the post-industrialised capitalist world of the late 20th century. It is therefore distinct from modernism. The reason why postmodernism is considered a break with modernism entirely is because while cultural modes (such as modernism and postmodernism) can exist at the same time, only one will dominate. Jameson argues that postmodernism is the cultural dominant of late capitalism (Jameson 1991: 55), and that the incredulity towards modernism and the cultural logic or attitude of postmodern society is a result of multinational capitalism and globalisation. For Jameson, pushing the modern aesthetic style to the extreme, postmodernism has created a culture of flatness, of depthlessness, a collapse of high culture (which was aligned with the playing with technique by modernist writers and artists) into pop (consumer) culture so that no distinction is left between the two. Moreover, for Jameson, postmodernism is a commercial culture that does not resist capitalism in the way modernism did, but rather submits, and thus reinforces and reproduces consumer culture (Jameson 1991: 85; Storey 1993: 171). Consequently, Jameson is one of postmodernism's major critics, arguing that not only is there a collapse of high and low (pop) culture, but a blurring of the distinction between culture and economic activity (Storey 1993: 171). This is a negative outcome for Jameson, who believes that these distinctions are important in order to resist abolishing 'any practical sense of the future and of the collective project' (Jameson 1991: 85). We could argue that in periodising postmodernism, Jameson implicitly homogenises it as only occurring in one particular period (and this is arguable).

On the positive side, supporters of postmodernism, like Lyotard, argue that by activating and attending the differences, and by realising that the subject is constituted in and through language and relations with others and with a world, we might cease to discrimate against others, and accept the fact that not all humans, cultures and societies are the same. Attending to the differences is precisely what postmodern art and literature enables. The various styles of writing, which enable reflection about the construction of a text and thus critical self-reflection about the construction of the subject and identity in and through that text (language), is precisely the means by which people are exposed to differences within the world more generally. For example, postmodernist style might include: the disruption of the omniscient narrator, which is also a disruption to the social, cultural and ideological metanarratives that defined traditional thought; multiple narratives that challenge the notion of totalising theories and unchanging subjects; the blurring of fact and fiction that functions to question 'reality' or the notion that there is one true reality that can be grasped if one delves deep enough, and so on. Supporters of postmodernism, then, do not believe that the collapse of high and low culture will be the death of the subject, far from it. Rather, what is dispensed with is not so much the subject, but the autonomous subject: the subject that is believed to exist outside language and therefore to exist before and apart from its relations with others and the world (texts, language, society, culture); one that is *not* constituted by its historical, social and cultural contexts. This does not mean that difference between individuals does not exist, but that these differences are also contingent and contextual. All in all, postmodernism is concerned with difference, with the ways in which differences are constructed and constituted in and through language and institutions.

# cultural studies and postmodernism ... where to next?

In the various stories of postmodernism I have outlined so far, I have attempted to discuss postmodernism as it developed in the 20th century, drawing on and exemplifying the work of what have been considered prominent postmodern philosophers and theorists, such as Lyotard and Jameson. I began by stating that even from the vantage point of the 21st century with the distance that this affords, postmodernism is difficult to define, because it has been taken up and applied in various ways across many differing disciplines. Therefore, there is no one postmodern theory, and no one postmodern approach one can take to analysing or discussing the world around us. Indeed, this is the point of postmodernism:

its varying interdisciplinary approaches and styles are a means of defying the metanarratives that are continually emerging and calcifying thought to produce one perspective; one view of the world. While the scholarship around trying to define postmodernism is not so prevalent in the 21st century, it is this aspect of postmodernism, the pluralistic perspectives that generate difference (in content, style, approach), that today continues to (in)form the way in which scholars, at least in Cultural Studies, write, think and respond to everyday life, to texts, as well as to the political events that unfold around them. What the three chapters in Part 3 offer is not an exposition of postmodernism (what it is, or its history). Rather, they take up some of postmodernism's central ideas (ideas about 'difference' and commodity culture) through a discussion of one or more 'postmodern' theorists, and then apply this to a discussion of various artistic works (as Elizabeth Stephens and Linnell Secomb do), or apply it as Greg Noble does to an analysis of what is considered mundane everyday domestic objects. Moreover, the styles of each chapter are very different, and consequently the chapters in this part also offer examples of an array of styles and theoretical approaches (which is considered postmodernist) to topics and events.

Greg Noble's Chapter 7 exemplifies a postmodern approach that draws on various disciplinary traditions and theoretical approaches and theorists on consumption, and applies them to a discussion of everyday 'things' or objects (that you might have in your lounge room, for instance). By drawing on a range of theoretical approaches, and by adopting a style (asking questions of the reader throughout the chapter, inserting these questions within a theoretical discussion) he produces an interesting performative application of postmodernism. As Noble argues, '[t]his movement performs the kind of self-reflection postmodern analysis demands of us. To create this self-reflective distance, we also need to adopt a kind of disciplinary and theoretical "pluralism" which is also typical of postmodern approaches'.

Continuing our consideration of bodies and embodiment in Part 1, both Stephens and Secomb reveal the implications of postmodernism for understanding bodies. For instance, Elizabeth Stephens brings various theoretical approaches to the issue of the 'post-human body'. Moving adeptly through various postmodern theorists, Stephens uses them to unravel the way in which contemporary performance art practices destabilise the fixed meanings constituted in and through **binary oppositions**. Binaries are one of the means by which metanarratives become naturalised and fixed. For instance, the collapsing of binary oppositions is precisely what Lyotard describes as characteristic of the postmodern condition, and what Baudrillard calls the 'hyper-real', where the original becomes indistinguishable from the copy. Stephens explores the destabilisation of the binary oppositions by various postmodern artists: from Barbra Kruger to Orlan to Critical Art Ensemble. It is the postmodern destabilisation of binary oppositions and thus fixed meaning especially around notions of the body by contemporary art and performance that occupies this chapter.

Like Stephens, Linnell Secomb's 'Rrapping Irigaray: Flesh, Passion, World' also explores the notion of the body, but this time the focus is on the gendered body. But unlike Noble or Stephens, Secomb draws on one particular philosopher, **Luce Irigaray**, and her notion of **embodiment**, applying this to artist Julie Rrap's photo of bodily orifices (*Blindspot*), her digital colour landscapes (*Fleshstones*) and through 'her *A-R-MOUR* photos series'. For Secomb:

> Australian artist Julie Rrap and French philosopher Luce Irigaray each provide commentaries on, and new imaginings of, the gendered body and the negotiations of erotic encounters between the self and the other. Their differing yet converging conceptual reflections on embodiment, on the relation between body and world, and on the affects of love, overturn conventional perceptions and create alternative pathways toward embodied, enamoured, being-with-others.

This alternative pathway towards 'enamoured being-with-others' is performed in and through Secombs' style and approach. Interestingly, rather than only apply a particular theorist's ideas to analysing a text or artwork, or applying an artist/writer to some particular theory, Secomb beautifully *entwines* Irigaray's philosophy with Rrap's art so that there is a simultaneous dance of contamination and separation between the two. In this performance Secomb not only produces a performative application of postmodern style and approach, but in doing so the performance underpins her argument about love between beings requiring simultaneous distance (a difference) and proximity. Thus Secomb's chapter performatively highlights the postmodern notion of 'difference', outlined earlier, between artist (Rrap) and philosopher (Irigaray); lover and beloved; subject and other.

# THINKING WITH PART 3

- Choose a 'thing' with which you would have an intimate relationship. It may be your iPod, your mobile phone, your watch, etc. Consider the mixture of ways in which you understand that thing as both a commodity and as an extension of yourself. What does this suggest about postmodern ideas about the self?
- Can you make a piece of anti-consumerist art? If you could do this, think about where you could exhibit or advertise the work. What would be the reasons for you not wanting to exhibit your anti-consumerist art?
- If the characteristic of the postmodern body would be a body that could disturb the controlling force of the nature/culture opposition, what would these bodies do? Can you imagine a performance or action or style of dress that would challenge where your body would fit?
- Reflect upon the styles of each chapter. In what ways could you identify and mimic postmodern writing?

# CHAPTER SEVEN

# living with things: consumption, material culture and everyday life.

AUTHOR: greg noble

## INTRODUCTION

Pick up any object in your home and it can tell you a lot about yourself and the world you live in. Was it a gift from someone or did you acquire it yourself? Was it made 'by hand' or was it a store-bought commodity? Was it made overseas? Have you changed it any way? Is it a domestic appliance or a tool with a particular use? Is it a memento from your earlier life, family history, lovers or friends? Is it beautiful or fashionable? Is it on display or stored away? Does it have a special meaning for you? Does it say something about you, your cultural background and beliefs? Do you wonder why you got it in the first place, or why you keep it? These questions may seem fairly banal, but they begin to show you how the most mundane objects might reveal how you are part of a complex chain of personal and social relationships in an increasingly globalised economic system, in which particular kinds of political values and cultural meanings circulate.

Human societies have long been defined by the objects they produce and use. Indeed, we have a long tradition of naming eras in terms of their key tools and technologies. Nevertheless, it has become common to point out that contemporary lives are increasingly filled with 'things': one commentator has argued that we are increasingly surrounded by objects, and less by other people (Baudrillard 1996). Branzi, a historian of design, has estimated that while a 'comfortable' home in the West contained 150–200 objects in the early 19th century, the equivalent home of the late 20th century had around 3000 items (1988).

figure 7.1: living with many things

*Count the number of objects in your living room. How many of these do you use each day?*

It is not simply that we live with more things, but that this relationship has changed: we live more and more in a society shaped by acts of consumption as well as processes of production. The consequences of this 'consumer society' are complex, and have been hotly debated for over a century. For some this abundance is the true indication of the extent of Western affluence and its values of freedom and choice; for others, it is a new type of economic enslavement and social debasement. Each new technology or consumer item—like the mobile phone today—evokes public concerns about the consequences of our preoccupation with consumption. As we shall see, however, we can't reduce the meaning of the things we live to simple, often moralistic claims: rather, we need to explore our relations with objects from a range of approaches and with a number of conceptual tools. We don't just consume things, but find ways of living with them (Dant 1999).

This need to address such social and cultural complexity through multiple perspectives is typical of postmodern analysis. In this chapter, we will accomplish this in two ways. On the one hand we will engage in a kind of double movement, moving from the discussion of various theorists on consumption and applying them to a discussion of everyday 'things'. Then, through the questions the chapter asks, we require you, the reader, to apply the discussion of theory and household objects to your own world of 'things' in your 'here and now'. This movement performs the kind of self-reflection that postmodern analysis demands of us. To create this self-reflective distance, we also need to adopt a kind of disciplinary and 'theoretical pluralism' which is also typical of postmodern approaches. To capture different facets at stake in understanding our relationship to 'things' we will draw on a range of disciplinary traditions (anthropology, sociology, cultural studies) and various methodological and theoretical approaches (Marxism, feminism, ethnography, semiotics, and so on).

But first we need to reflect upon why we worry so much about the consequences of living with things.

# the emergence of commodity culture.

The complex array of economic and technological changes that mark the emergence of industrial capitalism in early 19th-century Europe also brought with it new kinds of social experiences and relationships: a world where everyday life was organised less around small-scale communities where people either made what they needed or traded locally for what they couldn't provide, and more around large urban centres in which people increasingly bought what they needed from the wages they earned working for others (Hobsbawm 1969). By the middle of the 19th century, there was an emerging set of debates about the social, political and cultural consequences of industrialisation: the vast movements of people from country to city, from one nation to another; the growth of large towns and cities whose inhabitants knew fewer and fewer of the people they mixed with; the creation of modern forms of cultural production like newspapers that could be read across vast territories; and organisations of political activism demanding new and more democratic political structures. These changes entailed a feeling of the 'massness' of social organisation: a sense that people lived in nations, for example. There was a perception that these changes brought about the breakdown of local community life and its attendant social and moral order, a loss of religion, a preoccupation with consumer goods, and the dominance of the marketplace as the primary source of social values.

These concerns were voiced by conservative writers such as Matthew Arnold, a poet and school inspector who warned, in *Culture and Anarchy* (1869), of the repercussions of the social changes brought about by the massive growth of England's commercial activity and wealth. Arnold opposed 'culture' (what he saw as 'the best which has been thought and said in the world', found in high art and tradition) with 'anarchy'—the degraded forms of cultural and social life typified by the modern press and popular novels. For Arnold, the material affluence brought about by economic change represented a loss of social and moral order.

From the other end of the political spectrum, **Karl Marx** developed a powerful critique of contemporary society in *Capital* (1869/1976). Marx demonstrated the workings of capitalism through an analysis of the commodity. Capitalism is a system of generalised commodity production where things are produced primarily to be sold rather than made by the user for self-sustenance. Because the goal is capital accumulation (or profit), things have an exchange-value as well as a use-value. The rapid expansion of the capitalist system means that more and more aspects of life are increasingly commodified, and therefore brought under the logic of exchange rather than use. This system is also structured by class relations, which are relations of exploitation in the first instance and social relations of power in the second. They are exploitative because profits come out of the surplus value produced by the worker, hence reproducing class relations of power and inequality. Moreover, in the labour process workers are alienated from their own labour and from the products of their labour. Marx describes this in terms of what he calls 'commodity fetishism': a process whereby we only see the commodity as a thing, on the shelves of the store: we don't see the labour that has gone into the production of the thing, and hence we don't see the relations of exploitation that underlie it. As a consequence, the computer that sits on our desk appears to be simply the result of consumer abundance rather than the outcome of a worldwide system of production increasingly typical of **globalisation** that involves the exploitation of many workers, especially poor women and children, in third world countries (Klein 2000). It is important to remember that things like globalisation and economic and social inequality aren't 'out there', but are part and parcel of our everyday life.

*Pick up some of those mass-produced objects in your living room. Where do they come from? What do you know about the conditions under which they are made? (Or, if you don't know, what do you suspect about the conditions under which they are made?) Does this change how you feel about them?*

Marx's analysis is taken further in the 20th century by **Theodor Adorno** and **Max Horkheimer** in *The Dialectic of Enlightenment* (1947/1973), which argued that the most affluent nation in the world, the USA, is as unfree as the fascist Germany they had recently escaped from because it is marked by vast inequalities of wealth, poverty, racism and political apathy. They argue that the commodification of culture, captured in their notion of 'the culture industry', is a source of domination rather than fulfilling the Western promise of freedom and autonomy. The culture industry, typified by Hollywood, entails the standardisation of culture and its reduction to principles of economic exchange which require formulaic cultural products. This also standardises the consumer, producing a degraded culture of pseudo-individuality, an illusory belief in our power as consumers, and the transformation of utopian desires for a better world into the next hit song or movie, integrating us into larger relations of domination.

Just as with the conservative perspective, there are problems with Adorno and Horkheimer's view of the culture industry, but the significant point here is that, in very different ways, both analyses saw larger social and political issues behind the objects of increasing affluence. Yet, as insightful as the analysis of commodity culture is, does it tell us everything about the ways objects mediate our world? Can objects be mechanisms of connection as well as alienation? Part of the answer lies in examining the roles of objects in our everyday lives, the uses we put them to.

# the uses of things.

The anthropologist **Marcel Mauss** (1925/1967) famously explored the function of gift-giving in what he calls the gift economies of tribal societies, in contrast to modern economies based on commodities. He showed that in tribal societies gifts are predicated on a system of reciprocity and obligation and are intended to establish alliances, maintain social relationships within and between tribes, avoid conflict and preserve order. Yet because they entail specific obligations—to give, to receive and to reciprocate—and because they are also bound up in status contests, gifts are sometimes used to crush rivals by exhausting their resources. Feminist scholars have pointed out that this understanding of gift-giving is primarily about male relations, whereas the giving done by women is frequently invisible or devalued (Diprose 1996)—an issue of the gender dimensions of things we'll return to below.

Mauss' discussion of the gift may sound a long way from your notions of gift-giving, but the complex nature of gifts in Western societies may not be that different after all. We think of gifts as acts of love and intimacy, generosity and altruism, acts that are not meant to be motivated or calculating, yet what do we expect when we give gifts? Some people will say they expect nothing, but in fact an analysis of a ritual like Christmas will show that a system of reciprocity prevails which signals information about the relationships we have with others (Berking 1999).

*When you give a gift to family, or a friend or lover, do you expect anything in return? And do you expect something of comparable value? How would you feel if you gave your best friend or lover a gift that expressed your sense of intimacy and how you valued the friendship—say, a weekend away together—and they gave you a pair of socks? Or, indeed, nothing?*

Yet it is not simply the question of reciprocity per se here: we also make assumptions and judgments about people through gifts.

*What gifts would you give, and what wouldn't you give, your mother, your lover, a child, your boss, and so on? Which of these would you give a pair of sexy underpants? Similarly, from whom would you accept a pencil drawing of a barely recognisable dog? Try generating a list of the different kinds of things you would give specific categories of people, and would expect to be given in return. What do these things say about you and the others?*

We can summarise a couple of points from this exercise. In creating reciprocal bonds, gift-giving also does some other work:

- Gifts express and therefore help maintain personal relationships: family, friends, lover.
- These may also be *social* relationships: gift-giving between boss and employee, between colleagues or customers.
- Gifts allow us to express a sense of personal identity: this is the kind of person I am and the kind of person you are (a fan of hip hop, for example).
- These identities are also *social* categories; they define us in terms of gender, class, educational background, ethnicity, and so on. There are often quite clear *informal* rules about what we give men or women, for example.
- Gifts help create a corporate or group identity (our family, my friends, this subculture).
- They 'measure' relationships in terms of esteem and intimacy (through value of the gift, the type of gift, the care taken in its selection and presentation).
- Gifts express shared values and meanings (around notions of 'femininity', for example), similar tastes or mutual political and religious beliefs.

This list by no means exhausts what we can say about why and how we use gifts in a market-based society. Mauss' distinction between gifts and commodities can lead us to assume they are radically different things where in fact in our society they represent different moments in the life of an object. Most of us buy commodities to give as gifts, but we do certain things to erase, at least in part, their status as mass-produced commodities. We remove price tags, we wrap presents, tie them with ribbons and attach signed cards, or even transform the object in some way with a personal touch (Carrier 1993). This process of *decommodification* is a way through which we personalise and singularise an object, making it unique and marked by our humanity. We would be unlikely, for example, to give someone a domestic appliance for a present just in its cardboard box. This decommodification can be seen as an attempt to reclaim our economically driven social world as a human world, in contrast to the instrumental logic of the world of production and its profit motive.

Of course, these practices are not just about gifts, but are found in all our relations with objects. 'Appropriation' is the name some academics give to the ways we bring back objects into our domains, where we can exert control via the meanings we give them away from the dominance of the economic system or, as Miller (1987, 1988) points out, systems of government. Appropriation describes those material and symbolic transactions whereby a commodity becomes a personal possession, where it leaves the public world of exchange and becomes an object in our own worlds, fulfilling the purpose of self-creation in our private lives. These can be as simple as unpacking a new acquisition, giving it a place in the home or marking it in some way (like writing your name on it); and it may also involve ongoing acts of maintenance (like looking after your car) or re-use (like showing it to others, or wearing a favourite outfit).

Miller's analysis of appropriation draws on the work of the German philosopher **Georg Hegel**—the same source that Marx used to develop his notion of alienated labour. Hegel (1807/1977) showed how, through labour, humans not only transform nature to produce our means of subsistence, but in doing this, we produce ourselves as human beings. The essence of ourselves as human is realised through labour; we externalise or objectify ourselves into things we produce, things that we then reabsorb through use. Through this dialectical process we satisfy our needs and create new needs, developing our capacities as human beings that are the bases for our individuality and our sociality, and enable our recognition by others. The importance of this dialectical process is not simply that we reproduce ourselves as individuals, but that we reproduce our society and culture: its dominant relationships, meanings and practices.

Where Marx applied Hegel to an understanding of production, Miller (1987) uses Hegel to transform our understanding of consumption. Where Marx emphasises the way the world of work reduces our sense of autonomy, Miller shows how we attempt, if only symbolically, to regain some sense of our agency through consumption. We also realise ourselves as human through the labour of consumption, Miller suggests, because in the complex societies of late capitalism it provides powerful resources for shaping how we present ourselves. He characterises consumption as crucial to the process of *externalisation* of self into objects, and the absorption of those objects into self-image, or what he calls *sublation*. Externalisation or objectification is most clearly demonstrated when we make something, like a painting, but it can also be in the way we invest our labour and love into everyday items, like looking after our clothes or cars. Sublation refers to the ways those objects come back to help define who we are, reabsorbed into our self-image—our favourite T-shirt, a ring, the car. Yet while consumption involves, like production, the dialectic of externalisation and the sublation, Miller gives it greater agency by framing it as an act of *appropriation*, through which the object is de-alienated, personalised as a possession, recontextualised into our own world of meaning and use. This is central to both the production of our social worlds and to human self-actualisation, if in far more personal ways than production.

figure 7.2: personalising our spaces

*Go back to the things in your own home. Look around your bedroom or the lounge room and think about the things that mean most to you. What are your most prized possessions? Why do you value them? If your house was on fire, what objects would you try to save? Why?*

These prized possessions might be a favourite book or trinket you bought yourself as a reward for achieving something, or a memento from a lover or a favourite relative, a holiday overseas, a family heirloom, a photograph of yourself as a child, something you made, and so on. They were all probably commodities at some point, but they stopped being primarily a commodity in the processes by which we gave them new meanings and values. In fact one scholar even goes so far to talk about the 'biography' an object has as it moves from one condition to another, from commodity to personalised object, and from place to place, owner to owner (Kopytoff 1986). As many commentators have pointed out, consumption is not simply an act of buying something, but is ongoing work. McCracken (1988) describes what he calls rituals of possession and grooming which represent substantial investments of time, money and labour and which are crucial in transforming a mass-produced commodity such as a motor vehicle into a singularised, personalised possession. As Miller argues, this suggests that consumption, like production, involves acts by which we put ourselves *into* our objects.

figure 7.3. rituals of grooming

*What items do you have that you spend time looking after or working on? Why?*

Even though our favoured objects 'contain' a bit of us because we have put our love and care into them, this kind of work and the way we see it can be highly gendered. The very public 'grooming' of a car undertaken by some men is in sharp contrast to the invisibility of housework (Oakley 1974). Where those men may see their effort as a creative and productive investment 'in' the car, and may be seen this way by others, housework, which is still overwhelmingly the task of women, tends not to be perceived in these terms. Nevertheless, both cases capture the kinds of ongoing work that characterise our relations with objects; work that takes place over time and in particular spaces. To capture this sense of process, Silverstone et al. (1992) describe a cycle of consumption that moves through different moments: of acquisition, objectification (where we put an item in a particular space for use or display), incorporation (where the item is built into routines and uses) and conversion (where we, in a sense, relate the object back to the social world by, for example, talking about our latest CD or piece of clothing with friends).

Understanding the processes whereby we 'invest' ourselves in some objects may help explain why we even see some of these things as almost human: why, for example, we give some objects human names and characteristics. These acts of 'anthropomorphism'—seeing objects as human-like—are part of a wider process, however. Think of how and why we see particular kinds of objects in gendered terms, like giving ships and cars female names, or of how we often talk about computers as though they are thinking beings with emotional capacities (Noble 1999).

*Have you ever given an item a name, or do you think of some objects as having human characteristics? Which ones? Why?*

As we have seen in contrasting car care and housework, sometimes our objects can be gendered in various ways. As Livingstone (1992) points out in relation to domestic technologies, men and women tend (though not absolutely) to view objects and talk about them differently: women tend to see technologies in terms of facilitating social contact, while men see them more in terms of their functionality. Similarly, we often associate some objects with men, and others with women. In one quirky experiment where participants were asked to label household technologies as pink or blue (or in between) depending on whether they saw them as female or male, Gray (1992) found a clear patterning in the gendering of technologies and the divisions of labour around them.

*Do you think we tend to see some objects as being more 'male' or 'female'? If so, which ones, and why?*

Recognising the processes involved in our use of objects is important because it demonstrates that the meanings of the things we surround ourselves with have temporal and spatial dimensions, and link our personal worlds with the wider networks of social relations, the economy and globalisation.

# the meaning of things.

There is a tendency to think of the meaning of a commodity as it is defined by the world of advertising, yet as we have just seen, the meanings of things are much more complex. It is perhaps more accurate to say that the marketing of an object is a crucial way of selling something because it articulates social values and discourses. Anthropologists have long shown that goods express key cultural categories (Douglas & Isherwood 1980). Advertisements for cars, for example, tell us about the complex meanings that link this technology to modernity, power, speed, mobility, sexuality and gender (Bayley 1986; Wernick 1991). A dominant approach in the understanding of these social meanings has been to see advertising as central to the systems of social domination; as 'hidden persuasion' over which we have little control (Packard 1962). Much of this analysis has its links in the history of seeing consumption as a new form of social control and has centred on the ways we use commodities to express our social status.

*Think about a recent purchase. How important was advertising or marketing in convincing you to buy it? Why?*

In the late 19th century, as commentators were trying to make sense of new patterns of consumption, Veblen (1899/1998) coined the term 'conspicuous consumption' to describe the practices of increasingly wealthy middle-class people who used commodities to express their economic, social and cultural power. We talk about 'keeping up with Joneses' to express the same thing: the way some people purchase items, often new cars, fashionable clothing or technologies like plasma TVs, in a very demonstrative way, to display their social status. A nuanced understanding of this process is given by **Pierre Bourdieu**, a French scholar whose *Distinction* (1984) explored the ways people use such goods. While we like to think of our taste as very personal judgments of our own choosing, Bourdieu argued that taste—whether it is styles of music, the books we read or films we see—was part of a process of 'distinction' through which we differentiate ourselves within a class-based system of cultural and social values. As he argued, taste is a form of classification which classifies us just as much as the objects of our judgments. This process of achieving status through socially sanctified meanings is best seen today in our preoccupation with specific brands that don't simply represent a product, but a lifestyle and personality. These often mark us as belonging to a particular demographic (for example, surfie culture) that unites us with others, but, Klein (2000) argues, they also integrate us into a dehumanising, global economic and social system of vast inequalities.

figure 7.4: displaying our tastes

*Have you ever bought an item simply because it was fashionable or the right brand? Who were you trying to impress?*

More recently, as we have begun to see in the discussion of Miller, studies of consumption have focused less on the socially determined meanings of things offered through advertising and the ways consumption locks us into systems of social control, and more on the ways consumers negotiate and challenge these social meanings to resignify objects, participating in the production of meaning. The recent focus on this ongoing work of appropriation highlights the ways individuals and groups take commodities and their coding within design and marketing, and recontextualise them to transform them, both symbolically and physically, in a way that gives them specific types of meaning and makes these objects their own. Such meanings may even be actively involved in challenging conventional ways of thinking or resisting oppressive social relations. **Dick Hebdige** (1979) talks about how punks used banal, everyday items like safety pins and made them signify danger and threat to people outside the subculture, a shared value within the subculture.

Our objects are rarely so dramatic, but we do consign idiosyncratic meanings to objects that are only known to our immediate circle. A student some years ago nominated a chupa-chup as her prized possession because it was given to her by her first boyfriend. Not only did this significance have nothing to do with the ways the chupa-chup was advertised, its very banality was important in underlying the enormous significance she gave it. It was a meaning that only people she explained it to could understand. Similarly, some people put individually designed decals on their cars which, to others on the road, can only be nonsensical and meaningless (Noble & Baldwin 2001).

*Do you have a favourite item whose meaning would only make sense to you and your friends? How did this come about? How does this meaning relate to its original status as a store-bought commodity?*

So between the idea that advertising shapes the way we view our objects and the idea that we can grant peculiar meanings to these same objects lies the recognition that meaning-making is a complex process, and one that tells us something about how we relate to wider social structures and discourses. In fact, the further we explore the meanings of things the more we recognise just how complex this can become. Csikszentmihalyi and Rochberg-Halton (1981) asked people what their most prized possessions were and what they meant to them and found dozens and dozens of different kinds of significance of objects. Some items were more likely to be valued than others—like photo albums—and most commonly people talked about how these objects were used as memories, representing family relationships, friendships, past experiences and a sense of identity, but also much more. In one study I showed how in a married couple's display cabinet almost their entire networks of kinship, friends and significant acquaintances were captured, along with key family events (births, weddings, deaths) and life experiences (first job, current profession, hobbies) (Noble 2004). Indeed, I argued that these objects, taken as a whole, functioned as 'proof' of the depth and breadth of our existence, testimony to our relationships, experiences, values, and so on. Together they constituted a sense of ourselves as accumulating over time and space in complex networks of practices and relations; indeed, they grant us a degree of 'ontological security' in an increasingly insecure world (Dupuis & Thorns 1998).

figure 7.5: displaying our families

figure 7.6: displaying our histories

*Can you imagine your life without objects?*

Csikszentmihalyi and Rochberg-Halton (1981) summarise the complexity of meanings by grouping them into categories: how objects express identity, status and our experience of social integration at personal, social and 'cosmic' levels (cosmic here means how objects capture our sense of the world), and with different modalities: objects serve to differentiate us or to integrate us (think here of an item that signifies our membership of an ethnic or religious community, or a subculture). But these objects don't just represent our world to us and others, they also mediate it—think of how we use photos at family gatherings to form the basis of chitchat, collective memories and emotional ties. Think of how we also use the 'special crockery' to indicate to others how we esteem them and the occasion of their visit, or how we use our music CDs to experience shared tastes with others.

Objects mediate our relationships with others in many often banal ways. Miller (1998) demonstrates that the simple act of shopping for everyday items involves complex processes of sacrifice and indulgences through which we evaluate and produce our relations with others. He uses the way mothers choose to forgo things for themselves and yet buy special treats for their children as evidence of how we realise the emotional ties of love through objects. This is a far cry from the kinds of ego-centred activity we find in clothing shopping, where the focus is on an individuated self measured through the social dictates of fashion (Langman 1992).

# conclusion.

To explore the interface of humans and things, we need to embrace a kind of interdisciplinary, methodological and theoretical pluralism typical of contemporary postmodern analysis which engages with a range of ideas and approaches. One of the central tenets of postmodern theorising has been that there can be no single metanarrative that explains all aspects of our social existence. Therefore we need to avail ourselves of a variety of scholarly disciplines, conceptual tools and research methods to begin to capture the complexity of our lives by approaching the problem again and again from different perspectives. Much like the objects with which we began, we can approach the significance of material culture through the movement between and across different kinds of questions. This means we might end up with contradictory insights and findings, but this may tell us something about the contradictory nature of our social existence.

The study of 'things', in fact, leads us to a central paradox. On the one hand, we see in commodity culture a degree of inauthenticity and delusion, even an 'enfeeblement' of our self and our relations with others (Langman 1992); on the other, we have seen how we use these commodities to restore a sense of the human proportions of our existence and allay our anxieties about the anonymous world of globalised consumer capitalism, the erosion of social values and relationships. Acts of appropriation through consumption, rather than simply tying subjects into systems of capitalist production, constitute the ways through which we seek to recuperate forms of social power in the face of these capitalist relations of economic and social power (Miller 1988). In other words, we use objects to make ourselves at home in a world that is increasingly alien and hostile; indeed, the very system of producing and consuming things that makes those objects available also produces many of those feelings of alienation and hostility. Dant (1999) characterises this as a question of whether we consume or live with things but, as we have shown, we need to recognise this paradox and use it to reveal the complexity of our relations with material culture and with others.

## key readings

Dant, T. 1999. *Material Culture in the Social World*. Buckingham: Open University Press.

Featherstone, M. 1991. *Consumer Culture and Postmodernism*. London: Sage.

Lury, Celia 1996. *Consumer Culture*. Cambridge: Polity Press.

# CHAPTER EIGHT

# flesh machines: self-making and the postmodern body.

AUTHOR: elizabeth stephens

## INTRODUCTION

The advertising for the annual summer sale in Selfridges, a large department store chain in Britain, is unusually blunt. Written in large white capitals on a red background, the banner slogans include such statements as: 'Buy me. I'll change your life' and 'Money talks'. Given the frantic consumerism being played out beneath those banners, these slogans may seem merely descriptive of the commercial space they adorn, if somewhat jarringly so. Shoppers familiar with the artwork of **Barbara Kruger**, however, might be especially surprised to discover that Selfridges has appropriated her distinctive style, and somewhat confounded that Kruger's art, in particular, should come to be redeployed in such a context. Kruger's work famously superimposes anti-corporate, anti-sexist slogans over found photographs taken from mainstream beauty and lifestyle magazines—'I shop therefore I am' and 'Your body is a battleground' are two of her best-known pieces—always using the same white capitalised font on a red background seen in the Selfridges advertising. The appropriation of Kruger's anti-consumerist art by this commercial company raises a number of interesting questions about the relationship between activist art and capitalist culture in the early 21st century. Does this appropriation transform Kruger's artwork into the very thing it is designed to critique, erasing the irony and resistance encoded in her reworking of consumerist slogans? Are the banners found in Selfridges prescriptive, instructing its customers to indulge their materialism, or are they a form of subversive anti-advertising? That is to say, what is the functional status of these slogans as advertising, and what does it tell us about our own media literacy that advertising can play with its levels of meaning and problematise its own functionality in this way? What sense are we to make of an advertising campaign whose central conceit is a critique of advertising campaigns? We might wonder, further, to what extent our answers to such questions would change if we discovered that Kruger herself had designed this advertising campaign—as indeed she did do. Is this the ultimate sell-out or a canny subversion of capitalist rhetoric from within? What effect does this have on shoppers who recognise the advertising as Kruger's, or at least in her style: does it simply allow them to congratulate themselves on their cultural literacy while simultaneously continuing to enjoy shopping as a recreational activity?

If these questions seem unanswerable, it is primarily because they presuppose a yes/no response that, in turn, relies upon a clear distinction between two opposing sets of possibilities which seem increasingly blurred and problematic in the contemporary period. The Selfridges advertisements, the folding back of Kruger's anti-slogans onto the advertising discourse they both emerge from and critique, reflect as well as contribute to the collapse of such distinctions. This kind of destabilisation is central to what **Jean-François Lyotard** has famously termed 'the postmodern condition'; or, rather, it would be if postmodernism could be said to have a centre, if postmodernism did not, by definition in fact, describe the dispersal of such ideas of cultural centres. In *The Postmodern Condition: A Report on Knowledge*, Lyotard examines the shift in structures of knowledge, which is to say the changing ways in which we make sense of the world around us, that he identifies as having taken place since the 1950s and the emergence of a post-industrial culture. Prior to this time, Lyotard argues, knowledge was structured around 'metanarratives or 'grand narratives', by which he refers to the series of overarching stories that a culture tells itself about its practices and beliefs, and that provide a coherent interpretive framework within which subjects can understand their experiences and the events that occur around them. Examples of such metanarratives include the widespread conviction that human history is a story of progress and enlightenment, or that scientific knowledge is objective and an unmediated expression of truth, or that democracy will lead to universal human happiness. Postmodernism, Lyotard explains, is the condition in which these narratives have broken down, both because their cultural power is in decline and because the narratives themselves have become increasingly fragmented and incoherent. As a result, Steven Connor (1997: 8) explains, '[t]he postmodern condition … manifests itself in the multiplication of centres of power and activity and the dissolution of every kind of totalising narrative which claims to govern the whole complex field of social activity and representation'.

On the one hand, then, the characteristics most commonly associated with postmodernism are those of fragmentation and the destabilisation of previously coherent cultural centres, but on the other, a correspondingly changed relationship to, and interpretive practices for, the world around us. For **Jean Baudrillard**, postmodernism is the period in which traditional ideas of the 'real' dissolve, fundamentally transforming the way we understand the relationship between objects and representations, or between words and things. In the late 20th century, Baudrillard argues, something has disappeared: what we have is a world that produces images of a reality that have no 'real' origin. Baudrillard refers to this as the 'hyper-real' or the 'desert of the real'. The postmodern world, he writes, is constituted as and by a precession of simulacra, copies of things which have no original object, and which signal, moreover, 'the liquidation of their referents' (Baudrillard 1994: 11). Baudrillard cites Disneyland as an exemplar of this. Disneyland's material rendering of cartoon versions of pirate cultures, or of an American Wild West that never existed, or its now nostalgic visions of Future World, does not simply reproduce a series of cultural phantasms, Baudrillard contends, but exists to mask the fact that America itself *is* Disneyland. That is, Disneyland is an artifice of something that is itself already an artifice: 'Disneyland is represented as imaginary in order to make believe that the rest is real, when in fact Los Angeles and the America which surround it are themselves already not real, but of the order of the hyper-real and simulation' (Baudrillard 1994: 26). Thus postmodernism is widely identified with high levels of self-reflexivity and referentiality, of irony and playfulness: in place of a Romantic celebration of the natural world, we now have an embracing of the fabricated and artificial; in place of the modernist 'shock of the new' (such as Marcel Duchamp's public urinal exhibited as a found art object, or the futurist manifestos urging readers to burn down libraries and museums, both from the turn of the last century), we find critiques of traditional notions of originality and creativity.

We see a similar kind of destabilisation in Kruger's reworking of her own anti-consumerist art as advertising for a large international corporation. In the first place, her art derives from found photographs culled from popular women's magazines which are themselves simulacra: these photoshopped and airbrushed images of women are designed, precisely, to erase any signs of human imperfection—erasing shadows, lines and other such 'flaws', rendering the face an unblemished mask. Her slogans are designed to interrupt the production of such images by and while speaking in the language of crude capitalism ('I shop therefore I am'). The transformation of these critical artworks, which adopt the style of commercial advertising, into actual advertisements recognisable as famous artworks exactly encapsulates the multiple levels of signification and reflexivity that characterise postmodernism. Moreover, her advertisements are all the more effective *as advertising* for representing themselves as anti-adverts (whether or not one reads her campaign within the context of her wider art project). They play ironically with ideas both of selling products and of selling out in a way whose meaning cannot be fixed or stabilised. On the contrary, what Kruger's Selfridges campaign represents is an unstable proliferation of meaning, an explosion of semantic possibilities that cannot be reduced to a single position, much less positioned categorically on one side or another of a binary.

By blurring the boundary between what is art and what is advertising, and refusing the clear-cut distinction between previously irreconcilable categories, Kruger's work is thus emblematic of the shift in the structures of knowledge during the late 20th century identified by Lyotard. The consequences of this shift are by no means confined to the realm of artistic or commercial image production, however. Indeed, for many postmodern theorists, an issue of particular concern is the fate of the body in this context. In a post-industrial age characterised by simulacra and hyper-reality, in which almost all bodies contain some form of prosthesis or implant (from glasses and dental fillings to cosmetic injections, prosthetic limbs and transplanted organs), and in which bodies are routinely hooked up to technological apparatuses (such as computers, cars and personal stereo systems) or medically altered (through antidepressants, hormone therapy, the birth control pill and the like), traditional associations of the body with the natural seem increasingly fraught. Accordingly, postmodern theorists have been concerned to show that our understandings and experiences of the body—our own and those with which we interact—are highly mediated through cultural assumptions about corporeality. In this, postmodern theory draws upon a rethinking of the relationship between body and subject that underpins much contemporary critical and cultural theory as a whole. Reversing the centuries-old tendency to see our **subjectivities** as limited or constrained by our bodily needs and desires, **Michel Foucault** has famously argued, following Nietzsche, that it is not our bodies that imprison the 'soul', rather, 'the soul is the prison of the body' (1997: 30). That is to say, our sense of ourselves is produced through the series of cultural inscriptions and normalising technologies that are brought to bear on the body. We find this idea elaborated in Elizabeth Grosz's *Volatile Bodies*, in which she argues that '[a]ll the effects of depth and interiority can be explained in terms of the inscription and transformations of the subject's corporeal surface' (Grosz 1994: vii).

Within a specifically postmodern context, characterised by a rapid proliferation of the technologies brought to bear on the body, some theorists have claimed that the contemporary body has become 'post-human'. Judith Halberstam and Ira Livingston, for instance, argue that '[p]osthuman bodies are not slaves to masterdiscourses but emerge at nodes where bodies, bodies of discourse, and discourses of bodies intersect to foreclose any easy distinction between actor and stage, between sender/receiver, channel, code, message, context' (Halberstam & Livingston 1995: 2). Just as Baudrillard contends that we are living in a hyper-real culture, in which traditional assumptions about a clear distinction between original and copy, real and fake, object and representation have dissolved into a precession of simulacra, so too have previous concepts of the body as natural, self-contained and individual given way to the technologised, fabricated, post-human body whose relationship to the natural and the real is increasingly tenuous. We see this in the heavily photoshopped and airbrushed images of women found in fashion magazines that Kruger appropriates, and this is an issue further confronted by the theorists Arthur and Marilouise Kroker in their *Body Invaders: Sexuality and the Postmodern Condition*: 'why the concern over the body today if not to emphasise the fact that the (natural) body in the postmodern condition has *already* disappeared, and what we experience as the body is only a fantastic simulacrum of body rhetorics?' (Kroker & Kroker 1998: 21–2). Similarly, they argue:

> If, today, there can be such an intense fascination with the fate of the body, might this not be because the body no longer exists? For we live under the dark sign of Foucault's prophecy that the bourgeois body is a descent into the empty site of a dissociated ego, a 'volume in disintegration,' traced by language, lacerated by ideology, and invaded by the relational circuitry of the field of postmodern power. (Kroker & Kroker 1998: 20)

For **Donna Haraway**, it is more specifically a particular concept of the body that has disappeared: the humanist idea of the body as a natural, autonomous entity. In a world in which the traditional distinctions between nature and culture, art and science, world and self have become increasingly blurred, the contemporary body is always already a cyborg, she argues. Understood in the popular imagination to be human-machine hybrids, cyborgs, for Haraway, represent not a fusion of two opposing terms, but rather a breakdown of such binaries:

> The dichotomies between mind and body, animal and human, organism and machine, public and private, nature and culture, men and women, primitive and civilized are all in question ideologically ... The home, workplace, market, public arena, the body itself—all can be dispersed and interfaced in nearly infinite, polymorphous ways ... The cyborg is a kind of disassembled and reassembled, postmodern collective and personal self. (Haraway 1991: 163)

That is, the cyborg provides a new model for thinking about corporeality, one that does not rely on ideas of the natural and individual, one less focused on the question of what the body means than on what it can do and how it can be made. As Haraway recognises, although cyborgs are the product of the dominant capitalist culture, they can nonetheless be used against that culture, in the same way that, as we have already seen, Kruger's (anti-)advertisements both draw on and problematise traditional commercial images and rhetoric. 'The main trouble with cyborgs, of course, is that they are the illegitimate offspring of militarism and patriarchal capitalism, not to mention state socialism', Haraway writes. 'But illegitimate offspring are often exceedingly unfaithful to their origins. Their fathers, after all, are inessential' (Haraway 1991: 151).

This idea of the body as made or manufactured rather than born has important consequences, as Rosi Braidotti demonstrates in *Metamorphoses: Towards a Materialist Theory of Becoming*. Focusing on the subject's potential agency in remaking her own body within a postmodern cultural context characterised by constant change and transformation, Braidotti emphasises the way in which a post-industrial culture provides women with the ability to remake both themselves and the cultures within which such transformations take place, because 'self and society are mutually shaped by one another through the choreography of entitlements, prohibitions, desires and controls which constitute the socio-symbolic field' (Braidotti 2002: 144). The modes of becoming examined in *Metamorphoses*, she contends, have the capacity to enable an 'undoing [of] the structures of domination by careful, patient revisitations, re-adjustments, micro-changes' (2002: 116). The consequences and possibilities opened up by this approach, and its potential for a feminist theory of becoming, are evident in Braidotti's account of the post-human body, which draws on Halberstam and Livinstone's earlier work to argue that

> the post-human body is not merely split or knotted or in process: it is shot through with technologically-mediated social relations. It has undergone a meta(l)morphosis and is now positioned in the spaces in between the traditional dichotomies, including the body-machine binary opposition. In other words, it has become historically, scientifically and culturally impossible to distinguish bodies from their technologically-mediated extensions. (Braidotti 2002: 228)

Meta(l)morphoses are, Braidotti explains, forms of becoming-machine (2002: 215) that provide productive, positive figures through which to explore and rethink the 'social imaginary of post-industrial societies' (2002: 174). As Braidotti contends, meta(l)morphosed bodies problematise traditional concepts of the body as individual, self-contained and unchanging in a way that enabled new possibilities for subjectivity and corporeality.

This is a theme that has been thoroughly investigated in the contemporary arts. The French performance artist Orlan, for instance, undertook a series of surgical procedures as part of a project entitled *The Reincarnation of St Orlan*. These procedures were not intended to alter a physical characteristic perceived to be in need of 'correction' or 'perfection', but rather to reproduce on the artist's very body selected features of classic artworks celebrated for the idealisation of the female form: the chin from Botticelli's Venus, the forehead of Mona Lisa, and so on. Orlan's work, as her many critics have argued at length, demonstrates the extent to which enacting and undertaking cosmetic surgery popularly associated with the normative modification of the female body can itself be a form of cultural criticism of these practices. In this respect, Orlan's appropriation of traditional images of female beauty closely recalls Barbara Kruger's: both of these artists recontextualise conventional representations of the female body in a way that **denaturalises** these and transforms their signification. In keeping with the fragmentation and decentralisation that characterise postmodernism, however, work such as Orlan's does not constitute a new master narrative that would describe the 21st-century body since it is primarily contestatory, and cultural responses to the emergence of this body are accordingly not unified. On the one hand, then, we see the development of a vast array of cultural institutions designed to enable subjects to undertake the self-making of their own bodies (from private medical clinics to self-help books to television make-over programs). On the other, we see increasing public concern and government regulation surrounding reproductive technologies, commercial bio-banking and research involving the use of stem-cell material. While fears about the self-made body are hardly new (Victorian novels such as Mary Shelley's *Frankenstein* and Robert Louis Stevenson's *Strange Case of Dr Jekyll and Mr Hyde* explored these themes in the 1800s), the rapid proliferation of bio-technologies in the past few decades has intensified these concerns.

The very real tensions surrounding these issues are exemplified by the recent controversy surrounding the work of the Critical Art Ensemble (CAE, 1998, 2007) and the subsequent court case involving it. The Critical Art Ensemble is, in their own description, 'a collective of five artists of various specialisations dedicated to exploring the intersections between art, technology, radical politics and critical theory' (www.critical-art.net/index.html). Their work includes projects such as 'Flesh Machine', for which members of the audience were DNA-tested, the 'Cult of the New Eve', which explored recent reproductive technologies, and 'Contestational Biology', which included the 'reverse engineering' of genetically modified canola. In *The Flesh Machine*, the Critical Art Ensemble attempt to take account of the reconceptualisation of the body in and by contemporary cultural discourses and institutions. 'The Flesh Machine', the Ensemble writes, is

> a heavily funded liquid network of scientific and medical institutions with knowledge specializations in genetics, cell biology, biochemistry, human reproduction, neurology, pharmacology, etc., combined with nomadic technocracies of interior vision and surgical development ... It has two primary mandates—to completely invade the flesh with vision and mapping technologies (initiating a program of total body control from its wholistic [*sic*], exterior configuration to its microscopic constellations), and to develop the political and economic frontiers of flesh products and services. (1998: 4–5)

The economic, legal and medical frameworks within which the contemporary body signifies as a commercial assemblage of bio-materials is the focus of much of the CAE's work, a concern they share with a growing field of other artists and collectives, such as Bioteknica, Art Orienté Objet, the Tissue Culture and Art Project and, most famously, Stelarc (whose projects include the grafting of a third ear onto his body, a digital head installation employing artificial intelligence technologies, and a 'blender' of combined bio-materials).

Despite this established practice of using bio-materials within contemporary art practice, in May 2004 agents from several federal law enforcement agencies (including the FBI and the Joint Terrorism Taskforce) descended on the house of CAE's co-founder, Steve Kurtz, in hazmat suits. The area was cordoned off and quarantined, and materials including his car, cat, books, manuscripts and art equipment were confiscated. The focus of concern, however, were petrie dishes containing bacteria and laboratory equipment for monitoring genetically altered food, which were impounded under the Patriot Act. Although the bacteria from Kurtz's home were quickly established to be benign, Kurtz was originally charged with bio-terrorism: charges that were eventually downgraded to mail and wire fraud. The seized material, which was to be used in a (subsequently cancelled) exhibition, 'The Interventionalists: Art in the Social Sphere', has never been released. The case against Kurtz is ongoing.

While the legal response to the Critical Art Ensemble's work is clearly a reaction to a very specific set of contemporary circumstances—in particular fears about bioterrorism in the wake of 9/11 and subsequent scares concerning anthrax being sent through the US mail system—it is also evidence of the extent to which the bio-technologies emergent within postmodern culture remain the subject of intense scrutiny and concern. Artists whose work, like that of the Ensemble, involves an explicit referencing and critique of the historical and institutional contexts in which biomaterials have been produced and examined can find themselves the object of hostile legal, medical and journalistic attention. Like the Kruger advertisements with which this chapter began, then, the Ensemble's work destabilises fixed meaning in such a way that their work has the potential to be read in vastly different ways: as a dangerous deployment of bio-technologies or a subversive critique of their commercialisation. At the same time, the fate of the Ensemble's work alerts us to the high risks such strategies entail. It is perhaps precisely because traditional binarised categories are already breaking down, as noted by the postmodern theorists examined above, that attempts to further dismantle such categories can meet with such strong opposition and institutional resistance. As we see reflected in a wide range of contemporary cultural texts—from the idealised bodies appropriated in Kruger's anti-corporate artwork to the self-made body of body of artists like Orlan and the bio-art of groups such as the Critical Art Ensemble—the emergence of the post-human body remains a source of cultural fascination and fear, precisely because its emergence is not a completed process, but rather a site of ongoing struggle whose future significance is far from certain.

## key readings

Baudrillard, Jean 1994. *Simulacra and Simulation*, trans. Sheila Faria Glaser. Ann Arbor: University of Michigan Press.

Haraway, Donna 1991. 'A Cyborg Manifesto: Science, Technology, and Socialist-Feminism in the Late Twentieth Century.' In *Simians, Cyborgs and Women: The Reinvention of Nature*. New York: Routledge, pp. 149–81.

Lyotard, Jean-Francois 1984. *The Postmodern Condition: A Report on Knowledge*, trans. Geoff Bennington and Brian Massumi. Foreword Fedrick Jameson. Minneapolis, Minn.: University of Minnesota Press.

# rrapping irigaray: flesh, passion, world.

AUTHOR: linnell secomb

## INTRODUCTION

How do we understand, experience, express and perform the everyday sensations of the body: the phenomenology of living in and as a body and the embodied turmoil of love, desire and passion? Australian artist Julie Rrap and French philosopher Luce Irigaray each provide commentaries on, and new imaginings of, the gendered body and the negotiations of erotic encounters between the self and the other. Their differing yet converging conceptual reflections on embodiment, on the relation between body and world, and on the affects of love, overturn conventional perceptions and create alternative pathways towards embodied, enamoured, being-with-others.

Luce Irigaray has challenged the traditional conceptions of the human subject defined primarily as a thinking thing by emphasising the significance of the body and by focusing on the importance of embodied sexual difference. She critiques philosophical and psychoanalytic accounts of subjectivity, revealing the obliteration of femininity in these disciplines that speak from a masculine perspective about a seemingly sexually neutral human being that turns out to be based on masculine attributes and characteristics. Postmodern and poststructural feminisms are hugely indebted to Irigaray's ideas because she provides the basis for a feminism that seeks not only equality but also a recognition and revaluation of feminine difference. Julie Rrap's work has developed over the same period of the late 1900s and early 2000s, though she engages primarily with the limited representations of femininity within the visual arts and challenges the reduction of the feminine to a passive object of a voyeuristic gaze. Like Irigaray, she explores a positive feminine embodied difference and by using her own body in many of her artworks confounds the dichotomous opposition between artist and model, active creator and passive created, viewer and object of the gaze, masculine and feminine, and so on. Through their differing works each incarnates a new sensuous erotics of difference based on a feminine understood not as the opposite of man but as a differently embodied, passionate, active, creative becoming.

# blindspot.

Printed on adjustable Holland blinds, close-up images of the most intimate orifices of the human body repel and fascinate as the skin glistens in hyper-fleshy pink and orange tones. It is not immediately evident which body part is represented with the close-up rendering the familiar and intimate, strange and abject. Julie Rrap's *Blindspot* series of fifteen computer-generated iris prints printed on Holland blinds disturbingly renders ambiguous the boundaries between inside and outside as well as the distinctions between skin, flesh, organ and orifice. Hair of various sorts contrasts with the flesh—eyelashes, genital, scalp and body hair, ear and nose hair—providing clues for a possible reading of the bodily locations but also augmenting, through the exaggerated close-up and unusual perspective, the sense of the strange or foreign that imbues these images. Wrinkles, dimples, folds and fissures create further signposts, yet these so familiar locations nonetheless remain uncannily unfamiliar (Alexander et al. 1998: 104–5).

These images do not simply question the inside–outside boundary. Nor do they only evoke the *unheimlich* (uncanny, un-homely) experience of the body that is our dwelling place—both our own bodies, and the maternal body that envelops every human life. In addition to making the familiar strange they also introduce the strange within the familiar. Using calposcopic cameras, more commonly used for medical investigations of inner organs, Julie Rrap enters and represents the thresholds of the body, allowing the viewer to enter into the porous and penetrable body. The viewer's relation to the represented body remains ambiguous: is this a violation and violent entry into the body or is it an embracing by the open welcoming corporeal? The represented body seems to welcome, embrace and envelop the gazing eye of the viewer and at the same time remain vulnerable to ever-deeper invasions by the viewer. The viewer, a foreigner, a stranger to this body, imposes itself and/or is invited into this wet and glistening dwelling. It is as though the body and viewer, the self and other, were not completely separated. As though the viewing stranger were herself in the other's body, and part of that body. This intimacy, this proximity, disturbs the self–other boundary.

While Julie Rrap represents this *unheimlich* intimacy of body and stranger through visual images, Luce Irigaray evokes a similarly uncanny embodiment in words. Though Irigaray is perhaps better known as a theorist of sexual difference, her elaboration of difference avoids the problems of oppositional, dichotomous and dialectical difference by situating difference in relation to proximity.

Irigaray challenges the conventional representations of masculinity and femininity, arguing that in phallocentric cultures (those organised around the power of the phallus understood not as the male organ but as the signifier of male privilege) there is only one (valued) sex and that the feminine is constituted as either the negative reflection or diminutive lacking copy of this one masculine sex. Irigaray argues that woman is 'the sex which is not one'. This claim has a double meaning. It implies that 'woman' has multiple meanings, identities, and sexual pleasures and orientations: she is not one but multiple. It also suggests that 'woman' is not a sex; that she does not exist as an autonomous sex or meaning. Instead there is only one sex—the male sex—and woman is the unrepresentable or absence in masculine-dominated culture and discourse. Writing of the contemporary Western understandings of sexuality, Irigaray (1985a: 28) suggests that '[p]leasures … are somewhat misunderstood in sexual difference as it is imagined—or not imagined, the other sex [woman] being only the indispensable complement to the only sex [man]'. In contrast to this conventional understanding, in which the male sexual organ is valued while the female sexual organs are 'nothing-to-see' and 'are simply absent' (1985: 26), Irigaray insists that a new sexual imaginary could be constructed reflecting the female body, which she argues 'has sex organs more or less everywhere' (1985: 28) that enable multiple pleasures for a redefined feminine sexuality.

Instead of a monosexual culture in which only the male sex is recognised and valued, Irigaray advocates an ethics and culture of 'being-two' in which each sex is valued on the basis of its own attributes. This involves a recognition of the two and of the differences between the two and requires the reimagining or invention or creation of a new feminine subjectivity/sexuality as up to now, Irigaray contends, woman has only been man's diminutive copy or opposite mirror reflection. This new or alter-feminine is conceived by Irigaray as a multiplicity. The image of the two lips is an especially evocative one in Irigaray's arsenal of specifically feminine pleasures and morphologies. The two lips—both the lips of the mouth and of the genitals—cannot be separated into ones and they are in continuous contact, caressing and touching each other without need of mediation. Irigaray (1985a: 24) writes that 'Woman "touches herself" all the time … for her genitals are formed of two lips in continuous contact' and she adds that the 'contact of *at least two* (lips) … keeps woman in touch with herself, but without the possibility of distinguishing what is touching from what is touched' (1985: 26).

This image of the two lips not only recognises a specifically feminine corporeality and erotic pleasure, enabling woman to be constructed as a sex distinct from the male sex, but in addition it highlights the significance of the concept of proximity in Irigaray's work. The lips are neither only one nor divisible into two but are an organ of touch facilitated by the proximity of parts. While Irigaray is known as a theorist of sexual difference, the concept of proximity recurs in many of Irigaray's images and metaphors, including concepts such as mucous, love, angels and the sensible transcendental. This nearness obviates the tendency for difference to revert to opposition or to mirror reflection. While Irigaray stresses sexual difference, this is not a difference in which woman is simply man's opposite or reflection as this would install the one-sex society in which woman mirrors man. Rather, Irigaray's sexual difference insists on woman's autonomous difference; but importantly, this does not mean absolute separation, or the creation of boundaries between woman and man. Instead their difference is experienced through proximity and via the intermediaries that move between them facilitating being-two: intermediaries such as mucous, angels and love. As Krzysztof Ziarek (2000: 142) writes: 'Irigaray's work can be seen as literally fleshing out such relations in terms of the proximities of sexed, embodied beings.'

Nearness, caress, touch, proximity with the different other fleshy body is central to Irigaray's imagining of sexual difference. Imagining the enveloping caress of touch, the contact of flesh on flesh, the entwinement of limbs and bodies, Irigaray imagines the difference that would avoid merger or sameness by creating a proximity that enables the acknowledgment of alterity. Julie Rrap's 'Blindspot' expresses likewise an obsession with the flesh and its hidden dimensions, bringing the viewer into proximity with the body-image through the close-up that is not a merger but is a nearness so near that we almost touch, caress and feel the damp shiny folds and crevices, the voluptuous shapes and the sticky textures of the bodily orifices. Here there is the difference of the strange and foreign and simultaneously the caress and welcome of an uncannily familiar proximity.

Julie Rrap's *Blindspot* close-up photo series of bodily orifices creates a proximity between the viewing subject and viewed represented body. This semi-entry into the body, this almost-crossing of thresholds, this out-side-in positioning, parallels or echoes Irigaray's strategy of preserving difference while facilitating proximity and touch. This echoing is repeated through the similarity of themes: Rrap's orifices evoking and recalling Irigaray's doubled lips and multiple sites of feminine pleasure. Without reducing these two depictions of corporeality to the same, we may identify some proximities between Rrap's orifices and Irigaray's lips. Each refers to a blindspot, or an absence, a 'nothing-to-see', created by a culture that continues to overlook feminine pleasures and to shudder at the uncanny ambiguity (neither inside nor outside; neither of the body nor separate from the body) of the holes, the spaces, the thresholds and orifices of the body. Yet if there is a nearness between these two conceptualisations of the imaginary (or unimaginable) body there are also divergences. These divergences emerge most clearly in Irigaray and Rrap's varying depictions of the gendered materiality of the earth-world.

# fleshstones.

Diagnosing Socrates' story of the cave, recorded in Plato's *Republic*, Irigaray proposes that the philosophical search for knowledge and truth, and the quest to give birth to ideas, is facilitated by a repression of the original birth from the mother's body. Socrates tells of prisoners who, escaping imprisonment in a dark cave, find knowledge in the light of the sun. His pedagogical metaphorical narrative explains that the prisoners are chained in such a way that they are forced to face the back wall of the cave. Behind them guards move before a fire that throws shadows onto the back wall of the cave. The prisoners, having no other evidence, believe these shadows to be all reality and to contain all truth and knowledge. One prisoner escapes through a tunnel to the outside world where, in the sunlight, he sees the real world and is enabled to gain true knowledge (Plato 1998).

Irigaray reads the minutiae of this narrative, analysing each phrase, word and sentence to reveal another repressed metaphor within this metaphorical account of how most men live in a world of deception while truth may be found through the sunlight of philosophical knowledge. Irigaray's metaphor within a metaphor reads the cave as the womb, the escape as the rejection and repression of the maternal, and the light of knowledge as the privileging of the abstract transcendental over the materiality of the world, and of mind and thought over body and matter. Finally, the inner metaphor reveals the subordination of the feminine associated with maternity, materiality, body and earth, and the valorisation of masculinity and its associated attributes—mind, thought and transcendence of the mundane world. The philosophers, but also phallocentric culture more generally, 'get out of the "'maternal waters"' (Irigaray 1985b: 351) in order to create a reason divorced from the feminine. Phallocentric culture reproduces itself, through its inventions of thought and its birthing of ideas, by denying the maternal: 'Reproduction (of self) without matter, or mother' (1985: 251).

While Socrates tells the story of the cave as a metaphor of the quest for higher knowledge, achieved by escaping the dark and finding the light, Irigaray sees another repressed layer within the metaphor of the cave. This other metaphor reveals the repudiation of the feminine maternal who can henceforth only gain entry into the masculine universe through mimicry; that is, by adopting a pseudo-masculinity:

And what will be called the 'sensible,' or matter, or mother, or even 'other,' will have to yield if she wishes to have some face in this 'universe.' For she can only be known and recognized under guises that denature her; she borrows forms that are never her own and that she must yet mimic if she is to enter even a little way into knowledge. And when she does this, she will no doubt be stigmatized, after the fact, for owing her power of seduction to deceptive appearances. (Irigaray 1985b: 344)

Irigaray, then, identifies an association between cave and womb, the maternal and the earth, the feminine and the materiality of both body and world. In contrast, Julie Rrap's 2003 exhibition *Fleshstones* imagines a masculine body fused with and emerging from the earth. Her digital colour landscapes foreground (in scenes of beaches, bush, valleys and hills) stones that are flesh or that are wrapped in flesh—but here specifically in male flesh and body parts (www.roslynoxley9. com.au/artists/32/Julie_Rrap/338).

In the image titled 'Coogee Paul' the slightly sagging torso drapes around the rock form sitting on a cliff edge overlooking the horizon of the Pacific Ocean and summer-blue Sydney sky. The pink 'fleshstone' contrasts with the surrounding greys and greens of rock and grass yet casts a shadow confirming its locatedness in the scene. In 'Pearl Brian' a darker skin tone and more ambiguous morphology renders the merger from skin to stone indistinct. Surrounded by a scrubby background and lying on a sandy foreground, the rock-body evokes, through its colours and textures, other forms of matter—bone, wood, even perhaps some misshapen mutating inner organ.

Rrap has expressed an interest in interpretations of these images in which the rock-bodies are associated with the discarded bodies of stateless peoples whose rights as citizens are negated and who occupy a non-place between human life and non-human organic life. These rock-bodies are 'washed up on the shore', she says, and she elaborates referring to 'what Australia is now ... Tampa and detention centres' (quoted in Backhouse 2003). Rrap refers here to recent Australian policy and practice in relation to asylum seekers arriving by boat who were not allowed to land on Australian shores and were instead held in detention centres on various

figure 9.1: Julie Rrap, *Coogee Paul*, 2003, from the series *Fleshstones*. Digital print, 150 x 126 cm. Courtesy of the artist and Roslyn Oxley9 Gallery, Sydney.

Pacific islands in order to avoid Australia's responsibilities under international law to provide refuge for those genuinely fleeing from danger in their countries of origin. This policy commenced in 2001 when the Norwegian vessel, the *Tampa*, having saved refugees from a sinking boat, was refused permission to enter Australian waters (Marr & Wilkinson 2003: esp. 102–28).

While these images may thus be read as political comment, they simultaneously critique and engage with aesthetic traditions. Referencing the abstract sculptures of Auguste Rodin and Henry Moore, Rrap nonetheless fleshes out these abstractions, incarnating stone as skin and thereby juxtaposing abstraction with 'figurative sculpture in which stone is transformed through the skill of the artist and the desire of the gaze' (Parr 2003: 59).

Yet these 'fleshstones' are not just stone become flesh but are simultaneously bodies turned to stone. They oscillate undecidably between incarnation, animation and petrification. Is this an anthropomorphising of rock or an ossification of body? Either way the morphing between man and earth creates a counter-narrative to the more conventional stories of mother-earth that Irigaray exposes and elaborates. Rrap acknowledges a wish to challenge this conventional association: 'So much of the history of art is based on women in the landscape, I wanted to shift that way of thinking' (quoted in Backhouse 2003). Here, it is the male body that emerges from and recedes into matter, becoming one with the earth.

Where Irigaray reveals a repressed association between womb-cave-mother-earth, Rrap imagines a new alignment of masculinity with materiality. This new vision disturbs the conventional gendered alignments and oppositions while also questioning the division between the natural and the cultural or human.

Yet, while Irigaray and Rrap's strategies diverge, their concerns are similar. Each questions conventional gendered representations. Rrap overturns mother-earth by turning men to stone and/or transforming inert matter into masculine corporeality. Irigaray instead reinterprets and revalues gendered difference, opening a space for, and a recognition of, the maternal and the earth as the sites of original care, nurturance, welcome and hospitality. Despite their differences there remains a proximity between Rrap and Irigaray, for Irigaray writes, too, of men turned to stone. While analysing the Socratic cave metaphor she suggests that the repression of maternal femininity results in a masculine production that is deadly. The movement from matter to thought, abstraction and transcendence ('The climb up from the sensible to the intelligible—that is to say from the "lower abdomen" to the "head"' (Irigaray 1985b: 343)) replaces the living body with statues, deathly copies and corpses. The Socratic metaphorical cave is a dead cave because it has repressed the living maternal:

> Theatre of the cave, in which man's attributes figure only insofar as they have been made statues, immortalized in deathly copies ... The potency of the enchanter has always already been captured, made into a corpse by morphology ... The eye does not see to what sepulchral mummification it owes its enchantment. (1985b: 355)

Rrap's masculine 'fleshstones' may perhaps be interpreted otherwise, or as images of a sepulchral world in which man turns to stone in the forgetting of the feminine. Or broadening this line of thought: man turns to stone as a consequence of the forgetting of humanity and humanness. Rrap alludes to this possibility, associating the 'fleshstones' with 'the only people who can arrive (in Australia) now [who] are like dead bodies because then they're not going to cause any problems' (quoted in Backhouse 2003).

# A-R-MOUR.

While Rrap's *Fleshstones* ambiguously morph from man to rock and back, her *A-R-MOUR* photo series focuses on the morphing of the female body and depicts the becoming-armour of Hollywood sex starlets. These icons of desirable femininity are represented here as they transmogrify into their associated fetishes or as their fetish object becomes a form of protective shield. In each case Julie Rrap photographs herself dressed and posed as the Hollywood goddess-becoming-armour-fetish. In one image titled 'Marilyn' Rrap enacts the moment when Marilyn Monroe's dress is blown up around her thighs as a blast of hot air rises from a pavement air-duct. But here the folds of fabric have become corrugated Perspex, transforming the fetishistic not-quite-revealing of Marilyn's sex into a shield—though one that is tantalisingly transparent.

In 'Elizabeth' Rrap poses as the 16-year-old Elizabeth Taylor dressed in jodhpurs with riding crop neatly tucked underarm as she shapeshifts into her horse in the 1944 film *National Velvet*. Feet and hands have become hooves, creating defensive weaponry but also allowing a slide between the woman and the horse that is part of her seduction. Commenting on this work, George Alexander points to the association with Donna Haraway's becoming-cyborg:

> A-R-MOUR is a mausoleum of mutant goddesses (Liz Taylor, Sharon Stone, Catherine Deneuve, Ursula Andress, etc.). They are heirlooms of feminine power capable of becoming bestial,

f i g u r e 9 . 2 : Julia Rrap, *Camouflage #3 (Elizabeth) (A-R-MOUR)*, 2000. Digital Print, 195 x 122 cm. Courtesy of the artist and Roslyn Oxley9 Gallery, Sydney.

transgenic harbingers of some New Amazon, with mammalian fur, talons like birds of prey, amphibian scales, clover hoofs, unfinished tails and the space alien's mutability. Where there's a will, Donna Haraway. (Alexander 2002: 29)

The imaginary here puts in question the boundaries of the body and suggests that prosthetics, including sexualised fetish prosthetics, become part of the embodied corporeality of the subject. Woman is body, but this is a body inscribed by cultural codes—a body that is an entwining of animal, metal, Perspex and flesh—creating the cultural imagining of femininity.

The Hollywood goddess, the object of adoration, worship, sexual obsession, passionate amour, dons armour as defence and in the same gesture becomes explicitly the sexualised fetish she represents. Love, here, is both battle and game. There is armoury but there is also a flirty, if somewhat sarcastic, hyper-seduction.

Irigaray's reflections on feminine adornment and on love move in other directions. For Irigaray, woman's body provides a home for man—her sexual organs envelop his, her womb a dwelling for his becoming: 'If traditionally, and as a mother, woman represents *place* for man, such a limit means that she becomes a *thing* ... The maternal-feminine serves as an *envelope*, a *container*, the starting point from which man limits his things' (Irigaray 1993: 10). But he fails to provide a home for her becoming—except, perhaps, in providing a house that often functions as a prison—and so leaves her homeless and destitute. Woman, left defenceless, adorns herself, not with the armoury depicted by Rrap, but, in Irigaray's vision, in clothing, jewellery and makeup that protect and envelop, creating a dwelling place of her own making. Irigaray writes: 'Her clothes, her makeup, her jewels are the things with which she tries to create her container(s), her envelope(s). She cannot make use of the envelope that she is, and must create artificial ones' (Irigaray 1993: 11). Yet, while Rrap depicts a shielding and Irigaray a feminine adornment, perhaps both point to the feminine need for protection, for a mask, for a shield; and in each case a covering that is also an alluring revealing. The woman, left vulnerable, exposed, open, in danger of attack or penetration, covers herself with jewels and turns her fetishisation into armoury.

For both Rrap and Irigaray sexual love mutates into sexual war in which the feminine beguiles her lover-foe with her sexual allure while also safeguarding herself with gilded body armour. Yet if love between the sexes may become combat and contest it is also, for Irigaray, the possibility of a mutual becoming (Ziarek 1998: 71). In *I Love To You* Irigaray advocates an indirect expression of love: 'I-love-to-you' rather than the direct 'I-love-you'. The direct address 'I-love-you' implies ownership and union. It risks turning the beloved into an object-recipient of love. The insertion of 'to' is an attempt to open space, a little distance, a moment of difference, between lover and beloved. It avoids reducing the other to property and it sidesteps the merger or fusion of the two into one: the unification of self and other, lover and beloved, into one couple (Irigaray 1996: 109–113).

While the 'to' creates space and difference between the one and the other it also nevertheless retains a proximity. This is a small redirection of the expression of love. It does not found a complete exclusion or absolute disconnection but rather enables an encounter and engagement between that is neither conflation nor segregation. The 'to' signifies a space of proximity and a redirected movement between the lover and beloved. 'I-love-to-you' involves a double strategy creating space for difference while maintaining the proximity, intimacy and passionate exchanges required in love. Just as Irigaray invokes the two lips as a metaphor for simultaneous difference and proximity, 'I-love-to-you' likewise emphasises difference and proximity. The redirection through 'to', which echoes expressions such as 'I speak to you' (rather than 'at you' or 'for you'), creates a space or threshold that facilitates the relation between self and other and maintains separation while also enabling touch, caress and connection.

While Julie Rrap's *A-R-MOUR* reflects a concern with feminine armoury, and thus separation from the other, there remains here a reference to the pleasures and attractions of love. These iconic sex goddess figures do not simply mutate into protective shields but also into fetishistic armoury. The fetish, as the object that denies the 'castration' of the feminine—and thereby also denies her loss of phallic power—fascinates and eroticises her body. The fetish is the stiletto-heeled shoes, the undergarment, the fur coat that are the last objects perceived before the exposure to the 'lacking' female genitals. Rrap's mutating women become armour but also become fetish; become the hyper-object-of-desire that fascinates and attracts the lover/viewer. There is both distancing and irresistible allure; the woman becomes armour and fetish creating separation and attraction, repulsion and obsession, from and towards the feminine other. This oscillation creates a proximity that is both engagement, fascination obsession and at the same time protection, separation, difference. These mutant goddesses invite and simultaneously repel so that we are both near and at the same time far, and far while also near. Irigaray's proximity suggests a greater stability, always brushing and touching alongside the other. Rrap's representation of love oscillates and agitates but in so doing avoids merger while also facilitating encounter with the other: between lover and beloved, between viewing gaze and the mutant goddesses of love.

✳ ✳ ✳

Do the Australian artist and the French philosopher provide new knowledges about the body and its sensations? Yes and no. There are no facts here about the chemistry of the body, the organs, the pheromones, the blood and mucous. There are no statistics about courting rituals and sexual engagements, about which partnerships endure and which fall apart, about the percentages of individuals who marry, divorce, remarry or remain single. Yet there is a reflection on and speculation about the embodied self and other, their styles, their gestures, their habituated engagements, their characteristic ways of being. There is also a counter-discourse that reimagines passion, the body and the earth: a new perspective and interpretation that questions convention and opens possibilities in the present and for the future. Irigaray and Rrap embark on an adventurous exploration of embodied passion that recreates the experiences and performances of the body, gender, world and love otherwise.

We may learn from this new ways of imagining those things that we most often take for granted, and even assume to be natural: new ways of imagining the body, the relations between bodies, and the passions, desires, loves and complex entanglements of bodies. We may learn not so much to adopt Irigaray's and Rrap's visions as new orthodoxies but to be ever open to new possibilities and alternative incarnations as living, becoming, transforming subjectivities.

## key readings

Alexander, George, Catriona Moor, Terence Maloon and Sam Schoenbaum 1998. *Julie Rrap*. Australia: Piper Press.

Irigaray, Luce 1985a. *This Sex Which Is Not One*, trans. Catherine Porter. Ithaca, N.Y.: Cornell University Press.

Ziarek, Ewa Plonowska 1998. 'Toward a Radical Female Imaginary: Temporality and Embodiment in Irigaray's Ethics.' *Diacritics* 28(1).

# 4

# sex and sexuality.

# the stories so far.

AUTHOR: katrina **schlunke**

## the problem of heterosexuality.

What is heterosexuality? A theory? A desire? A set of practices? A way in which power works through the invention (and reinvention) of 'the normal' and 'the natural'? Can we think of heterosexuality without also imagining at least two sexes, woman and man? Can we think of heterosexuality without also thinking change? Noting shifts in matters of sex and sexuality are key ways in which we identify past eras and they are crucial in understanding responses to contemporary cultural change. For example, we know about the rise of Christian fundamentalism in a very particular, sexed and gendered way because of the contemporary re-emergence of the 'virgin', no-sex-before-marriage movement. By exploring notions of sex and sexuality we can often arrive very quickly at the lived experience of different times and cultures.

Some ways of thinking about and practising sex and sexuality that appear in the following chapters will show how sex and sexuality are imagined through different cultural and historical materials, through different reading practices and diverse points of identification. Styles of pleasure, the rereadings and repractising of popular phenomena and the ways in which thinking about those phenomena also invent particular communities of sexuality can also show us the deep inventiveness of the categories of sex and sexuality. Taken together, these three chapters demonstrate the great variety of ways in which we can understand ourselves and others, our bodies and pleasure. This diversity needs to be appreciated within a history of thinking about sex, which was driven less by ideas of diversity and pleasure than by ideas of certainty, limit and universalism. The following provides a short introduction to those histories.

# the biological.

One of the ways in which sex and sexuality have been controlled and ordered is through the use of oppositions, through imagining that women and men can be clearly identified through their biological differences. For example, all women have breasts; all men have testicles. This idea of female and male as opposites culminates in the early 18th century when the body replaced the soul as the point of differentiation (Laquer 1990). This was then extended to the idea that men and women have a vastly different genetic, hormonal and physiological makeup which is basically unchangeable across time and culture. The shift from soul to body was itself indicative of changing modes of oppression that required different ways of understanding sexes and bodies to operate effectively. That is, when ideas about the status of godliness organised the sense culture made of women and men, the quality of a person's soul was paramount. As the importance of the soul diminished the value of the body and how it was interpreted rose. As an organising principle that produces oppression, these sexed oppositions are then put into operation across the material environment and small day-to-day practices. Think about the ways in which plumbing parts can be referred to as having boy and girl parts and that an explanation of how velcro works is that is requires a 'boy' strip and a 'girl' strip. Within this biological model of sex, the physical differences then give rise to a natural gender—a natural set of behaviours that all men and women share. As a result of their biology women will be nurturing, non-aggressive and value the emotions, while men, as a result of their biology, will be combative and value the intellect. These two different sets of biologically driven behaviour will result in a 'natural' heterosexuality; the aggressive initiating sex drive of the male will be met by a submissive and receptive female resulting in a 'natural' act. Is this how we would all understand heterosexuality today? Who would and who wouldn't? Women and men in this model are complementary opposites who are defined by one another. This model is an **essentialist** one, because it conceives of the behaviours of men and women as the same across history and culture. This means we can apply the same criteria of judgment to the question of who and what is a man or masculine, or a woman or feminine, across time and across the world.

There are some obvious difficulties with this model, even as many religious and social groups continue to depend on it as evidence of the naturalness of their own cultural practices. The usefulness of a model of a constant sex and unchanging sexual role to any organisation that wants to make claims to a perpetual existence is obvious: such a model precludes any idea of political challenge or reform. Individuals and specific groups who are entirely 'hard-wired' sexually must simply exist, because no practice, no thinking can change them. The key objections to this thinking have come from history, science and anthropology, or cultural observation.

Many people have traced the historical specificity of certain sorts of sexual behaviour and shown that it has not always been the same. For example, relations between older men and younger ones in 5th-century Greece were sexual but they did not understand themselves, and were not understood by others, as homosexual (that term was yet to be invented). Their behaviour was understood as manly and appropriate as long as (like relations between women and men) it conformed to certain cultural rules. Another example might be the obvious shifts in how our sex has been 'performed' through fashion. In one era the wearing of wigs and copious white makeup that once marked the aristocratic male might now be understood as female behaviour or perhaps 'goth'. Science has also argued that women and men have much more in common biologically than they have differences. Variations between men can be as acute as those between men and women. Boys and girls are born with similar muscle mass and there is huge diversity in hormonal makeup within both sexes. Ongoing gene mapping has also challenged simple sexed divisions with the discovery of just how much of our genetic makeup we share with other species, let alone with other sexes. Sexuality and what a man and woman are cannot therefore be entirely known in biological terms. As Gayle Rubin puts it:

> The body, the brain, the genitalia, and the capacity for language are all necessary for human sexuality. But they do not determine its content, its experiences or its institutional forms. Moreover we never encounter the body unmediated by the meanings that culture gives to it. (Rubin 1984: 276)

# sex and gender.

Perhaps in part to explain the diversity of behaviours that biology alone could not account for, the idea of gender came into being as a repository for all the socially acquired characteristics that were seen as distinct from biology. Another way of saying this is that we may be born a particular sex (female or male) but we 'become' women and men, feminine or masculine. This means that we are taught particular roles according to our biological sex and these roles become our gender (see **Judith Butler**, *Bodies that Matter*, 1993; Moira Gatens, *Imaginary Bodies*, 1996). So gender (woman/man or feminine/masculine) is understood as a distinctly social category and sex (female, male), a distinctly biological one. This idea of 'becoming' a woman appeared in **Simone de Beauvoir's** *The Second Sex* as 'One is not born, one becomes woman' in 1949 and was developed throughout second-wave feminism in the 1970s, with radical results. Besides de Beauvoir, the writings of Betty Friedan, **Germaine Greer**, Gloria Steinman, **Mary Daly** and Kate Millet among many others were powerful examples of the ways in which this 'theory' was practised in the areas of law, policy, ethics, literature and daily life. The development of 'gender' politics, particularly via 'women's liberation', gave rise to demonstrations and the demand for acknowledgment of domestic violence and rape in war, for state-sponsored childcare, rights to abortion and women's refuges; it also opened the way for lesbian separatist politics, reformation of university and school curricula, equal employment and pay legislations, and major shifts in how women and men connected and imagined one another.

The great strength of this argument is that it is an anti-essentialist one, which states that there is no single, essential 'thing' that is women, but rather a category, 'woman', that is constructed within society through trainings, organisation of power and systemic practices. Therefore these practices can be challenged and changed, and women can be 'liberated' from their effects through critique or 'consciousness raising'. It also means that much of the so-called differences between men and women are created through these same means and that those differences are organised for the benefit of men. Or as de Beauvoir put it: 'She [i.e. woman] is defined and differentiated with reference to man and not he with reference to her; she is the incidental, the inessential as opposed to the essential. He is the Subject, he is the Absolute—she is the other.'

Biology within this sex/gender model became reduced to a simple citation of reproductive differences and sometimes the site of an assumed sameness or androgyny in babies that was worked over through the social world to produce 'man' and 'woman'. The roles of 'woman' and 'man' were actively learnt through a system of socialisation that rewarded gender-appropriate behaviours and punished deviant ones. The simple examples of such trainings include the punishing of boys who cry and play with dolls, the discouragement of girls from hitting anyone and the endorsement of girls playing quietly. You should easily be able to think of your own examples here. It also assumes that sexual desire is learnt and that the style of conducting one's body in sexual situations will be the result of social training. The two established roles, then, produce a heterosexual act. A homosexual act will result from refusing and critiquing the social role to some extent, hence the importance of 'political' lesbianism in this period. This model of thinking was, however, less concerned with a rich account of sexuality than with why and how the role of women came to be understood as subordinate to men and why it continued to be reproduced as subordinate.

One of the difficulties with this model of thinking was its seemingly simple assumption about the constancy of the social environment that would produce these constant genders. Aren't the rewards for certain kinds of gendered behaviour more diverse then this? Are the processes of reward and punishment likely to be entirely the same? A division between a biological sex and a social gender also seemed to suggest that the body in some way didn't matter, because it was merely an undifferentiated mass that became shaped by the social. However, Moira Gatens in 'A Critique of the Sex/Gender Distinction' (1996) shows that sexed bodies are always already understood as gendered. Even if liberal feminism could establish the right for men and women to undertake the same tasks, the already gendered bodies of the women and men undertaking those tasks would be understood differently. So, if sex is already gendered the distinction between sex and gender does not exist. Think about the ways in which men and women do similar work but how their bodies are understood differently in the same context. For example, how do women and men appear very differently as preschool teachers, as drinkers of beer in pubs or as ball throwers and catchers? So for Gatens the questions came to be: how are bodies constituted and lived as sexually different from one another?

There were also critiques of this gender-based political movement as one that privileged sex over race or class. **bell hooks** in the USA and Jackie Huggins in Australia were key critics of the theories and practices that claimed a) to include all women and b) saw sex oppression as the most fundamental form of oppression. Black women and Indigenous women saw immediately that many of the specific issues being fought for were not ones relevant to them. In Australia, for example, amid the effects of the **Stolen Generations** and poor health conditions, Indigenous women were fighting as Black women to keep their children and give birth to children in conditions that did not produce high child mortality rates, while the largely white feminist movement were seeking rights to abortion and alternative birthing practices. Indigenous and black feminist responses to issues of race and colonialism continue to be one of the very productive spaces for thinking about gender that enacts new politics. This is, in part, due to the ways in which raced politics cross national, gender and sexuality boundaries while still needing to account for the force of white privilege within those changing formations. Working-class critiques have also continued to transform the meanings of sex and sexuality and have re-emerged in the politics of globalisation. The connecting point between these eras has been what work it was assumed women do and what wages they are paid, and whether a socialist politics can meet the demands of new labour formations that consist almost entirely of women, such as global domestic workers and an internationally connected and organised sex industry. Indigenous, working-class, black and migrant women continue to critique and thus drive the practices and theories of gender, particularly through the challenges of contextual difference and the specificity of raced and gendered 'performances'.

Judith Butler articulated the idea of gender as a particular kind of performance in her book *Gender Trouble*. In her terms, gender is a performative effect that arises from repeated acts. These acts then 'congeal over time to produce the appearance of a substance, of a natural sort of being' (Butler 1999: 33). There was no 'original' or essential gender or sex but rather a set of body and social practices that were endlessly repeated. This could range from the 'natural' application of lipstick to the 'natural' inclination to pee sitting down. Each of these is a different kind of performance, but a performance all the same. The usefulness of thinking of both sex and gender as 'performed' was that it articulated the possibility of intervening in narrow definitions of sexed behaviour by imagining and participating in different performances that were always both 'biological' *and* 'social'. Butler (2007: 11) came to say: 'Indeed, sex, by definition, will be shown to have been gender all along.' That is, there is no 'real' or definitive gender that has a beginning point in a sexed body to which we can return. Sexed performances could never be only social or only bodily, but always included both. The body offers no 'original' set of drives that could be understood outside culture or represented outside language. (See Part 1 for a greater account of the body.)

Butler's work also asked us to pay greater attention to alternative performances of gender such as drag kings and drag queens (see Chapters 2 and 10), to think not only about how we could do gender/sex differently, but also to see that gender is an effect of the action of the performance. Therefore we can see 'ordinary' gender as an effect of day-to-day performances that become a regulating fiction. This gender fiction enables rewards and punishments within a frame of heterosexuality so that heterosexuality is sustained as an organising discourse. This analysis also means that other sexual categories are also cultural fictions, such as homosexual and heterosexual. In the place of any of these categorisations Butler posits that our gendered identities come into being through our relations with others and the world and thus will be contextual, dispersed and in process. This has sometimes been called '**queer**' and we will consider that idea further below.

# sex as discourse.

Another key idea—driving ideas of sexed diversity and thinking of our sexed bodies as sites of diverse pleasure—came as a reaction to the realisation that sex and sexuality are discourses, that is, ways in which power is practised. This idea was formulated most extensively by **Michel Foucault**. His argument suggests that in the 19th century the family came to operate as an institution that would discipline and normalise sexuality. It would do this through ideas and practices such as regular medical checks of children, a moral discourse concerning the need to control children's sexuality, and the creation in the child's mind of a sense of self-scrutiny as to what were good and bad sexual practices. In the 19th century this produced a disjuncture between a medical system that denied the existence of childhood sexuality and a moral discourse that was telling parents to be very aware of and try to prevent children from participating in morally dangerous activities such as masturbation. So what was on the one hand denied (sexual activity in children) was on the other hand acknowledged (stop the child masturbating). This mix of negation and moral instruction led, Foucault believed, to a greater public awareness of what sexuality might be and extended the limits of social control. Through the positing of a 'normal' sexuality that was arrived at through medical and psychological study and regulated via families, schools and the idea of the individual, sexuality became the means by which control was organised in small individual ways across and through numerous social sites to produce an ordered social institution. Another way of saying this would be to think of the ways in which the knowledge 'discovered' and circulated by doctors, psychologists, priests and parents produced a particular kind of sexual subject—the child in this instance—who would need to be watched and checked for breaks with an established norm. The subject (the child) would him/herself in various ways take up the order she/he would learn and understand and regulate her/himself through it. The sexed identity would become internalised (I am a boy or a girl) and made natural, and therefore naturally controlled. For example, being told 'girls don't sit with their legs apart' or 'boys should play football' would be understood as natural and something that made one a 'proper' girl or boy; and we would desire to be a 'good' and 'proper' girl or boy. Thus we become a product of our relationship with power. The danger for the individual who can accept being told whether they are good or bad according to a power/knowledge formation was what Foucault tried to undo. This included a suspicion (Foucault also loved men) of a gay liberation movement that could insist on a project of 'making same', of insisting that only one particular set of activities enabled you to call yourself gay. That is, to have 'gay liberation' one needed to 'discover' an original gay identity that could only be identified by limiting what gay could mean (for example, only those sexed partners, only those practices of the body). Instead Foucault supported the idea of discovering and practising new ways of being that were open-ended and uncertain. It was in such directions that Butler developed these ideas further.

This idea of sexuality and subjectivity as a field of possibility of multiple forms can be described as 'queer', as understood within queer theory. This is a theory, with a radically available subject, which is ideally never decided on. Or as David Halperin suggests: 'There is nothing (that is, no 'normal', no ordinary, no natural, no public figure or historical archetype) to which it [queer theory] necessarily refers'. This is an idea of a sexed subject which cannot be checked or examined for how little or how much it is queer (or how good or proper it is), for no such system of knowledge/power will be produced through queer theory. This is also another way of thinking of sexual desire.

Ideas about desire have also shifted through various models from a set of biological impulses to a much more fluid and yet productive idea of what desire is and does. Many of the earlier formulations of desire were based on ideas of desire being in some way a means by which we substitute desire as a stand-in for something we lack. In **Freudian** terms this was practised through a fraught and often incomplete process marked by threat and repudiation and figured around the power of the phallus that took the child through an **Oedipal** stage which would or perhaps should produce heterosexual attraction. Boys had to switch their desire from the mother to other women through fear of castration (they lack the power of the father over their desired object the mother) and girls had to switch their desire from their mother to the father and so to other men out of a desire for the penis (they lack phallic power without it). But Deleuze and Guattari in *Anti-Oedipus: Capitalism and Schizophrenia* (1972) posit a different model of desire. In their thinking desire is a positive force that is always social from birth and is a means by which things are connected, brought together and transformed. The subject within this thinking is a 'becoming', that is, has no absolutely fixed identity but is mutable and multiple. Think perhaps of who you are when you participate in an online forum, when you put your earphones in, buy a drink or party with friends. Are all of these versions of 'you' exactly the same? Or is the need to think constantly of oneself as a single unchanging entity the way in which you are disciplined and discipline yourself to imagine only family and capitalism as ways through which you can make sense of yourself? A useful guide to appreciating the ways in which sex acts are understood is to look at Gayle Rubin's five discursive formations that she lists in 'Thinking Sex' (1984), which include sex negativity, the fallacy of misplaced scale, the hierarchical valuation of sex acts, the domino theory of sexual peril, and the lack of a benign concept of sexual variation. This last formation is the idea that there is only one standard of sexuality (heterosexuality) against which all else is measured as more or less legitimate and so more or less real and valued. But because these are discursive formations there is also variation within them. Heterosexuality can include home-owning white picket fence dwellers as well as green-voting, shared household dwellers, and the sexual practices of each group may vary enormously. The seeming variety within any discourse works to hide the larger and yet often more localised productions of power that continue to sustain the idea of 'normal' sexuality and sex.

In the three chapters that follow we see that sex and gender are no longer seen as in any way existing outside culture and that the effort now is to identify the diversity of ways in which new forms of sexed behaviour are coming into being. This diversity is particularly marked now compared to other periods because of the globalised (see Part 5) circulation of images, books and other texts as well as individuals' capacity to participate in subcultures across different time zones and geographical locations. Widely circulated figures such as celebrities can become the new sites for alternative readings as different groups and individuals make a version of the world that has a place in it for their emerging desires. Through these desires new configurations appear of how gender and/or sex work. Sex with its deep connections to the body, to ideas of private and public worlds, and as the most often articulated site of desire, remains an ongoing source of creative and imaginative intervention in the world and a highly productive means for individual practices of thinking.

In the chapters by Audrey Yue and Brett Farmer we are able to see the explicit sexed engagement with two very different celebrities—Bruce Lee and Kylie

Minogue. Yue traces the ways in which Lee has been understood through national ideas of what is masculine, through the sheer spectacle of his 'actioning' and his particular uptake by Black Americans and diasporic drag kings. Because of his global celebrity, because of the way his body is seen and admired and because he is a well-known Asian star, further formations of masculinity are made through him. What are your experiences of Bruce Lee? How could you learn to move your body like his? This chapter also shows the ways in which different kinds of masculinity can be negotiated and managed through performances of the body and by reading masculine performances differently. In the spectacle of Bruce Lee's body on film there seems to be an available excess that enables others to recross into a different order of desire and a different performance of masculinity. But is this about individual invention or a way of contesting, of struggling against dominant ideologies that seek to control groups in both Asia and the West?

In a very different way Farmer explores the ways in which another celebrity, Kylie Minogue, 'works' as a gay icon. How does a 'pop princess' contribute to the destabilisation of any simple and stable idea of sexuality? Farmer outlines the features through which Minogue is read by gay men in particular, but also reads herself to produce **camp**. Camp (and other negotiations) can show the way in which homosexuality works as an expansive and productive force to open up phenomena otherwise closed and bounded by heterosexual claims. This in turn reminds the consumer and reader of all cultural texts of the possibility of making cultural community through how you theorise and practise your thinking about what you 'consume'. Farmer calls this the 'extraordinary everyday creativity of their (popular celebrities) multiple audiences'.

In Chapter 12 Fran Martin looks at another kind of creative counter-reading in 'The Counterpublic World of Taiwanese Women fans of Japanese Homoerotic *Manga*'. As the title suggests, this is a geographically specific group of women consumers of 'boys' love' (BL) *manga* who articulate the multiple reasons why such publications give them pleasure across gender and sexuality boundaries. An important aspect of this chapter is that the author quickly recognised that one of the pleasures of this activity was the collective, informal theorising that accompanied the reading of the texts. What kinds of selves are made possible by reading BL? What are the processes that enable the women to produce helpful ideas about their own agency, sexuality and gender that also enable them to challenge dominant, public representations of young women that they disagree with?

It is obvious that sex and sexuality fit within larger projects concerning the philosophy of the subject and the organisation of power, but they also extend and critique dominant thinking about how the world works. On the one hand we recognise that the very particular histories of how sex and sexuality have been and continue to be understood make this a category through which individual bodies have been tortured, confined and killed for failing to conform to a very particular discipline of power. We could say that through the category of sex, the most minute and the most marked lines of power are drawn through the private and public worlds of individual and groups. But equally and precisely, because of how power has operated through sex, it is a site where new ideas about what bodies, what genders, what selves could be, get worked out and reformulated. Sex is always an imaginative site where culture itself can be temporarily reconsidered or reassured but never closed down. Sex and sexuality are also sites where people practise and theorise at once in a productive and embodied way that is exciting and contagious.

# THINKING WITH PART 4

○ Try to consciously 'perform' masculinity. What props do you reach for? What tones of voice do you employ and how do you rearrange your limbs?

○ Think about what would be involved in designing and rehearsing a Bruce Lee drag king performance. How can the spectacular actions of Bruce Lee be 'translated' respectfully across genders and races?

○ Identify the gendered appeal of any celebrity icon. How does the celebrity produce a particular appeal to men and women, queers and straights? How stable is that appeal?

○ Conduct a 'camp' reading of other celebrities and identify why they succeed or fail within a camp frame.

○ Find and read some examples of BL *manga*. Where did you have to go to find it? What internet sites did you explore? What fan groups did you encounter?

○ Where have you found pleasure with reading with others? (A book club or study group perhaps?) What part does your gender or sexuality play in these reading pleasures?

# kung fu fighting: doing action and negotiating masculinity.

AUTHOR: audrey yue

## INTRODUCTION

In the thirty-five years since the sudden death of Bruce Lee in 1973, the cult of Lee has sparked a transnational action culture, not only through the global circulation of kung fu cinema, but also through the kung fu genre as a public space for meditating on the ethics of everyday action. In America, his films have empowered black and working-class audiences with their portrayal of a Chinese underdog fighting and overcoming colonial oppressors. In India, they have inspired Tamil villagers in Andhra Pradesh to form martial arts schools and create new collective public spaces (Srinivas 2003). In the city of Mostar in Bosnia, a solid gold statue of Bruce Lee graces the town square and christening one's child with 'Brucelee' as a first name has become a common practice. In the **queer diaspora**, drag kings and tomboys mime his every pose in adulation and adoration. As his fans eagerly await the 2009 opening of the Lee-themed park in the star's ancestral town of Shunde in China, it is clear that, whether it is through cinema, the wider kung fu culture, or even sampled in Hollywood as kitsch (Pang 2006), Lee has become a repository for new ways of imagining and doing action. This chapter examines Bruce Lee as a site for constituting new modes of 'doing action'. Central to this is the way Lee reinvents his body to negotiate **hegemonic** masculinity.

Bruce Lee is arguably one of the world's most widely acclaimed and highly imitated icons. He is a symbolic and representative signifier for thinking about action as a genre of cinema, as a style of martial arts and as a cultural practice of 'doing'. His films have done more to bridge the gap between the East and the West than any other star, director or genre. Having only made four films in his short career, his premature death elevated him instantaneously to a legend. Like James Dean and Marilyn Monroe, '[w]ith his death, Lee became an object, even a fetish' (Teo 1997: 20). Widely emulated and copied, he sparked a global 'kung fu craze' (Desser 2000) with the mushrooming of martial arts schools, fan clubs and even a series of 'Bruceploitation' (Kenny 2001) films with 'Leealike' clones (Logan 1995: 24).

Kung fu films, unlike swordplay films, emphasise the body and training rather than the supernatural. Marilyn Mintz (1978: 11) refers to the film as one in which 'competence as martial arts performer determines role and behaviour in the plot'. Leon Hunt (2003) extends this by focusing on how the performance of the body constructs the pace, exhilaration and excitement of action. He borrows the concept of the body genre from feminist film scholar Linda Williams to classify kung fu films as 'a genre of bodies: extraordinary, expressive, spectacular, sometimes even grotesque bodies' (2003: 2). The way Lee shrieks and roars, and how his body twists and swishes, resonates with what Williams (1995: 140) describes as a 'display of sensations that are on the edge of respectable'. The kung fu body, like the deviant bodies in horror films and pornography, is excessive and transgressive. Formalist film theorist David Bordwell (1997) claims it is precisely this aesthetics of action that makes the genre so popular and infectious in the West. Unlike the classical realism and continuity editing of Hollywood action cinema, the kung fu action film is closer to Eisensteinian montage. Using the discontinuous pause-burst-pause rhythm of editing, this form of montage relies on the spectacle of action rather than the story of the narrative to create the thrill of action and effect of motion. It is an 'ecstatic cinema' where 'the *expressive amplification* of action ... felicitously exaggerates the most emotion-arousing features of pursuit of combat' (Bordwell 1997: 86). Kung fu action is an **affective genre** that focuses on the body as a repository of desire. Located in the performative skill of a culturally and historically specific body, stardom is important to this genre because the action hero personifies a society's aspirations, values and beliefs. Lee's powerful and strong masculinity, as a representation of the fantasy of Chinese nationalism, is incisive here.

Masculinity refers to a set of socially constructed cultural traits associated with the gendered role of men in society. Dominant or hegemonic masculinity is synonymous with manhood, power, legitimacy, privilege, patriarchy (Connell

1995). Dominant Confucian Chinese masculinity is also complicit in these gender and sex role discourses where a daughter is subordinated to her father when young, a wife to her husband when married, and a mother to her son when old. Kam Louie (2002) highlights two ideal types of Chinese masculinity: a *wen* masculinity that refers to the soft intellectual ability of a scholar, and a *wu* masculinity that refers to the hard, active, physical and military ability of the warrior. The analogy of patriarchal *wen-wu* masculinity to nationhood is understood through the etymology of the Chinese word for 'nation', '*guojia*'. '*Guo*' means 'country'; '*jia*' means 'family'. As a compound word, '*guojia*' refers to how the nation is imagined as composed of families. In this relation, a weak patriarch (neither *wen* nor *wu*) is thus constitutive of a weak nation.

The association of the body with the nation can be further understood through the concept of the body-politic. It refers to how the unity of the nation is imagined by producing and circulating dominant ideas and images about the bodies available in the culture. The body is imagined as a site of physical and symbolic geographical and cultural penetration. The stronger the body, the harder it is to invade, hence the stronger the nation. Kung fu action is also an exemplary model to demonstrate the body-politic because it is a form of contact sports about strong, skilled and hard bodies, as well as a contact zone of international fights and tournaments. *Fist of Fury* (Lo Wei, 1972), set in the international settlement of Shanghai in 1908, is noted for two sequences that reflected the weak Chinese nation. One is the 'Sick Man of Asia' plaque delivered to Lee's school by a rival Japanese school in the wake of his master's death; the other is when Lee is refused entry to a park displaying a sign that reads 'No Dogs and Chinese Allowed'. These racist slogans mock China and subordinate the nation to foreign concessions and colonial power. By cultivating and reinventing his body as hard and powerful, Lee uses the skill, strength and power of his racialised body to fight the colonial oppression of the Japanese and the West. His empowered masculinity can be considered a form of **postcolonial** masculinity, which is a discourse of producing new representations of the male body as strong and liberated in order to challenge the colonial stereotype of the oppressed colonised male body. Lee not only single-handedly crushes the karate school; he also trounces a Russian martial arts champion enlisted to protect the school. He plays the anti-foreign underdog who redeems the honour lost through colonial prejudices and humiliation. As Hong Kong film theorist Siu Leung Li reiterates, 'In kung fu cinema, the restoration of a strong China and of national pride under colonial conditions is often effected through a fetishisation of the male kung fu body imagined as an empowering fighting and self-defensive skill' (Li 2001: 516). This type of postcolonial and cross-cultural fight sequences have become *de rigueur* in all his films.

Lee's postcolonial reinvention of his racialised body as strong and powerful perpetuates the Chinese ideal of *wu* masculinity and rekindles the fantasy of Chinese nationalism. It also inverts the stereotype of weak diasporic Chinese masculinity. Action cinema scholar Yvonne Tasker introduces the term 'remasculinization' to refer to how Lee's display of strength, muscles, agility and speed challenges the dominant construction of Chinese masculinity in the West: 'Lee's image speaks of a struggle to become hard, to negate an imputed soft' (Tasker 1997: 325). She traces the racist stereotypes of Asian men in Hollywood using images such as the inscrutable Charlie Chan, the vicious Fu Manchu and the yellowface 'bucktooth Chinaman' played by Mickey Rooney in *Breakfast at Tiffany's* (Blake Edwards, 1961) to show how they are usually represented as desexualised, feminised and hence 'soft'.

The cultural practice of 'doing action' or 'actioning' can be summarised through how the remasculinised body reproduces the ideal of Confucian Chinese masculinity and inverts the subjugation of diasporic Chinese effeminacy. It refers to how the learning of martial arts and the strengthening of one's body can enable one to refashion one's identity through what **Michel Foucault** (1997) identifies as the ethics of self-cultivation and self-empowerment. It also refers to how a collective identification with an action hero can help to foster and maintain a group's imagined community. Central here is the way postcolonial masculinity functions as an ethnic and gendered site to contest different ideologies of power within China, in Asia and in the West. The popularity of action cinema among ethnic minority and working-class audiences in America further demonstrates this.

Black audiences in America were among the earliest fans of kung fu action cinema in the 1970s. David Desser elucidates how Lee's subalternity enabled black audiences, who were alienated by mainstream film and culture, to identify with him:

> This was the genre of the underdog, the underdog of colour, often fighting against colonialist enemies, white culture, or the Japanese. The one, often unarmed combatant fighting a foe with greater economic clout who represented the status quo provides an obvious but nonetheless real connection between kung fu films and black audiences. (Desser 2000: 38)

David Bordwell (2000: 50) also notes that 'many a black or Hispanic youth was inspired by Lee's fearless confrontation with white power'. Stuart Kaminsky (1974) points to how Lee uses the underdog to justify the violence of revenge and promote the myth of the ghetto. This myth repeats the ritual of the racial minority groups who redress a social injustice and gain dignity through vengeance and destruction. Bill Brown stresses that it is not the specificity of Lee's racialised body but his 'generic ethnicity' that fulfils the fantasies of liberation and empowerment to audiences who are racially and marginally oppressed (Brown 1997: 33). **Meaghan Morris** (2004: 186) emphasises that these films address Western working-class audiences by creating 'a model of learning based on emulation'. The affiliation between the subcultures of the 'foreign' kung fu action film, and other diasporic ethnic minority and working-class communities, highlights how the ethnic masculinity of the kung fu action body is a site for generating new minor transnational alliances.

These exchanges continued into contemporary times with the successful crossover of the kung fu comedy of Jackie Chan. Chan actively cultivated black spectatorship by setting his films in Africa or the African diaspora, collaborating with black actors and incorporating black popular cultural references in his films. Afro-Asian aesthetics now include the rave scene of hop-fu, the music of Wu Tang Clan, and the new collaborations between hip hop artists and kung fu action stars such as DMX and Jet Li in *Cradle 2 the Grave* (Andrzej Barkowiak, 2003) and RZA's endorsement of Tony Jaa in the Thai action blockbuster *Ong Bak* (Prachya Pinkaew, 2003). These minor transnationalisms, from cross-cultural and subcultural identifications to new cultural productions, express new ethics of 'doing action'. They embody action as a practice of the care of the self, as well as a style of life, and show how minority groups can learn from and collaborate with each other to carve out their own 'practices of freedom' in their tactics of everyday survival (Foucault 1997: 285). While these diasporic identifications create affective life politics and distinctive new cultural styles, they are also constituted by the forces of global capital and the national body-politic. The impact of the genre on mainstream action cinema and the social history of reception provide a context in which to situate this.

Nineteen seventy-three, the year when *Enter The Dragon* was released and topped American charts, was also the year America withdrew its troops from Vietnam. Despite its box office success, the genre was only popular among black, Hispanic and working-class audiences, and consigned to a B-subculture of chop socky and blaxploitation films. It was not until the Rambo films of the 1980s, which saw a white American hero invading Vietnam, that action cinema grew to become a significant mainstream genre in Hollywood (Desser 2000: 39). The mainstream and the subcultural action heroes highlight two competing ideologies of masculinity. While the mainstream action hero appropriates the physicality of the martial arts body to remasculinise the traumatic body-politic of an America recovering in the wake of Vietnam (Jeffords 1989, 1994), the ethnic masculinity of the subcultural action hero can be argued as remasculinising the 'counternation' (Brown 1997: 36). In this complex positioning, the hyper-muscularity of the Rambo-like American action hero has the hegemonic effect of displacing the ethnic populism of the subcultural action hero. This is evident in the exoticisation of ethnic action as a B-film commodity and the use of labels such as '**camp**' or 'kitsch' by academics, cinephiles, fans and journalists to classify the Hong Kong action film (Stringer 1997). Lee's ethnic masculinity is decentred, and even 'refeminised' to fit the history of Asian-American emasculation. Black action heroes and heroines in films such as the *Black Belt Jones* (Robert Clouse, 1974) and *Cleopatra Jones* (Jack Starrett, 1973) series are also hyper-sexualised to fit the stereotypes of excessive black masculinity and femininity. Gina Marchetti, writing about Jackie Chan's subcultural connection with black audiences, argues that Asians in America function as '"buffers" or "middlemen" between black and white communities' (Marchetti 2001: 144). James Kim, examining the role of

Jet Li in *Romeo Must Die* (Andrzej Barkowiak, 2000), furthers this by suggesting that Asian-American masculinity functions as a 'third term' that 'facilitates white racial fantasies about black masculinity' (Kim 2004: 155). Because Asian-American masculinity disrupts the black and white racial hierarchy, he argues it must be erased to maintain the white desire for and disavowal of black masculinity.

In these debates, the postcolonial masculinity of the action body, as a site of African/Latino-Asian subcultural identification, or Hollywood incorporation, is clearly a critical discourse embedded in the uneven flows of spectatorial desire, national body-politic and global capital. As action cinema becomes global popular culture, it is also a site 'where capital organizes and distributes the kind of generative desire or fantasy that enables production and accumulation to take place' (Ching 2000: 256). From ethno-nationalist desires in Asia, minor transnational lifestyles in the diaspora to the spectacle cinema of Hollywood (Arroyo 2000), postcolonial masculinity is reinvented, appropriated and co-opted. In the life-worlds of the Chinese diaspora in Australia, its hegemonic status as patriarchal Chinese masculinity is also contested. The subversion of Bruce Lee by diasporic drag kings provides a useful example to demonstrate further how postcolonial masculinity is also challenged by diasporic Asian female masculinity.

# Lee Bruce Lee.

Lee Bruce Lee is a disco-dancing, kung fu prancing Melbourne-based Malay-Chinese drag king.[1] Just like the real thing, he begins his act by ripping off his Bonds singlet, revealing a bound chest, but unlike the real thing or even the movies, nothing much else is hard-boiled or hard-bodied. The kok is synthetic, homemade. Made in China. Lee Bruce Lee performs best to a Barry White croon. He gyrates the Travolta swagger with the balletic grace of the real thing. He chopsticks a fly in slo-mo tai chi precision. He even tops it off with the trademark squeal. The chicks at the Star Hotel love their chinky boi. None of these hormone-puffed transmen, just a subtle modern touch, like the unassuming little Nokia that Lee Bruce Lee carries in the palm of her handsome clutch.

figure 10.1: Lee Bruce Lee (Ray Jalil) with Dr La Fist (Elizabeth Eldridge)

Lee Bruce Lee (Ray Jalil) (LBL) (Figure 10.1) is a regular drag king at King Victoria, a weekly Friday night cabaret and translesbian show in Melbourne, Australia. A drag king is 'a female (usually) who dresses up in a recognizably male costume and performs theatrically in that costume' (Halberstam 1998: 232). Judith Halberstam uses the term 'female masculinity' to refer to the drag king's theatrical performance of masculinity. She describes female masculinity as 'gender deviant' or 'gender-ambiguous': a hybrid identity that is 'not-woman and not-man' but 'an unholy union of femaleness and masculinity' (Halberstam 1998: 21, 29). King Victoria's co-founder, Bumpy (Elizabeth Eldridge) further elaborates this identity as 'transient boy stuff', and drag is 'whatever the boygrrl or grrlboy wanted to make of it'. Subverting the spelling of 'grrl' but keeping the normative spelling of 'boy', the practice of drag kinging has 'the power to reorganize masculinity' by challenging 'how masculinity is constructed as masculinity' (Halberstam 1998: 29, 1).

As the name suggests, LBL performs the recognisable male persona of Lee. He carries a mobile phone and wears a 1970s-styled polyester striped shirt, high-waisted bell-bottomed pants, a white flat cap, moustache and very little makeup. His main act consists of lip-syncing and dancing. Sometimes, he slows down in mid-act with a stylised display of kung fu fist fights in the air. At other times, he continues by taking off his clothes to reveal a singleted flat chest and a stuffed crotch or a strap-on. LBL also performs as Dirk ReDiggler, a post-adolescent boy in an Afro wig wearing a self-named tight yellow T-shirt with an oversized foam penis over his white jocks. LBL's other alter-egos also include Annabel Lee and Tiger Lee; the former a blond-wigged Hong Kong socialite travelling the festivals of the world; the latter a sex slave/nymph with long black hair.

At its basic, LBL's fist-fighting appropriates the style of Lee as a style of performance. This act can be read as an earnest copy of kung fu masculinity and a homage to the kung fu king. Such a worship reflects the pre-eminent place Lee holds in the popular imagination. As the trailer to Lee's final film *Enter the Dragon* (Robert Clouse, 1973) eulogises, Lee the legend is 'part man, part myth, part magic'. This myth is exposed as a social construction when the term 'kung fu' is rendered in the Chinese language. Its Chinese term, '*gong fu*', translates as 'a learned skill from hard work'. This translation exposes the myth behind the muscles that support the body, resonating with Meaghan Morris' suggestion that it is Lee's status as 'an iconic film teacher' rather than a 'generic action hero' that makes him an ideal teacher to learn from (Morris 2001: 178). Against this, although LBL's imitation of kung fu can be read as a form of appropriated flattery (LBL admits to being a fan of martial arts in his star biography), LBL's tactic of copying-as-kinging in this instance reveals there is no essence to kung fu masculinity except as a physiological form of body training that can be acquired. Writing on the differences between white and black king performances in America, Halberstam suggests many drag-king-of-color performances are not as successful as white performances because they imitate rather than parody (Halberstam 1998: 257). Here, LBL's copying-as-kinging is subversive because it reveals that the postcolonial masculinity connoted by hardness, strength and power is indeed a skill that can be learned. LBL's mimicry of the kung fu king displaces the patriarchy of Lee's Chinese masculinity by inscribing it with the gender deviance of diasporic Asian female masculinity. Diasporic Asian female masculinity is a hybrid sexual identity that combines and contests dominant representations of Asian femaleness and Asian maleness in the homeland (for example, China) and the hostland (for example, Australia). As a female cross-dressing performance of parodying the tough masculinity embodied by Lee, it challenges the sexist exclusion of Confucian Chinese *wu* masculinity. By visually embodying the physicality of the sexed and racialised body, this practice also exposes the stereotyped constructions of these genders in the West, and queers heteronormative and colonial desire.

Consider, for example, LBL preening as he prepares to lip-sync to the deep soul bass of Barry White and gyrate the Travolta groove. This authenticates the 1970s set by a staging a realism that intertextualises not the scene in Tony Manero's (Travolta) room in *Saturday Night Fever* (John Badman, 1977), but a similar scene in the Singapore action film *Forever Fever* (Glen Goei, 1998) where, repeating a similar narrative, the male protagonist is framed preening himself as he prepares for a disco dance competition. *Forever Fever's* bedroom, similar to the mise en scène in *Saturday Night Fever*, is walled by a row of posters that includes Tony Manero, Rocky (Sylvester Stallone) and Bruce Lee. LBL's quotation shows the kinging tactic of understatement where realism strips the stage of props to convey masculinity through the body, rather than the spectacle of the costume. His impersonation stages the theatricality of a hybrid masculinity personified by Lee, Travolta and Stallone in a genre characterised by the physicality of the body. This performativity stages the past ('homeland') through a present ('hostland') where Travolta returns as a king role model imagined in the diasporic circuits of *Forever Fever* and Bruce Lee. By quoting the actions of Travolta and Lee from a Singapore film, rather than referencing Lee directly from the original, it displaces the hegemonic location of Lee's nationalist Chinese masculinity. This performance also sexualises the diasporic Asian male body to expose the history of the construction of Asian-Australian men as weak and effeminate. LBL also uses the gender deviance of diasporic Asian female masculinity to challenge Western stereotypes of excessive Asian femininity. As Annabel and Tiger Lee, LBL's repertoire parodies a wide range of these stereotypes including Singapore porn star Annabel Chong, Hong Kong film star Maggie Cheung and Filipino Australian reality television icon Rose Porteous. These stereotypes Orientalise the Asian woman through a hyper-sexuality sensationalised by the media representations of pornography, sex work and mail-order brides. Similar interventions include LBL's reinvention of the 1970s porn king Dirk Diggler. These performances use racialised sex and gender to reflect and disrupt the excessive sexuality of the Asian woman in Australia.

The border-crossing drag king performances of LBL describe a range of dissonances surrounding gender, sex, appearance and reality. Drag kings parody male stereotypes, exaggerate heterosexual gender, destabilise the intelligibility of heteronormative masculinity and reveal how the gendered body itself is performative. Diasporic Asian drag kings in Australia problematise the dominant racialised masculinities that produce the social histories of gender relations, questioning the reciprocities surrounding patriarchy, privilege and female empowerment. For LBL, the actioning inspired by the kung fu icon has produced a new hybrid sexual identity that challenges normative genders and sexualities in both Asia and Australia. The emergence of the diasporic Asian tomboy in the Australian queer cultures is an example of how diasporic Asian female masculinity has become a desirable hybrid sexual identity (Yue 2008). In Canada, Asian tomboys have also seized the iconicity of Lee. Donna Lee's queer film *Enter the Mullet* (2003) explores how the patriarchy of the kung fu dragon is refashioned by the tomboy's mullet hairstyle as form of diasporic queer Asian identity. Like the straight projects of remasculinisation, diasporic queer Asian action is also a practice of self-fashioning the ethics of a queer life.

✷✷✷

This chapter has critically discussed how Lee has become a platform for fashioning new selves and actioning new practices of freedom. It has examined the postcolonial masculine body in the kung fu film to show how it functions as a site for symbolic and everyday remasculinisation. From the textual representation of the body, the audience consumption of the genre in the everyday, diasporic, global and queer Asian popular, to the political economy of transnational action cinema, postcolonial masculinity has challenged, resisted and facilitated the logics of capital and desire. Lee's pedagogy embodies the ethics of action as considered practices of freedom. Through emulation, self-cultivation, appropriation and subversion, these practices are the ways by which the self learns to know itself in its conduct with others.

## key readings

Hunt, Leon 2003. *Kung Fu Cult Masters: From Bruce Lee to Crouching Tiger*. London: Wallflower Press.

Morris, Meaghan, Siu Leung Li and Stephen Ching-kiu Chan (eds) 2005. *Hong Kong Connections: Transnational Imagination in Action Cinema*. Durham, N.C.: Duke University Press.

Tasker, Yvonne 1997. 'Fists of Fury: Discourses of Race and Masculinity in the Martial Arts Cinema.' In Harry Stecopoulos and Michael Uebel (eds) *Race and The Subject of Masculinities*. Durham, N.C.: Duke University Press, pp. 315–36.

## notes

[1] This section is rewritten from a longer essay on Asian drag kings in Australia. See Yue 2008.

# can't get you out of my head: consuming celebrity, producing sexual identity.

AUTHOR brett farmer

## INTRODUCTION

In late 2006, the international market research company Onepoll.com surveyed 5000 UK-based gay men and women, asking them to nominate their favourite entertainment celebrity. When results of the survey were released early the following year, they were carried by media services around the world in brief stories such as British tabloid *The Sun*'s front page headline, 'Kylie's Greatest Gay Icon Ever' (2007). That Australian pop star Kylie Minogue was revealed as the polled favourite is possibly less surprising than that a market survey of gay tastes should have been deemed sufficiently newsworthy to gain global media attention. Using Minogue as an illustrative case study, this chapter seeks to explore the meanings and values of 'the gay icon'. It starts from the premise that, while the issue of celebrity consumption in gay subcultures may seem narrow in focus, it actually engages a range of issues—the nature of social identity and sexualities in postmodern cultures, practices of media representation and consumption, sexual commodification, and so forth—that resonate powerfully with broader social and historical patterns, and that therein lies its appeal and significance for tabloid readers and cultural theorists alike.

# step back in time: charting the gay icon.

When *The Sun* newspaper trumpeted that Kylie Minogue had been voted the 'greatest gay icon', it was actually referencing a cultural practice of long standing wherein certain entertainment celebrities have been appropriated by Anglo-American homosexual communities and recoded with a range of specifically **queer** values to the point of assuming 'iconic' gay status. If Kylie Minogue is one of the more recent recipients of such processes of gay iconicisation, she is far from the first. Some historians claim the tradition of the gay icon goes back centuries, but most agree the practice largely emerges with the consolidation of homosexuality as an identity-based category of modern sexualities in the late 19th century and the subsequent development of identifiable homosexual subcultures in the metropolitan centres of the industrialising world (Beemyn 1997; Chisholm 2004). Throughout this period, homosexual subcultures cultivated increasingly significant fan followings of various celebrity figures from opera and theatre divas to the dazzling personalities of the then novel medium of cinema (Koestenbaum 1993). Indeed, as the first truly international mass cultural medium, film was instrumental in furnishing developing queer subcultures with a common set of cultural forms and figures through which to develop shared subcultural tastes (White 1999; Farmer 2000). By mid-century gay cult film star receptions were so entrenched that a simple allusion to a particular Hollywood personality could function as a coded subcultural sign of homosexuality itself, such as the popular expression 'friend of Dorothy'—a direct reference to the character in *The Wizard of Oz* (1939) played by Judy Garland, one of the most popular gay icons of the time—which was widely used in gay argot then, and indeed still now, to identify someone as gay (Grahn 1984). As the mass media proliferated and diversified across the 20th century, gay icons were drawn from an ever widening range of sources: film (Marlene Dietrich, Bette Davis, Julie Andrews), musical theatre (Ethel Merman, Carol Channing), popular music (Barbra Streisand, Diana Ross, Dolly Parton), television (Lucille Ball, Mary Tyler Moore), and even sport (Billie Jean King, Martina Navratilova).

We will be discussing shortly what it was about this eclectic assortment of celebrities that attracted gay audiences and enabled their widespread celebration in queer subcultures. For the moment, it is their structural function as sites of collective gay investment that is of interest. What these stars offered to gay audiences were topoi of identification, figures with which to identify in a sociohistorical context generally devoid of acceptable homosexual reference points. It is often claimed that one of the distinctive aspects of gayness is its extreme social marginalisation. Unlike other cultural minorities, gays and lesbians generally grow up isolated from others who share their identities, and thus they don't have the benefit of communal structures such as family, religion or school through which to consolidate their developing sense of queer selfhood (Harris 1998; Sullivan 2006). This isolation is further compounded by the pervasive cultural vilification of homosexuality: the fact that, until very recently, few positive images, let alone role models, of homosexuality were publicly available. The gay icon has been one of the ways in which gay people and cultures have responded to this situation. Through the cult of the gay icon, gays and lesbians have seized upon various celebrities to fill the discursive void of queer isolation, recoding these stars with queer-affirmative values and using them to perform the sort of foundational identity-building work that is crucial to everyone.

The growing social, political and economic significance of gay communities meant that, from about the 1980s onward, an increasing number of celebrities started not only to acknowledge and accept gay iconicity, but to actively court it (Sender 2004). A high-profile band of contemporary stars such as Cher, Bette Midler and Madonna, for example, have responded very positively to their popularity with gay audiences and have marketed quite explicitly to them. Kylie Minogue is part of this newer breed of self-aware gay icon. While there is evidence to suggest she had a discernible gay following almost from the outset of her musical career in the mid-1980s—and Minogue herself is fond of claiming this with statements like '[m]y gay audience has been with me from the beginning … they kind of adopted me' (Ives & Bottomley 2004)—it wasn't really till the mid-1990s with her move from bouncy teen pop to a funkier-sounding dance music, itself a style with strong gay subcultural associations (Thornton 1996; Amico 2001), and her development of a sexier, more sophisticated image that Minogue's popularisation in gay subcultures achieved appreciable mass. A strategic gay address became an increasingly overt aspect of the Minogue star image throughout the 1990s: she gave exclusive interviews to leading gay magazines, came out in strong support of AIDS charities and gay rights, incorporated visual signs of gay culture into her videos and headlined at queer events such as London's Gay Pride and the Sydney Gay and Lesbian Mardi Gras (Baker & Minogue 2003). None of which, of course, compromises the legitimacy of her gay iconicity and certainly doesn't explain it. All the marketing in the world won't ensure popularity with any audience segment, and it is at this point that the crucial question persists: what is it about Kylie Minogue, as indeed of other celebrities, that has proved so popular with gay fans? What is it that makes the gay icon … well, a gay icon?

# put yourself in my place: reading the gay icon.

In one of the earliest studies of the gay icon, Richard Dyer (1987) analyses the queer appeal of Judy Garland, a star widely regarded as an historical paradigm of gay iconicity. He starts by noting a seeming paradox at the heart of the gay cult of Garland—as indeed of many gay icons, Minogue included—in that she was, by all accounts, heterosexual. As such, he suggests, the construction of Garland and others as figures of queer identification—as, precisely, gay icons—is rooted not so much in a **hermeneutics** of **mimesis**, that is to say a literal or denotative reading, as in a hermeneutics of metaphor. Gay and lesbian subcultures identify with and celebrate certain celebrities as icons not because they *are* gay in any real or evidential sense but because they can be *read as* gay, or to put it more specifically, their star personae contain elements that resonate with gayness and that can therefore be engaged as analogous to gay lives and experiences.

In this sense, the history of the gay icon is effectively one of 'textual poaching' in the meaning given by **Michel de Certeau** and popularised through the fandom theory of Henry Jenkins (1992) as a mode of cultural consumption where audiences 'poach' texts from the dominant culture and rework them to better accommodate or serve their own personal needs. This process of textual poaching is widely practised by all sorts of consumers but it assumes intensified form in the context of what Jenkins (1992: 26), following de Certeau, calls the 'weak': 'those barred from or subordinated within the regimes of public culture and who, therefore, operate from a cultural position of marginality'. For these groups, simple acts of textual appropriation and repurposing are not only necessary in order to assert their own, otherwise invisible, meanings and desires but literally life-affirming because they enable them to 'construct their cultural and social identity through borrowing and inflecting mass culture images' (Jenkins 1992: 23).

So what are the elements of the Kylie Minogue star image 'poached' by queer audiences in their metaphoric readings and reconstructions of her as gay icon? Here again, Dyer's analysis of Garland proves instructive. He argues that while the Garland persona was undeniably diverse, it presented four key interrelated attributes or qualities that 'were homologous with male gay culture' (Dyer 1987: 156) of the mid-20th century and that furnished the principal grounds for her reconstruction as queer icon: emotionalism, ordinariness, androgyny and camp. Garland and Minogue are, to be sure, markedly variant stars inhabiting contrasting sociohistorical contexts and produced in and for significantly different industrial economic systems and mediascapes. But there are enough points of potential correspondence between them to suggest that Dyer's four analytic categories may, with some conceptual and historical revision, function as a useful entry into thinking more specifically about queer receptions of Kylie Minogue.

# hand on your heart: emotionalism.

The first category Dyer identifies as crucial to gay popularisations of Garland is 'emotionalism', a shorthand term for a set of affective dynamics central to the personae and performance style of certain celebrities: 'an emotional register of great intensity which seems to bespeak equally suffering and survival, vulnerability and strength, theatricality and authenticity, passion and irony' (Dyer 1987: 149). This dynamic of intense emotionalism has been widely claimed as pivotal to **discourses** of gay iconicity in all its forms, where it is generally seen to serve as the affective grounds through which queer audiences forge bonds with the star figure in question. The implicit logic is that the emotional intensity of the star mirrors and gives voice to the correlative mix of strong feelings—from pain and anxiety to hope and excitement—that gays and lesbians experience in coming to terms with their sexuality but may not feel licensed to express or even acknowledge.

Defined too narrowly, the dynamic of emotionalism in gay iconicity can easily inspire charges of masochism and self-loathing. More than one commentator has used the accent on emotional intensity to characterise the cult of the gay icon as possessed of an unhealthy predilection for tragedy and morbidity (Harris 1998). The emotionalism of the gay icon, however, has never been solely or even principally about suffering in isolation but rather suffering as a precondition for survivalism and forbearance. It is, as Dyer (1987: 149) writes, always 'a combination of strength and suffering, and precisely the one in the face of the other' and, as such, reveals the emotionalism of gay iconicity to be anchored in a logic of optimistic triumphalism much more than any alleged self-pitying masochism.

Minogue is a clear exemplar of the survivalist strain of emotionalism at work in gay iconicity. Her persona is certainly more complex than often acknowledged, but it is constitutively marked by what can only be described as an affective register of plucky optimism as clearly evidenced in the range of affectionate monikers with which she has been dubbed over the years: 'Pop's Princess', 'The Singing Budgie', 'Smiley Kylie'. Indeed, Minogue is fond of highlighting the extent to which her persona is far removed from the stereotypical image of suffering artist popularly, if erroneously, associated with the gay icon, commenting in interview: 'I am not the traditional gay icon. There has been no tragedy in my life, only tragic outfits' (Ives & Bottomley 2004). The disarming self-effacement on display here, itself further testament to Minogue's upbeat breeziness, should not draw away from a recognition of either the deep emotionalism that nevertheless courses through the Minogue persona—perhaps most overtly articulated through her music which, for all its pop accessibility and dancefloor rhythms, deals with a diverse range of profound affects—or the steely survivalism and grit that has been an equally significant aspect of that persona. As regards the latter, the sheer longevity of Minogue's celebrity career, as well as recent widely publicised events in her personal life such as her successful battle with breast cancer and subsequent triumphal 'comeback' global concert tour, has arguably served to make a discourse of survivalism one of the dominant signs governing her star image and, by extension, her status as icon in gay subcultures (Figure 11.1).

figure 11.1: Kylie fights back: the gay icon as triumphant survivor

(*Bent Magazine*, issue 96, January 2007)

# word is out: ordinariness.

Ordinariness is not generally the sort of term one associates with gay icons, nor with gay people for that matter, and it might be more fitting to rename this second of Dyer's affective qualities of the gay icon 'extra/ordinariness' because he actually uses it to refer to a process of structural transformation that besets certain star images leading to radically different perceptions and readings. With Garland again as example, Dyer argues that when her ongoing struggles with depression and substance abuse became widespread news in the 1950s and after, the Garland persona shifted dramatically from an initial image of benign small-town ordinariness—think of Dorothy in *The Wizard of Oz*—to one of extraordinary difference and abnormality. It was a shift that spoke powerfully to gay audiences of the time because it presented intense homologies to gay experiences. 'To turn out not-ordinary after being saturated with the values of ordinariness', contends Dyer, 'structures Garland's career and the standard gay biography alike' (1987: 159). This dynamic of transformative rupture remains strikingly similar in contemporary queer life experiences and arguably feeds into more recent gay icons as well. Most gays and lesbians continue to grow up and operate in fiercely **heteronormative** contexts—families of origin, school, work—where the presumption is almost universally that one is straight. To declare a homosexual identity therefore is to rupture a postulated image of presumed normative heterosexuality; in other words, to transform ordinariness into extraordinariness, normality into difference.

A metamorphosing movement from ordinariness to extraordinariness is a crucial aspect of both the **diachronic** evolution of the Minogue persona and her gay iconicity. Minogue first rose to celebrity as a teen star on a number of family-oriented soap operas in the 1980s, most famously *Neighbours*, where she played the bubbly girl-next-door, Charlene. The resultant image of decorous suburban cuteness was further compounded with her subsequent foray into popular music where, under the direction of British production team Stock, Aitken and Waterman, Minogue released a series of bouncy bubblegum pop hits which were extremely successful in mainstream charts around the world but which, combined with the peppy codings of her visual and performance styles at the time, cemented an easily derided teenybopper persona of antiseptic sweetness. This initial persona changed rather dramatically, however, in the early 1990s when Minogue quit Stock, Aitken and Waterman and signed a new contract with deConstruction Records. Minogue started to experiment with a more soulful style of hardcore dance music, which was matched by a substantially transformed star image: one that was more stylistically sophisticated, 'out there' and explicitly sexualised both in studio, on stage, and, as a series of highly publicised romantic liaisons with celebrity playboys seemed to suggest, in real life as well. It is precisely during this period of radical transformation that, as previously remarked, the gay cult of Minogue effectively materialised, imputing an apparent, if overdetermined, causal dynamic between the two. Her mid-1990s transformation from teenybopper pop princess to radical dance diva, from the whitebread heteronormativity of the suburbs to the wayward eroticism of the urban dance club, arguably mirrors the broadly parallel life trajectories of many queers, turning her into a figure with whom they could relate and identify.

# body language: androgyny.

Homosexuality has long been conceived and thus frequently experienced as a form of gender and sexual aberrance which is the source of Dyer's third common attribute of gay iconicity, androgyny. In its literal sense of combining male and female characteristics, androgyny is a descriptor that might seem readily applicable to the personae of some gay icons but less so to the deeply eroticised, conventionally feminine 'sex symbol' styling of a celebrity like Kylie Minogue. The gender ambiguities of androgyny can, however, assume multiple forms that need not always be expressed explicitly but might be articulated in more subtle, subtextual ways such as at the level of discursive or ideological coding. To the extent that the very discourse of stardom turns on an inherent possession, and often quite spectacular display, of cultural power, authority and activity—attributes all traditionally coded as masculine—the category of *female stardom* arguably obtains a strong structural capacity, even predilection, for androgynous effect. It is for this reason, perhaps, that female stars can evoke considerable ideological anxiety. Feted and adored, on the one hand, the figure of the female star is also prone to widespread vilification and pillory, on the other—think, for instance, of the popular stereotype of the diva as excessive, emasculating shrew—largely due to her perceived disruption of received sexual hierarchies.

As a contemporary female superstar of the highest order, Minogue inherits the androgynising capacities of divadom and they inform her persona in diverse ways. Consider as just one example what has become a veritable hallmark of the Minogue performance style: her use of scantily clad male back-up dancers. A direct inversion of the longstanding practice of the female chorine, Minogue's signature chorus boys serve at once to accentuate her position of empowered diva femininity while at the same time offering a potentially transgressive spectacle of subordinated, objectified masculinity. An equal tinge of androgynous spectacle informs the visual styling of Minogue in many of her photographic texts as well. The cover of her self-titled 1994 CD, 'Kylie Minogue', for example, which was incidentally her first release for deConstruction Records and part of her attempt to break out of the earlier teenybopper image, features a decidedly gender-ambiguous Minogue, bespectacled and dressed in a dark three-piece business suit, hair slicked back as she crawls towards the camera with her tongue lasciviously licking her upper lip.

# spinning around: camp.

Notoriously resistant to simple definition, camp, Dyer's fourth and final attribute of gay iconicity, is perhaps best characterised as an aesthetic discourse that seeks to produce **denaturalising** effects through disruptive representational strategies such as irony, parody, pastiche and mimicry (Farmer 2000). Closely associated with Western homosexual subcultures of the early and mid-20th century, camp has been widely cast as an aesthetic sensibility informed by queer experiences. Living in the context of what was described earlier as an aggressively heteronormative world, gays and lesbians, it is suggested, have been uniquely positioned to recognise the fully artificial—by which is meant, culturally and historically constructed— nature of social and sexual hegemonies. With its accent on artifice and stylised theatricality, camp signals an aesthetic correlative to this paradigm of queer experience. It unmoors signifiers of identity, especially as these pertain to gender and sexuality, from their perceived anchorage in ontological categories such as nature and the body, and recasts them as performative moments of social role-playing and masquerade. The longstanding queer practice of drag, of male and female impersonation, is a classic instance of the camp aesthetic in practice. The function and appeal of drag turns on its subversive display of sexual performativity: it exaggerates and parodies the conventional signs of hegemonic gender (anatomy, fashion, comportment) and mixes them in often grotesquely ironic ways to the point where they become incoherent and denaturalised. It is a disruptive logic that camp extends to all facets of cultural selfhood, rewriting identity itself as a fluid series of reiterative performances and masks, helping explain why camp is so frequently associated in cultural theory with postmodernist notions of decentred, pluralised **subjectivity** (Cleto 1999).

'Kylie Chameleon', as she was dubbed by one journalist (Wallace 1998), or 'the mother of reinvention' by another (Dubecki 2006), has fashioned a persona in which a camp logic of pluralised identity and multiple performativities is crucial. Consider the celebrated video for her 1997 hit 'What Do I Have To Do' where, through the magic of digital compositing, Minogue appears simultaneously as the four major incarnations of her persona to date—Cute Kylie, Dance Kylie, Indie Kylie and Sex Kylie—each battling for prominence without, significantly, any one winning. It is a wry play on the radical pluralism of her celebrity text repeated elsewhere: the video for her 2002 release, 'Come Into My World', ups the ante with its digital spectacle of a repeatedly self-duplicating Minogue who, cell-like, splits into multiple Kylies in a continuous regenerative cycle with no apparent promise of fixity or completion. That the changeling multiplicity and playful irony of her persona obtains strong allegiances to discourses of queer camp is evidenced through Minogue's widespread appropriation and celebration of gay drag. As early as 1990 and the mildly controversial video 'What Do I Have To Do'—it featured Minogue impersonating a series of classic female sex archetypes in the ambiguous space of a queer nightclub, complete with drag queens and lipstick lesbians—the camp spectacle of drag has been central to Minogue's thematic of protean self-fashioning. It is a strategic borrowing that has intensified across the years—especially through her long professional liaison with stylist William Baker and their collaborative attempt to create a constantly morphing catalogue of high glam looks and stylised posturings they have collectively described as 'artificial femininity' (Baker & Minogue 2003: 12)—and that achieved a certain knowing apogee at the Closing Ceremony of the Sydney Olympics in 2000 when, bedecked in pink feathers and sequined showgirl outfit, Minogue sang a cover of ABBA's 'Dancing Queen', itself a gay camp anthem, while a bevy of drag queens dressed in emulative showgirl style circuited the stadium. Within such a context, it becomes difficult to ascertain the precise order of gender signification and decide just who is imitating whom, thus potentially throwing awry the whole normative assumption of originary, stable sexuality, which is of course the intended effect of camp and why it plays such a fecund role in Kylie's queer iconicity.

The point of camp is not just a mischievous destabilisation of orthodox sexual structures for its own sake, but rather the strategic use of such a destabilisation to open up a more expansive range of sexed ways of being than is otherwise accommodated in heteronormative economies. As such, while I don't mean to prioritise camp unnecessarily or accord it the definitive, final say on gay readings of Minogue or traditions of the gay icon more generally, these arguments help return us to the opening claims about the basic functions and values of gay iconicity. If, as is often argued, the principal cultural role of celebrities is to help 'articulate what it means to be a human being in contemporary society' (Dyer 1987: 8), the gay icon highlights how that role has been realised in the specific context of queer lives and cultures. In a world that has, more often than not, refused to legitimate their identities and frequently expressed a generalised wish that they simply not exist, gays and lesbians have mined the rich fields of mediatised stardom for vital social and political sustenance, seizing upon a select range of resonant celebrity texts and reconstructing them as icons of queer self-definition and valorisation. Through their resistant consumption of celebrity, gays and lesbians have refused the strictures of heteronormative marginalisation and wilfully set about fashioning cultural tools with which to pursue their own projects of queer identity production. The gay icon is thus a sure testament to the enduring significance of popular celebrities in contemporary culture and to the extraordinary everyday creativity of their multiple audiences.

key  readings

Creekmur, Corey K., and Alexander Doty (eds) 1995. *Out in Culture: Gay, Lesbian, and Queer Essays on Popular Culture*. Durham, N.C.: Duke University Press.

Dyer, Richard 1987. *Heavenly Bodies: Film Stars and Society*. Basingstoke: Macmillan.

Whiteley, Sheila, and Jennifer Rycenga (eds) 2006. *Queering the Popular Pitch*. London and New York: Routledge.

# comics as everyday theory: the counterpublic world of taiwanese women fans of japanese homoerotic manga.

AUTHOR: fran martin

## INTRODUCTION

In Taiwan today, as in many other parts of east Asia from mainland China to South Korea to Japan, tens of thousands of young women are passionately engaged in consuming, producing, trading, talking about and even re-enacting comic-book narratives of love and sex between boys and young men. These homoerotic manga comics are known among their Taiwanese fans as 'BL,' for 'boys' love' (Figures 11.1–11.4). This chapter proposes that interaction with BL texts enables women fans to engage actively with questions of gender and sexuality which are central to their own everyday experience as young female-bodied social subjects, and which can be negotiated 'at one remove' through the BL stories of male homoerotic romance.

figures 12.1 and 12.2: cover and excerpt from the
Taiwan edition of Hiromi Sakuta's BL manga *1,2,3*

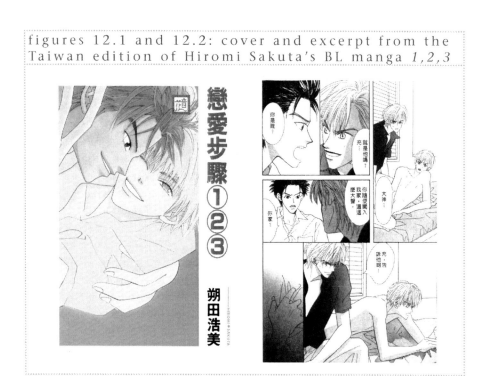

Taipei: Daran, 1999..

figures 12.3 and 12.4: cover and artwork from a
Taiwanese fan-produced (*tongrenzhi*) BL manga
series by dokoshu, based on narratives of male
same-sex love among members of Johnny's
Jimusho, a talent agency in Japan famous
for producing male idols and boy-bands.

Taipei, 2004 and 2005, self-published. Reproduced with kind permission sb dokushu.

The BL subculture is based originally on Taiwanese women readers' fandom of Japanese homoerotic manga, known in Japanese as *shonenai, bishonen* or YAOI manga, which first appeared in Japan from the pens of a pioneering generation of women manga artists in the 1970s (Fujimoto 1991; McLelland 2000; Orbaugh 2003; Welker 2006, 2008a,b). Today in Taiwan, BL manga form a major niche market within the broader category of girls' manga (*shaonü manhua*), and are generally displayed openly in a dedicated section of the girls' manga area in manga rental libraries, rather than being aimed—as one might initially assume—at a gay male niche readership. There are hundreds if not thousands of titles available, covering a spectrum from the 'pure love' (*chun qing*) subgenre, with its emphasis on chaste, child-like romance, right through to the 'H' (hard/*hentai*) subgenre with its combination of romantic plots and pornographic-style explicit sex scenes.[1] More than two decades after the initial appearance of the Japanese works in pirated editions in Taiwan in the late 1970s, today Taiwan's BL culture encompasses a wide range of texts, practices and sites far exceeding its original instance in the Japanese comics (Lent 1999; Zhong 1999). The BL scene includes not just fandom of commercially produced Japanese *shonenai* manga (in Chinese translation or in the original Japanese), but also Taiwanese fans' do-it-yourself production of amateur spin-offs, in both comic and popular novel form. It includes a flourishing fan culture known as *tongrenzhi* (from the Japanese *dojinsha*) that holds regular conventions and swap-meets for the fan-produced products, and intersects with the broader COSplay (costume-play) youth culture, in which fans dress up *en masse* in elaborate home-made costumes representing favourite manga characters. Taiwan's BL scene also extends into an additional transnational dimension in a lively internet culture where fans chat and swap artwork and stories with their counterparts in Japan, Hong Kong, South Korea, mainland China, and beyond.[2]

This chapter presents some of the results of an interview-based study I conducted of female fans of homoerotic manga in Taiwan in 2005. I spoke with thirty women between the ages of 19 and 34, including some who produced their own fan editions and were otherwise active in the *tongrenzhi* subculture, plus one professional male manga editor.[3] Participants were interviewed both singly and in friendship groups, with each semi-structured interview lasting between one and two hours. What follows is a condensed account of some of the extremely rich and complex range of responses that were given in interview discussions about the possible motivation of readers of homoerotic manga.[4] Like most researchers of BL, YAOI and slash cultures, one of my own motivating questions when I commenced the study was precisely the question of reader motivation: why should young women flock in such numbers to texts about love and sex between men? What did they get out of their BL fandom? How did it impact on their understanding of real-life gay cultures? How did it contribute to their understanding of their own genders and sexualities? In short, what could it reveal about the cultural constitution of the readers themselves, as young, female subjects in Taiwan? But as our conversations progressed, through the sophistication and complexity of their own thinking on precisely these issues, the readers began to teach me that my own desire, as researcher, to uncover concrete and accurate answers to these questions might be obscuring a more interesting point about the readers' *own* proficiency and pleasure in asking and debating exactly these questions. I began to think that one of the main things that readers get out of reading BL and participating in BL subcultures might be precisely the chance to be part of this collective, ongoing process of thinking about, discussing and hypothesising on—in an informal sense, theorising—important elements of their own social experience as young, feminine-gendered social and sexual subjects, via the mediation of their BL consumption.

The importance of the indirect and collective elements of this everyday theorising was brought home to me by the extremely different kinds of response I tended to receive to two of my standard questions. The question 'what is it that you like about BL manga?'—addressed directly to the respondent as an individual—in many (not all) cases tended to elicit one-dimensional, dead-end responses such as 'I enjoy their artistic style,' or 'I find the stories interesting'. In contrast, the question 'Why do you think that so many young women enjoy BL?'—addressing the readers indirectly and as members of a community of readers—was far more productive. The second question plainly solicits what might be called a theoretical response: it asks for the respondent's hypothesis on an abstracted social phenomenon, while the first question aims at uncovering an individualised, 'authentic' motivation on the part of the respondent herself. While the respondents' preference for the second kind of question might simply be seen as evidence of some women's shyness in directly confessing individual preferences and desires to a relatively unknown researcher, I think that the verve with which they leapt at the second question also indicates a real pleasure in this kind of folk-theorising, with the level of abstraction it entails, and respondents' preference for seeing themselves in relation to a community.

Given this, I would frame the accounts that follow as reflexive **discourses**—theories of self routed through and made possible by BL readership—rather than as authentic reflections of reader motivation and practices. That is, I am not proposing that the *content* of these accounts be taken at face value as an accurate explanation of why and how Taiwanese women read BL manga; rather, I want to foreground the immense complexity and richness of the *process* of producing these discourses or 'folk-theories' about young women's gender, sexuality and cultural agency. Such theories are continually arising and being contested, defended and refined as a direct result of the women's participation in the richly productive world of BL and its Taiwanese fandom, suggesting that BL manga could productively be understood as '**goods to think with**' for this group of readers.

Crucially for understanding the specificities of feminine-directed BL (*nüxingxiang* BL), these manga were considered by the vast majority of interviewees to be clearly and obviously distinct from gay (*tongzhi*) narratives. Giselle, a 24-year-old university student, encapsulated the distinction succinctly when I asked her whether she'd classify BL as 'gay':

*NO!* They're totally different. I've got a gay friend who says BL is totally not the same thing as gay, he says [BL] is really just a bunch of boy-girl love stories. It's a bunch of stories that wouldn't really happen in real life. To put it bluntly, BL is a kind of fantasy, it's different from [what] those gay guys [do]. BL is mostly written and drawn by girls.[5]

The distinction from gay identity politics occurs at a textual level as well: a virtual set piece in many BL manga is the speech—in a way, the opposite of the gay coming-out speech—in which one or both of the members of the central male couple vociferously declare himself/themselves *not* to be homosexual (making the current same-sex entanglement the exception rather than the rule for him/them). Although there clearly exists a very general, conceptual link between BL manga and the homosexual topic, it is equally clear that *nüxingxiang* BL was not generally understood by this group of respondents as offering social-realist accounts of actual gay lives.[6] If not primarily this, then what are these young women looking for in BL narratives?[7]

The question of reader motivation is evidently much discussed within the fandom itself, as the theories offered, while multiple and varied, nevertheless began to show a certain consistency over time, with a handful emerging as the strongest, repeatedly cited hypotheses. The idea that interaction with BL texts enabled young women to engage actively with questions of *gender and sexuality* was among the most frequently expressed, and it is on this aspect that I will concentrate here.[8] Specifically, clusters of theories emerged on BL fandom as a form of proto-feminist cultural critique, on the one hand, and as a means of readers symbolically negotiating their own gendered and sexual self-understandings, on the other.[9]

# theory 1: BL manga as gender and genre critique.

On the question of why straight girls should prefer stories about love between two boys over stories about love between a boy and a girl, several interviewees offered critiques of the representation of girl characters in mainstream girls' manga. Musing on the relative popularity of boy-boy manga romance, Zirong, a 25-year-old project manager, connects the general lameness of girl characters in boy-girl romance manga specifically to the generic conventions of mainstream romance:

In the mainstream of girls' comics and romance novels, in order to let the reader identify with the female protagonist, they make her a character totally without good points, with nothing at all going for her, while the male protagonist is outstanding in every way. And then, by some miracle, he falls in love with this loser girl. Some people can identify with a character like that, but others think that kind of female protagonist is just plain dumb.

Petit, a 29-year-old worker in a games company who was very critical of what she saw as the extreme sexism of mainstream boys' manga, went further to frame the collective girls' culture of BL as a slap in the face for the masculinism of older genres of manga:

> Nowadays at a lot of *tongrenzhi* conventions, men tend to feel sort of as if they've been marginalised by the women—because everyone's reading BL manga now, and it's as if their regular comics have been pushed aside. It's really interesting—at that sort of gathering, BL comics are totally the mainstream, and BL are even quite prominent among the comics you can find at regular outlets, as well. Whereas before [the culture was] very much dominated by masculinist manga.

As these comments indicate, the implied gender critique that many readers find in BL frequently relates to *genre* critique: BL is interpreted as a rectification of, or a critical commentary on, the limitations of conventional genres of girl-directed popular culture.[10] Several respondents cited the deadening predictability of representations of heterosexual relations in standard BG (boy-girl) romance as a possible motivating factor for their own or other young women's enthusiasm for BL. Vicky, a 24-year-old university student, was especially taken with the gender and sexual ambiguity represented in BL, in contrast to the rigidity of sexual and gender roles in straight romance:

> [I like the] ambiguity [of BL], I think it leaves more space for the imagination. As soon as the relation [between characters] becomes too defined, it gets just like ordinary heterosexual culture; it gets limited down to an ordinary *love story*.[11] But if they don't define the gender roles too clearly, it's really fun.
>
> [Later:] If both characters are very clearly defined as homosexuals, in my opinion that makes the whole thing more or less the same as a heterosexual relation; I mean if right from the start they're defined as lovers, and there's no real space for ambiguity, then their relation is no different from a standard heterosexual one … But if there is some space for ambiguity, then that comes closer to my own sense of what same-sex relations should feel like.

While Vicky values the ambiguity (*aimei*) in both gender roles and sexual identity for which pure-love BL is well known, Petit enjoys the assertiveness that is often permitted to feminised bottom/insertee characters, which she contrasts critically with the passivity of girl characters in standard straight romance:

> I think most of those [heterosexual mangas] are pretty stupid … The girl characters in them have no brains at all. I guess this might actually be a problem with Japanese manga in general. When the male characters do things to them; hold them down or whatever, they never put up any resistance—that's really weird, to me [laughs]. For some reason they seem to have absolutely zero brains and zero physical strength. But when you read BL manga, if [the top/inserter character] tries anything, [the bottom] gets to resist, he gets to fight back. That seems more like it, to me—in that regard, [BL] seems closer to reality … It's because I don't like that kind of [powerless] girl character that I don't read those 'normal boy-girl' mangas.

Giselle, meanwhile, cites the greater level of social realism available in BL narratives, as compared with the hidebound clichés of straight romance, as a key reason for her enjoyment of them:

> The reason I started reading BL is because I'd gotten a bit sick of ordinary manga. It was right around that time that [BL] books began to appear [in Taiwan], and so I started to read them. Then once I'd read some, they brought me some different sort of feelings. Aside from their novelty value, their plots were more attractive, too. BL novels add a bit of social context, or discussion of social morality—things like that. It was quite different from the sort of romances I'd read before, where the boy and girl always just fall in love at first sight and walk off into the sunset to live happily every after. By contrast, [BL] feels a bit more realist.

# theory 2: BL manga as enabling creative negotiation with readers' own gendered identities.

In addition to the various forms of implicit gender and genre critique that these readers interpreted in the popularity of the BL phenomenon, other responses suggested that BL could be useful to young women readers for the ways in which it facilitates negotiations with readers' own gendered and sexual identities. Readers discussed how they felt that reading 'transvestite', BL, GL (girls' love), and related forms of 'gender-bending' manga when young had helped them formulate both counter-hegemonic forms of femininity and proto-queer gendered and sexual identities. Linking both of these themes, Malfoy, a 19-year-old university student, related:

> When I was young I just loved [Osamu Tezuka's] *Princess Knight*, because actually that was a dream of mine—to grow up from a little girl into a king. I was very excited by the idea at the time, I was all like—oh wow! Can that really happen? Because I didn't like wearing lacy puff-skirts, or acting all sweet and gentle—and your Mum and Dad would always be on your back, if you played outside: 'hey—remember you're a girl!' What they meant was that you should act dignified and not make too much noise, just sit there like a goody-goody, with a little bow on your head, or whatever. I just hated all that. Where the hell did they get off, [saying] you're a girl, so you can't run around like the boys? And when I was a bit older, Oscar [the 'transvestite' protagonist of Riyoko Ikeda's *The Rose of Versailles*] came into my life. Back then I was like: Wow! She's so handsome! She's so cool! In my opinion, girls had the same level of ability as boys. But later when I heard that [Oscar] fell in love with Andre, I was just heartbroken, I felt: you've betrayed me! You don't love Marie Antoinette!

Lesbian or 'T' (butch) identifying respondents also quite frequently cited BL, GL and other gender-bending manga as a source of alternative gender representations that they felt had related to their own formulation of a gendered and sexual identity. July Monster, a 23-year-old nursing student who self-identified as a T, described her reactions to non-conventionally gendered characters in manga:

Well, if it's a boy [character], but yet he's drawn very feminised, or a girl character who's very masculinised, then what I feel is—that I'd like to meet people like that in real life! ... Basically, I myself am a girl whose behaviour is quite masculine, so mostly when I come across characters like that, I classify them in the same category as myself ... When I was little I certainly [used to identify with manga characters]! For example I was a fan of [Rumiko Takahashi's] *Ranma*—Ranma could turn herself into a boy just by wishing for it, or turn himself into a girl! It reminds me of myself today: if I want to seem feminine for some reason then I dress more girly, or if I want to be more casual then I can do that too. [What I really identified with as a child was] the ability to change genders at will—don't you think that would come in pretty handy?

Simao, another T-identifying interviewee, had the following exchange with Lucifer, an assistant at some of the interviews and herself a prominent personality in Taiwan's **queer** manga cyber-fandom:

S: I identify most strongly with Seiya, from [Masumi Kurumada's] *Saint Seiya* [a.k.a. *Knights of the Zodiac*]. I actually have a dream someday to transform from Seiya into Dragon Shiryu.

L: Well you've no hope of that in this life as far as I can see [laughs]. So I guess right now we're really talking about T [butch]-style characters. Maybe Seiya represents what we might call a 'hot-blooded young T,' while Dragon Shiryu is more like a 'beautiful youth T'?

S: Exactly. Among the five main characters, Seiya is the one who's always fighting, always struggling, and who has greater strength than all the others. Also he tends to explode without warning. But Dragon Shiryu is more the silent type, more like a 'master of martial virtue', in the Chinese tradition.

L: More like the young Kuan Yin [Avalokiteshvara].[12]

S: No, that's got nothing to do with it. I think that the characters in *Saint Seiya* are undergoing a Chinese-style development—the process of becoming a 'man of culture' (*wenren*) ... Dragon Shiryu is more like the man-of-culture type, whereas Seiya is more like a kid from the sticks who's come for the fighting—he'll never grow up.

Simao and Lucifer's translation of the personality and gender traits of the various male mythical characters in the *Saint Seiya* manga into the 'nonce taxonomies' of Taiwanese lesbian secondary gender (hot-blooded young T; beautiful-youth T; cultured T; martial T, etc.) provides an exemplary illustration of BL's utility as goods to think with.[13] The fictional characters function as quasi-totemic figures enabling a symbolic processing of Simao's relationship with available identity categories within a local sex-gender subsystem.

# theory 3: BL as enabling sexual agency and exploration.

Another folk-theory about BL's popularity among young, straight women, which was so common as to approach a kind of common sense among this group of readers, proposes that BL can be seen as the expression of a common feminine sexual fantasy: the visual possession of two beautiful male bodies at once. This 'two-for-one' theory is neatly encapsulated by Malfoy:

> Mostly, *danmei* ['aesthetic'] works require both of the lead characters to be aesthetically beautiful. Their primary purpose is to fulfil straight girls' fantasy: if I can look at two cute guys at once, why would I waste my time with [works that] include a female character? ... [*Danmei* works] are purely the product of the imaginations of straight girls lying locked away in their bedrooms.

Malfoy's characterisation is slightly condescending in tone: at other points in the interview she made clear that she herself was impatient with what she perceived as the unrealistic qualities of these feminine sexual fantasies, especially their strict demarcation of active and passive sexual roles. But other respondents who cited a specifically sexual motive for their own consumption of BL were quite upfront about the genre's fantasy status, and clear about the distinct pleasures this enabled. Fiona, a 25-year-old worker in a design firm, made the following straightforward statement:

> Actually, [sexual] objectification is not necessarily a bad thing, because it reflects reality quite directly: people's psychology really does include an element [that desires] it. Take me, for example: when I rent manga, I'll choose ones that are *H* ['hard'; perverse; sexually explicit] through and through, because I'm very clear about my own desire to read material that is thoroughly *H*. Of course if I were reading for the plot then I'd rent manga with more plot development. It just depends what you feel like reading that day—each to her own!

Reflecting a similarly liberal, utilitarian view of *H*-style BL manga as enablers of sexual pleasure rather than aspirants towards social realism, Shaomo, a 21-year-old university student, spoke even more frankly about the kind of sexual fantasy she prefers her manga to deliver:

What I like is flat chests! That's right! The ones with flat chests. And I prefer it if they have hermaphrodite genitals, too … BL doesn't have that, but at least they get the flat chest part right! I have no interest in breasts … The whole point is the flat chest … The genitals on the lower part of the body are also extremely important. Because I don't have that much interest in girls' genitals, I think it's best if [the characters] can have both kinds of genitals at the same time. Like there's this Japanese *danmei* novelist … that's right, Yamaai Shikiko. I don't like her plots, I can't accept them at all. But in her stories the bottom/insertee character mostly has hermaphrodite genitals. That's the one thing I like about her stories.

Such frank accounts bespeak a shared theory that BL readership facilitates a mediated sexual agency in its female fans: not simply the power to consume and enjoy explicit sexual fantasies—a power not readily granted to young feminine subjects in the wider culture—but also the power to become a connoisseur of such fantasies and to share them among a community of similarly minded friends.

# counterpublics and parallel worlds.

Writing on the phenomenon of women's and girls' fandom of Japanese YAOI comics in Japan and beyond, Mark McLelland and Seunghyun Yoo aptly draw on Michael Warner's concept of the *counterpublic* to theorise the community of readers enabled by YAOI readership (McLelland 2005; McLelland & Yoo 2007). Critically modifying Jurgen Habermas' influential theory of the public sphere as a feature of emerging modern Western democracies, Warner writes:

> [S]ome publics are defined by their tension with a larger public. Their participants are marked off from persons or citizens in general. Discussion within such a public is understood to contravene the rules obtaining in the world at large, being structured by alternative positions or protocols, making different assumptions about what can be said and what goes without saying. This kind of public is, in effect, a counterpublic: it maintains at some level, conscious or not, an awareness of its subordinate status. (Warner 2002: 56)

As McLelland and Yoo (2007) astutely observe, female YAOI fans can be seen as a counterpublic not only by virtue of their feminine gender—in itself a guarantee of subordinate status in patriarchal societies—but more specifically, in that the collective discourses on gender, sexuality and women's agency they elaborate through their interaction with YAOI texts critically interrogate 'hegemonic (that is, **patriarchal**, masculinist, heterosexist) codes governing the public expression of gender and sexuality' (2007: 100) in the societies in which they live. The Taiwanese study discussed in this chapter certainly supports this contention. We have seen how these women's interactions with BL cultures enable them to voice criticism of the representation of girls and women in mainstream, heterosexual romance novels and manga narratives; to argue with the ways in which female subjects are socialised into hegemonic forms of 'proper' femininity, and to imagine and sometimes enact alternatives to this in creative formations of androgynous, fluid or transgender sexuality; and to think through and assertively express their own explicit sexual desires in a culture that tends to position feminine subjects as the objects, rather than the subjects, of sexual desire and self-expression.

As a way of concluding this discussion, I would like to extend the notion of the counterpublic by proposing the notion of '**worlding**' as a name for the cumulative effect of the specific kinds of imaginative and material practices that these women are engaged in. As I intend it, 'worlding' refers to the creation of parallel worlds, both in imagination—as in the texts themselves, with their invention of a parallel universe of male homoerotic love—and in subcultural practice. On a textual level, BL manga present their readers with a world of sex-gender ambiguity, fluidity and sometimes resistance, where beautiful boys enact fantasy romance narratives and enjoy passionate sex with each other. In subcultural practice, alternative worlds of feminine sociality are created through *tongrenzhi* BL fan culture in a whole range of activities, from reading, COSplay, amateur manga and novel production, and internet communities to swap-meets, conventions and the specialised Japanese-Chinese-English hybrid subcultural argot that creates an effective exclusionary cordon around 'BL girls' interacting with each other in mainstream public space.[14] In all of the imaginative and material uses to which Taiwanese women fans put these narratives, we have seen how BL manga function for these women as 'goods to think with': material commodities that enable creative, pleasurable and self-reflexive practices of everyday theorisation.

## key readings

McLelland, Mark 2000. 'The Love Between "Beautiful Boys" in Japanese Women's Comics.' *Journal of Gender Studies* 9(1): 13–25.

Penley, Constance 1991. 'Brownian Motion: Women, Tactics and Technology.' In C. Penley and A. Ross (eds), *Technoculture*. Minneapolis, Minn.: University of Minnesota Press.

Warner, Michael 2002. *Publics and Counterpublics*. New York: Zone Books.

## notes

[1] This bipartite classification is something of a simplification: further distinctions can be made between 'hard/*hentai*' (H) BL works and the commercial genre of male homosexual pornography. In addition to—and somewhat distinct from—all of these categories there also exist gay (*tongzhi*) manga that aim to offer realistic depictions of gay male life and target male readerships as well as female 'BL girls.'

[2] BL culture is perhaps broadly comparable to, albeit also distinct from, 'slash' cultures in the USA and elsewhere. Slash is the subject of an extensive field of critical commentary. Some key texts include Russ 1985; Penley 1991a,b, 1997; Bacon-Smith 1992; Green, Jenkins & Jenkins 1998; Cicioni 1998; Brooker 2003. A comparative study of English-language slash and Japanese and Chinese-language BL is outside the scope of this chapter; one clear difference, however, is the relatively high degree of commercialisation of Japanese-originating BL publications as distinct from the still almost purely amateur status of Euro-American slash publications.

[3] The study also targeted fans of the much smaller, less codified group of texts classifiable as 'GL' (girls' love/ female homoerotic manga), but discussion of this aspect falls beyond the scope of this chapter.

[4] The discussion covered both BL and GL, but most discussions concerned the larger cultural phenomenon of BL.

[5] All original responses were in Chinese; these translations are the authors'. Pseudonyms have been used for all interviewees.

[6] This is in distinction to the *nantongzhi* (gay male) subgenre, which unlike *nüxingxiang* (female-directed) BL, *is* concerned with more or less social-realist depictions of gay life.

[7] Some interviewees *were* looking specifically for social-realist accounts of gay lives; these respondents noted critically that *nüxingxiang* BL is not the right place to seek such accounts—as a group, they preferred the relative realism of *nantongzhi* manga.

[8] Other theories linked BL consumption with specific aesthetic and generic pleasures, with negotiations around ethnicity and nationality, and with a generalised social rebellion or anti-conformism. A full exploration of all of these elements is material for a more extensive paper.

[9] The fans in fact produced a far wider and more complex array of 'folk-theories' on these subjects than can be done justice in a paper of this length; for this reason, I concentrate here on three common sets of theories as outlined above, that is: BL as gender/genre critique; BL as enabling readers symbolically to 'process' or negotiate with their own gendered identities; and BL as enabling women readers to enact particular forms of sexual agency.

[10] Cf. BL manga artist Moto Hagio's comments on BL as an antidote to the predictability of straight romance; cited in Fujimoto, 1991.

[11] Vicky said the phrase 'love story' in English.

[12] A key deity in East Asian Buddhism: the Goddess of Compassion, who underwent a process of transgendering from her origins as the male Sanskrit deity Avalokiteshvara. As such, Kuan Yin sometimes functions as a symbol for Taiwanese queer youth.

[13] On 'nonce taxonomy' as a creative queer world-making practice, see Sedgwick 1991. She defines nonce taxonomy as 'the making and unmaking and remaking and redissolution of hundreds of old and new categorical imaginings concerning all the kinds it may take to make up a world' (23).

[14] These terms include BL (boys' love), GL (girls' love), BG (boy-girl romance), *shoujun* (insertee), *gongjun* (inserter), *funü* or *funüzi* (serious female BL fan); *danmei* ('aesthetic'-style; referring to sensuous, but not pornographic, BL texts with drawings of delicate, feminine young men); *baihe* (a code-word for GL manga); *qiangwei* (a code word for BL manga); *Zhengtai/Zhengtailang/Zhengtaikong* (Shota/ Shotaro/ Shotacon in Japanese: refers to erotic interest in younger men or boys, and manga that represent this); *Luoli/luolikong* (Lolicon in Japanese: refers to the 'Lolita complex', i.e. erotic interest in younger women or girls, and manga that represent this), and so on. Many of these terms are based on Japanese *kanji* but in Taiwan are pronounced in Mandarin pronunciation.

# 5

# empire and globalisation.

# the stories so far.
AUTHOR: katrina schlunke

## difference and circulation.

Empire and globalisation bring together in a single heading the evolving appreciation of the ways in which a globalised world can operate as a new kind of empire
that produces raced individuals and mediascapes as well as particular economic
environments. Some of the key ways in which we come to participate actively
in globalisation (as well as being unconsciously folded into globalisation) are by
understanding systems of meaning that emerged in an earlier imperial period.
What race do you consider yourself to be? White? Black? Australian? European?
These are all kinds of identities that were produced by empire from the 1500s
to the 1800s. But what meaning do they have in an environment where raced
and national identities move and are moved around the world as both workers
and images? How can we connect with the very different experience of others
while acknowledging our own position, which is also informed by that diversity?
The tensions and pleasures in this diversity and difference are part of what Stuart
Hall (1996: 251) suggests results from placing 'colonisation in the framework of
"globalisation"'. For Hall the hybridities and syncretisms, the translations and
two-way traffic between the global cities we have now were always characteristics
of the contact zones of all the kinds of colonialism that existed. As Hulme suggests,
'[i]f "post-colonial" is a useful word, then it refers to a process of disengagement
from the whole colonial syndrome which takes many forms ...' (quoted in Hall
1996: 246). Part 5 suggests that that 'disengagement' from a 'colonial syndrome' is
an uneven process complicated by the speed and movement of global capital and

its accompanying images, cultures and modes of meaning-making. As we begin to think about what global capital has produced it is easy to imagine a disembodied environment of financial flows, but those flows of capital also transport ways of making meaning that in turn produce racial and ethnic identities in new and old ways. Sometimes it seems the question to ask of globalisation is: what of this is not colonialism? What changes when a representation is global or globalised? What new forms of racial or ethnic *being* have arisen or been further enforced?

# globalisation.

**Globalisation** can be described by many different models and vocabularies that would to varying degrees emphasise politics, identities and power. Globalisation as understood through cultural theory can be described as consisting of at least the following three characteristics, which bring together the key work of Zygmunt Bauman (1998) and Arjun Appadurai (2001). Globalisation is marked by a collapse of time and space, by a division between the mobile and immobile class, and by the way in which meaning circulates its multiple products across local and global communities within sets of flows or 'scapes.

## time and space.

The idea of a 'collapse' in time and space simply refers to the ways in which technologies like the internet, when linked to an idea of global share and finance trading, enables certain sorts of processes and activities to be no longer bounded by geography or nationhood. This is perhaps better understood through a shift in how something like manufacturing has been understood, so let me start with a non-globalised example. Say, for example, you occupy a middling rural town which produces green peas. Someone seeing the opportunity to expand employment in the town and their own profit borrows money and builds a pea-processing plant that produces canned and frozen peas. The factory grows, employment rises and while the boss and the workers may live in very different parts of town they are all connected geographically to the town. Equally, the factory will reflect the original connection to a pea-producing area and so the sense of the town as a key pea place may be taken up by town promotion policies (and in Australia and America the suggestion of the building of the 'Big Pea' will surely follow). As the factory continues its work it comes to be understood as a stable source of employment (albeit with seasonal variation), and personal identities develop that reflect the factory's role in the lives of generations of people in the local area. The town bank and other local lending institutions are themselves invested in the factory's management and are aware of the natural rises and falls in possible profits depending on the quality of the seasons. Given the dependence on local labour and seasonal variation in the supply of peas, this factory is tied both by the place it occupies and the seasonal times to make money. Given these ties it is the sort of business that during a drought, for example, one could imagine the local community undertaking to work at lower pay and adopting other strategies to ensure the long-term success of the factory. And in good times the local factory might in turn donate land or money for local parks or sporting grounds. This idea of how a factory might once have worked has now to be compared with what is possible in a globalised environment. The key shift is that the company is now owned by a globally spread set of share owners and investors who will support or abandon the company depending on its profit, as is shown in the share return gained by the investor. No set of share owners will necessarily know or care exactly where an individual company is located, or what time zone or seasonal system it may move within. Bauman begins his book *Globalisation* with a quote from A.J. Dunlop that sums this up: 'The Company belongs to people who invest in it—not to its employees, suppliers, nor the locality in which it is situated.'

Thus a pea company needs to be performing at a profit at all times for a set of globally dispersed investors, and to do so needs to be willing to shift its operation or parts of its operation at any time. So if there is a drought one year in Australia but a bumper crop in Argentina the investors' money is withdrawn from the Australian operation and put into the Argentinian one. If this means the collapse of the Australian pea plant this is of no concern to the investor, who simply sees a rise or fall in their share return. In a similar way, if one part of the pea-producing process requires specialist equipment it may be best to have all the peas from all over the world have that part of their preparation performed in a low-wage, low-tax environment that may be quite disconnected from where the peas were first picked. In this way the peas themselves become globalised as they are shifted from one economic site to another. Because of the mobility of the capital and the precariousness of any commitment from the pea production companies, towns (but also particular nations) will compete with one another to offer more infrastructure or lower wages to keep the business in their area or within their nation. Some versions of this model would see the nation becoming increasingly reduced to the supplier of infrastructure, and this has led to debates about whether or not globalisation has superseded ideas of nationhood and to what extent nations can any longer control the activities of global business and finance.

## mobile and immobile classes.

Once the above model is clear it is easy to see that the next characteristic of globalisation, a division between the mobile and immobile classes, simply identifies those people who can move easily around the world following flows of money via international corporations and those who remain committed to geography through familiar ties, traditional relationships with particular places and/or the inability to move anywhere else due to their economic position. Think, for example, of the person who lives in a small cottage in the country costed at about $30 000 trying to buy in a major capital city—immobility is not simply about choice. But think also of the thousands of people each year who are forced from their homes due to warfare, poverty, illness and environmental collapse. These people are forced to be mobile but are then highly contained in refugee camps, in exile or at staging posts within certain international processes. We could also consider the ways in which guest workers and other identified immigrant labour are attracted into wealthier countries from poorer ones. They certainly move away from their original homes but are then left relatively immobile with low wages and minimum conditions, and little chance of easy returns home. When we think about mobility we have to think about the style and conditions of that mobility and whether or not it can be understood as enduring mobility. Certain kinds of air travel between key sites of capitalist production, for example, are thoroughly supported with an infrastructure that eases ideas of difference and makes for effortless flow between time zones via generic ideas of comfort, rest and support, all these manifested by the similarity of hotels, airport layout, service mentality and luxury travel.

## flows and 'scapes.

The final characteristic of globalisation refers to the ways in which meanings (and so understandings and readings of each other as well as products) flow through local and global communities via various 'scapes. This makes the important point that globalisation produces particular kinds of culture or, for Arjun Appadurai, a particular kind of cultural activity called the social imaginary, which consists of five particular flows. These five flows are 1) ethnoscapes: flows of people across the globe, e.g. tourists, refugees, immigrants, guest workers; 2) technoscapes: movement of machinery such as VCRs, computers, mobile phones; 3) financescapes: currents of money via markets, stock exchanges, the drug trade; 4) mediascapes: flows of images and information; and 5) ideoscapes: flows of ideologies and ideas, for example democracy and human rights. This sense of the global as simultaneously an imagining and a style of economy make up the strong sense that Hardt and Negri (2000) communicate in their idea of empire that there is nothing 'outside' this kind of globalisation. This does not mean that there is not strong and organised opposition to certain sorts of American cultural domination or worldwide environmental assault, but that the means of opposition are also likely to be global in their style. Groups will organise via the internet and local Indigenous communities will join with international Indigenous groups, for example, to produce results that have local and international effects.

## old and new empires.

In the chapters that follow it is useful to remember at all times that all these flows are operating to differing degrees at any one moment in our global environment. If we think about what images do in this environment we need already to appreciate that media product (news, music, film, advertising) is as dependent as the globalised pea upon making global profit. This means that the attempts by local interest groups or indeed national governments to create images and ideas about themselves may have lessened, since what is shown to make global profits are generic and multiconnected (i.e. productive of multiple spin-offs) media products. But the media products produced are also a key way in which people make up new globalised identities, even down to the ways in which we organise and direct our individual lives. Thus ideologies, images and machinery all come together and reconnect through people and money, but these flows are not simple unchecked flows but become particularly contested, embraced or ignored. Osuri's chapter, for example, asks us to think about the ways in which an idea of 'beauty' has become embedded in our global culture through ideas of race that emerged from an older notion of imperialism that has joined with newer orders of empire that now connect 'whiteness' to a state achievable by the practice of particular beauty regimes including the use of 'whitening' creams. This, for Hardt and Negri, is one of the ways in which the existing empire differs from the older imperial order that was understood much more as a purely economic or regulatory system. For them the new empire is one that operates through a 'global form of sovereignty composed of agencies which operate in diverse arenas (national, regional and global), yet interlock to form a single framework of governance for the entire world' (Marks 2003: 461). One example of this interlocking would be the ways in which the same media company might be engaged in producing very local newspapers as well as international forms like the reality TV 'product', which in turn creates particular kinds of identities that produce stories at a local level which might be featured in the local newspaper.

The understanding that the global works in very local ways and indeed through individuals is also one of the ways in which the new and old empires need to be differentiated. Older versions of empire occupied a centre which was partially reproduced in their colonies to bring into being a class of like-minded 'colonised' bureaucrats or to cater for expatriate settlers and workers who needed some of the reassurance of 'home'. A civil service, universities, communications system and other infrastructure were styled on the model of the imperial centre and put into place to (in part) produce knowledge about the colonised. These institutions were then subject to the underlying, usually racist, principles that motivated their construction. Some were for 'whites only', some for 'English educated' and they generally depended on dichotomies and hierarchies that reproduced the colonial order. But in the current order of globalisation, empire no longer depends on simple oppositions, for the hold of a single centre no longer works. There is no stable 'home' for many to return to and in many cases no stable home to begin with. Oppositions between colony and centre (or centre and periphery) are now cut across not only by migrational flows but also competing ideas about what it means to be English, for example as the Cornish, Scottish and Welsh (and many other groups) question the overarching idea of England that the earlier empire bought into being and circulated internationally. Now we would have to think of the ways in which people participate globally in modes of identification that are more complex, often contain multiple points of opposition and connection, and produce further styles of being that nonetheless are still circumscribed and informed by racialised orders. Has your own 'ethnic' identity shifted in your lifetime or that of your parents? Do you wear clothing or eat food that you recognise as belonging to other cultures? How are those differences negotiated?

The first of the chapters to follow, by Fiona Nicoll, is indicative of that global complexity and its limitations when we look at a specific practice of globalising empire. You will notice from the start that this is a comparative piece that still presents the USA and Australia as very different places. This accentuates the global reality that although certain forms or representation and decades of American media product flow into Australia to create a common language of characters such as *The Simpsons* or *Friends*, the different experiences of those products will shift their meanings in sometimes radical ways. The **glocal**, or the localising of global (most often American) content, occurs simultaneously with the reading of the media product. But besides signalling the ongoing usefulness of cross-national comparisons, the chapter brings together three seemingly disconnected ideas: gambling, white possession and popular culture. This alerts us to the fact that a globalising empire will produce new logics and thus bring people and things together in new and unexpected ways. Would the ways in which non-Indigenous Australians assume the possession of Australia have previously been connected to gambling and popular culture? White possession of Australia and the elision of Indigenous sovereignty would perhaps previously have been seen as something belonging wholly within the discourses of ideology and law, but as Nicoll makes clear, these ideas are now being played out via global ideas of Indigeneity that leak across national borders to prevent (in this instance) alternative imaginings of what a recognition of Indigenous sovereignty and Indigenous gambling might look like. That is, the satirising of Northern American Indigenous groups' use of their recognised land does many things in the cartoon itself, but in Australia it contributes to what we rule in or out as imaginable in the Australian setting with quite a different history of Indigenous–colonial relations. This is a nuanced chapter and requires the reader to recognise our own possible attachments to denying Indigenous sovereignty alongside our possible pleasure in popular 'politically incorrect' cartoon shows such as *South Park* or *Family Man*. Does our easy consumption of global cartoon content enable us to feel at home within global media as long as we assume that we are in some way included as fellow 'white' global citizens?

Understanding the global endurance of certain styles of racism has required some shifts. As Nicoll says:

To understand surviving and new patterns of racial inequality between and within peoples and nations, critical race and whiteness theory moves beyond a focus on cultural 'difference' to explore how *whiteness* functions as a gendered system of power that works ideologically through discourse and social institutions to promote, legitimate and protect the interests of white people as members of a racialised collective in Europe and its ex-settler colonies.

This shift in how to think about race assumes that although the central organising ethos of colonialism may have been displaced (e.g. any simple idea of motherland and colonies), this does not mean that the independent nations that emerged after colonialism, for example, will necessarily cease to be colonising in their laws and ideologies, particularly towards Indigenous populations. The study of whiteness emerged within this environment. As Nicoll further says:

> [T]he critical study of whiteness simultaneously builds on and represents a departure from earlier research on the violence associated with policies and practices of white racism. From the late 20th century to the present, white dominance has necessarily operated through processes of invisibility, ex-nomination and normalisation rather than through the exclusionary 'whites only' practices of the segregated American South or Apartheid-era South Africa.

Paying attention to how a figuration such as 'white' works not only locally and globally, via traditions of racist segregations, but also, in the contemporary moment, through conjoined modes of representation to keep on occupying the invisible norm, means that whiteness manifests itself in many ways. Would you now identify as 'white'? Why? Why not? One example of whiteness at work can be seen throughout Chapter 14 where Goldie Osuri looks at the ways in which Aishwarya Rai works within discourses of beauty, whiteness and commodification at once. For Osuri:

> Contemporary cultural theories can help us read the ways in which some of these non-white representations of beauty circulate transnationally. Using whiteness theory, in particular, this chapter will examine how Aishwarya Rai (Miss World 1994 and a Bollywood star), packaged as an icon of Bollywood Indianness abroad, is simultaneously represented as an assimilable, marketable form of cultural difference in contemporary Western locations.

As Osuri begins to unpack how these ideas of 'global' beauty came into being she identifies four elements that constitute the generative matrix which enable the transnational circulation of Aishwarya Rai as a world beauty. These are:

1   Aishwarya Rai's status as a Bollywood star
2   the construction of white femininity in Western contexts
3   the economic liberalisation process in India as partly responsible for validating and idealising the cultural form of beauty pageants and beauty queens
4   intensified discourses of skin-whitening and lightening in the Indian context.

You can see in this list the ways in which a single globalised figure moves through and is seen as indicative of cultural forms that arise through specific individual histories, large philosophical movements, political and economic processes, and particular products aimed at national markets. Although the list is highly diverse it is not unlimited. Analyses of globalised phenomena as cultural forms will still render rich, coherent readings that can be the grounds of global interventions or globalised support. It is very important to remember that globalisation is not a single force that overwhelms us but an environment that we are all within and in which we act. One of the ways we act is to produce new kinds of knowledges: in the Osuri chapter, for example, new ideas about what beauty could mean. At this moment can you write down what you think beauty is? Have you thought of it as a racial or ethnic category before? Is the application of lipstick a 'racial' act? (Or even racist?)

Knowledge as power has also been a key way in which the world was ordered throughout the colonial era via the intermeshing of cultural forms and colonial practices. The discourse of **Orientalism** as articulated by **Edward Said** is used by Joseph Pugliese in Chapter 15 to look at the images of torture that came from Abu Ghraib. As Pugliese shows us, these images emerged not only as one part of a global flow of media images but began with the domestic and ubiquitous phone camera. This in turn connects new digital machinery with older styles of photography that included the photos taken of lynchings of black Americans in the USA as well as the many colonial tableaux that staged Indigenous and colonised peoples for the ready consumption of those in power. But the displays of power enacted through physical and digital means on the bodies of the Iraqi prisoners are also reflective of the globalised moment we are currently within. The claims that the tortures were done 'just for the fun of it' and the evidence that certain shots of the scenes were sent home to family alongside conventional tourist snapshots of local markets and landscapes requires us to see the utter colonisation of the space of the Abu Ghraib prison. Even when the means used to torture is 'global' in both the style of machinery and ways the images were circulated we are reminded that bodies do not and often cannot move at the rate of digital images or transnational finance and in fact are further invaded and immobilised by the mobile image when taken in this environment. As Pugliese writes:

> 'Imperialism and the culture associated with it,' Said (1994: 93) argues, 'affirms both the primacy of geography and an ideology about control of territory'. In the colonised sector of Abu Ghraib prison, the Orientalised bodies of the Iraqi prisoners in the torture photographs become symbolically coextensive with the invaded territory of Iraq: they are the ground upon which violent military operations are physically performed and through which control of the colonised country is symbolically secured, even as outside the prison US imperial rule is violently contested and destabilised.

This speaks of the endurability of Said's analysis that power is organised through ways of knowing difference. That knowing includes stereotypes and 'othering' but also now the intense circulation of those knowledges in sometimes unpredictable conglomerations where styles of racism exercised over black American bodies morph into ideas of the Arab as circulated in earlier colonial times with styles of 'fun' and domination to make new kinds of torture that centre again and again on how something or someone can be made to be seen and so known.

This idea of a stylisation of knowledge/power moves through each of these chapters linking images and politics and their joint circulation in new ways. We see the new and old empire in globalisation and the globalising and historicising forces within a new idea of empire. Along with the emergence of new identities and new critiques we also have newly refigured modes of racism, new styles of colonisation, and circulating forms of exploitation that limit what can be imagined. Globalisation expands and contracts what is possible.

# THINKING WITH PART 5

- Are you white? Why? Why not? How does the meaning of white change between countries colonised at different times and adopting different racial politics?
- Can you think of other examples where globalisation has bought together ideas that would not have previously been considered together? Can you see where popularly circulated ideas in cartoons or other popular media have constrained how we imagine national policy?
- Imagine you are particularly beautiful. How will you now move your body, talk, dress or shop? Can you identify how these acts are racial? Are you 'acting white'?
- What is a 'post-colonial' body? Name its characteristics and try and draw them.
- How does looking at images of and 'knowing' about other races and cultures also help us erase the experience of 'others'?
- Take a series of photos with your mobile phone at parties and other places where you are having fun and you are being encouraged to take photos as a part of the fun. Review them later and consider the ways in which this very ordinary activity also confirms particular ethnic identities or even displays of power. Who is in the centre of the frame? How do these images compare with mass-circulated news photos? Is race or ethnicity erased in these private images? Why? Why not?

# what's so funny about indian casinos? comparative notes on gambling, white possession and popular culture in australia and the usa.

AUTHOR: fiona nicoll

## INTRODUCTION

Successful tribes and new forms of Indian capitalism are forcing white Americans to reassess their relationship to and preoccupations with Native American peoples, and along the way are helping to forge a cultural revitalization within all Native American communities, which remain the most impoverished and deprived in the United States. (Darian-Smith 2004: 109)

Wow, man—Indians have it good!—Eric upon arriving at the 'Three Feathers' casino on *South Park*. (quoted in Light & Rand 2005: 1)

[These] people took 24 dollars for the Isle of Manhattan. They have no idea what things are worth!—Peter Griffin after losing the family car to 'Geronimo's Palace' on *Family Guy*, ep. 6, season 1.

This chapter will explore two apparently different things: a lack of cultural research on everyday representations, practices, spaces and identities related to gambling in Australia; and the fact that references to gambling in American animated sitcoms almost always occur in the context of a central storyline about Indian casinos. While *South Park*'s episode 'The Red Man's Greed' (season 7, 2003), in which the demolition of the entire community is planned to allow a superhighway leading directly to the door of the 'Three Feathers' Tribal casino, is arguably the most vicious representation, the storyline of white Americans being taken for a ride in native casinos has the force of an established convention, with two episodes of *The Simpsons* addressing it (ep. 10, season 5 and ep. 17, season 11) as well as an episode of *Family Guy* (ep. 6, season 1), which will be discussed in greater detail below. I will conclude with some comparative reflections on how Indigenous people in Australia in are positioned in relation to economic, political and cultural aspects of gambling.

In considering the meanings of Indigeneity generated within animated sitcoms featuring representations of Indian casinos, we can turn to an interdisciplinary and international field of research that has emerged over the past two decades. Critical race and **whiteness** studies provide ways of understanding the relationship between aspects of our embodiment such as race and gender which are already inscribed with certain meanings, and the cultural tools and processes through which we might actively disrupt or challenge these meanings. Whether we experience our social identities as restrictive or even as violating of our individual and group agency depends on the relations of dominance in any given society at any given historical moment. This is why Stuart Hall (1997) argues that the symbolic violence entailed in stereotyping is not a universal effect of the process of identity construction itself but, rather, is a result of the cultural hierarchies which order different social identities at particular moments and places.

Building on the work of Hall and an established tradition of critical theorists of race, from Franz Fanon (1982) to **bell hooks** (1992), critical race and whiteness studies begin at the point where existing cultural theories of globalisation and post-colonialism fail to provide convincing explanations for the persistence of racialised relations of dominance. To understand surviving and new patterns of racial inequality between and within peoples and nations, critical race and whiteness theory moves beyond a focus on cultural 'difference' to explore how *whiteness* functions as a gendered system of power that works ideologically through discourse and social institutions to promote, legitimate and protect the interests of white people as members of a racialised collective in Europe and its ex-settler colonies.

In her ground-breaking article 'Whiteness as Property', Cheryl Harris (1993) explains how the American state constructed the position and status of slaves and first nations differentially in relation to whiteness, which operated as an inalienable property right to African persons, on the one hand, and Indian lands on the other. It is with reference to relations of property and possession that we can understand how the critical study of whiteness simultaneously builds on and represents a departure from earlier research on the violence associated with policies and practices of white racism. From the late 20th century to the present, white dominance has necessarily operated through processes of invisibility, ex-nomination and normalisation rather than through the exclusionary 'whites only' practices of the segregated American South or Apartheid-era South Africa. As Richard Dyer articulates the contemporary challenge:

> Whites are everywhere in representation. Yet precisely because of this and their placing as the norm they seem not to be represented to themselves *as* whites but as people who are variously gendered, classed, sexualized and abled. At the level of racial representation, in other words, whites are [apparently] not of a certain race they're just the human race ... This is why studying whiteness matters. (quoted in Rothenberg 2002: 12)

It is because whiteness tends to operate beneath the radar of everyday life that its effects are often apparent less in relation to the things white people actively *do* than by the actions we *fail* to take to support positive changes to the status and situations of people racialised as Indigenous and non-white. 'But what can we do'? is a frequently voiced question of white people when our privilege is bought into clear view. Aileen Moreton-Robinson (2000: xvii) is an Indigenous Australian theorist of whiteness who disarmingly challenges such disingenuous protestations of powerlessness by posing a question of her own: 'What are the limits to what you would do?'

In a range of case studies from interviews with white academic feminists to analyses of legal decisions over anti-discrimination and native title law, Moreton-Robinson (2004) identifies 'a possessive investment in patriarchal white sovereignty' as a limit to the collective white agency required to commit the nation to a positive process of 'post-colonising'. In her analysis of the High Court's Yorta Yorta Decision in 2001 that found Indigenous claimants' rights to native title had been 'washed away by the tide of history', she argues:

> The possessive logic of patriarchal white sovereignty is predicated on exclusion; that is it denies and refuses what it does not own—the sovereignty of the Indigenous other. Here I use the concept 'possessive logic' to denote a mode of rationalization ... that is underpinned by an excessive desire to invest in reproducing and reaffirming the nation-state's ownership, control and domination. As such it is operationalised to circulate sets of meanings about white ownership of the nation, as part of common sense knowledge, decision making and socially produced conventions. (Moreton-Robinson 2004: para 5)

Toula Nicolacopoulos and George Vassilacopoulos (2004: 32) build on Moreton-Robinson's arguments to show how the exclusion of Indigenous people from the status of property-owning subjects 'make possible distinctively white Australian constructions of whiteness'.

The possessive investment in patriarchal white sovereignty is perhaps most obvious in the language used in everyday life to refer to Indigenous people and their affairs by white people official and non-official positions across the political spectrum. As Minister for Immigration and Indigenous Affairs, Amanda Vanstone justified the abolition of the elected Indigenous representative body the Aboriginal and Torres Strait Islander Commission (ATSIC) in 2004 by saying: 'the whole notion of separateness puts indigenous Australians into a different category and they are not. *They are first Australians, they are ours* … and they deserve to get the treatment that everybody else gets' (*Australian*, 17–18 April 2004: 6, italics added) And Tony Abbott, Minister for Health, urged remote Indigenous communities to accept greater responsibility in the fight against petrol-sniffing by describing Aboriginal people as '*an asset to be cherished*' (*Australian*, 24 September 2005: 6, italics added). More recently, an emailed letter to the editor of *The Australian* about the federal invasion of Indigenous communities in the Northern Territory on the pretext of saving children from sexual abuse by 'Robert of Roseville' complained that, 'Past governments have failed *our indigenous people*, each for a variety of reasons' (italics added).[1] These everyday examples illustrate how intimately a sense of Australian citizenship is entangled with a possessive relationship to Indigenous people. Such pervasive understanding of Indigenous people as 'ours', as the property of a white nation, explain 1) why representations of Indigenous gambling are virtually non-existent in Australian popular cultural texts and 2) why representations of Indigenous gambling in American animated sitcoms are so fraught.

# 'the son also draws': authenticating white possession in *Family Guy*.

The sleeve of the DVD of the first season of *Family Guy* promotes it as 'Uncut, Un-PC, Unsuitable for Kids' and wears a recommendation from *Entertainment Weekly*: 'Family Guy is what you'd get if you put Hank Hill, Homer Simpson and Cartman in a Blender.' A brief analysis of the episode summarised below will be used to generate new understandings of how the value of white possession circulates through the production and consumption of popular culture in America and Australia. I will argue that the failure to recognise Indigenous people as self-possessed and possessing subjects makes possible the deployment of 'authenticity' as a weapon of white cultural power within discourses of national identity that inform these popular texts. To pose issues in terms of 'authenticity' is to ask whether a given thing is, in the definitions of the *Concise Oxford Dictionary*, 'reliable', 'trustworthy' or 'genuine'. We will see that, while the usually white male subject we encounter at the narrative heart of animated American comedies may be (and regularly is) experiencing a crisis of identity at the moment of his encounter with Indigenous gambling, this crisis is at least partly resolved by emphasising the (usually male) Indigenous subject's cultural inauthenticity (see Chaney 2004).

# *Family Guy.*

## product description.

Meet the Griffins: Peter, the big, lovable oaf who always says what's on his mind. Lois, the doting mother who can't figure out why her baby son keeps trying to kill her. Their daughter Meg, the teen drama queen who's constantly embarrassed by her family. Chris, the beefy 13-year-old who wouldn't hurt a fly, unless it landed on his hot dog. Stewie, the maniacal 1-year-old bent on world domination. And Brian, the sarcastic dog with a wit as dry as the martinis he drinks. The animated adventures of this outrageous family will have your whole family laughing out loud.[2]

## plot summary.

Chris hates being in the 'Scouts' (a parody of the Boy Scouts of America) and wants to quit, but is afraid to tell Peter. He is finally kicked out, and Peter insists on driving the family to Scout headquarters in New York to get Chris readmitted.

While they are gone, Brian is unable to find the television's remote control and his intelligence drops sharply after watching daytime programming.

The family stops at a Native American casino for a bathroom break, but Lois quickly becomes addicted to gambling and loses the car. Peter tries to get the car back by claiming to be Native American ('My great-grandfather's name was Jeep Grand Cherokee.'), and the doubtful elders demand that he go on a vision quest to prove his heritage.

Chris accompanies Peter into the wilderness, hoping to tell him that he only wants to draw instead of being in the Scouts. Delirious from hunger, Peter begins talking to trees and sees a vision of his spiritual guide, The Fonz.

He finally listens to Chris' complaints and realises that his son is a talented artist. They return to the casino and reclaim their car, ending the episode with a parody of NBC's 'The More You Know' public service announcements.[3]

The narrative uses authenticity to support the possessive investment in patriarchal white sovereignty in several ways. The plot trigger that leads to the family's encounter with Indigenous gambling is Chris' desire to express an authentic artistic self rather than the limiting version of male identity imposed by the Scouts. And the troubled relationship between father and son is healed through the 'Indian' ritual of self-discovery entailed by a vision quest in a 'wilderness' just beyond the casino. Lois' character is used to feminise political sympathy for the casino's owners as well as to embody gambling addiction through her compulsive attachment to the slot machines. Her role as the white dupe of Indigenous enterprise, coupled with the exclusion of Indigenous women from the cast of casino powerbrokers with whom the Griffin family has dealings, has the effect of associating questions of cultural authenticity with masculinity or rendering them 'men's business' (see Churchill 2003: 223–44)

Supporting this narrative are many details of the text that highlight the use of authenticity judgments in securing the prerogative of white possession in America by invalidating contemporary expressions of Indigeneity. The casino's name, 'Geronimo's Palace', combines references to post-colonial resistance with a nostalgic nod to 'Caesar's Palace', that icon of Mafia-ruled Vegas. And kitsch signifiers of 'Indian-ness' abound within this space. What appears at first to be a sculptured towel caddy for which Peter reaches after having relieved himself in the bathroom turns out to be a living employee who is name-tagged as 'Watch-As-You-Pee'. Nostalgic references to pre-colonial 'noble savagery' are juxtaposed with allusions to current developments in Indigenous or Indian welfare in the dialogue. Consider this exchange between Lois and a gaming machine attendant after he invites her to gamble.

> Lois:       Thanks. But I don't—you know—approve of gambling.
> Attendant: Technically it's not really gambling; it's just us trying to rebuild our shattered culture after you raped our land and defiled our women.
> Lois:       Well as long as you're not using it for fire-water!

On other occasions the naive primitivism of the white characters is satirised. After Lois tells Peter she has gambled the family car, he makes the 'indecent proposal' of finding a high-roller who will sleep with his wife for a million dollars.

> Lois:     That's ridiculous
> Peter:    Come on Lois, these people took 24 dollars for the Isle of Manhattan. They have no idea what things are worth!

Following the decision to send Peter on a 'vision quest' to prove membership of the tribe which he has claimed in order to repossess his car, the casino's owners send him packing through the door making spooky 'spiritual noises' and then collapse laughing at having taken Peter for a 'sucker'. These and other details accumulate throughout the episode to produce a vision of Indian casinos as a cynical capitulation to the commodification of Indigenous culture and traditions which, in turn, supports the episode's larger premise: successful Indian enterprises are a threat to the white man's family and his other material possessions, which is, in turn, countered by attacking the authenticity of the casino owners on *their* grounds of identity and possession.

While the depiction of 'knowing natives' does acknowledge Indigenous agency, the focus is on the characters' resistance to this awareness, required for the plot device of the epiphanic 'vision quest' with which the episode achieves closure. With white father and son rebonded and the losses incurred through the white mother and wife's initial desire to support the casino venture and her subsequent addiction reversed, the car drives away and the Indian casino fades into the distance to make way for the next adventure of this ordinary white American family. My argument here is that the episode's depiction of the 'knowing' exploitation of white subjects lured into Indian casino gambling for all the 'right reasons' (guilt, pity, benevolence, not to mention the violent 'call of nature' that causes Peter to make an urgent bathroom stop at the casino in the first place) consistently translates political questions about Indigenous economic rights and self-governance into questions of 'authenticity'. The absence of competing definitions of 'Indian-ness' not only enables the casino's owners to be presented as wily captives of non-Indigenous popular cultural representations of what it means to be Indian (see Cuillier & Dente Ross 2007), but also precludes Indigenous articulations of the relationship between possession, authenticity and gambling, both historical and contemporary, from entering the picture.

The point of this analysis has not been to view this text simply as a mimetic reflection of the value of white possession within American culture but rather to use it to consider how certain racialised values might gather power as popular cultural texts travel between different national contexts. This is to focus on the *relationship* between those ideas and things that circulate most easily within globalisation and those that seem to remain stubbornly confined to their domestic contexts. Animated sitcoms are massively popular in Australia; many of my students (most of whom are under 25) are able to recite whole passages of dialogue from them. In spite of the popularity of these shows and media discussions about the appeal of 'politically incorrect humour' which has attended this popularity (Anderson 2005), serious debates raging in America, and more recently in Canada, about gambling's role in facilitating Indigenous economic development and self-governance are virtually inaudible here. My concern is that, at a moment when radical neo-liberal solutions to Indigenous poverty and disadvantage are increasingly prominent topics of political and news discourses in Australia, the depiction of Indian casinos as the epitome of inauthenticity in *Family Guy*, *South Park* and *The Simpsons* makes serious discussion of the relationship between white possession, Indigenous sovereignty and gambling less likely.

# comparative articulations of indigenous rights and gambling in Australia and the USA.

Since 1988, the year in which two centuries of uninvited British presence was variously celebrated and protested by non-Indigenous and Indigenous people across Australia, Indigenous people in the USA have been enabled through the

Indian Gaming Regulatory Act (IGRA) to own and operate gambling venues on reserves. Rather than representing the fulfilment of 'tribal sovereignty', however, this right is the product of a compromise negotiated with state and federal governments after the IGRA was passed, and it has played a part in making several impoverished reservation communities financially viable (Light & Rand 2005: 9). In some cases, Indian gaming businesses have generated such significant economic and cultural resources that established gambling moguls such as Donald Trump have protested themselves to be the 'victims' of Indian casino interests (2005: 105). The situation in Australia could not be more different. In contrast to America where 200 tribes own and operate 350 gaming establishments (see Light & Rand 2005), as the most impoverished community in Australia, Indigenous people seem to have everything to lose from the expansion of legal gambling forms under current constitutional arrangements and taxation regimes and almost nothing to gain unless they are in a financial position to become owners of gaming businesses as private individuals.

Whereas the ownership of gambling businesses as a major economic resource has been viewed by members of first nations in North America as one vehicle through which enduring aspirations to self-governance are being realised, the value of self-governance for Indigenous Australians itself came under sustained political and ideological attack over the period of the Howard government. Private home ownership was promoted as a solution to the problems experienced by Indigenous people living in public housing in remote communities, and Shared Responsibility Agreements that made welfare contingent on behavioral change were implemented. These Agreements were implemented as a weapon of 'tough love' designed to break a cycle of a 'culture of welfare dependence'. The idea that gambling might be anything but a vehicle for dysfunctional behaviours in Indigenous communities has almost never been mooted within public debates on Indigenous policy. Much more common are statements such as the following by Noel Pearson, lawyer, Indigenous spokesperson and head of the Cape York Institute, who enjoyed support from the Howard government, supporting the banning of welfare payments to parents in Indigenous communities 'who use it on the pokies or use it down at the tavern'.[4]

Perhaps the best way of illustrating the comparative position of Indigenous people in Australia and America in relation to gambling is to invoke the figure of the 'house'. Gambling businesses are premised on the fact that 'the house' always has the edge on the gamblers who play against it and hope to win. Colonial processes driven by the prerogative of white possession have enabled non-Indigenous interests to acquire more than a 'house edge' against Indigenous claims to a share of national resources. That the gap in life expectancy between Indigenous and non-Indigenous people has narrowed to seven years in the USA and Canada[5] (seventeen years in Australia), both of which recognise limited rights to self-governance from which collective ownership of legal gambling enterprises flows, is worth considering in the current context of legalised gambling in Australia where one poker machine is valued at around $227 000 or the price of the average suburban family home (*Courier-Mail*, 4 August 2006). While the global gambling boom persists and continues to generate revenue through online ventures and intra- and international cultural tourism, Indigenous ownership of the house will bring collective benefits not available to individual gamblers who would attempt to beat casinos and other legal gambling businesses at their own games.

I have brought critical race and whiteness theory to bear on popular cultural representations of Indigenous gambling produced in a nation with close cultural, economic and military ties to this one. In the absence of research on the way Australians interpret such representations I can only end with the following speculation: it is possible that the pleasures we might experience in consuming representations of Indian gaming in American animated sitcoms have their source less in their subversive challenge to political correctness than in their parodic representations of what Moreton-Robinson describes as 'the possessive investment in patriarchal white sovereignty'. I will end this chapter with two questions: Do we laugh at Indian casinos because allowing Indigenous people to own and operate legal gambling businesses marks the limit of what white people will collectively do to redress the living legacies of colonial dispossession in Australia? And is laughter about this limit the only thing we can do about these legacies?

## key readings

Hage, Ghassan 1998. *White Nation: Fantasies of White Supremacy in a Multicultural Society.* Sydney: Pluto Press.

Harris, Cheryl 1993. 'Whiteness as Property.' *Harvard Law Review* 106(8): 1707.

Moreton-Robinson, Aileen 2007. 'Writing Off Indigenous Sovereignty: The Discourse of Security and Patriarchal White Sovereignty.' In *Sovereign Subjects*. Sydney: Allen & Unwin.

## notes

[1] <http://blogs.theaustralian.news.com.au/letters/index.php/theaustralian/comments/long_term_bipartisan_action_needed_and_no_more_talk/ >, 6 July 2007.

[2] <http://www.amazon.com/Family-Guy-Vol-Seasons/dp/B000083C6V>, 12 April 2007.

[3] <http://en.wikipedia.org/wiki/The_Son_Also_Draws>, 12 April 2007.

[4] <http://www.kooriweb.org/foley/resources/politics/age22jul05.html>, 22 July 2007.

[5] <http://www.news.com.au/couriermail/story/0,23739,21488643-953,00.html>, 25 July 2005.

# CHAPTER FOURTEEN

# beauty and the bollywood star: stories of skin colour and transnational circulations of whiteness.

AUTHOR: goldie osuri

## INTRODUCTION

Conventional icons of beauty in Hollywood have included the likes of Grace Kelly and Elizabeth Taylor. Many of these women embodied an 'iconic' status, not simply because they were beautiful according to the judgments of the day, but also because a white skin colour has historically been associated with the norms of beauty. These norms have shifted in the context of discourses about diversity and multiculturalism through advertising, beauty contests and women's magazines which now seek to validate non-white women as beautiful.

Contemporary cultural theories can help us read the ways in which some of these non-white representations of beauty circulate transnationally. Using whiteness theory, in particular, this chapter will examine how Aishwarya Rai (Miss World 1994 and a Bollywood star), packaged as an icon of Bollywood Indianness abroad, is simultaneously represented as an assimilable, marketable form of cultural difference in contemporary Western locations. Representations of Rai's beauty and skin colour, in particular, appear to resonate with investments in an aesthetics of whiteness which govern gendered notions of beauty, especially in Western locations. Some of the questions this chapter will examine are: How do racialised ideals of white beauty within Western contexts shift as well as entrench, include and exclude 'multicultural' 'cosmopolitan' femininities? How are Bollywood ideals of beauty transfigured in a transnational context?

Perhaps one of the most widely quoted statements about Aishwarya Rai in various media in the last few years is the endorsement of Aishwarya as 'the most beautiful woman in the world' by Julia Roberts, the Hollywood actress. It may be an appropriate statement as Aishwarya Rai did win the Miss World beauty contest in 1994. But the statement is not just about having won the Miss World contest. Many websites appear to have devoted their energies into asserting this fact in nationalist statements about Indian women and beauty. Some of these statements imply that Indian women are some of the most beautiful women in the world in relation to women from other nations. If beauty was a phenomenon naturally related to geographical territory, it wouldn't explain why ideas about beauty are always shifting as well as contested. These statements suggest that the concept of beauty is worth examining because it is related to a set of norms or rules about what can be considered beautiful in a cultural and/or historical context. In this sense, it is interesting to examine the transnational (across national boundaries) circulation of Aishwarya Rai as an icon of Indian and 'world' beauty.

In 2005, a CBS news interview conducted with Aishwarya Rai also made reference to the territorial boundaries of beauty. The interview was framed as a question, 'The World's Most Beautiful Woman?', signalling the issue of Aishwarya Rai's world beauty status as somewhat of a puzzle. According to the presenter, 'Half a century ago, Hollywood would have presented her to us. Grace Kelly, Ingrid Bergman or perhaps Elizabeth Taylor'. But today, it's someone 'you've never heard of' (Simon 2005). This was the lead-in to the interview with Aishwarya Rai. The foil of Hollywood stars as an introduction to the recognition of a Bollywood star as the most beautiful woman in the world is interesting. *CBS News* appeared to be making an announcement that a Bollywood star and an Indian woman could now be recognised as a beauty and femininity worthy of international validation. Previously, the news story suggests, only 'white' Hollywood actresses like Grace Kelly, Ingrid Bergman or Elizabeth Taylor could be thought of as world beauties. Such a framing of the story demonstrates that historically, in a Euro-American cultural context, only 'white' women could lay claim to becoming icons of 'world' beauty.

In order to understand how such statements are possible in popular culture or in the news, it is necessary to examine some of the norms of beauty that have been pervasive in historical terms. How is it possible that previously only 'white' women could lay claim to becoming international icons of beauty? And if only 'white' women could lay claim to this, what contemporary conditions have made it possible to shift ideas about these norms in Western locations so that Bollywood stars like Aishwarya Rai can not only lay claim to being a world beauty, but also claim other kinds of recognition? Apart from her cinematic roles, Rai circulates as an icon of beauty through advertisements for cosmetic multinational companies like L'Oreal, and stories about her appear in transnational women's magazines. Theories of norms of beauty and whiteness become necessary in explaining these transnational circulations of Aishwarya Rai. But there are a number of other elements that enable this circulation. And in order to identify these elements, it is necessary to theorise how transnational circulations are made possible within global cultural flows.

# global cultural flows as transnational circulations.

Dilip Gaonkar and Elizabeth Povinelli (2003) comment on the circulation of cultural forms as a specific way of reading global cultural flows. Referring to Benjamin Lee and Edward Lipuma's (2002) term 'cultures of circulation', Gaonkar and Povinelli suggest that 'there is a growing recognition of the importance of circulation as the enabling matrix within which social forms, both textual and topical, emerge and are recognizable when they emerge' (2003: 388). A matrix, in the way that Gaonkar and Povinelli discuss it, is that from which something else develops or takes form. This enabling matrix needs to be identified in the case of the circulation of Aishwarya Rai. Or the question can be phrased as: What is the enabling matrix of circulation within which Aishwarya Rai as a cultural/social form (celebrity icon and world beauty) moves transnationally?

Matrixes are made up of interlinked synergies (compatible elements) or transnational connectivities (Grewal 2005) which link forms (the cultural/social form of the star quality of Aishwarya Rai), historicised discourses (shifting norms of beauty) and their interpretive communities (readers/viewers of women's magazines), the movements of multinational capital through multinational cosmetic companies, and the constitution of identities, subjectivities, nationalisms and **cosmopolitanisms** with reference to beauty. For instance, the CBS news interview referred to international standards of beauty which could only be embodied previously by Euro-American stars, thus presenting shifting racial definitions of beauty as a puzzle. Assertions about Indian women and beauty on blog discussions suggest national identity as a frame of reference.

The transnational connectivities that constitute the generative matrix include:

1   Aishwarya Rai's status as a Bollywood star
2   the construction of white femininity in Western contexts

3   the economic liberalisation process in India as partly responsible for validating and idealising the cultural form of beauty pageants and beauty queens

4   intensified discourses of skin-whitening and lightening in the Indian context.

These four elements, I would argue, constitute the generative matrix that has enabled the transnational circulation of Aishwarya Rai as a world beauty.

# transnationalising whiteness and femininity.

To read the generative matrix that enables Aishwarya Rai to circulate, it is necessary to trace the implications of the transnational connectivity between the Bollywood aura that Aishwarya Rai wears and its conjunction with Euro-American hyper-white ideals of beauty, in Western contexts. Let's face it, the most powerfully seductive technology deployed by almost every multinational company selling anything from cars to beer to toothpaste or diamonds appears to be a white woman: mostly blonde and almost always thin and tall. This white femininity has a colonial history of hierarchy in Eurocentric classificatory systems of race, colour and class. Whiteness, in this context, is a complex identity born out of differentiations of race, colour and class. This femininity was idealised and privileged precisely through its differentiation from those that were considered non-white women or those who were working-class women. In this sense, it is important to remember that whiteness does not refer simply to a naturalised idea of skin colour. Whiteness is the construction of a group of people as white as they are differentiated from those who are named as black. Furthermore, whiteness emerges as a way of identifying groups of people associated with superiority. In terms of norms of beauty, whiteness classifies some groups of people as capable of being beautiful as opposed to others who cannot. Bridget Heneghan (2003) traces these differentiations in her reading of 19th-century delineations of white femininity in the American context. She suggests that even the word 'female' in guides to becoming ladylike during the time referred only to upper-class white women. Heneghan states that upper-class white femininity was expressed through a relationship to valuable things in the feminine sphere. So, claiming material things 'took the form for women of visually allying themselves with their household goods' and 'clothing fashion, which followed a constantly varying design, and travelled throughout the feminine sphere tying all things together visually' (Heneghan 2003: 89). White women, especially through advertising, became managers of goods in the feminine sphere.

In contemporary terms, this construction of white femininity and its relationship to material goods has been transfigured. White femininity is still validated through the possession of goods, but this possessive relationship has been expanded greatly. White femininity is used to market the desirability and seductiveness of the possessions themselves, whether this be commodities or bodies, even experiences. In fact, we could say that femininity itself is marketed as a desirable commodity, as a path to success, through associations with whiteness. It is this historical trajectory of the relationship between white femininity and the world of commodities that informs the Euro-American advertising industry's penchant for deploying white women as a transnational seductive technology. In other words, this upper-class idealised white femininity informs the aesthetic that we experience pervasively through advertising and the entertainment industry in Western locations.

How is this legacy recoded in the circulation of Aishwarya Rai? Carrie Smith (2006) comments on how assessments of beauty, bodily qualities and auras of celebrities in popular magazines and entertainment shows refer to non-white celebrities through a classificatory system. A white celebrity, for instance, is not racialised or differentiated. However, a non-white celebrity is almost always differentiated, often in coded terms with reference to national or cultural difference. Smith outlines how Salma Hayek has been referred to as a 'hot tamale' and 'Penelope Cruz epitomized the "Spanish beauty"'. She also describes how 'the talking heads raved over the "mysterious and exotic" Aishwarya Rai'. In Aishwarya Rai's case, the fact that one could not place her racial/ethnic background appeared to be part of her allure. Such classificatory regimes associated with non-white aesthetics of beauty in Western locations appear to both protect white femininity from incursions while simultaneously disavowing whiteness as a standard of beauty. That is, by not commenting on the whiteness of the celebrity, whiteness appears to govern standards of beauty, while naming national or cultural differentiations protects the white picket-fenced standards of beauty itself. And if Aishwarya Rai is validated through the inability to place her appearance, she is also named as a Bollywood star in entertainment magazines precisely to place her Indianness. But her Indianness, in fact, becomes attractive because it can be dissociated from Indianness. Comments that describe Aishwarya Rai as a Greek goddess or the fact that she cannot be placed as Indian appear to make her a more attractive Indian celebrity. And it is precisely this approximation to whiteness which can be read as a dislocated transnational whiteness that appears to intrigue and seduce media and fans. It is this dislocated transnational quality of whiteness which appears to form a connectivity with the construction of an Indian cosmopolitan femininity. I will now turn to a discussion of contemporary **discourses** of an Indian cosmopolitan femininity as they emerge from the cultural form of beauty pageants, beauty queens and their connection to discourses of skin-whitening creams.

# beauty queens and indian transnational femininities.

A number of theorists have attempted to discuss the effects of the liberalisation of the Indian economy from the late 1980s in the cultural sphere in relation to the manner in which advertising for beauty or cosmetic products has participated in emergent discourses and consumption practices around femininity. Radhika Parameswaran suggests that 'middle-class women themselves have become a much sought-after market in the global economy'. And 'the loud voices of multinational cosmetic companies like Revlon, Oriflame, Avon, L'Oreal and Bencksier have begun to present a serious threat to the previous monopoly of Lakme and Ponds' (Parameswaran 2004: 376). For instance, Parameswaran suggests that Revlon managed to secure 18 per cent of the market share in 1995 alone. In this boom of local and multinational beauty and cosmetic industries, Parameswaran points out that 'beauty pageants and beauty queens have become symbols of Indian women's new visibility in the public sphere' (2004: 377). In fact, Priya Lal argues that the winning of international beauty contests by Indian contestants is not simply a happy accident. She suggests that *Femina*, India's largest women's magazine, 'actually initiated a national campaign ... to change the way local beauty pageants were run' (Lal 2003). According to Lal, judges

> were instructed to choose women with an 'international' rather than merely Indian looks in order to increase the chances that the next Miss India would become the next Miss World. Hence the entire pageant business in India underwent a transformation into a virtual industry in which companies from the beauty industry 'invested'; and the result was a product that was fairer, taller, slimmer, and straighter-haired, and much more likely to be well-received on the global scene.

What Parameshwaran and Lal appear to be identifying is a transnational connectivity where liberalisation, the cosmetic industry, and national and transnational beauty pageants interact to produce a new cosmopolitan Indian femininity in the figure of the beauty queen. The figure of the beauty queen promotes and visibly advertises India's 'success' on an international stage, and this success, I would suggest, is associated with a lighter skin colour.

This transnational connectivity is enacted on a number of levels. In terms of actually promoting skin-lightening or whitening creams, there were already national industries advertising the benefits of skin-lightening. Lal (2003) notes that the skin-whitening cream Fair and Lovely was launched by Hindustan Lever in 1976. But there appears to be a boom in the skin-whitening industry after liberalisation, and it appears to be specifically associated with the beauty queen phenomenon. Fair and Lovely is now marketed in over thirty-eight countries, but its 'biggest customer concentration remains in South Asia itself', and current estimates place 'fairness products at up to 40% of profits of India's entire cosmetic industry'. In 2001, Hindustan Lever's 'skin care business grew by over 20% … led by Fair and Lovely'. Lal's claims are given substance by a 2002 report in *The Business Line*. In 2002, Hindustan Lever's business grew by 12.9 per cent (Challapalli 2002). Umesh Naidu, national sales manager of the Himalaya Drug Company, explains: 'Ever since Sushmita Sen and Aishwarya Rai made it big in international beauty pageants, there's been a lot of interest in "good looks"' (quoted in Challapalli 2002). Good looks here appear to be equated with skin-whitening or -lightening.

Transnationally, Aishwarya Rai was the face of L'Oreal in 2004–05. In the Indian context, she appeared in L'Oreal's White Perfect, a skin-whitening cream advertisement. As one *Hindustan Times* writer (2005) notes, the advertisement was 'a chilling mixture of biology-class jargon and measured reassurance' about a cream that constitutes a 'breakthrough in whitening' by reducing 'melanin production' and 'gently exfoliating dark, dead cells', so that the skin darkening process is policed—'regulated' is the word the copywriter uses—to produce a 'perfectly fair, transparent and even complexion'. The heading, 'For a smooth, fair skin', seems to have come to the copywriter in a simple 'revelation'. The writer goes on to note, 'I haven't seen a comparable advertisement in Britain or America. I don't think L'Oreal would, in those countries, have the temerity to advertise a product called White Perfect'.

Many of the Indian representatives of whitening or skin-lightening products justify the marketing and sale of these products. Soumitro Banerjee, executive vice-president of the Himalaya Drugs Company, says, 'This hang up with fair skin is a core need, we can't wish it away. Anyhow nothing is radically wrong with it. Look at all the Europeans and Scandinavians trying to get a tan. The grass is always greener on the other side' (quoted in Challapalli 2002). The manager director of Godrej Consumer strengthens this individual consumer choice narrative by saying:

> We do not believe that fair skin as such is more beautiful than dark skin. It's the people who decide what is really more beautiful. If a particular consumer believes that fair and blemish-free skin would make her more beautiful, our FairGlow would help her get it. (quoted in Challapalli 2002)

Such individualist, consumer choice claims not only ignore but completely disavow the extent to which the fair, light-skinned or 'wheatish'-complexioned woman has been historically privileged through various cultural forms in the Indian cultural sphere: Bollywood has been one of the major cultural forms through which this discursive embodied validation of light-skinned women is manifested. This is not to say that other cinemas in India do not validate these kinds of skin colours and female bodies. Or even that we don't have the occasional supposedly darker-skinned actress like Nandita Das, who is respected and celebrated. However, the dominant aesthetics of beauty and skin colour privileged in Bollywood favour lighter-skinned women. Here ideas about gender and nation have consistently been replayed and acted through the bodies of light-skinned film actresses over the years. It is here that the 'traditional' national female body coded and valued by skin colour and an idealised notion of Indian femininity has continually succeeded within a **heteronormative patriarchal** order. If she does lose, as in the genre of a tragedy, she may have been a courtesan with a heart of gold. However, she was and still is beautiful and light-skinned. Lal (2003) suggests that this preference for light skin is very much part of 'South Asia's patriarchal history'. And perhaps the value of lighter skin was and still is attached to a higher socio-economic status. This is the industry where Aishwarya Rai has found success as an actress and a celebrity, and is one of its megastars.

This transnational cosmopolitan Indian femininity therefore forms a complicity and a connectivity with a Euro-American ideal of white femininity. And it is this ideal that Aishwarya Rai appears to embody. This femininity participates in a capitalist transnational economy and signals India's modernity, yet tries to approximate a white femininity and its possessive relationship to the world goods and commodities through a whiter, lighter skin colour. It is telling, therefore, that Aishwarya Rai circulated as the face of L'Oreal in Western contexts, symbolising a triumphal Indian Bollywood cosmopolitanism. Yet, in the Indian context, she appeared as the face of L'Oreal's White Perfect skin—a whitening cream which invited Indian gendered middle-class subjects to participate in this cosmopolitan transnational femininity by lightening or whitening their skin. Rai circulates, therefore, as transfiguring *and* complicit in the relationship between an Indian capitalist modernity and a Euro-American capitalist modernity. This complicity also works at the level of South Asian patriarchal class structures as well as Euro-American discourses of diversity, which are eager to embrace an approximation of whiteness in the form of Aishwarya Rai as an assimilable marketable form of cultural difference.

# dialogues: transnational whiteness and norms of beauty.

A transnational dialogue about Aishwarya Rai, Bollywood, white femininity and skin-whitening creams did emerge on chat forums, blogs and various articles and postings on the internet. The internet enables such an interactive dialogic space even though this space is accessible only to those who have the time, money and resources to engage with these issues. Some of these conversations idealised Aishwarya Rai and promoted her through nationalist sentiment, while others interrogated the hierarchies of skin colour visible in Bollywood, the imperatives of the cosmetic industry and the Western aesthetics of white beauty with their tokenistic gestures towards diversity and cultural difference. One blogger, who calls himself Niraj, took the route of asserting Indian nationalism in a diasporic context. He apparently saw Aishwarya Rai on a L'Oreal ad in the USA, and says:

It was an odd thing to see on American television considering the South Asians you do see are mostly racist stereotypes: convenience store owners, heavy accents, and other such nonsense. I was simply floored when I saw it. She is simply smashing. (Niraj 2004)

Others on the blog were also quite excited to see the face of an Indian woman circulating transnationally. Arma says, 'dude it was amazing. It was like not only she took over the American adv. She is also the cover of swiz mag!' (Niraj 2004) Although this is an uncritical response to the L'Oreal ads, I am slightly sympathetic to it in the sense that the bloggers appear to point out the absence of Indians on American television who do not fit racist stereotypes.

However, a more critical dialogue appears to have occurred on a blog discussing comments by Bollywood actress Rimi Sen, suggesting that a specific Bollywood director could 'even make a black African look pretty' (t-hype 2006). The comment sparked off blog discussions about the dominant obsession with a light skin colour in the Indian context, and situated it in the transnational context of race, colour and gender. The conversation led to a discussion on the use of skin-whitening creams in the African-American as well as the Indian context. One blogger, calling him/herself 'the technophobic Geek', said: 'The sadder part than the actual comment is that this is treated as such a no-brainer by most Indians, of both older and younger generations: I mean the "fact" that African people are not beautiful' (t-hype 2006). Rimi Sen's comments appear to illustrate an ongoing history of privileging lighter-skinned women within the Bollywood context as I discussed earlier. However, the very fact that these comments were being linked to ideas about race by bloggers such as 'technophobic Geek' as well as linked to African-American contexts suggests that the issue of privileging a lighter skin colour in the Indian context was being questioned. This questioning process through 'everyday life' formats such the net blog is of immense value. As a blogger called 'Anonymous' stated, 'yeah, it's really sad that that kind of [bullshit] is just taken for granted and is accepted in Indian media ... it really makes my blood boil. Unfortunately such an attitude is all too widespread ... it stinks ... and it feels like those of us who actually can smell are in the minority' (t-hype 2006).

## key readings

Laforteza, Elaine 2007. 'The Whitening of Brown Skins and the Darkening of Whiteness.' *Reconstruction* 7(1), <http://reconstruction.eserver.org/071/laforteza.shtml> 11 April 2007.

McClintock, Anne 1995. *Imperial Leather: Race, Gender and Sexuality in the Colonial Contest.* New York and London: Routledge.

Mire, Amine 2000. 'Skin-Bleaching: Poison, Beauty, Power and Politics of the Colour Line.' *New Feminist Research* 28(3–4): 13–38.

websites

For images of Aishwarya Rai, see the follwing websites:

<www.redhotcurry.com/archive/style/beauty/l_oreal.htm> Story about Aishwarya Rai joining the L'Oreal dream team of women

<http://iamrainbow.wordpress.com/2007/01/06/> Story about L'Oreal's 'White Perfect' advertisement

<www.oprah.com/tows/slide/200504/20050425/slide_20050425_101.jhtml> Aishwarya Rai on Oprah Winfrey's Women across the Globe

<www.rediff.com/search/2001/mar/14ash.htm> Story on number of Aishwarya Rai sites online

<www.aishwaryaworld.com> Official Aishwarya Rai website

<www.aishwarya-forever.com/home.html> Fansite

<www.aishwarya-forever.com/multimedia/commercials.html> Adsite

Fansite

# visual cultures of orientalism and empire: the abu ghraib images.

AUTHOR: joseph pugliese

## INTRODUCTION

## introduction: Orientalism as knowledge/power.

First published in 1978, **Edward Said**'s *Orientalism* has continued to exercise a critical influence across a wide range of disciplines, including cultural studies, philosophy, anthropology, political science, literary studies and art history. The transdisciplinary value of Said's book emerges from his detailed mapping of the relation between knowledge and power. In locating his analysis of the relation between knowledge and power in the texts, images and archives that the West has produced in its study of the East, Said coined the term '**Orientalism**'. Orientalism refers to the ways in which the West objectifies the East, constructing it as a subjugated object of the colonial gaze. For Said (1991: 57), the European view of the Orient is a 'vast, amorphous Asiatic sprawl' that stretches from the Middle East, encompasses the Indian subcontinent and reaches to the archipelagos of South-East Asia. In Said's work, the Orient is discursively constituted both as a geographic space (for example 'Turkey') and as a racially charged place inhabited by Europe's Others (for example 'the Arab'). In his analysis of the operations of Orientalism, Said demonstrates how geopolitical understandings of place necessarily inform 'aesthetic, scholarly, economic, sociological, and philological texts' (1991: 12).

In his work, Said (1991: 40) maps the wide range of Orientalist stereotypical representations that function to reduce the East to the status of inferior other of the West. Inscribed in this **othering** of the East is a structure of unequal relations of power in which the West occupies the superior and governing term in relation to the East. So, for example, in the context of the war in Iraq, Western powers such as the USA represent the Iraqi nation as a lawless and barbaric state that needs the intervention of the West in order to achieve the status of a 'civilised' nation. Viewed in this light, Orientalism functions as a knowledge/power system driven by what Said (1991: 14) identifies as 'a certain will ... to control' and govern the Orient. Understood in these terms, Orientalism must be seen as a regime through which colonial and imperial relations of power are reproduced and secured.

In this chapter, I will deploy Said's theory of Orientalism to examine the Abu Ghraib torture photographs. These photographs were taken in the context of the war in Iraq, which commenced on 20 March 2003.[1] The so-called 'coalition of the willing's' war in Iraq, a coalition constituted by US, British and Australian military forces, was launched on the basis of removing 'weapons of mass destruction' from the hands of the Iraqi regime; liquidating its ruler, Saddam Hussein, because of his purported links to al Quaeda; and, finally, securing American national security in the face of the 9/11 terrorist attacks. As was consequently disclosed, there were no weapons of mass destruction found in Iraq; there were no links evidenced between al Qaeda and Saddam Hussein; and international security has been put at risk precisely because of the war in Iraq (see Danner 2005: 57). The scale of the violence perpetrated by the 'coalition of the willing's' war in Iraq did not register in the West, despite ongoing reports of massive civilian deaths (see Pugliese 2006), until the disclosure of the Abu Ghraib torture photographs on the CBS News program *60 Minutes II* on 28 April 2004. Published by *The New Yorker* in the days that followed, the torture photographs quickly circulated across global news media.

# the camera as adjunct weapon
# of torture.

At one point in *Torture and Truth*, a harrowing testimonial account of the torture of Arab prisoners by the American military at Abu Ghraib, Mark Danner draws attention to what he appositely calls 'that ultimate third party': 'the ubiquitous digital camera with its inescapable flash, there to let the detainee know that the humiliation would not stop when the act itself did but would be preserved into the future in a way that the detainee would not be able to control' (Danner 2005: 19). In the context of the Abu Ghraib torture photographs, Danner's naming of the camera as a 'third party' brings into focus the voyeuristic intrusion of the camera within the relation of torturer and tortured. The voyeuristic optics of the camera as third party are reproduced in the material text of the digital photograph, as the ocular apex originally occupied by the photographer is reproduced by virtually every spectator who views the images. 'Ocular apex' refers to the reproduction of the position of the photographer as the 'taker' of the photograph; in the viewing of the photographs, the enframing and voyeuristic position of the photographer is necessarily reproduced by the viewer. This voyeuristic economy is problematised, however, by the viewing of the photographs by the victims of torture. Their relation, as both subjects and objects of these photographs, functions to short-circuit this voyeuristic economy.

The use of the camera in the Abu Ghraib torture photographs must be situated within the discursive matrix of Orientalist visual culture practices. The photographs are all characterised by a cinematic desire, on the part of the torturers, reflexively to 'shoot' and 'stage' the practices of torture performed on the victims. This reflexivity on the part of the torturers, in terms of their use of the camera as a type of adjunct weapon in their arsenal of torture implements (guns, sticks, ropes, electrical wires and so on), is something that is repeatedly drawn attention to in the testimonies of the victims. The testimonies reveal both the intrusive and amplificatory role of the camera in the process of being tortured, and the way in which the victims feel themselves to be violently positioned as having to perform 'roles' in 'porn movies':

> They beat him a lot then they removed his clothing then they put wire up his ass and they started taking pictures of him. (Greenberg & Dratel 2005: 511)

> They tied him to the bed and they inserted the phosphoric light in his ass and he was yelling for God's help ... The female officer was taking pictures. (2005: 504)

> After they removed the sandbags they stripped us naked as a newborn baby. Then they ordered us to hold our penises and stroke it and this was only during the night. They started to take photographs as if it was a porn movie. (2005: 516)

Situated within prison contexts governed by the suspension of fundamental human rights, the prisoners at Abu Ghraib are, at one and the same time, tortured *and* photographed; as such, their torture becomes available as a visual commodity that renders the victims of the torture a spectacle to be consumed within global networks of visual consumption (Pugliese 2007a). I would include the prisoners of Guantanamo Bay within this violent economy of visual commodification as the regime of torture practised there clearly parallels what was perpetrated at Abu Ghraib: in the words of General Mark Schmidt, appointed to investigate reports of torture at Guantanamo, 'You know, if you really think about Guantanamo, but for a camera … it was Abu Ghraib' (Democracy Now! 2007).

The cinematic framing of the victims of torture in the Abu Ghraib photographs, as if they are characters in a porn movie, needs to be historically contextualised in order to draw out its enmeshment within visual regimes of Orientalism. The Orientalist archive that informs the visual production of the Abu Ghraib photographs includes the Hollywood film industry, with its long history of racist representations of Arabs—as so many mad, bad and fanatical characters (Shaheen 2001; Sennerling 2006).

# the Orientalist 'bordello' of Abu Ghraib and the phantasm of the harem.

In the study of visual culture, visual regimes refer to the discursive frames that influence what we see and how we make sense of what we see (Bryson 1988: 91–2). There is nothing 'natural' or 'innocent' about the process of seeing. Seeing is at all times mediated by multiple **discourses** that regulate the meanings we make of images. At the schematised level of visual regimes, the Abu Ghraib photographs reproduce the colonial tableaux of 19th-century imperial photography (Maxwell 1999), in which the colonised natives, naked and shackled, are choreographed as mute and erotic trophies of imperial conquest. The Abu Ghraib photographs compel the viewer to bear testimony to the deployment and enactment of US imperial power on the bodies of the Iraqi prisoners through the organising principles of Eurocentric aesthetics that intertwine violence and sexuality with Orientalist spectacle. Orientalism, Said argues, is characterised by 'an almost uniform association of the Orient and sex' (1991: 188). Orientalist discourses invariably represent the Orient as phallocentrically 'feminine,' that is, as passive and sexually available; the Western subject, in contrast, is represented as phallocentrically 'masculine,' that is, as active and in control.

In keeping with the gendered power relations of Orientalism, the bodies of the Arab men in the Abu Ghraib photographs are phallocentrically transgendered and theatrically arranged into passive and available feminised bodies; the way in which the Iraqi prisoners were compelled to wear women's underwear over their heads underscores the transcoding of their bodies from male to female. Situated in the context of Orientalist imagery, the photographs of the feminised Iraqi men must be seen to belong to the 'phantasm of the harem' (Alloula 1986: 4; see also Puar 2005[2]). Malek Alloula articulates what is at stake in the transcription of space and bodies in terms of the phantasm of the harem: 'What is remembered about the harem … [is] the sexual excess to which it gives rise and which it promotes—a universe of generalised perversion and of absolute limitlessness of pleasure' (Alloula 1986: 95). What is operative in such instances is what Medya Yegenoglu (1998: 73) calls the 'interlocking of the representation of cultural and sexual difference'; this interlocking 'is secured through mapping the discourse of Orientalism onto the phallocentric discourse of femininity'.

Inscribing the Abu Ghraib photographs are the conventions of Orientalist tableaux that represent the Arab subject as the manacled slave, the erotic captive, the vanquished enemy as corpse-trophy, and so on. In the context of the visual genres of Orientalist representation, the pyramid of nude male Arab bodies, lasciviously intertwined, reproduces the Abu Ghraib equivalent of Orientalist visions of the harem, with their excess of naked and pornographically arranged Arab women's bodies. The transposition of this phantasm of the harem onto the space of the Abu Ghraib prison evidences the points of intersection between multiform colonial relations of power invested with the production of subjugated subjects 'where bodies are taken without any possibility of refusal' (Alloula 1986: 122). As a phantasm of the harem, Abu Ghraib embodies what Alloula calls in her analysis of the colonial dynamics of the harem 'the very space of the orgy: the one that the soldier and colonizer obsessively dream of establishing on the territory of the colony, transformed for the occasion into a bordello' (1986: 22).

In many of the Abu Ghraib photographs, the Iraqi prisoners have their heads covered in hoods. In keeping with the unequal relations of power reproduced by Orientalist visual regimes, the victim that is being photographed is rarely allowed to stare back into the camera and, by implication, agentically address the voyeuristic gaze of the viewer; rather, the victim's gaze is entirely occluded by hoods or, alternatively, the victim is compelled to be photographed with an averted look that undermines his or her power (a)symmetrically to return the gaze and thereby disrupt an unequal relation of visual power (Alloula 1986: 131). In foreclosing the right for the victim of torture to return the gaze, a unidirectional relation of **scopic power** is preserved; in other words, the right to look remains the sole prerogative of the voyeuristic photographer/spectator. By formally foreclosing the possibility for the torture victim to return the gaze, what is effectively precluded is the right of acknowledgment, if not appeal, that would be enunciated in the eyes of the victim—a right of acknowledgment regarding their categorical status as human in the face of subhuman acts of torture.

In the rare instances within the Abu Ghraib photographs that the Iraqi victim of torture is allowed to stare back at the camera there is inscribed the possibility of agency in minimally interrogating, if not disrupting, these violently unequal relations of visual power. Exercised in such instances is what Yengenoglu (1998: 63) terms a 'counter-gaze' that attempts to disrupt Orientalist relations of visual power: 'Instead of being looked at, the object now looks at.' For example, one of the Abu Ghraib photographs shows a smiling US soldier sitting on an Iraqi prisoner sandwiched between two stretchers (see <www.guardian. co.uk/gall/0,8542,1211872,00.html>). In this photo, the prisoner is stripped naked, immobilised between the stretchers and crushed under the weight of the triumphant soldier. On a symbolic level, the Iraqi prisoner is made to embody a subjugated and imperially vanquished nation: Iraq. The prisoner, however, simultaneously stares directly into the camera at both the photographer and the presumed viewers of this picture. The prisoner's direct stare constitutes a counter-gaze as it articulates two critical things: an anguished injunction to the viewer to bear witness to the violence and humiliation that he is forced to endure and an indictment of the US soldier's scripting of this scene of torture as celebratory and humorous.

# Orientalist exteriority: the hyper-visible body of the Arab prisoner.

The theatricalised visual coding that inscribes the Abu Ghraib torture photographs is exemplified, as I outlined above, by the repeated use of the colonial genre of the tableau. This genre is a hyper-real genre that is self-conscious of its own staged and choreographed effects. It is a genre that theatricalises its subject and renders it as spectacle. The discursive dimensions of this Orientalist aesthetic are constituted by the intertwining of torture, pain, sexuality and death in the service of spectacle and entertainment.

The desire to produce images, in this context, augments the physical rituals of torture as the victim is compelled to 'hold a pose' while undergoing the torture in order for the image to be produced. The testimony of one of the Abu Ghraib torture victims evidences as much:

On the third day, after five o'clock, Mr. Grainer came and took me to Room #37, which is the shower room, and he started punishing me. Then he brought a box of food and he made me stand on it with no clothing, except a blanket. Then a tall black soldier came and put electrical wires on my fingers and toes and on my penis, and I had a bag over my head. Then he was saying 'which switch is on for electricity.' And he came with a loudspeaker and he was shouting near my ear and then he brought a camera and he took some pictures of me, which I knew because of the flash of the camera. And he took the hood off and he was describing some of the poses he wanted me to do. (Greenberg & Dratel 2005: 526)

Here the victim of torture is compelled to participate in what goes by the name of 'no-touch torture', wherein the victim is so positioned as to self-generate their own intense and crippling pain (McCoy 2006: 9). In keeping with this codification of torture-as-violent-aesthetics, the victim of torture is compelled to participate in the theatricalisation of his or her own torture as he or she is commanded to assume specific poses by the torturer for the benefit of the camera. This theatricalisation of the subjugated subject is constitutive of the way in which Orientalism works. In Orientalism, Said (1991: 63) argues, the 'idea of representation is a theatrical one: the Orient is the stage on which the whole of the East is confined ... The Orient then seems to be ... a theatrical stage affixed to Europe'. In the context of this theatricalised setting of torture, the Iraqi prisoner is positioned in terms of a subhuman subject who cannot possibly experience the same level of pain, hurt or humiliation as his 'human' torturer. In the demand to 'hold the pose' while being tortured, an asymmetrical system of value is operating: the pleasure of the torturer/spectator is procured and secured through the logic of diminishing the possibility that the other has an equivalent capacity to feel pain. The victim of torture is also compelled to experience the very objectification of their body-in-pain as a type of visual commodity put to use for the gratification of the torturers and their fellow spectators (see Scarry 1987).

The camera, in this context, is instrumentalised into another weapon of torture, as it extends the duration of the regime of torture for the sake of producing the perfect picture. The camera and the flash are here mobilised within a regime of absolute power predicated on maximum visibility. The flash of the camera symbolically amplifies the stripping naked of the victim of torture as it produces an inescapable regime of hyper-visibility. In Abu Ghraib, the flash of the camera immobilises its victims at the same time as it transfixes them within a hyper-visible regime of complete exposure that underscores their complete vulnerability and object-status. In the torture photographs, every aspect of the Iraqi prisoners' bodies is rendered available for visual consumption. This regime of hyper-visibility, in which the Orientalist subject is rendered as absolutely exposed and exteriorised as an object of knowledge, is constitutive of the operations of Orientalism. 'Orientalism', writes Said (1991: 20–1), 'is premised upon exteriority', that is, Orientalism renders the 'mysteries' of its objects of knowledge as 'plain for and to the West ... The principal of this exteriority is of course representation'.

This scripting of Orientalism's objects of knowledge as immediately knowable to the West is enabled by their framing in stereotypical terms: for example, the sexually promiscuous Arab, the duplicitous Indian and so on.

One of the torture victims describes a regime of torture that included being bashed, being sat upon, then spat upon and urinated on by one of the military police, who 'was pissing on me and laughing' (Danner 2005: 240). The torture session concludes with the anal rape of the prisoner by one of the MPs using his police baton—and '[t]hen they broke the glowing finger [a fluorescent tube] and spread it on me until I was glowing and they were laughing ... And they were taking pictures of me during all these instances' (2005: 240). After the multiple violences performed on his body, the victim of torture is finally instrumentalised into a light-emitting object that renders the flash of the camera redundant: he becomes his own source of radiant light in a scopic regime that demands absolute exposure and visibility of the tortured body. The closing statement of this man's testimony, 'And they were taking pictures of me during all these instances', serves to indict the role of the camera as one more weapon of torture deployed against him by his torturers. This is a weapon that will be productive, during and after the brutal fact of torture itself, of an ongoing secondary trauma. This is the secondary trauma of knowing that the images that bear testimony to the victim being reduced to the status of objecthood will have taken on a life of their own, endlessly circulating the spectacle of the victim's pain and torture within globalised circuits of visual consumption.

In other words, the effect of image-as-augmentation-of-torture is amplified, in turn, by the networks of circulation, exchange and consumption within which these images are inscribed. Inserted within US networks of circulation and visual consumption, these images of torture become, like the white supremacist 'souvenir' photographs of the lynching of African-Americans (see Allen et al. 2005), Orientalist 'souvenirs' of symbolic violence that effectively legitimate the actual acts of physical violence and torture through the interpelation of an imperial anti-Arab spectatorship that will appreciate the 'sport' and get the 'joke'—and I refer here to the unforgettable words of one of the participants in the torture of the Iraqi prisoners who, when questioned, remarked that they tortured their victims at Abu Ghraib 'just for the fun of it' (Danner 2005: 323).

## Orientalism, homophobia and sexual assault.

Repeated throughout both the Abu Ghraib torture photographs and the documented testimonies of the victims is what Lee Edelman (1994: 173) calls the 'spectacle of sodomy'. The rape and sexual assault of the male Iraqi prisoners by the US guards must be seen as homophobically transcoding homosexuality: in other words, sexual practices (sodomy) and sexualities (homosexuality) that challenge regimes of heteronormativity are transcoded as 'aberrant' and 'perverse' and are thus absorbed into an homophobic eroticisation and aestheticisation of torture that targets the homosexual, the cross-dresser, the feminised Oriental male, and so on. In this economy of homophobic and phallocentric violence, anal penetration is performed in order to debase and humiliate the prisoners. In homophobic terms, '[t]o be penetrated', writes Leo Bersani (1987: 212, 217–18), 'is to abdicate power'; its intended effects are a 'radical disintegration and humiliation of the self'. Operative in this homophobic and phallocentric scripting of anal penetration are both gendered and racialised inflections: the subject of anal penetration is marked as 'feminine' in being positioned as 'passive' and 'receptive', and this marking is, in turn, overcoded by Orientalist fantasies designed to render the Arab male a 'woman'. The transcoding of homosexual sexual desire into acts of homophobic violence, which are still compelled to reproduce homoerotically coded practices (such as anal penetration), enables the violent disavowal of this self-same desire. '[M]utilation and sadism', Steve Neale (1992: 281) argues, 'are marks both of the repression involved and of a means by which the male body may be disqualified, so to speak, as an object of erotic contemplation and desire'.

The American military's naming of the Iraqi prisoners at Abu Ghraib as 'sand niggers' (Bacevich 2006) must be seen, in the context I outlined above, as activating a long and entrenched US racialised history predicated on sexualised violence exercised against Blacks in the contexts of both public lynchings and the systemic sexual assault in prisons (see also Davis 2005: 55). Reflecting on this intersection of sexual assault, race, colonialism and histories of slavery, Kobena Mercer (1996: 139) raises this critical question:

> Why does sodomy, or anal rape, come to acquire such an overdetermined and intolerable emotional significance in representations of colonisation? This requires more than an understanding of sexualization in a Foucauldian sense, and the way in which, through slavery and imperialism, the black body is opened up for power, primarily through the gaze, by being constituted as a specular object for the other who is also master.

The 'opening up for power' that Mercer draws attention to in his analysis of sexualised colonial practices resonates with the cases of anal rape of the Iraqi prisoners perpetrated by US soldiers at Abu Ghraib.

# geocorpographies
# of imperialism.

In marking the bodies of the Iraqi prisoners as coextensive with the imperially invaded territory of Iraq, anal rape is resignified, homophobically, as another instantiation of opening up the occupied territory for power. William Pinar (2001: 571), in his exhaustive analysis of the racialised, gendered and sexualised dimensions of the history of lynchings in the USA, brings into sharp focus precisely what was at stake in the practices of sexual mutilation of black men that accompanied lynchings: 'the definitive element of rape centers around male-defined loss, not coincidentally also upon the way men define loss of exclusive access'. The rape of both female and male Arab prisoners in Abu Ghraib is predicated—once the bodies of the prisoners are seen as symbolically situated within Orientalist matrices of territorial invasion and occupation—on continuing to exercise the imperial prerogative of 'exclusive access' in the face of resistance and contestation by those at the receiving end of this exercise of imperial power.

As I argue elsewhere, what was perpetrated at Abu Ghraib prison was a 'geocorpography' of torture (Pugliese 2007b). In coining this term, my aim is to bring into focus the violent enmeshment of the flesh and blood of the body within the geopolitics of war and empire. 'Imperialism and the culture associated with it', Said (1994: 93) argues, 'affirms both the primacy of geography and an ideology about control of territory'. In the colonised sector of Abu Ghraib prison, the Orientalised bodies of the Iraqi prisoners in the torture photographs become symbolically coextensive with the invaded territory of Iraq: they are the ground upon which violent military operations are physically performed and through which control of the colonised country is symbolically secured, even as outside the prison US imperial rule is violently contested and destabilised.

## key readings

Alloula, Malek 1986. *The Colonial Harem*. Minneapolis, Minn.: University of Minnesota Press.

Said, Edward 1991. *Orientalism*. London: Penguin.

Said, Edward 1994. *Culture and Imperialism*. London: Vintage.

notes

1  Web archives of the Abu Ghraib images are available at: <http://www.guardian.co.uk/
   gall/0,80542,1211872,00.html> and <http://www.antiwar.com/news/?articleid=244>
   20 March 2007. They are also reproduced in Danner 2005.

2  I am grateful to Goldie Osuri for bringing the Puar article to my attention.

# 6

# ethnography.

# the stories so far.
AUTHOR: katrina **schlunke**

## strangely familiar.

Ethnography offers a way of studying culture and a way of thinking about culture. In this way ethnography is both a methodology or practice and a theory or way of imagining the world. There is therefore no conclusion to ethnography, that is, only one way of doing it, but instead you might imagine it as a space where you find new ways of relating to objects of ethnography and new ways of writing those relationships. Think about sitting around with friends for a moment and imagine taking off your shoes and socks and putting a sock on your head. There may be consternation—a sock doesn't (in our culture) belong on our head. There may be worry—you will get all those yucky, sweaty sock germs on your head. Seeing the sock out of place reminds us of other bodily excretions that we also culturally hide such as sweat and snot and, classically, shit. Mary Douglas, an anthropologist and ethnographer, suggested that dirt is simply 'matter out of place' and we can actually feel the way that the dirt of the sock becomes seen when it is on the head but not on the foot. Why would you put your sock on your head?—to experience for a moment how very, very easily we can make the familiar strange. And in making the familiar strange, this ethnographically charged experiment shows us some of the key practices that organise our culture. We see that a proper order of dress suggests sanity, that we practise rituals of containing our bodily excretions, that the sock is usually understood as a kind of undergarment so should be kept hidden (except at festival times when a certain reversal can occur like children hanging socks up for Santa to leave presents in) and so on. What other kind of simple cultural experiment can you think of? How could you come to know your own culture better though such experiments?

The traditional practice of ethnography typically involved the study by an outsider of a small group of people in their own environment. The ethnographer attempted through a process called 'participant observation' to get a detailed understanding of the very particular culture (the ordinary lives, contested codes and **representations**) of those he/she was living with. That understanding was processed by keeping notes (field notes) and then writing those notes up into a comprehensive account called an ethnography. The key markers of an ethnography as opposed to other forms of research are personal involvement, time spent, and the centrality of culture as an organising mode of thinking. To understand better the changes in ethnography we will arbitrarily divide its history into three parts: making the strange familiar, making the familiar strange, and a third movement that I will call familiar/strange, which seeks to expose in the doing and writing of the ethnography the philosophical assumptions and acts of power that sustain ethnography's status as knowledge. You should be aware that these divisions are not neat and that assumptions from each part may leak back and forth between the selected headings.

# making the strange familiar.

Bob Hodge, in Chapter 16, traces very carefully the invention of the word 'ethnography' in 1834 and the different origins of its constitutive parts, *ethnos* and *graphe*. By tracking how the word and practice itself came into being Hodge is able to show the various uses to which the word has been put. This includes the ways in which knowledge about cultures other than those in the colonial centres was used for ruling over colonised peoples. Ethnography therefore has a very particular origin as a way of making knowledge about others that enabled colonial powers to rule others, and to represent and produce Indigenous peoples as colonised **subjects**. A clear example of this would be the ways in which ethnography assisted in the production of **Orientalism** through careful studies of seemingly exotic phenomena such as the harems and religious rites of the Middle East. As ethnography developed, however, the cultures that were most sought after for study were those understood as being the most removed from Western 'civilisation' and so most untouched by historical processes. It was thought that these ahistorical, 'primitive' peoples would reveal something of the origin of culture itself.

Ethnography was also seen as the key way in which the ancient idea of anthropology could become a discipline and fulfil its promise of being a scientific (and therefore worthwhile) study of humankind. Think about the following quote from Bronislaw Malinowski, who was working in the mid-20th century and is seen as one of the 'fathers' of modern anthropology.

> Finally, the ethnographic field-worker cannot observe unless he knows what is relevant and essential, and is thus able to discard adventitious and fortuitous happenings. Thus, the scientific quota in all anthroplogical work consists in the theory of culture with reference to the method of observation in the field and to the meaning of culture as process and product. (Malinowski 1944: 126)

Here Malinowski has a very clear idea that a 'core' of culture can be identified through a clear method of observation that will record only what is essential and relevant to how a people understand themselves. This idea assumes that all cultures operate through repeated practices, for example the eating of pies or the beating of breasts in mourning, which produce what is definitive about that culture. For the ethnographer working in this way it is vital that only those key elements are identified and that occurrences that happen by chance or don't fit this pattern are dismissed. In this way the ethnographer arrives at a positivist and therefore scientifically unassailable view of the operations and actions that produce the culture of a people. As Hodge notes, the discovery of the 'deep rules' of a group are established by trusting 'a small number of informants, an act of complex communication that cannot be reduced to quantitative, positivistic science': thus the seeming paradox that ethnography had within 'scientific' anthropology—a qualitative method being asked to produce a quantitative result. The need for the ethnographer to be intimate and accepted by the culture she/ he was researching, and yet create scientific knowledge that was presumed to be neutral, repeatable and without the differentiation of changing personal relations, was always a tension and slowly exposed the role of the field notes and final written ethnography in their production of 'scientific' outcomes.

Another idea underpinning the efforts of the ethnographer in pursuit of a scientific account of culture was the structural division of all cultures into the binary categories that have organised Western culture. These included ideas of men/women, insider/outsider and other presumed categories of Western knowledge. However, ethnography also provided much of the evidence to disprove the universalism of these categories. What was categorised as male and female, for instance, was deeply challenged by the realisation that other cultural organisations were not easily translated into the bounded boxes of Western imagination. It was not so much that **structuralism** was exploded, but that it leaked away across the imagined divisions so necessary to **binary oppositions**. (See Part 2 for an outline of structuralism, and Part 1 for an account of binary thought.) But the dream of what ethnography could achieve when put to this structuralist purpose was great: 'Ethnographic analysis tries to arrive at invariants beyond the empirical diversity of societies', said Claude Lévi-Strauss in 1966 in his classic book *The Savage Mind*.

In this way it would be ethnography that would for the first time provide the world with rules of culture that all societies could share. Our question now might be: at what cost?

# making the familiar strange.

The historical complicity of ethnography in the knowledge production of colonialism was to come slowly undone as global politics shifted the conditions that made ethnographies of so-called 'primitive' groups more and more difficult. The assumption that groups of people remote from the seeming centres of Western civilisation were outside historical processes was proved to be glaringly untrue as those very same people became a part of nationalist governments that overthrew colonial regimes. The new national governments were not interested in work that may have previously categorised them as curious savages, and so access to foreign field sites became more difficult. At the same time questions of ethics and method became sharply political as those who were the subjects were heard speaking back to the centre and the ethnography that had until then partially produced how they were understood in the West and elsewhere. There also arose within the West itself a growing sense of the politics of difference and a proliferation of **subcultures** that began to be actively formed and named after World War II and continue in different forms now. Science was increasingly seen as driving destructive technologies such as nuclear warfare, and scientific explanations for race, sometimes using ethnographic 'data', were seen as having made the Holocaust possible. 'Scientific' studies of people with their emphasis on the unchangeable were therefore increasingly seen as a problem and as inappropriate to the study of human cultures.

Ethnographies, if asked for or carried out by minority groups, were now seen as potential ways in which the richness of a national culture could be understood, critiqued and hopefully enriched. In some aspects this transformation of ethnography into a cultural criticism that was subversive of national norms was nothing more than the continuation of the idea of ethnography that had developed through Surrealism in 1920s France and Germany. There ethnography's task was to be 'restlessly subversive of surface realities' as **Marcel Mauss** said, and to constantly question what 'normal' was.

Just as the Surrealists had done with their abandonment of the high/low distinction in art, so too ethnographers emerged from the new disciplines, such as sociology and cultural studies but also 'new' anthropology, and looked into institutions (schools, asylums, hospitals, defence forces), subcultures (mods and rockers, teenage gangs, bikies) and government itself to discover how new kinds of cultures came about and were sustained. How were particular kinds of identity such as 'working class' or 'girl' reproduced or resisted in the cultural forms that such groups developed? This necessitated the careful questioning by the contemporary ethnographer of why and how they are researching what they are researching. Will the knowledge they produce be used to assist the group under study? Will the knowledge contribute something to a rethinking of how familiar categories of behaviour operate in the 'home' culture? What form of writing will best evoke the mixture of translation, silences and disruption that the conduct of an ethnography will produce?

It became increasingly usual that the ethnographer might be from the sub-culture that was being looked at or have some kind of existing insider relationship. The ethnographer might also be an active participant rather than simply a participant observer. The reasons for the ethnography might also have arisen less through intellectual or disciplinary curiosity than through a desire for advocacy or as part of a government contract to provide information that would contribute to policy. The length of time once considered a minimum to understand a culture (one to three years living within the culture) was now reduced to short bursts of some months or an ongoing commuter encounter. When the ethnographies became more 'across' than 'downward' oriented the realities of 'living with' shifted. Who could be asked to have their lives observed and recorded while also coughing up for food and rent? If the ethnographer was to try and anonymously blend in, what was the ethics of doing so and with what justification?

But at the same time the very aspects of ethnography that had troubled the positivistic claims of anthropology (the personal, sensual and particular form of the ethnographic encounter) were now positively revalued. The ethnographer was understood to be a sensate, **acculturated** individual who could give an account of a cultural situation that was specific and grounded in the encounter of bodies. It was therefore possible for ethnographers in their role as cultural translator to provide details not only of ritualistic activities but also of the surprising and the incomprehensible. Precisely because the ethnographer was now only able to produce 'partial truths' (Clifford & Marcus 1986: Intro), the omnipotence of the scientist-ethnographer could give way to the particular, sensate individual translating the **embodied**, emotional, daily complexity of ordinary life that he/she was within. The capacity of ethnographers to reflect on their own position and what they might represent coming into the cultural moments they were recording was now vital if their account was to be properly situated. Were they there at the request of the group? If not, what politics or intellectual histories had informed their decisions to come to this group? What were the institutional and financial arrangements that had gone into making the contact possible? If the group were also known through other representations and histories, how had these textual parts of the group been accounted for?

If all this was to be written down, what was the best way of representing this multiple experience? Should the film, book or video be co-authored with the participants? How could the silences and the banalities of the experience be best communicated? What might make one group's everyday experience a way of critiquing larger normative structures and make the effects of governing 'norms' less dangerous and pervasive?

# familiar/strange.

The final set of questions posed above still assumes that an experience can be represented and that a single ethnographer can attempt to reflect on her/himself to useful effect. But ethnography is now at a moment in history when assumptions about representation and self should not be easily made. The first point concerns the idea of experience. Experience is certainly something that the ethnographer will have, but it is now recognised that any encounter or experience will be a result of a particular set of circumstances that may also produce other meanings that have not, or perhaps cannot, be recorded. Once the instability of the idea of experience itself is revealed, the idea of representation also comes to be uncertain. Ethnography depended a great deal on the idea of 'going there': the authentic encounter with a group, who in some cases had not been written about before. Now the ethnographer will have an experience within a group who are themselves active meaning-makers: creators of their own representations who together occupy an acknowledged field of textuality. For example, an ethnography of any bikie gang must be aware of the ways in which popularly circulated meanings of bikie gangs emerge from magazines, film, histories of police control, modes of consumption, and dress and language. An ethnography is therefore just one site of meaning-making among many and can make no claim to being the single authentic account. It will, however, be a further productive possibility that could carry the particular force of the emotionality, the in-situ translations of existing representations, and the embodied negotiations that come with emplaced humans doing culture. Think about the ways in which Jean Duruz in Chapter 17 shows the changing meaning of food, sociality and sexuality across countries and differing ideas of domestication and 'at homeness'. Think of the ways in which Hodge carefully unpacks what he thought he knew in one small celebration, his parents' Golden Wedding, to show the limits of self-reflection and the difficulties of ever completing knowing what has occurred. The cultures that are now represented no longer work within the easy binaries of Western knowledge. The trouble that ethnography always gave to such simple binaries is now thoroughly distributed within Western thinking itself. That is, easy oppositions and ideas of difference are already undone by globalised activity that shifts cultures and cultural artefacts around the world to land in unpredictable places and where a usual form of being would be that of a **glocal** connective **hybridity**. The ethnographer him/herself has no easy recourse to the bounded imagining of the Western individual who steps back and writes up what has been found. Although this thinking is now identified as part of a set of poststructural theories of the **subject**, the dilemma with self-representation within fieldwork was well made in the Surrealist 1930s by **Michel Leiris**'s writing. His work, as James Clifford notes,

> largely devoted to a heterodox, endless autobiography, reinforced the ethnographic point. How could Leiris presume to represent another culture when he had trouble enough representing himself? Such an attitude made sustained fieldwork impossible. (Clifford 1988: 233)

The contemporary ethnographer, like all 'individuals', is more than a multiple subject and is perhaps better understood as a site of incomplete possibility. Certain forms of ethnographic becoming will produce words and exchanges while other styles of interaction will be unrepresentable or silent. No whole culture can emerge from such encounters and now it would be unlikely that any group would want such knowledge when that style of knowing seems only useful for ruling over others in an authoritarian manner.

But perhaps precisely because ethnography today must occur in between multiple discourses and through intimate engagement with people, place or subject over time, it may give rise to new ways of communicating difference, initiating new ethical imaginaries and providing a more sustaining and diverse idea of culture.

# ethnography now.

Ethnography has continued to drive experiments in writing, in styles of 'doing research' and in considerations of how knowledge works through power.

Various kinds of **fictocritical** writing, such as much of Michael Taussig's work on weather, shamanism, defacement, political systems, South America etc., is also ethnographic. Many of his efforts to copy in his writing something of the place and people he is engaged with reveals that desire to find a means by which the force of the opposition between 'us' and 'them' is radically deferred to enable new forms of thinking to emerge. As Taussig writes about shamanism, colonialism and the Wild Man he seems also to be conjuring up a shamanistic poetics, which happens not through recourse to a single magical figure, but is something that happens to the reader as we read one tale after another, thus entering a different point of knowledge possibility. There a dream, there the vomit of envy, and here and there—in the way the words fall on the page—the cultural sinuosity which makes for reading as an 'in-between' experience. Perhaps there is a relationship here between Taussig's writing and the films of **Jean Rouch**. Consider *Les Maîtres Fous* (The Mad Masters), his 1955 film about some Hauka ceremonies where members of the group undergo a violent possession by spirits that assume the identities of their colonial masters. This film is now understood as an early example of a kind of ethnography that works not through an appeal to the mind, but through an effort to disorder the senses and subvert habitual ways of thinking so we can know differently. As Grimshaw (2001) describes it,

> Rouch recreates the Hauka ceremony with each screening, trying to disorientate his audience and persuade us to surrender conventional patterns of thought and reconnect with mind and body through a ritual experience. We thus make community with our fellow viewers and with those who are on screen and so ideally we become active participants in the creation of an expanded notion of human society. (Grimshaw 2001: 101)

So although this film does not make the strangeness of possession 'familiar' it might allow us to see where possession has been made 'ordinary' through colonial rule. We could think about Australia and Possession Island where Captain Cook 'claimed' the entire east coast, and so the film may do as Rouch intended and expand our thinking of ways we participate in and can subvert certain forms of power through our bodily performances.

In a different way Katrina Schlunke, in Chapter 18, attempts to show fictocritically how an ethnography of an historical figure like Cook enables an appreciation of the ways in which 'normal' white culture is anything but. At the same time she invites the reader to rearrange her writings to produce the 'ethnograft' she aspires to, which would imagine a **postcolonial** white culture that would assume Indigenous sovereignty. How can we arrive at new ways of writing and new ways of relating to 'ordinary' or ordinary history or life via the ethnographic?

All these examples highlight the capacity of ethnography to provide a much more embodied idea of culture. The practice of ethnography assumes that bodies meet with other bodies and that the emotions will be engaged in communicating through difference. Even when reports of emotions and embodied affects were underplayed in earlier ethnographic work, those works were still haunted by them. Now the 'sensual scholarship' of Paul Stoller (1997) and others is seen as one way of providing an adequate cultural space to the ongoing project of an expanded idea of the human that is also related to particular landscapes and economic terrains. The senses may currently provide a more useful site of connection between competing ideas of difference and capital because so much of what we consume and produce, through multiple scapes of meaning, comes to us in a sensual form. Ethnographies that produce accounts of sensual cultures are therefore beginning to appear as we 'feel out' new environments produced through a new order of globalisation.

Another ongoing area, particularly within Cultural Studies, is the work that ethnography has done in the area of audience research. Once texts (that is, books as well as films and other representations) were understood as entities available to multiple readings, and not dependent on the directorial or authorial power for their single authentic meaning, what form of study would tell us what meanings were being made by readers? Ethnographic research on audiences could reveal new patterns of reading that might suggest the ways in which cultures shifted between old and new representation and readers acted as **bricoleurs** to create new culture through combinatory readings. This work marks an appreciation of the ways in which it is now not only dress and language that make cultures distinct, but also styles of 'doing' texts, that is, ways of listening, reading and in some cases smelling and touching them. (See Part 7 for more on 'texts' and 'touch'.)

To believe in the benefits of what ethnography can produce is to believe in the value of 'hanging around' and casually picking things up. There should be a natural humility in such an undertaking where what will happen is unknown. In this sense ethnography may require a participation that asks the writer or translator to work at the edge of his/her skin.

So in this brief exploration of the idea of ethnography you should already be getting a sense of ethnography as a kind of recorded scratching. The ethnographer scratches into different groups and worlds, and those worlds or cultures or groups of individuals and artefacts scratch back. These marks affect the physical body and also the body of knowledge that is created. Ethnography is an exciting idea, a volatile practice and a great questioner of how and from where we write.

This incomplete account of ethnography hopes to have conveyed to you some sense of the historical baggage that ethnography carries. It has been and is used to oppress and control often vulnerable peoples. It has also been used to reimagine the world, as a challenge to how we communicate difference ethically, and indeed how we communicate at all. Its history offers a very real caution to accepted ideas that are embedded in expressions like 'my subject group' or 'my field notes suggest'. Nothing within ethnography is entirely the product of the viewer or the writer. Ethnography is the practice of being caught up with one another in the process of communicating culture. Your whole self is always at play when you are engaging in this constant translative process, and it will be very exciting to learn what you do with that knowledge in the research contexts in which you find yourself. Ethnography in its formation (sometimes in its anthropological, and often in its surrealist, form), radically questioned what was normal. It abandoned distinctions between high and low culture and it worked to put the ethnographer 'in between' life. The early ethnographers did this in part by conducting experiments in the workshops of their own 'normality'. These are not bad ideas for any researcher wanting to change the world a little. Ethnography asks us always to imagine that another reality, another explanation of what might be happening, exists. It asks us at the same time to be curious about the ways in which our own desires and seemingly natural understandings of the world may be mistaken, or one story among many. It asks us to take time and move slowly within difference. It demands we be as curious about ourselves as we are about the world and others—all the time thinking through culture, thinking through the ways people make meaning for themselves with others. The following three chapters illustrate different styles of ethnography, different kinds of writing and different cultural sites. Together there is the space for you to imagine what else ethnography could be.

# THINKING WITH PART 6

1   Write an account of an intimate family memory (A shared holiday? An eventful celebration?). Show it to those people who shared the event with you and record their comments. Was there complete agreement with your account? Radical or nuanced differences? How is your position changed by their reading?

2   Consider all the ingredients, raw or dried foodstuffs in your cupboards or pantry. What do they suggest about your cultural situation? Now think about what actually happens when those foods are transformed through the cultural ritual of cooking. Who does what? Are the roles sexed, ethically imbued, hierarchically dictated? How? Why? What happens to a particular ingredient as it moves from Coles-bought tomato to spaghetti bolognaise or home-made tomato sauce or kasundi or …? What story can you write about the cooked food and how does it differ from the first?

3   Read the stories of Captain Cook that come from Indigenous Australia as collected by Chips Mackinolty, Penny Macdonald and Deborah Bird Rose. Then read the stories about Cook as you find them on monuments and in museums. What further cultural stories can you make by reading them together? Do either set of stories reflect your relationship with Cook? Observe what happens around you and what other people say when you look at public Cook material.

4   Make some ordinary, familiar cultural act strange (Sock on head? Eat without any utensil?). What do you discover? What cultural rules do you encounter? How can you write the experience up in a way that is honest to the sensations you experience on attempting this experiment?

# CHAPTER SIXTEEN

# from other to self and back: the curious history of ethnography.

AUTHOR: bob hodge

## INTRODUCTION

This chapter will begin with a deceptively simple question: What is ethnography? I will then proceed to fail at some length to answer it exactly. It has been many things in its history, meanings that have shifted and changed as a result of the many different contexts in which it has been used. This trajectory has contributed many unresolved differences and contradictions to the meaning and uses of the word today. Yet these contradictions create a methodological space that is rich and capacious, allowing you to make sense of a variety of different practices, issues and traditions in cultural research today. Ethnography is a subtle and powerful form of cultural research precisely because of its contradictions.

# origins.

I begin with the word. The *Oxford English Dictionary* defines it as 'the scientific description of peoples and cultures with their customs, habits and mutual differences' and derives it from the Greek words *ethnos*, which it translates as 'nation', and *graphe*, writing. This seems simple enough. Yet the full story is more complex. First, it sounds like a Greek word, but it was not. The *OED* reports 1834 as its earliest appearance. It was a 19th-century English invention. Nor is it 'scientific'. Ethnography has never been scientific, but the contrary, as we will see. The (mis)use of Greek has been a clever trick, to make ethnography seem ancient and scientific when it is neither.

Yet *ethnos* and *graphe* do exist in Greek, with interesting separate histories, which exist irrespective of when ethnography itself was born. Etymology (the study of the origin of words) is always illuminating for students of culture, though not because it always resolves the issues.

*Ethnos* referred to all groups who live together, such as tribes or families, and also nations. This sense still survives as a root meaning in the modern English word 'ethnic', often used for a group whose identity is set against the nation. In this respect it is like the **Marxist** 'class', a group conscious of its own identity. 'Ethnic (group)' today is often opposed to a Marxist class analysis, but in its earlier sense it overlaps.

In another use of 'ethnic' in Greek, especially in the New Testament, the word refers to everyone but Jews and Christians. This submeaning survives in modern English, where 'ethnic' is commonly used in English-speaking societies to refer to everyone other than those belonging to the dominant culture.

There is another trick behind 'ethnography'. The idea of 'customs', which is now part of its definition, does not come from *ethnos*. The best explanation I can come up with for this is that it comes from a different but related Greek word, *ethos*, or custom, habit. Somehow, taking advantage of the English deferential ignorance of Greek, this other word and meaning slipped into the mix, and no one noticed. The English word *ethnos* strictly should be written *eth(n)os* to distinguish it from the Greek, though I will not do so here.

*Ethos* referred to anything customary or habitual, patterns of life and belief: something like 'culture' in its broad sense. The French sociologist **Bourdieu** (1977) coined the term *habitus* from Latin, to describe learnt patterns of behaviour of a group. He could have used *ethos* to capture the same sense. *Ethnos*, what is written by 'ethnography', refers not only to a group but also to what holds groups together, patterns of belief and behaviour. The group can be of any size, from small and close to large and distant. It can be a nation, but if so, it is a nation functioning as a group, gathering other groups within it. What holds it together is a product of repetition, acts reflecting beliefs and patterns of relationships: the *ethos* within the *ethnos*.

*Graphe* completes the meaning of 'ethnography'. It comes from another Greek word, *grapho*. This could be 'writing' in the modern sense; 'writing about the *ethnos*'. But the word had a broader scope in Greek, to include painting, and today it can be used of film. Its root referred to scratching and scraping (letters or other marks), as in modern English 'engrave'. 'Carve' has a similar origin and meaning. *Grapho* referred to any way of making a mark to communicate.

The word 'groove' comes from a similar root. So does *kharakter*, 'character', someone or something that carves or engraves, and also the results, 'characters', letters. For Greeks as in modern English, *kharakter* could also refer to typical patterns of behaviour of individuals, understood as graven or grooved into them. In this way *kharakter* has a similar meaning to *ethnos*: patterns grooved by repetition.

From *grapho* comes *grammar*: underlying patterns grooved into a language, its 'grammar' in the modern sense. Modern anthropologists have taken this analogy further, to talk of underlying patterns in other media which function the same way: for example, the 'grammar' of music, art, film, cooking, and so on. This development converges on the same phenomenon as *ethnos:* a mysterious object that has no reason to exist, that holds together a group, a language, a culture, through *deep rules* of which most people are mostly unconscious. The best way of establishing this mysterious object is to trust a small number of informants, an act of complex communication that cannot be reduced to quantitative, positivistic science. This form of research seems profoundly unscientific for positivists, though it is 'scientific' in another meaning of science, as 'knowledge' (for example of the structure of atoms or DNA; Latin *scientia*, knowledge).

*Graphe* in this context can refer to a range of relationships between ethnographer and subject, from distant and power-laden to a visceral engagement that mirrors and reproduces relationships within the *ethnos*. 'Writing' the *ethnos* (recording in any medium, visual, verbal, behavioural) is also what someone within the *ethnos* does, grooving (carving, scratching, inscribing) or being grooved (carved, scratched, inscribed) through many repetitions of the characteristic, identifying acts that hold that group (*ethnos*) together. 'Informants' are also ethnographers, active in reporting the *ethnos* as well as living it.

Ethnographers always participate in the *ethnos*. The 'deep rules' they uncover are inscribed within them, to some degree, and cannot be known otherwise. Their bodies and minds are marked by the experience, and that experience (real or claimed) is a crucial basis to their capacity and right to know and speak. They also mark, wound the *ethnos* as they describe it. Ethnography is not innocent.

## contexts.

Ethnography, as word and practice, has existed in a number of different contexts, each of which has inflected its meanings, cumulatively producing the rich, complex, contradictory set of meanings it has today. This outcome is a problem for those who like their meanings simple, fixed and clear, but offers many rich possibilities for those who happily accept these multiple meanings.

The 19th-century context for ethnography was so potent in defining it that for some this context is inseparable from the word. European powers subjugated vast territories, like India, China and Egypt, and displaced native populations in settler colonies like Australia and South Africa (as happened earlier in America). In both cases, the *ethnos* of rulers and ruled were so different that the rulers needed to understand these other populations, pragmatically and emotionally. The practices around which 'ethnography' crystallised I call *wild ethnography*. Sir Richard Burton, adventurer and linguist, journeyed to Mecca in disguise, and translated the *Kama Sutra*. Dr Livingstone explored 'darkest Africa'. Daisy Bates lived for many years near Aboriginal camps in Australia. Such people, marginal in their home communities, ambivalent advocates for the foreign *ethnos*, brought back new understanding for administrators, fascinating stories for domestic consumption. They risked their lives, learning the language, talking to 'natives', reporting what otherwise the metropolis could not know. The difference in *ethnos* was extreme, and the typical *graphe* was sensational and polemical.

By the beginning of the 20th century, wild ethnography was becoming *classic ethnography,* an academic practice with more in common with wild ethnography than it acknowledged, successfully claiming a scientific status it did not have. This claim was accepted because ethnography provided such valuable knowledge, both to colonial administrators (of foreign territories and increasingly of objects of internal colonisation, like Indians in America and Australian Aborigines) and to metropolitan populations. The difference of *ethnos* was still extreme, and practitioners still wrote bestsellers, like Margaret Mead (1943) on sexual freedom on Samoa, but most writing now was specialist and scholarly.

The post-colonial theorist **Edward Said** (1978) used one term, '**Orientalism**', to cover both these practices. Both, he said, supported the imperialist project of the major European powers, especially France and England, constructing colonised peoples as populations for rule, represented as **Others** who, however fascinating, were unable to understand, represent or rule themselves, needing Europeans to do so on their behalf. I call this composite form of ethnography *Orientalist*.

Political events after World War II created a new context in which Orientalist ethnography was challenged. Most former colonies gained independence, and subjugated *ethnia* in settler nations protested and resisted. They attacked the ideologically charged term 'informants', used patronisingly of those whose appropriated knowledge formed the real basis of classic ethnographies. *Counter-Orientalist ethnography* arose as a mirror image of Orientalist ethnography, in which the Other refused the dominant gaze, claiming exclusive rights to speak and know their *ethnos*, exposing the mechanisms of power inherent in the academic *graphe*.

Yet ethnography like so much else migrated into new contexts, and thrived in new forms in the ample spaces outside the colonial binary, whether the *ethnos* was a workplace or a subcultural group, consumers or elites, rebels or bosses—any group that could be understood to have a 'culture'. It promoted the ideas of the *ethnos* and its rules as complex objects of 'writing', and *graphe* as new forms and genres to engage in effective, reflexive forms of critique and resistance. *Critical ethnography* allowed many different relationships between ethnographer and *ethnos*, none free of power, but avoiding the absolute difference that constituted Orientalist ethnography. In this new context it is clear that no *ethnos* is static and homogeneous, but is always in a state of tension, even crisis, always inflected by relations of power.

None of these forms is obsolete. Orientalism is still a potential trap within all other forms, even the most 'critical'. Yet new contexts can transform earlier contexts and their effects. As contexts change, so does the *ethnos* and the relationships that link it to the observer. In all forms of ethnography the *ethnos* is located ambiguously in relation to self and other, always partly inside both, binding ethnographers to those being studied, just as an *ethnos* binds each to others.

One form of critical ethnography, *auto-ethnography*, illustrates especially vividly the problems of self and other in all ethnography. Self and other meet in the same person, generating complex relationships with others in the 'same' *ethnos*, productively held apart by, and revealing, tensions and differences that make up both the ethnographic relationship and the *ethnos* itself. Auto-ethnography insistently reveals the scandalous secret of ethnography, that the self is always bound up in ethnographic practice, exposing the illusion that ethnography is 'scientific'.

But ethnography has survived and flourished in cultural research not because it is a good word (it isn't) nor because it refers to a consistent set of principles (it doesn't). For all its imperfections, it is an illuminating research practice, especially in contemporary contexts where the blindspots and operations of power of Orientalism are more visible, easier to critique through counter-Orientalist tactics.

I will outline some elements of this practice through the work of Clifford Geertz, a distinguished 'classic' ethnographer whose work foreshadowed many features of later forms of ethnography. His ethnography of Balinese cockfights (1973) begins with the story of how he encountered his subject, auto-ethnography before the name. This narrative (*graphe*) tells how he and his wife were watching a cockfight in Bali, his chosen ethnographic area, when the local police appeared, breaking up what was a criminal activity. Geertz tells how he and his wife ran in undignified terror like everyone else.

One accidental outcome of the incident was to create the 'mysterious necessity of anthropological fieldwork, rapport', at the same time giving him insight into the 'inner nature' (*ethos*) of Balinese society (Geertz 1973: 416–17). This 'rapport' is mysterious because it will soon become the basis of his Orientalist claim to deeply know these people and their *ethnos*. Yet in the moment he reports, the culture was 'written onto' his adrenaline-charged body. It so affected him that his research changed to include Balinese cockfights. They enacted the site of conflict between two *ethnia*, representing the play of colonial powers: the Dutch, whose prohibitions on cockfighting were taken over by the new rulers, against the Balinese, themselves also stratified by gender and class.

Geertz fleeing was a 'wild' ethnographer, yet he also remained a classic ethnographer. He switched from first-person story to the 'objective' style of 'scientific' ethnography, using his difficult experience to legitimate himself as an authentic 'other', claiming, as Orientalist ethnographers do, to be so totally an insider that the Other has no need to speak.

Geertz coined the term 'thick description' to capture how to 'write' complex instances of the *ethnos*. 'Thick description' sees the intersection of different systems of value and meaning in incidents and objects, like cockfights that go wrong. The 'thick explanatory space' surrounding these elements brings out what holds the different participants together and apart, not as individuals but as struggling representatives of an *ethnos* in conflict or crisis.

Geertz performs typical ethnographic actions—he observes, joins in, enacts, asks questions, of his own marked body and behaviour as well as others, and puts things together, talks and writes, and proposes 'deep rules'. He also includes, as inherent qualities of the *ethnos*, its ambiguities, indeterminacies and instabilities, the continual effects on and in it of power, struggle, conflict. The result is insightful, persuasive, problematic; a fine example of the strengths and weaknesses of classic ethnography, a bridge to different forms of critical ethnography.

# an ethnographic fragment.

I will finish this introduction to ethnography with a personal story. My conservative parents celebrated their Golden Wedding in 1985, but I was not invited, for reasons that will emerge. Initially I chose this theme and site intuitively, sensing something important here for me and my *ethnos*, which might be useful, in some as yet unknown way, to readers of this book. It is no accident that it concerns an event. The best ethnographies, like Geertz's cockfight, describe disturbing events, not typical customs or objects.

The *ethnos* I am examining was a middle-class, conservative Anglo family in Australia: 'postcolonial nouveau-riche' as my son later labelled them. I think of them as more postcolonial, less rich, desperately keeping their *ethnos* pure out of duty to a fading empire in this alien land, the Australian colonies. A core part of their *ethos*, what held them together, the 'deep rules' that ethnography aims to articulate, was a commitment to 'traditional' patriarchal family structures, where hierarchy and official status were all-important, interacting with gender rules that assigned status and obligations. This particular celebration functioned to publicly affirm these values, as exemplified by the fidelity and fruitfulness of the Patriarch and his wife, the Matriarch. I represented an acute problem to this structure because five years previously I had divorced and remarried.

This event was repugnant to the *ethnos*, yet I was the second son of this marriage, who until five years ago had been loved and admired, father of three grandchildren who till then had seemed the most attractive and talented of the next generation, who should have been on show in this celebration, jewels in the Golden Couple's crown. How could I be there, having betrayed the *ethos* which otherwise held everyone together? Yet how could I not, given my structural role in the *ethnos*?

Strong, mainly painful feelings were involved over this incident, but that makes it only more suited to ethnography. Feelings, a scandal for 'scientific' research, are important data about an *ethnos*, which prescribes feelings as well as relationships. Splits between prescribed and actual feelings and relationships are common and always significant. In this case, the split in the *ethnos* was especially deep because everyone felt strongly, much as the *ethnos* prescribed. My parents loved me deeply, as I loved them. My love for my children was as strong as the *ethnos* required, as the *ethnos* on this occasion forbade. My father the Patriarch acted as he should, but with great personal distress. This event crucially split feelings organised by the *ethnos* from actual feelings, with a terrible cost for everyone.

Auto-ethnographies need more than one report, for many reasons. As will emerge, my own understanding of the *ethnos*, my memory and reading of the incident, proved unreliable. One source is not enough, not because large numbers make it quantitative or objective, but because the complexities of subjectivity are filtered by single perspectives. Differences are essential in thick description, because they are traces of struggle, conflict, multiple frameworks. I asked my three children for their accounts, as members of the same *ethnos*, partly to build up a consensus narrative, partly to identify differences.

My elder daughter, then 18, began her version (ethnography) by noting the pain of 'being from the black sheep of the family'. Like all good ethnographers, she is a natural semiotician. She focused on the dress code. All her cousins wore school uniforms to the celebration. This signifier has many possible meanings. For my daughter on that occasion it signified the fact that they belonged to the dominant *ethnos*. Following this line, I could see that it connected them with a larger *ethnos* beyond this particular family, conservative middle-class parents who sent their children to private schools.

Her younger sister remembers with pride the blue dress she wore, and how odd she felt her cousins' clothes were, for this occasion. The response reflected her different relationship to the competing *ethnia* at that time, her confidence that she belonged to the *ethnos* that mattered. This 14-year-old delivered a famous put-down to a pretentious second cousin from England. 'I'm a hydraulic engineer,' he told her. 'Oh, you mean a plumber?' she asked. My son, then aged 17, was similarly unimpressed by his cousins' clothes, ('them and their little aspirations'), and by the visiting 'hooray Henrys'. The term comes from a popular Australian rejection of colonial pretensions and public school connections: two *ethnia* that were at stake.

Symbols are rich sites for thick description. My elder daughter focused on the flowers. The Matriarch liked flowers to be fresh. In spite of this stated position by the supposedly dominant woman in the *ethnos*, she said, my brother's wife pushed for artificial flowers, although they signified exactly that capitulation to modernity which I symbolised. She remembers that my brother's wife's artificial flowers triumphed. My younger daughter doubts this. Whatever the outcome, the fact of the struggle reveals the dynamics around this event. The meaning of the flowers was not 'given' by the culture but created in context, as reported by participants.

There was another event, part of the system precisely because it was kept separate. My father persuaded me and my second wife to come to a 'special' meal in a local restaurant. Reluctantly we agreed, because my father insisted. The actual occasion was as bad as I should have expected, and time has erased all the dreadful details. I know the Golden Couple were there, and my wife and I. Recalling it later, I always presumed my children were there, but my elder daughter says no. Her grandmother explained to her that her brother was invited, as a male companion for a significant aunt, and since there had to be a gender balance, the two girls were not invited.

From this comment she thought her brother went, but he does not remember this. She is reporting only a conversation, not the occasion. Perhaps my son was asked and didn't go, and no longer remembers the invitation, though he thinks not. Surely he would have remembered if he had gone. At the time I didn't know the reasons for anyone's presence or absence, and now I can't even remember. Yet for an

ethnography details can be significant even if (because) they are disputed. The Matriarch's remembered words are ethnographic facts, as are my son's and daughter's differing memories, whatever actually happened.

This occasion was an anti-Golden Wedding, replicating the structure of the actual Golden Wedding, whose 'bridal table' replicated the reception from the actual wedding, adding the absent element that was the reason for the actual wedding (sons and lines of male heirs). The Golden Wedding was a rule-governed event, no doubt typical of such occasions at that time, in that society. The anti-Golden wedding was invented on the run in a desperate attempt to correct the errors of the Golden Wedding, further distorted by unresolved conflicts between the principals: nothing less than bizarre. Yet the two events form part of a single system, which together reveal the properties and tensions of the *ethnos*, the scope and contradictions of its deep rules, better than either on their own.

I gave this description to my children. Their responses, respected, not assimilated into my homogenising narrative, make this a better ethnography, if more difficult for me as ethnographer. All objected to how I had constructed them. The quotations were accurate, they said, but selected and put together to imply a narrative and judgment that was mine, not theirs. In spite of what I wished, I had Orientalised them. As I said, but was unable to live up to, there are no innocent ethnographies.

They reminded me that this was my crisis, not theirs. For my son it was just part of 'a whole string of events', which he labelled 'the cold war, normalised'. I came to realise that they were generously recreating this painful event for my sake more than theirs. Talking about it raised many other memories that would have been more prominent in their own ethnographies. As my elder daughter said, 'everyone behaved badly', me included. They remembered me as harsh, ungenerous, judgmental, a more typical product of this *ethnos*, more a traditional patriarch than I'd thought.

It had been bizarre that I wasn't there, but I came to realise that it was equally bizarre that I'd used this ethnography to be there vicariously after all. The *ethnos* that I repudiated then obviously still held me. I realised (better late than never) that I didn't know what this *ethnos* was, what were its boundaries, inside or outside myself. It was like a nested set of boxes, related by complex webs of similarity and difference, hostility and love, no level complete in itself.

This is a critical ethnography. My 'informants' were themselves participants and ethnographers, marked by the *ethnos* and its divisions. I was an insider, yet as far outside this *ethnos* as if it were in another country, a 'wild' ethnographer who did not even make it to this strange land. The *ethnos* in the first place was a small group, but at every level lacked a single or stable identity. This self-division meant that some parts of the *ethnos* belonged to and owned it more than others, though this ownership and power were always contested, as this event showed. This is not a problem for (critical) ethnography, but its proper object. Ethnography and thick description are good at describing such complexity.

This point is the chief lesson I draw from this account of ethnography. It is precisely its inconsistencies and contradictions, its successful lack of a 'sound' academic basis and scientific method, that makes ethnography so vital and flexible a resource for cultural research today.

\*\*\*\*\*\*\*

**Acknowledgments:** As is obvious, this ethnography owes more to Anna Notley, John Hodge and Jennifer Sultana than I can adequately express.

key readings

Bourdieu, Pierre 1977. *Outline of a Theory of Practice*. Cambridge University Press.
Geertz, Clifford 1973. *The Interpretation of Cultures*. London: Fontana.
Said, Edward 1978. *Orientalism*. Harmondsworth: Penguin.

# talk table: doing–ethnography in the kitchen.

AUTHOR: jean duruz

## INTRODUCTION

'I'm telling you stories. Trust me', says Jeanette Winterson in the opening pages of her novel *The Passion* (1988); a book interwoven with tales of Napoleon's chicken chef, a tender lesbian romance, the surreal beauty of Venice and, above all, food: fish, chicken, cakes and wine. In my chapter on food, conversation and cultural analysis, the stories will be more homely. There'll be no trace of Winterson's signature magic realism here. Nevertheless, her dictum about the power of storytelling—its capacities to beguile—will prevail as we approach the kitchen table, icon of the West's desire for nurturance; an everyday site of catharsis and renewal.[1]

Lately this table has become a nostalgic symbol of loss, inscribed with spectres of kitchenless apartments, children who can't cook and absent mother-figures— echoing spaces haunted by the ghost of 'cooking woman' (see Duruz 2004), who is meant to stand comfortingly at the kitchen table, kneading pastry and 'fashioning the world' (Giard 1998a: 222). As Nora Seton says about this form of kitchen romancing and yearning, 'It is like the staging of a child's favourite story. We conjure images of hot ovens, splashy sinks, baskets of onions and potatoes, bins of fresh bread, fleshy women and merry faces' (Seton 2000: 173).

Nevertheless, while myths have a powerful hold on the cultural imaginary and how people live their lives, in this chapter I'm interested in different kinds of stories. These stories are ones that are 'not-fitting', stories of contradictory details that creep up on you and, sometimes, give the myths a shake. This is in keeping with Ben Highmore's conceptualisation of everyday life as a paradox: a curious blend of the mundane and strange. Highmore claims it is the capacity to 'make strange' the familiar, the obvious, the boring, that lies at the heart of productive analyses of 'everyday life as a lived experience' (Highmore 2002: 16).

In my case I am searching out narrative moments in stories that challenge assumptions of who sits around the table, who cooks, who eats, the foods that are eaten and the pleasure in eating them. As well, I want to reflect on stories that travel beyond their tables, beyond their dishes, and beyond households of cooks and eaters to question frameworks of analysis. How are mundane acts of preparing food and eating together shaped, in sometimes unexpected ways, by intersecting meanings of gender, class, ethnicity, sexuality, and so on? In other words, we'll examine moments when the 'talk' of the table meets the 'talk' of cultural theory, together with the intriguing possibilities embodied in these exchanges.[2] Finally, I want to think about the 'doing' of storytelling as a process, in which rich nuances from ethnographic practice intersect with the curiosities of everyday life, offering productive spaces for cultural theorising.

To track those phantoms of domestic nurturance, together with the everyday's messy response, we'll visit two kitchens. One is close to Green Lanes, Haringey—popularly known as north London's 'Little Istanbul'—and the other, near King Street, the territory of the 'tribes' of Newtown, a suburb in Sydney's inner west. Each kitchen is 'different' from those imagined ones peopled by 'fleshy women with merry faces', and each offers digestive possibilities for its 'different' identities in the making. Sitting at these kitchen tables we'll piece together narrative fragments that include idiosyncratic moments, compelling images, occasional comments, drifts of conversation, laughter and jokes that are a tasting menu for 'different' belonging vested in sexuality. At the same time, through 'food talk' at the table, this menu expands to include other dimensions of difference. Here conversational exchanges emerging from the shared pleasures (or otherwise) of cooking and eating, chart a gastronomic map of how complicated, and sometimes tricky, processes of identity-making and identification can be.

# Rachel and Miriam: too many cooks, and too few.

*To set the scene:* Green Lanes, a quintessential London high street. It stretches from its multicultural southern end, busy with Greek bakeries, Cypriot greengrocers spilling onto the street, Turkish cafés and the legendary Turkish grocer/patisserie/delicatessen of Yasir Halim (see Rista 2000: 136), to its English northern end that includes such stalwarts as Marks & Spencer.

*Introductions:* The kitchen we are entering is Miriam and Rachel's workspace.[3] The two women have been in a lesbian relationship for some years and living together for the last year. Both had been married previously, and now, as a couple, maintain strong links with their extended families. As a result, and drawing substantially on food rituals to maintain social bonds, these women occupy a significant emotional place in their community of relatives and close friends. At the time of my interviews, Miriam and Rachel own two houses—the one we are in now is in a side street off Green Lanes, a convenient distance from Miriam's workplace, while the other is in a small country town not far from Bristol where Rachel works. Both women are employed as professionals; both would see themselves as decidedly middle class. As well, while not practising as orthodox Jews, Miriam (born in South Africa) and Rachel (born in England), both identify culturally as Jewish, observing holidays such as Yom Kippur and Passover.[4]

*Food maps:* Food trails and networks are complicated. Rachel and Miriam divide their time between the two houses, and circulate food between the two kitchens: organic vegetables from the country, for example, are taken to London, while Green Lanes' luscious olives end up in the cottage in the 'cutesy little Cotswold village'. Sometimes these are traded for dates that the Algerian mother of one of Rachel's colleagues brings with her when she visits her daughter in England. The dates, in their turn, become Haroset, the traditional paste prepared for Passover Seder and shared with Rachel and Miriam's extended family.

*Stories:* At the table, the conversation moves from city to countryside; class, ethnicity and religion; life histories, marriages, lesbian relationships, children and grandchildren; it reflects on how one develops a taste for organic, ethnic or exotic food. So, in the multilayered nuances of this kitchen, how do cooking, eating and food form a 'different' landscape of nourishment, set a 'different' table? At this point you'll have to imagine the many delicious dinners and sociable evenings spent in these women's company; there is only space here to tease out a few moments in their storytelling. First, let's consider the dynamics of two cooks in the kitchen.

*Too many cooks?* Miriam has a reputation as a fine cook within her community. This prompts my curiosity about Rachel's reaction to this. How does a woman live with another woman, particularly a good cook? Between two women, how are iconic meanings of femininity, enacted in daily rituals of emotional work for others' comfort, managed? Who owns the kitchen and its cultures of giving? In the following fragment of table talk, Rachel outlines a curious dilemma:

Jean:     [Tell us about] when you moved in with Miriam ... She's obviously a keen cook.

Rachel:   Gorgeous.

Jean:     [D]id you have to do any negotiations about who cooks or what gets cooked?

Rachel:   I think at first [that] ... that got kind of competitive.

          [T]here's still a kind of ... power ... dynamic ... [F]or ... [Miriam, cooking is] ... [an] act of caring ... in a very very strong way ... [Y]ou wouldn't be allowed to have some bread and cheese for lunch ... She's got to make a salad, you know, it's got to be nice ... and sometimes if you're in a hurry ... its vaguely aggravating. You have to let her do it and now ... we tend to always cook together. Umm which is all right but she's bossier ...

          I'm the *sous-chef* (laughing). We have quite different styles in the kitchen—I'm kind of incredibly ... neat and methodical and I work clean ... [W]hen I've finished cooking a meal the kitchen's pristine ... Whereas [with] Miriam, it looks like utter catastrophe, it looks like there's been a riot. ... But we work well around each other ... It works.

It would be easy to romanticise this story. Remember Nigella Lawson's kitchen goddess who 'trail[s] ... nutmeggy fumes of baking pie in ... [her] languorous wake' as she effortlessly produces golden puddings and sugar-crusted piecrusts (Lawson 2000: vii)? Here in our Green Lanes kitchen, instead of one kitchen goddess, there are two. Each vies to nurture friends, family, each other. It's every eater's fantasy, with our literature full of accounts of childhood at the kitchen table—all those sensory moments of tasting, smelling, touching, watching and listening—while armies of good women prepare and serve. Whether 'cooking woman' appears to be a cast of stylish 'goddesses' or Seton's less ethereal, more earthy image of 'fleshy women with merry faces', a 'different' relationship of two women cooks certainly benefits its hungry guests.

Nevertheless, there's trouble in paradise. While Miriam and Rachel embrace the pleasures of women's traditional work, there are hints in Rachel's story that their years of sharing a kitchen have not been unproblematic ('competitive ... power dynamic ... aggravating ... bossier'). At this point, Highmore's tension of the everyday as mundane-strange is significant, with the unexpected detail undercutting the obvious direction of the plot. Here, the mythical image of the cook's 'gorgeousness' is in turn disrupted by her irritating behaviour, and the tendency to produce a '**queer**' romance of two-radiant-cooks-for-the-price-of-one is challenged. One cook's exacting approach to food preparation produces, for the other, a 'riot' of kitchen disorder. So, this kitchen table story becomes more prickly than we would have imagined. And this is not the end of the story. Reminiscent of **de Certeau**'s 'tactics' as everyday, creative ways of negotiating pleasure within the constraints of social order, Rachel describes microcosmic balancing acts of living and working together (de Certeau 1984: xix–xx). Here, with effort, good humour and an easy acknowledgment of the other's 'gorgeous' qualities, 'it works'. So these women are not goddesses, but neither are they doormats. In a kitchen where the 'neat and methodical' faces 'utter catastrophe' and 'riot', a 'different' resolution from conventional heterosexuality is achieved.[5] Both cook, and cook together—they give, they take. However, this should not be seen as an all-to-easy romanticised reciprocity but as a work-in-progress.

*Too few invitations?* As well as the question of too many cooks, there is also the question of the rituals of exchange with others, especially other women. Not surprisingly, we find that among their circle of lesbian friends, Rachel and Miriam have achieved a reputation for generous hospitality. In fact their dinner parties are legendary, with large numbers of women invited for evenings marked by a program of small 'performances'—stories, party games, gossip and jokes—accompanied by much noise and hilarity. Of course, there is food and wine in abundance, with menus planned to cater for all dietary needs and passions. But, I ask Rachel, 'do the others … [ask] you back?'

Rachel continues:

> [N]ot as often. I think that they sometimes don't enjoy it the way that we do. It doesn't matter, so we … just like doing it and that's what we do, and that's fine, and they can entertain us in other ways … [A] lot of our friends find cooking quite stressful, for other people. So … we're quite happy to give that, that's what we do, it's a gift.

Here the conventional rules of dinner party obligations are challenged, and, interestingly, 'different' forms of reciprocity exchanged. As **Emmanuel Levinas** reminds us, true gifts are simply that—given without expectation of return (Levinas 1982: 101; Derrida 2001: 17–18).[6] The problem is that such an argument might confirm the traditional figuring of femininity as selflessness or sacrifice. Rachel's account is more complex than this.

Once again ethnography hints at different analytical directions to take. Narrative fragments, such as 'enjoy it the way we do', 'we just like', 'entertain us in other ways', indicate the pleasure of gift-giving for the giver or, if exchange is required, the alternative forms this can take. Nevertheless, I do not want to argue that these everyday 'tactics' of altering social 'rules' are exclusively owned by particular cultures of sexuality—in this case cultures of lesbian or queer identity-making. The point is rather that such stories provide possibilities for reflecting on how a 'different' community experiments with 'different' exchanges and 'different' forms of belonging. Other communities, other people, might adopt similar 'tactics' or different ones entirely.

# Katie: cuisine tracky dack.

*Introductions:* So, in spite of readiness to accept 'gifts' of hospitality, not everyone wants to cook. Seated at our second kitchen table, we're about to hear tales of not-cooking, or rather of creative responses to appetites for 'home' cooking. Katie lives in a tiny Victorian cottage in Sydney's Newtown, a suburb celebrated for its ethnic diversity and culinary opportunity. Its main street, King Street, is known as a meeting place for 'tribes'—ferals, greenies, gay men and lesbians. There are 'grungey university students riddled with body piercings, yuppie professional couples, black-draped goths and punks' (Reiden 2000: 32). In keeping with its reputation for diversity, the street boasts a wide range of restaurants and food outlets that include Thai, Vietnamese, Malaysian, Chinese, Indian, Pakistani, Fijian, Japanese, Italian, Greek, Lebanese, African and Mexican cuisines.

*Home alone:* In our conversation with Katie the question of home cooking produces a poignant story:

| | |
|---|---|
| Katie: | I went through a period of time where I ate out a lot … I had gone through a relationship breakup and I actually didn't want to be at home on my own because you know the relationship had broken up and your partner leaves, and it's sort of like … |
| Jean: | You're lonely? |
| Katie: | Yeah, and my ex-partner at that time was quite a good cook. |
| Jean: | Oh Katie, what a loss. |
| Katie: | Oh, it was. I think I was devastated. You know, I could have got over the loss of the love and all that sort of thing, but the bloody cooking, I tell you. You'd come home from work at night and what do you find—a dog and … an empty fridge. |

Here, the mythical nexus of cooking, nurturance and love, with its complicated relationship to women, appears to have been broken. Without a woman (mother, wife, daughter, lesbian lover) to prepare comforting meals at the end of the day, there is only the dog and the empty fridge. Or at least, that's how the story goes. Obviously, everyday life offers different accounts, or all men in single-person households, and gay men in live-in relationships, would starve! So, is Katie's story simply one in which her lesbian relationship mirrors traditional divisions of labour, with one good woman assuming the role of 'cooking woman'? Perhaps. Is Katie exaggerating her predicament for the purpose of a good story? Again, perhaps.

*Eating out:* Either way, Katie doesn't starve. Fortunately, her 'eating out' is no longer a gesture against loneliness; instead, more recently it has become a significant route to strengthening community bonds. As a working-class Irish-Koori (Indigenous) lesbian who was born near where she lives, Katie has complex threads of attachment with Newtown's various 'tribes' and well-defined spaces of eating and pleasure. Everyday cultural practices range from eating 'real tucker' (heart-stopping helpings of schnitzel and mashed potato) with Koori friends at George's, one of King Street's oldest and best-known cafés, to vetoing cafés whose staff Katie perceives as 'unfriendly'—as racist and/or homophobic. On the other hand, unnatural 'friendliness' is to be avoided, with Katie refusing to accept the position of exotic 'other':

> [S]ome of the cafés you go in with a Koori mob and all these people [are] going 'Oh, it's lovely to have you in here' and all that, and you just think 'Give us a break ... [I]t's not a reconciliation event. I'm just going in for a bloody cup of tea'.

*Eating in:* Interestingly, it is the ritual of the dinner party and its cultural politics that Katie approaches in a creative, non-cooking way. With irony, she describes the form it takes—amiable competition—as a group of friends attempt to outdo each other on takeaway knowledge:

> [W]e will get some takeaway and watch a new vid, you know, and you'll say 'Well, there's this new, sort of, upmarket, you know, Middle Eastern restaurant that does ... sweet lamb on ... fresh Turkish bread with ... prunes' ... and then someone else will say 'I know this great Thai restaurant that does ... hand-fed duck in ... Tasmanian oranges with sort of like you know sweet chilli sauce from Thailand' ... and so ... you'll have this sort of fun evening ... [in your tracky dacks] that's sort of like an eating out evening at home.[7]

Here, Katie could be accused of celebrating difference as a form of commodification. Is she reworking signs of ethnic belonging simply as a choice of different takeaway 'styles'? After all, **bell hooks** in her classic criticism of cultural appropriation warns against the mainstream's greedy consumption of 'ethnic' dishes, in which 'ethnicity becomes spice, seasoning that can liven up a dull dish that is mainstream white culture' (hooks 1992: 21). Since hooks' injunction, other writers, focusing on the politics underlying a culture's taste for exotic foods, have developed similar arguments (see Cook et al. 1999: 230–1; Probyn 2000; Heldke 2003). However, Katie is saved by her own strong sense of irony. Her storytelling parodies both the language of food writing (with its breathless pronouncements about food 'discoveries') and the phenomenon of the dinner party itself. So, here, in tracky dacks, talking 'foodie' talk and, significantly, with *no woman cooking*,[8] a community can comfortably tweak (if not break) the rules of feminine responsibility for food preparation. Together, its members 'eat out at home'.

*Refusals:* The rules are broken in other ways. In spite of Katie's mockery of ostentatious food talk, she also asserts, as a working-class woman, her right of access to certain forms of cultural capital—food knowledge, food tastes, food language—normally regarded as the province of the middle classes. Likewise, on political grounds (as an Indigenous lesbian), she reserves the right to bestow patronage on, or withdraw it from, particular restaurants and cafés. Although it could be argued that such actions simply uphold **discourses**, images and meanings of consumer choice and sovereignty, these 'choices', in Katie's storytelling, assume the qualities of 'tactics'. These become ways of negotiating identity formation and comfort within the constraints imposed by relations of class, ethnicity, gender and sexuality. This continual balancing of pleasure and constraint through imaginative yet mundane 'tactics' returns us again to de Certeau, who describes this holding-in-tension as 'the microscopic, multiform, and innumerable connections between *manipulating and enjoying*, the fleeting and massive reality of a social activity at play with the order that contains it' (de Certeau: xxiv; original emphasis). There is much more toughness, struggle and cunning being exhibited here than a simple narrative of consumer choice would suggest.

# Luce Giard: kitchen doings.

Our third kitchen visit is brief—a final moment for reflection on the complex connections of cultural theory, narratives of everyday practices and ethnographic tools of analysis. Imagine we're sitting at the kitchen table of **Luce Giard**, French cultural theorist and co-writer with Michel de Certeau. Growing up with a well-developed feminist consciousness, Giard remembers, in the second volume of *The Practice of Everyday Life*, her childhood as one marked by a stubborn refusal to learn to cook. Later, as an adult preparing meals in her own kitchen, Giard experiences an epiphany:

> Yet my childhood gaze had seen and memorized certain gestures, and my sense memory had kept track of certain tastes, smells and colors. I already knew all the sounds … [Now, as an adult,] I learned the tranquil joy of anticipated hospitality … with moving hands, careful fingers, the whole body inhabited with the rhythm of working, and the mind awakening, freed from its own ponderousness … Thus, surreptitiously and without suspecting it, I had been invested with the secret, tenacious pleasure of *doing-cooking*. (Giard 1998a: 153)

While it might be suggested that Giard's discussion of 'doing-cooking' is overly romantic, Giard protests that she is not assuming that cooking is fundamentally women's work (1998a: 151).[9] Her project instead is to retrieve from the mundane, undervalued and overlooked routines of everyday, possibilities for inventiveness and pleasure.[10] Much of this pleasure for the cook is derived from the sensory satisfaction of *doing* something ('hands', for example, 'that slowly knead pastry dough'). Pleasure also is derived from a sense of competence: knowing 'the exact moment when the custard has begun to coat the back of the spoon'. Finally, cooking as an activity affirms the cook's identity and emotional connections ('a … practice … rooted in the fabric of relationships to others and to one's self, bound to childhood memory just like rhythms and seasons' [1998a: 157]). Nevertheless, in these tones of celebration it is hard not to detect the shadow of Nigella's goddess, or of Miriam at her most 'gorgeous', or even of Katie's now-departed cook-lover, mourned for her absence in the kitchen, if not in other respects.

Even so, Giard turns the tables on her own romance by including a full interview transcript of research she and others conducted with twelve French women in the late 1970s. Reading the interview with Irène, we immediately sense contradiction: the power of cooking to reassure the cook of her capacity to nurture, yet, at the same time, to arouse performance anxiety:

> When it comes down to it, cooking worries me, I don't know why ... On Saturdays
> I still take the trouble, especially when [my husband] Jean's kids are coming to eat
> ... On Saturday nights, it's almost a celebration when one of them comes over ...
> What I really like about having company over is having guests who are no bother,
> who can stop by unexpectedly; that way ... you manage with what you can find in
> the fridge ... [W]hen it comes down to it, I don't really feel very much at ease in the
> kitchen ... In the end, I'm not very inventive. (Giard 1998b: 225–6)

Worry and celebration, anxiety and ease: the emotional comforts of offering hospitality versus the psychic costs of giving; the satisfactions of impromptu meals versus the stresses of culinary 'theatre': all of these feelings infiltrate the dynamics of this account, with its cautious balancing of desire and constraint. In her storytelling, Irène joins a chorus of voices to which, says Giard, cultural theorists should pay more attention:

> diverse living voices that approve of, are moved, and remember themselves; voices
> that regret, answer and contradict themselves. They are voices that talk simply
> about ordinary practices with everyday words, women's voices that talk about the
> lives of people and things. Voices. (Giard 1998a: 161)

By tracking the ways voices 'regret, answer and contradict', we find that a much more subtle analysis of 'enjoying and manipulating' emerges than one simply shaped by 'good' and 'bad' cooks.

We leave the table, then, with a sense of the analytical possibilities of storytelling, of ways that everyday talk at the kitchen table can challenge taken-for-granted theoretical assertions. Nevertheless, the 'different' table, in itself, does not provide easy answers for heterosexuality's ghosts and for cultures of mother-yearning. As well, it provides no collection of recipes for queer cuisine as such. Instead, by doing ethnography as a situated, resonant practice, we have traced the multiplicity of identities brought to the kitchen table and the inventive performances produced (whether these performances involve negotiations between the kitchen's chef and *sous-chef*; the unconditional offer of 'gifts'; the simultaneous parodying and raiding of middle-class restaurant culture; the refusal to make indigenous identity exotic over an 'ordinary' cup of tea).

This returns us to that messiness of the everyday as a rich source of storytelling and reflection and, in turn, to the power of kitchen talk, in fact any talk—conversation, stories, memories, images, dreaming—to trace the ways we 'live' the everyday. Unlike that phenomenon of baking, the perfect sponge cake (with its golden surfaces, vanilla-scented sweetness and light-as-a feather textures),[11]

I suspect no story, if it is to be interesting and meaningful, is ever perfect. In fact, it is probably its 'imperfections'—those rough edges, ambivalences, tensions, those curious, quirky or simply odd details—that provide food, even whole meals, for thoughtful digestion.

## key readings

Abarca, Meredith E. 2006. *Voices in the Kitchen: Views of Food and the World from Working-Class Mexican and Mexican American Woman.* College Station, Texas: Texas A & M University Press, pp. 18–49.

Giard, Luce 1998. 'The Nourishing Arts.' In Michel de Certeau, Luce Giard and Pierre Mayol, *The Practice of Everyday Life*, vol. 2. Minneapolis, Minn.: University of Minnesota Press, pp. 151–69.

Highmore, Ben 2002. *Everyday Life and Cultural Theory: An Introduction.* London: Routledge, pp. 1–16.

## notes

[1] The significance of the kitchen table for collective remembering is elaborated in Duruz 2004.

[2] This is not to assume that everyday talk at the kitchen table is not shaped by its own frameworks of analysis. In *Voices in the Kitchen*, Meredith Abarca, examining the culinary remembering or working-class Mexican and Mexican American women, discusses the politics informing her own research practice. Abarca says that one of her decisions, methodologically speaking, 'is not to think of the women in the *charlas* [*culinarias*, culinary chats] as 'informants' for my research agenda, but as critical thinkers in their own right who use the language of food to formulate their theories' (Abarca 2006: 4).

[3] Research for this chapter is drawn from a continuing project that focuses on everyday identity negotiations through food in global cities such as Sydney, New York, London and Singapore. Specifically, this chapter is based on an extended informal interview with 'Rachel' in 2001, when she was visiting Adelaide, and one with 'Katie' in Sydney, also in 2001. In the interests of confidentiality, the real names of 'Rachel', 'Miriam' and 'Katie' have not been used in this chapter. Interviews were taped, and tapes and transcriptions are in the author's possession. All quotations attributed to 'Rachel' or 'Katie' in the chapter are drawn from the interview transcripts.

[4] Pesach (Passover) is a festival celebrating the Jews' exodus from Egypt. Families gather for a ritual meal (Seder) and prayers on the evening before Passover. Yom Kippur (Day of Atonement) is a day of fasting and contemplation, marked by a festive meal prior to the day itself and another to break the fast in the evening of that day. See Koval 2001: 10.

⁵ Historical assumptions of gendered divisions of labour—men as chefs and women as home cooks—underpin Michael Symons' (1998) analysis of the development of cooking as cultural practice. This distinction persists within the hospitality industry, with Meredith Abarca noting the comparatively small number of women who train as chefs at one of America's leading culinary institutes. See Abarca 2006: 85. Domestically, this division could translate as assumptions that women cook everyday meals while men cook the more elaborate meals for those occasions when company is expected. Nevertheless, I want to emphasise that here I am referring to 'conventional' household arrangements in regard to cooking. This is not to deny the diverse practices households (containing members of whatever sexualities, personal attachments) bring into play to handle the task of everyday food provision.

⁶ In relation to practices of giving food, especially home cooking, as gifts, see Lupton 1996: 46–9; Sutton 2001: 50–3. See also Belk's summary of classic anthropological literature, as well as literature arising from consumer research, on gifts and gift-giving (1996: 69).

⁷ 'Tracky dacks' (track pants, sweat pants) are alluded to elsewhere in Katie's interview as a phenomenon of casual evenings at home for the lesbian community, though Katie is anxious to distance herself from the wearing of these as streetwear. (She refers to friends who organise 'evenings where everyone has to wear their tracky dacks and come around looking absolute dags, you know, so you go there wearing a long coat so no one will know, [and so] … you're not on the street looking like a dag'.)

⁸ This 'no woman cooking' applies only to this example of the domestic kitchen, and is not to deny the substantial labour of working-class women in support of the fast food industry.

⁹ Probyn (2000: 38) points out that elsewhere Giard portrays the family meal as a battleground—a site of generational struggles (parents and children) over food.

¹⁰ Giard's primary criticism of Bourdieu's classic account of class-based differences in meals in *Distinction* (Giard 1988c: 183) is his failure to take dimensions of gender into account ('as is often the case with Bourdieu, feminine activities are a place of silence or disinterest') (Bourdieu 1984: 194–200).

¹¹ Santich (1996: 110–11), tracing the history of the sponge as an integral feature of afternoon teas in Australia, says, 'One particular cake became more Australian than the rest: the high and handsome sponge'.

# ethnografts.

AUTHOR: katrina schlunke

## INTRODUCTION

How does one conduct and write an ethnography of a Captain Cook in Australia? That is, how do we look at Cook as a cultural figure that produces cultural effects? The difficulty with looking at the culture that produces Cook as an important but deeply ordinary figure is that that culture is 'my' culture—white Australia. So how can I practise a kind of writing and research that will enable you to see Cook as both within 'my' culture but not only there? Is it possible to show how Cook works as both normalising touchstone for white Australia and as one potential point of opening into a proper acknowledgment of Indigenous sovereignty? This ethnography of Cook wants to show how white race claims to sovereignty in Australia work partly through a generalised, ordinary experience of white belonging and partly through the theatrical acknowledgment of the Cook story in monument and re-enactment. Thus we find Cook popping up in conversation as well as in national claims by white Australians to 'possess' Australia because

Cook 'discovered' Australia. Can the particularity of the ethnographic experience of Cook give rise to an appreciation of the ways in which normalising white culture is an onging active reinvention and a form of identity haunted by original dispossession worked through the figure of Cook? Ethnography in this piece is the studying and writing of mainstream white culture in such a way as to defamiliarise it and make it available to reformulations and reimagining. In this sense this is a simple effort to make the familiar figure of Cook strange by following Cook about as he runs into incommensurate Indigenous experience.

# the coming of Captain Cook.

It wasn't a formal thing. We were to have met for morning tea, but the Director was late and then his daughter played too long with a friend so we decided to have lunch the next day. I am being introduced to the Director through good friends who are also neighbours. They know the Director because the man of this lovely couple worked as a location manager on one of his films. The Director has bought or is thinking of buying or has just read—it is not quite clear—Anne Salmond's *Cannibal Dog*, which traces the story of Cook from Indigenous perspectives. He wants to do a Cook film. My friends and their kids are very good cooks.

The day is clear and blue and we eat outside on a rough table my friend has made. Wine is poured. Somewhere we talk about the 1960s *Oz* magazine days. A magazine that challenged ideas of what could be said or shown within the laws on censorship and obscenity and the role the Director had in those events. He is charming and self-deprecating. We drink some more and are having a very fine time. I love lunch. I love my old friends. I love my new friends. I love our conversation. Perhaps the segue was from *Oz* to Cook, for it seems sudden but appropriate that he says: 'Look I've been down to Antarctica for six weeks and I've been to Tahiti and you can't tell me Cook didn't have sex.' I have had three glasses of Sav Blanc. I don't even hesitate. 'Oh come on, think about the times, the Reformation, his contact with Yorkshire Quakers and maybe the wildness, the incredible newness of having a direct relationship with God. Not having sex with anyone but his wife might be the proof of his radicalness. Who had sex? The aristocratic Banks and the working-class sailors—the new emerging radicals were the self-made with their private God.' I am completely lucid and completely certain that I am completely right and that everyone will completely agree with me. I want to say more. I can see a whole picture of shipboard life and the play of Gods that land with them as they are told of other Gods and how the whole journey could be read as Greek parable, as odyssey not discovery.

I stop and no one notices if it was sudden or there was more to say and after a heartbeat even I have forgotten how I intended to go on. 'Who else didn't have sex?' I have no idea but because I am the Cook expert I say: 'Well, maybe Parkinson but I think Banks actually went with the idea of sleeping with the Tahitian Queen he had already heard about. And I think there was an Irish sailor on the Dolphin who had sex upon landing in front of his Captain.' Thus I say everything I know about sex and Captain Cook. Then we begin a rave about sex with strangers and we are back to assumed ideas about what sailors would have done. Some hours later as I leave I am overcome by how wonderful it could be to have an i-max high image of Cook having sex with a beautiful Tahitian woman and I tell John so (we are all on first name terms now): 'It would be great—what about Cook is true anyway? Just do it—it's fantastic, it's great.' I am sorry to leave baby boomer land where everything was possible. What is *true* about Cook?

# the coming of ethnography.

The relationship between ethnography (see the introduction to Part 6 for more on what ethnography means) and Cultural Studies has been central and ongoing. But perhaps typically of the anti-discipline discipline of Cultural Studies, the places where you find specifically ethnographic work being undertaken are varied and unpredictable. Some of the foundational texts of Cultural Studies could be described as particularly ethnographic. These are the works by Willis (1981/1977) and Jefferson and Hall (1976) with titles such as *Learning to Labour: How Working Class Kids get Working Class Jobs* and *Resistance Through Ritual*. Ethnography, with its grounded involvement with real people in a very particular cultural context, was 'crucially important in moving beyond the text' (McEachern 1998: 253, paraphrasing Willis), showing the ways in which subcultures were active cultures formed within a political project of resistance; not simply figures organised through existing representations (texts) but rather active makers of their own cultural meanings and texts.

In a similar way, but critical of the male-centred spectacles others had looked at, was Radway's work, which looked at how working-class teenage girls read their romances and created unspectacular, highly feminised cultures of the bedroom. It was the careful, ethnographic engagement with these different subcultures that revealed the deep gendered differences in how teenagers performed their cultures of rebellion. A crude summation would be that boys rode bikes and made noise and public displays and girls gossiped, smoked and rebelled privately, using their bedrooms as sites of invention where they could become teenagers together. Elsewhere ethnography became connected with audience research. For if cultural studies contended that after the author died, that is after the single authoritive power of the author to decide what a text meant was displaced by an idea that people were creative, active readers of text, we would have to discover what people did with those texts. How did they actively understand what they read, watched or listened to?[1]

Ethnographic exploration of how people understood texts (whether the text was a book, film, house, car or street) reflected Cultural Studies, interest in how new collective meanings arose and so how new cultural formations (subcultures, new imaginings of existing spaces, etc.) came into being. That is, there was and still is an interest in identifying what meanings are shared between groups and cultures as well as disputed. So Eric Michaels' finding that central Australian communities were reading Rambo (usually understood as a conservative, reactionary figure) as a rebellious, anti-establishment, Indigenous-type figure was typical of the excitement Cultural Studies experienced in finding out how people made different meanings of common texts through specific cultural contexts and particular local cultures. Is Cook a 'common text'? What meanings are made with him? How do we manage a figure around which there are both subcultural and hegemonic cultural formations?

This broad interest in how meaning was made took on a particular flavour through the influence of the Clifford and Marcus book *Writing Culture: The Poetics and Politics of Ethnography* (1986), which emerged from American anthropology and made an important textual point about ethnography. Their insight was that ethnography was, in its transmission and representation, a textual production (that is, for something to appear as an ethnography authors had to render ideas of here and there in writing), that ethnography is 'actively situated between powerful systems of meaning' (that is, it occurs between discourses of sameness and difference, centre and periphery) and that ethnographic truths are inherently partial (that is, they emerge from systems of thinking that enable the ethnography to be carried out and understood as knowledge, but it must be recognised that this knowledge is only one way of thinking and ethnography only one way of organising knowledge of others). These ideas seemed to open up ways in which ethnography could be re-engaged in a transnational, multimigrational world of competing histories and local/global identities with their multiple modes of representation. Clifford and Marcus' concern with writing also encouraged experiments and play with how an ethnography could be represented so that some of the assumptions that were traditionally hidden (like what the ethnographer's cultural context was) were exposed so that the appreciation of ethnography as a translation between cultures could be better understood. This contributed to ways of thinking that were less about discovering meanings than performing a critical creativity in relation to difference. That is, our readings of any of these texts, including Cook, require a creative recontextualisation to establish its meaning for us. This means there was no single meaning to discover that would enable a definitive knowing of any culture but ethnography could be an active participant in creating lines of translation between differences. Alternative histories of ethnography via travel writing and surrealism were '(re)discovered' to solve the crisis of representation that was said to arise once an ethnography was no longer understood as the single authoritative account of a culture. The politics of what the ethnographer was doing and why now needed to be more clearly understood to re-establish the worth of undertaking such work. Surrealism offered its politics of an expanding idea of what it is to be human and a sharp critique of 'normal society', and travel writing re-established the ethics of 'passing through' rather than acting on a different culture.

These ideas also had a particular effect within history where ethnographic history and versions of new historicism were both trying to render the story of the other side, the forgotten 'anecdote' and the need to show 'their' present in our present. They also argued that the cultural responses revealed in close textual readings of historical documents were as important for understanding the past in the present as recorded events were assumed to be. For cultural studies then, ethnography has been a practice (a methodology of interview, participation, observation), an ethos (making the familiar strange, the strange familiar), an ideology (people make cultures as they make meaning) and a style of interpretation (the ethnographic imagination gives us an impetus to imagine ourselves always in the act of translation to multiple audiences).

Finally, ethnography was a way of re-exposing the role of the ethnographer. What was our speaking position now that the taken-for-granted category of 'ethnographer' had been removed? From what cultural context were we undertaking the task of being with others? Where did 'we' come from? What possible self could be so certain of its containability and continuity that I/we/ you could be 'self-reflective of our own position'? Did we really only occupy one position, or were there many?[2] Anthropologists may have become self-critical about their disciplinary habits, but for those scholars coming to ethnography through Cultural Studies, potentially post-feminist, **postcolonialist**, post-**heteronormative**, an awareness of our own speaking position is an ordinary part of what we hope can be a supple sensitive practice. But does that help with Cook, who is all around us?

# Cook's feet.

One day a friend and ex-Shire (the shire being the Tolkienesque name given to the Sutherland Shire which includes Cronulla, where the race riots of 2003 occurred, and Botany Bay, where Cook landed) girl laughs across something I am saying and says: 'You know they used to take us on excursions to Botany Bay. And I'm sure I even saw Cook's footprints in the rock where he landed.' We both laugh and stop. And say—goddd!

# after our talk at the Cook society.

After our[3] talk at the Cook Society a woman asks: But why are people so fascinated with Cook? *Why do we love him?*[4] In our collected files we have a small desktop-published booklet made by an older woman, another friend's aunt, called, *My Love Affair with Captain Cook*. This is charismatic Cook, loved Cook. How does he appear?

# what do I do?

I am working on a project called 'Captain Cook in the Popular Imagination'. The conception of this project is partly dependent on an Indigenous perspective of Cook as a multiple, living thing. The claims that Cook made and the path into Australia that he mapped for millions of non-Indigenous Australians that would come means that every arriving non-Indigenous person is another Captain Cook, as is the very law that assumes white sovereignty over the land. There are 'too many captain cooks'—as Paddy Wainburranga says (Wainburranga & Mackinolty 1982). Cook is a force of proliferation in this thinking; he is living reproduction and at each point of reproduction he continues to break Indigenous law as he did on his first visit. We[5] therefore wanted to investigate places where Cook was recogniseably alive  and paid attention to in non-Indigenous culture. Where was he ritually bought back, revivified in mimetic, imagined performances at re-enactments and festivals but also in archives and exhibitions and everyday life? Where was the force of proliferation, of more and more Captain Cooks that he represented to Indigenous peoples to be found in non-Indigenous settings? We visited particular places, have had specific Cook experiences and seen him come to us out of the ordinary, suddenly noticeable within our ethnographic task where before he was all wallpaper. It is through Indigenous ideas about what white people do that we begin to see ourselves as more Captain Cooks, too.

The ordinary Cook, who looks a lot like me, is certainly of interest, but you will see how this day-to-day Cook is a concept? An idea? A moveable brand? an image or taste that does not have the seemingly satisfying idea of developing an intimate and personal relationship with people or persons that ethnography usually presumes? Cook is not distinct enough and not alive enough to report his individual peculiarities—we can only encounter the way in which white Australia makes him live on as many of us live on. Cook will not be able to be queried by an ethics committee—did Schlunke conduct herself ethically in the field, for he is long dead? But who I am having verifiable relations with are those people who attend the Cooktown re-enactment, who sail in the *Endeavour*, who themselves somehow been linked to him or made a deliberate home with him.

# the event of history.

Quite clearly the project of thinking about Cook in the popular imagination is one where we do not simply 'look at Cook', although the visual is a very important part of the work. And I am not simply 'reading' Cook, though the textual turn is assumed in my approach to artefacts and journals. Instead I would claim that we experience Cook. He is an event rather than an historical figure. He happens across bodies, he is 'a processual becoming'.[6] As an organism arising in a naturalised history he gathers diversities together in (sometimes momentary) unities. Thus Cook, when depicted as the 'discoverer' of Australia, brings together and resolves the deep differences between invasion, violence, enlightenment thinking, Indigenous response, the difference between the east coast and the Australian nation, and so on. To think of Cook in this way way gives his claims a magic that has not been nationally denied or undone, and so he lives on in those claims. There has been no identified break that a treaty with Indigenous people might produce, for example, that enables us to think of Cook as 'past'.

It begins to seem peculiar to refer to this Cook as 'he' when he is so surely not a 'thing', and yet that unifying gender helps to establish the physicality, the responsiveness, the livingness, the changefulness of the creature and the sense that Cook is a series of events that both reproduce existing orders of whiteness and provide enough variety to belie the unchanging order of white tenure of Australia.

Perhaps in a similar way I hesitate at the word 'whole', but how else to refer to the evolving colonialism, the formation of fan clubs, the volunteers, the flows of money, the everyday, the acts of 'preservation', the private and public, the 'immanent system of capitalism'[7] that come together in 'Cook'. Does it become obvious why I would claim that my approach is ethnographic? In traditional ethnographic terms I would claim that I live with Cook. I would claim that this event has persistently and consistently challenged my own cultural assumptions about who I am and what I might become. That he was always there and so therefore I did not need to leave home to find him makes his presence more painful, for as he is revealed in his white original claim to Australia, which was hinged on violence, so is mine. He is not still enough to operate as simply a screen upon which I can project my fears and doubts and connect to other mediated beings, but neither is he stable enough to wholly attach to. As a temporal organism he refuses to be 'got'. To be 'got' would be to have the authoritative knowledge of him that would hold him in place to be known and displaced, but since he works as a plurality, as many, that can never be done. Ethnography has also traditionally valued time—years in the field—and time must be spent working one's way with this time-travelling creature. In a more prosaic way, spending time is also an antidote to a language of 'outcome' and 'profit'. Like slow food, the principles of slow thinking are suitable for a moment in time where earth and human have to renegotiate relationships and we have to consider how much time we can spend learning to evoke difference adequately and ethically. 'Doing ethnographic research' is an expensive enterprise in an economy where time has been given a dollar value.

But still I will have to communicate the experiences of these Cooks and so I would like to think about the *grapho* (see Chapter 16) of ethnography for a moment. To write about is very different from writing with or even within. Ideally perhaps we should be able to 'duplicate in the writing something about the culture itself' to quote Taussig.[8] But the cultures of this event, this Cook, with its similar, same, ordinary parts might also require some other techniques lest we fail to notice the Cookism that white Australia operates through. So how to ethnographise that which is made ordinary? One path is to return to the writing of the ethnography and display more accurately the desirous and connecting relationships that come into being through that writing. I think of the writing and the relationships that come into being through those inscriptions as 'ethnografts'.

# ethnografts.

The first meaning of the verb 'graft' is to insert a shoot or scion (a descendant) into a groove or slit made in another stock so as to allow the sap of the latter to circulate through the former. Think of this historically. Something inserted into a groove (like in the groove, swinging)—have you got the particular cultural space where lives can mingle (in the groove, swinging)? Think of this culturally. Something inserted into a slit (a. open along a line) (b. render into strips) (*Colloq.* vagina) so that the sap, the life force, the blood/knowledge can circulate through the former (to be settled *into* or in a routine of work) (to dance, to listen with great pleasure, to make good progress, to make love, to give pleasure, to get on well *with* someone).

The second meaning of 'graft' refers only to the 'twig or off-shoot for use in grafting; a scion, a sucker'.[9] A descendant and a parasite making new life or monsters or making something that would have to be called graft growths and graft hybrids. With 'ethno' preceding this graft we have an emphasis on what is productive. What relationships through what slits and grooves will make for 'the sort of sensible actuality' that 'makes it possible to think not only realistically and concretely *about*' our 'mega concepts', but 'what is more important, creatively and imaginatively *with* them'.[10] Exactly, Professor Geertz. But what choice can we have to think *with* or not when the sap of another runs through the sucker, the pliable part of ourselves able to produce? And is *with* powerful enough to let us see the tiny intracellular forms coming into being? We do not have writing, we have production. In other words, how can we think *with* when we are also within Cook? The ethnograft makes a space for where Cook re-enters my culture, where I can see him where I could never see him before. The graft marks the space of encounter and struggle as his insertion is seen within 'our' culture. We have grafts, ethnografts. These are cultural makings that will enable the ordinary of Cook to become extraordinary and thus seen in his relatedness to a power grid of representation that is actively producing that ordinariness. We can do such work by how we perform him, by placing incommensurate things beside one and other as Muecke (1992) suggests, or even a use of allegory as Clifford (1986) and Benjamin[11] do, or we can sit with him rather than within him and practise new ways of not so white culture.

# days before the re-enactment of Cook taking possession of the east coast of Australia at Cooktown, Queensland.

In a shop where you can send a fax and buy bait I am talking to the man who fires the cannon in the re-enactment. It is, he says, the only cannon like it in the state. At one stage he had to travel down to Brisbane and make a direct and personal visit to the state minister to get permission to go on firing the cannon. There is a suspicion of terrorism when someone owns gunpowder these days. Conversation that ran around this Cook point was all about the National Park locking land up and the Alcohol Management Plan. My notes are not good:

We could lose the Cooktown festival.

Too many bloody cops, too much paperwork.

Lots of others have been here—I'm happy to see Chinese or Arab landings.

Before this terrorism nonsense you could carry as much black powder as you wished, now it's a permit for everything.

The police stopping all the cars in and out of Cooktown—that was payback.

We stopped the spread of the Alcohol Management Plan from DOGITS (something he explains is a kind of land tenure that exists on Aboriginal land) 'cause it is about equal rights. The AMPs are unconstitutional, everyone has a right to drink. Cooktown is part of the catchment area where people come from dry areas to drink. But if they don't let them drink at home where it's safe where are they going to go?

# talking to Pastor George at Hopevale.

Stephen is recording Pastor George, an elder of the Indigenous Hopevale community outside Cooktown, and one of the stories he tells is about how his people were poisoned. The only reason I'm here, he says, is because my grandfather (great grandfather?) was at school. That other woman who was here, she (her mother? grandmother?) survived because she was too small. She didn't need any of that flour.

# the day of the re-enactment.

At 6.10 a.m. the lights come on at the Cook's Landing Kiosk, Cooktown, northern Queensland for a 7 a.m. start. With the lights the pigeons begin to coo. At 10 a.m. the outdoor church service is held. It is somewhere in the order of Pentecostal. People call oh Jesus after some sentences or sometimes just a word. Sometimes it is oh, oh Jesus like a Hollywood orgasm. The preacher's point on Cook is that he brought supplies. Some of the supplies they didn't like, like sauerkraut, but it kept them safe. God's supply is infinite—it never ends even if you don't always like it. Oh Jesus, oh, oh, Jesus.

# earlier on the day of the re-enactment.

Hilda, a woman from Hopevale, who carefully made the green turtles from papier mâché that will feature in the show, the re-enactment, is sewing leaves together. Another woman sits quietly watching. Hilda says: 'I'll make sure I turn my back to them Cook. Next time we might take that Cook on a honeymoon.'

This ethnograft is both the writing and what it might do with you the reader. At worst it is a set of overheard statements, mundane activities and possibilities that are sat next to one and other in a puzzling way. At best this writing is also a productive relation that bends time around so that we can imagine Cook in more useful ways—in ways that give proper weight to his aliveness while asking why white Australia feeds so consistently upon the dead. The ethnograft actively seeks to defamiliarise the ordinary Cook so that the culture that would make him ordinary and unremarkable is itself rendered strange. This is doing ethnography.

# days before the enactment.

In the CWA tea rooms an older man reminisces about another re-enactment—could have been twenty years before. When the local guy playing Cook landed someone yelled out, 'Go home ya pommie bastard!'

## key readings

Clifford, James 1986. 'On Ethnographic Allegory.' In *Writing Culture: The Poetics and Politics of Ethnography*. Berkeley: University of California Press.

Dening, Greg 1996. *Performances*. Melbourne University Press.

Wainburranga, Paddy, and Chips Mackinolty 1982. 'Too Many Captain Cooks.' In *Aboriginal Australians and Christian Missions: Ethnographic and Historical Studies*, Special Studies in Religion, No. 6.

## notes

[1] See critiques and questions of the ethnographic status of this work in Nightingale (1993) and McEachern (1998).

[2] See Leiris's *Manhood* for what an inconsistent self might produce. Or see Probyn (1993) for another tack on this idea.

[3] These talks are a part of the dissemination of the research undertaken by myself, Stephen Muecke and Jan Idle.

[4] We are waiting for the video of this event to confirm the exact words.

[5] This project is being conducted with Stephen Muecke with research assistance from Jan Idle.

[6] Barbara Kennedy (2002) uses the idea of event with regard to cinema to displace the film from the representational and visual with that of the technologised or assembled body. Similarly, when looking at places and times where Cook arises even within a formal national, institutional setting the effort is not to think representationally but 'sensationally' about what we not only see but 'feel' and inscribe into legislation.

[7] Deleuze's useful description of capital whose only limit is itself.

[8] Taussig as quoted by Emily Eakin in the *New York Times*, 21 April 2001.

[9] Adapted from Oxford English Dictionary Online. Oxford University Press, 2007

[10] Geertz, quoted in Eipper 1998: 323.

[11] Walter Benjamin's use of allegory is neatly summarised in Geyer-Ryan 1994: 21.

# 7

# text, sensation and writing.

# the stories so far.

AUTHOR: katrina **schlunke**

## redoing the world.

Why would we think about the sensations the voice produces? The ways we could reimagine a city? The possibilities of conversation on a fabulous tram? The following three chapters put us into the world as participants, readers and makers of meanings. They challenge us to look again at what we think we might know and know it differently. That different knowing may arise from a different way of making sound with our voice, a different way of walking the already known city, and lead to a different way of writing that is not so much a critical reflection as an embodied infection! All three chapters explore in very different ways the extension of established thinking about the world working through 'texts' to consider instead how sensation, forms of writing and sound could enable us to re-order, re-enchant and thus re-know the world around us. Perhaps unlike previous parts of the book, Part 7 emphasises *how* we listen, work and write as large experimental categories rather than the more organised headings you have previously encountered. In this sense there may be a greater emphasis on doing rather than reading, or doing as reading that you might want to think about as you read.

# text.

The idea of the text has been central to how Cultural Studies has enabled multiple ideas and practices to be recognised in the richness of their multiple meanings. A text can be defined as anything that can be analysed or produces meaning, whether it be a book, a film, multimedia (websites, advertising, etc.), architecture, the environment or the body, or even more abstract things like ideas, concepts, feelings, the senses. If we are able to think of the body or a car as a 'text' we can begin to 'read' those entities in multiple ways. Thus we can begin to think of a body 'written' upon in particular ways, for example by the wearing of certain clothing, literal inscription in the form of tattoos (see Chapter 6) and even obeying certain codes so that the body might work 'like a language' and become identified as a body that belongs to a particular culture; surfer or Australian for example. Similarly, a car can be read not only by how it appears but the uses to which it is put in a particular context. Therefore the same car that is correctly read as a V8 Holden will within the language and practices of a street race become understood as a potential threat to public order by police or as a participant in a subcultural activity by fellow racers. Equally, phenomena that have been traditionally dismissed as mass or popular culture items such as Mills and Boon romances or *Big Brother* can be examined for the ways they work through genre conventions and audience responses and how they might challenge larger cultural values about high and low culture. Saying and showing that something has meaning is a very political act, as is the dismissal of something as meaningless. Think for a moment about who and why one group will say opera is without meaning and another that hip hop is. What access to funding, venues and participation does such a judgment bring forth? Think about the different people who will make up those groups. To 'read' a text is a very different act from simply understanding a 'text' as a part within an act of communication. Beyond simply communication the text becomes understood as a pleasure, intervention and strategy. That is (to return to the body and car example) the possibilities of what the body or car *could* mean are returned to them instead of leaving them stuck in a single discourse of the 'natural' or the 'mechanical', for example.

The reading of things and making meanings from them is an extension of **Roland Barthes'** thinking about authors and books. In his chapter *The Death of the Author*, Barthes took up **Saussure's** notion of the arbitrariness of the sign to argue that there is no one true meaning in a text and that meaning does not only reside in the text itself or in the meaning intended by the author (see Part 2 for more on this). Genre and grammatical conventions will of course organise the meanings given to particular texts and potentially limit the possibilities of what it could mean, but it is the act of reading/interpreting those possibilities that produces the 'meaning of the text'. As Barthes (1977) put it: 'The reader is the space and where all the quotations that make up a writing are inscribed without any of them being lost: a text's unity lies not in its origin (author) but in its destination.' There is no single reference to which we can return for the 'correct' meaning; rather, the meaning of any text is produced by readings conducted with the text. As a result of Barthes' focus on the reader, the phrase 'death of the author' has become shorthand for the elevation of interpretation over intention, and is seen crudely as a characteristic of poststructuralism. But perhaps more tellingly, Barthes' insight has provided a means by which texts (including traditional works of literature such as Shakespeare) become even more richly appreciated as we see what meanings are given to them in contexts as diverse as India and prisons. It has also led to the positive recognition of diverse populations and cultures as creative meaning-makers. As Threadgold puts it:

> The consequences of such a theory (e.g. intertextual and non-referential nature of the production of meaning) for the critic are immense: no longer able to 'read' the meaning in 'the words on the page', critical activity becomes a creative activity of recontextualisation, thus making the critic as much responsible for the production of meaning as is the originary text or author. The line between creative and critical work all but disappears, as both become part of the larger human processes of language and meaning production. (Threadgold 2005: 345)

Threadgold's identification of this style of reading as critical and creative is key to appreciating the enabling practice of 'textual analysis'. It also leaves a space for the more contemporary and global use of text, which can be deliberately or through multiple cultural translations become cut up, reorganised and moved around the world in a huge variety of ways.

# representation.

Meaning-making is also connected to the idea of representation, since how we represent something has traditionally reflected how we will display and communicate the meanings we have made. But to represent something requires an appreciation that we share certain cultural codes (as we can all more or less agree what a pair of spectacles is even if the specific colours or shapes differ) and that communicating the meaning of any object uses language that itself depends on codes of grammar and styles of usage. Representation is therefore a re-presenting of something within culture and language in order to communicate or share meaning.

The recognition that we are limited in the meanings we can articulate by underlying systems that rule language and the possible was one of the profound insights of structuralism (see Part 2). Structuralism suggested that we know everything relationally. That is, we know something by what it is not. That is, we understand a cat is a cat because it is not a dog and also because it is not a tiger.

The particular identity of our pet cat can be expressed only by knowing it is not someone else's cat or a wild cat. Within structuralist thinking the pet cat has no 'true' meaning but can be considered as a site of explanation. What conditions enable this cat to be understood as 'pet'? These might include that it is allowed inside rather than outside, that it is domestic rather than wild and that a market exists that supplies pet food, cat trays and pet shops that confirms 'pet cats' are a recognisable category. Structuralism also recognised that these relational systems worked with people (**subjects**) and things (materiality) and indeed made them up, constituted them, but in ways that were not necessarily obvious to the individual. Think, for example, of the ways in which 'white' and 'heterosexual' can work very powerfully precisely because they are in many ways unseen or assumed (see Part 5). Without specific markings—for example, 'This makeup is for white skin only' or 'Viewers should be warned: the following film contains heterosexual themes'—the culture enables the naturalisation of those categories. People will not be reminded on a daily basis that they are not black, are not homosexual and therefore not a usual representation. This limits what it is possible to imagine. Structuralism did not therefore accept that there was an essential 'human nature' or that historical narrative could be an assumed explanation of why events occurred; rather, the question to be asked was why do we explain the past in terms of a narrative of progress?

Poststructuralism has been understood very generally (see Part 2 for more detailed explanation) as an unwillingness to explain phenomena via a dependence on an underlying structure, and to explore instead the ways in which texts are always escaping or exceeding the relational system that they exist within. Another way of thinking this would be to say that language is a self-sustaining system in which words have no necessary relation to things. We need to have these general ideas in the back of our minds to appreciate the different kind of texts that these three chapters explore.

# voice.

So far the brief examples I have given have been things of various material orders: cars, bodies, cats, and so on, but what if you want to think about the meaning of something that is a sense, a corporeal phenomenon rather than a thing? How can we think about voice? Does it still make sense to consider it some sort of text, or rather as something that generates its own meaning? To propose as Theo van Leeuwen does that we can tense our vocal musculature to make a sound? 'The resulting sound not only *is* tense, it also *means* tense and *makes* tense.' Van Leeuwen uses John Shepherd's term 'physiologically coded' semiotics of the voice to describe a semiotics in 'which the voice is what it means and means what it is, and in which meaning is made with the body, and understood on the basis of bodily experience'. But this is not a chapter that argues that 'voice' is in some way outside representation or beyond representation, but rather that 'speech is material and experiential as well as semiotic and social'. That is, the meaning that the body makes of sound as well as the experience of producing sound needs to be accounted for as much as the way in which speech gains meaning through a system of recognisable signs and cultural context. So, on the one hand you could understand this chapter as a reconfigured and extended structural account, one that seeks to extend and enhance what the possibilities are in how we can understand the meanings of voice within a relational system. On the other hand you could understand this as a poststructural account in that it is interested in disturbing the opposition between the voice as physiological and voice as social communication. In 'adding in' the body and physicality of voice production to the meaning of speech, the idea and the experience of speech open up and reveal what had been assumed but not spoken of: that sound includes the body and the effects it produces needs accounting for in this context. By listening we interpolate the text that is speech into our world, but equally perhaps as the sound is produced there develops a range of physiological phenomena that resonate, touch or move us. Accounting for both the affective and reflective within communication is to potentially change the ways in which we assume meaning can be made. By concentrating on voice we can also appreciate that we are always making meaning, even when that meaning is usually recognised as physical, as a sensation and as produced with the body. But perhaps sound as text rather than speech as text already enables us to appreciate that the subject is sensate as well as cognate, feeler as well as thinker, and that these two realities cannot really be divided when we hear.

# flaneur.

But maybe before we can write or think the sensational we have to experience it or become aware that we are experiencing it. In Tara Forrest's chapter this is articulated through the example of the practice of the flaneur, a practice that is a 'rejuvenation of the capacity for perception and imagination'. This is the advocacy of a practice that will change how you think. It is an experiment in disrupting the habitual practice and theory of how we move within and know the city. This challenge is to our very conception of the world. Forrest uses the thinking of **Walter Benjamin**, a figure who was identified with the Frankfurt School rather than any school of structuralism. The thinkers of the Frankfurt School were concerned with providing a critical theory of **Marxism** and were curious about how consciousness shapes how we understand the world. The city has never been a 'text' in Benjamin's thinking, but his thinking is connected to the more expanded semiology and poststructuralist efforts explained above through the emphasis on the radical possibilities of sensation. Forrest begins by imagining Benjamin coming out of the cinema, which Benjamin also believed could reconfigure how we experienced the world. In this correlation with film it is perhaps easier to see the ways in which the idea of experience can transform how we think and practise something like a film. To understand a film as an experience rather than a set of moving images makes us rethink not only what a film is but also question the assumed separation between 'film' and 'viewer'. In this chapter film and a style of walking the city can make the ordinary extraordinary. This volatility of cultural surroundings is something that connects with ideas of postmodernity (see Parts 3 and 5) and the idea that we live within multiple gazes and mediascapes, none of which promises an entire cultural reality. But the point for Benjamin in re-experiencing the city as sensational was to expose the daily habits that kept a certain bourgeois order in place and prevented people becoming aware of alternatives to those inscribed habits. These experiments would let us expand our imaginations and 'blast the prison of conventional reality'.

# beyond writing.

When we think about something like voice and recognise that it is also something produced through cultural forms we challenge any easy idea of the 'truths' of experience. The experience of closeness when we listen to the breathless chanteuse can be 'explained', as van Leeuwen has shown. But equally, our experience of the voice may not be wholly contained by a 'feeling' of closeness. Certain voices combined with music or memory or both may render us estatic, morbid or formless. In a different kind of way, the experiments we conduct on how we do or could experience the city may excite or disturb us, give rise to an excess of responsiveness and shatter our sense of our own capacity to represent in any ordinary way that particular experience. In this sense certain kinds of experience challenge representation. If representation usually assumes the making of meaning and often the bringing together of different contexts in that act of meaning-making, there must also be moments when new sensations come into the world that cannot easily be assimilated to an idea of representation per se. It is not quite that language fails but that it stutters, is unable to summon together enough shared concepts and enough coherently connected historical experience with which to communicate our sensational event. The situations where such embodied moments arise may not all be catastrophic, like the failure of 'progress' that was the Holocaust, but the way your foot may start tapping after you pass through a shop playing a music you don't know but your toes do. This is a kind of contagion rather than representation and its unconscious immediacy suggests a body presenting rather than re-presenting. This idea of an immediate knowing, and finding ways to mimic such moments to continue the contagion rather than contain it, is the inspiration for numerous efforts to both experience the world differently and write the world differently.

# fictocriticism.

What if you want to think and so write your material differently? What if you want to write in a way that reflects the experience that arises from the coming together of events with histories of hierarchies of knowledge and you want to do something more than represent something but rather evoke an event or sensation or new politics? Stephen Muecke's piece of **fictocritical** writing can be understood as both post-representational and perhaps post-textual, which should not make the pleasure you take in it any less! But it is useful to consider what a certain sort of writing tries to achieve when it wants to both be the argument and make the argument. This kind of writing is not representational, as Muecke makes clear; the effort here is not to set one meaning of the tram text against another and another and to reflect which one works the best, but rather to 'create momentum'. What might this mean? You will remember how above in the brief outline of structuralism one of its key insights was that we know the world relationally—that is, through knowing something is not something else, we know a cat because it is not a dog and so on, and that poststructuralism can be characterised as an intervention into that system of oppositions. But what if you 'know' something neither through relations of difference nor through a language system where words and things have become disconnected? What if instead you claim to experience (not necessarily to know) an event through sensation and by thinking the particular difference of a particular experience? Now here we do not mean the relational difference (something is not something else) but the changeability, multiplicity and chance that difference can also produce when recognised within a thinkable chaos, as Deleuze has written about. A tram is not a cat or a car but it has a particular kind of smell, a rare beauty in this case, a place for talking; like a train, it is connected to tracks, to the world, to fears of terrorism. Connect this thinking with Muecke's radically flat Latourian environment where people and things, nature and culture are always entwined and neither is privileged and you have a particular kind of event. This is where matter, material and movement meld together as momentum: something that carries that new meld, that assemblage somewhere else. The work of this kind of writer is to create the momentum that will allow this new meld to move between other spaces, knowledges and worlds. This writing seeks to capture the processual (what was arriving and what is coming next and next) and not the representative where meaning coalesces in text. It is also a call to trust the demands of the situation we might find ourselves in to change our writing practices. In this way we will be able to respond directly to the truth that is particular to the tram itself and not a larger idea of the social or the political, although the tram's truth will ideally move those others along. Practising fictocriticism might produce a mutant thinking, a sensational engagement and encourage a rethinking and re-enchantment within our lives.

Thus we have here in these last three chapters three very different takes on what sensation can produce. It can expand what semiotics could be, it can challenge us to write differently, and it can transform how we inhabit the world. Each of these chapters shares an ethic of experimentation. Experiments on the body to show we can make and be tense through the production of voice; experiments with writing to produce momentum that will flatten hierarchies between orders of nature and culture and pay attention to the contingent; and connective realities and experiments on our own experience of the city to see if we can re-sensationalise the world around us.

# THINKING WITH PART 7

1   Listen to several pieces of vocal music and try through experiments with constrictions and loosening of the throat to imitate the sound. Do the sounds you produce have a bodily, emotional resonance? Can you name them?
2   Experiment with a friend by talking about something intimate and walking closer and further away. Do the same thing while talking about the weather. What do you observe?
3   Become a flaneur. Walk your usual path to the train or bus stop but do it very, very slowly. What happens? Does your appreciation of the city begin to change? Conduct other experiments that might help you re-experience the usual rhythms of the city. For example, sit quietly (and safely) on the corner of the busiest city intersection and write some poems. Come up with your own ideas and see if they fit with Forrest's point.
4   Find a thing that makes you think (and eventually write) differently. The paths to doing this might be many. For example, think about the shoes you wear, who made them, what they do, what they let you do—can you see how you are a part of shoesness? When you are in your shoes where do they end and you begin? Do they speak or connect with you and you with them?

# CHAPTER NINETEEN

# metaphors of voice quality.

AUTHOR: theo van leeuwen

## INTRODUCTION

The Gwen Stefani song 'Bubble Pop Electric' evokes a 1950s teenage date: 'Drive in movie. Drive in move me'. The setting, that era of 'penny loafers and poodle skirts', and the impatient anticipation of 'petting' in the backseat of a car are portrayed not just by the lyrics but also by the timbre of Gwen Stefani's voice, which alternates between seduction, as she addresses her boyfriend in a low, breathy voice ('Tonight I'm falling, won't you catch me'), and a teenage pop feel as she repeats the words 'Bubble Pop Electric' in a higher, tenser voice with a somewhat artificial ('electric') sheen. Just as her music combines many different styles, so her voice has many different registers, allowing her to express complex feelings and complex identities.

In this chapter I will suggest a way of understanding and appreciating how meanings are made with the voice itself, rather than with the words it speaks or the notes it sings. To do so I use two key concepts, metaphor and **connotation**, starting with the former.

# metaphors of voice quality.

Many writers on metaphor follow the age-old example of Aristotle in seeing metaphor as a key source of semiotic innovation. 'Ordinary words convey only what we already know', said Aristotle, in the 4th century BC (Aristotle 1954: 1410b), 'but it is from metaphor that we can best get hold of something new'. In his view this was less a matter of creating new ideas than of creating new ways of *expressing* ideas, though we will see that metaphors can also create new ideas and new practices. In literary theory this Aristotelian concept of metaphor has been dominant. According to Terence Hawkes:

> We think of metaphor as a direct linguistic realization of personal experience. Even banalities such as 'like a sledgehammer', 'a hot knife through butter', 'a bull in a china shop' aim at a 'vivid', 'striking' and 'physical' quality that relates *accurately* to events in the world. (Hawkes 1972: 17)

But Hawkes also points out that many philosophers and poets see metaphors not as depicting reality, as in the quote above, but as *creating* reality. The 18th-century Italian philosopher Giambattista Vico, for instance, wrote that abstract and analytical modes of thinking and writing evolved out of the metaphors, symbols and myths that, long ago, created the reality we experience and that are still deeply ingrained in the language we use today. This idea has been taken up in a number of ways in the 20th century, for instance by anthropologists such as Lévi-Strauss (1962) and linguists such as Benjamin Lee Whorf (1956), and more recently by Lakoff and Johnson (1980: 211), who see metaphor as 'one of the most basic mechanisms we have for understanding and expressing experience'. Most metaphors, they say, were once innovative, but are no longer. We do not even think of them as metaphors. They are the 'metaphors we live by', to use their telling phrase. Lakoff and Johnson call such metaphors 'structural', because they entail a whole complex of ideas. The metaphor 'theories are buildings', for example, entails such a complex of ideas, making it possible to say things like 'we've got the *framework* for a *solid* argument', 'if you don't *support* your argument with *solid* facts, the whole thing will *collapse*', and so on (Lakoff & Johnson 1980: 98). In other words, the structure of a building can become a vehicle for understanding the structure of theories.

A key element in Lakoff and Johnson's metaphor theory is their view that we understand metaphors on the basis of our concrete experience: 'No metaphor can ever be comprehended or even adequately represented independently of its experiential basis' (Lakoff & Johnson 1980: 19). This is a crucial point, because it suggests that new metaphors, and hence new concepts, can be founded on the affordances of direct, concrete experiences. These experiences may be bodily experiences that are shared by all humans, for example walking upright. But they may also be interactions with our environment. The experience of transporting goods, for instance, can become a basis for understanding communication, as when we speak of the *senders* and *receivers* of messages, the *sign vehicle*, and so on. Such experiences are likely to be less universal than physical experiences, and metaphors based on them will therefore be less likely to be universally understood. Finally, they may be interactions with people, and these will be even more culturally specific, even more determined by specific social, political, economic and religious practices, as in the case of Susan Sontag's discussion of the way illness can be understood on the basis of practices of colonialism and military conquest:

> Cancer cells do not simply multiply, they are '*invasive*' ('malignant tumors *invade* even when they grow slowly', as one textbook puts it). Cancer cells '*colonise*' from the original tumor *to far sites* in the body, first *setting up tiny outposts* ('micrometastases', whose presence is assumed, though they cannot be detected). Rarely are the body's '*defences*' vigorous enough to obliterate a tumor that has *established its* own blood *supplies* and consists of billions of destructive cells. (Sontag 1979: 64–5; italics mine)

In each case, concrete experiences, some purely physical, some culturally mediated, form the basis for metaphors that create a certain way of understanding some aspect of the world we live in.

Metaphors of voice quality are based on the physical experience of articulating sounds and therefore quite widely understood, which does not mean of course that they are always valued in the same way. Vocal tension is a good example of such a physical, bodily metaphor. Try it. When you tense your vocal musculature, your voice becomes higher, sharper and brighter, because in their tensed state the walls of the throat cavity dampen the sound less than they would in their relaxed state—an equivalent difference would be that between footsteps in a hollow tiled corridor and a heavily carpeted room. The resulting sound not only *is* tense, it also *means* tense and *makes* tense. We can recognise tension in our own voice and in the voices of others, and we also know *when* our voice is likely to become tense: when we are nervous, or anxious, or intimidated, or threatened, for instance. This complex of bodily experiences constitutes the meaning potential of vocal tension. It allows a metaphorical transfer from the domain of experience to the domain of more abstract ideas and values and identities. Literal tension can become metaphorical tension, expressing anything that can be said to have a component of tension in its meaning. Alan Lomax wrote of the high degree of tension in the preferred female singing styles of cultures with severe sexual repression of women:

> It is as if one of the assignments of the favoured singer is to act out the level of sexual tension which the customs of the society establish as normal. The content of this message may be painful and anxiety-producing, but the effect upon the culture member may be stimulating, erotic and pleasurable since the song reminds of familiar sexual emotions and experiences. (Lomax 1968: 194)

In the next few sections I will explore some further metaphors of voice quality. It should of course be remembered that voices combine a *range* of vocal features, each one deriving from specific articulatory gestures. Voices are high or low *and* soft or loud *and* tense or lax and so on, and all these features are capable of fine gradation: there are many different pitch registers and many degrees of loudness and tension. And meaning derives from all of these features, in their specific combinations.

# pitch range.

Our experience of pitch range tells us two things: men's voices are, on average, lower than those of women and children, and smaller resonating chambers (for example violins) produce higher sounds than larger resonating chambers (for example double basses). As a result low voices can be threatening (in operas the tenor is the hero and the bass or baritone the villain), while high voices can be used to make ourselves small and harmless, as in talking to children. But people can adjust the pitch range they use, whether to suit the context or to express more permanent identities. This inflects the gendered meanings of pitch range in complex ways. Men use the higher regions of their pitch range to assert themselves and to dominate; only the very highest regions (for example the counter-tenor) may become ambiguous in gender terms. A man who speaks low is trying not to be dominant, trying to make himself vocally small by mumbling, and the booming bass is usually considered overbearing. Women, on the other hand, use the lower end of their pitch range to be assertive. But, as it is difficult to be low and loud at the same time, they face a dilemma. They must either speak low (which is assertive) and soft (which is intimate), which can evoke the 'dangerous woman' stereotype, or high (belittling themselves) and loud (being assertive), which may be considered 'shrill'. In either case the dominant norms of the public, assertive (and 'masculine') voice are at odds with the dominant norms of the private, intimate (and 'feminine') voice.

Male news readers speak at a higher pitch level when they are on air than in their ordinary 'low-key' speech (Van Leeuwen 1983). Women news readers do the opposite. Poynton (1996: 8) describes how the same announcer, as 'Patricia Hughes', used 'a dark voice (the voice of authority) in reading the news on the Tasmanian "highbrow" station 7ZL', while as 'Patti, your Thursday bird', she used 'a lighter hyper-feminized voice to introduce herself on the "popular" station 7ZR'. Iconic female voices enshrine such meanings in public consciousness. Marilyn Monroe used a high yet breathy voice, combining 'feminine' vulnerability and seductiveness. Lauren Bacall used a sensuous low voice. In her autobiography she recalls how Howard Hawks conceived of her character for *To Have and Have Not* (1944) as 'a masculine approach—insolent. Give as good as she got, no capitulation, no helplessness' (Bacall 1979: 87). To this end Hawks not only invented 'the look' for her—a quizzical look upwards with the head slightly bowed, suggesting feminine deference as well as insolence—but also told her to work on her voice, to 'practice shouting, keeping my register low' (1979: 92).

# voice level.

The loudness of the voice relates to social distance, both literally and figuratively. As explained by Edward Hall (1964, 1966: 184–5), at 'very close range' (3–6 inches) our voice will be a soft whisper, whether for reasons of intimacy or conspiracy. At 'close range' (8–12 inches) our voice is still a whisper, still meant to be heard by one person only. At 'near range' (12–20 inches) our voice will be soft indoors, and 'full' outdoors, but still low enough not to be overheard by strangers. At 'close neutral range' (20–36 inches) we still tend to speak about 'personal matters', and softly, while at 'far neutral range' (4.5–5 feet) we tend to speak about 'non-personal matters' in a 'fuller' voice. At 'public distance' (5.5–8 feet) our voice will be 'full with slight over-loudness', conveying 'public information, for others to hear'. Beyond that we are no longer talking to one person but to a whole group.

Before amplification, there was a one-to-one relation between voice level and social distance. Voice level would signify actual relationships, along the lines suggested by Hall. Amplification has changed that. A soft, breathy whisper can now be heard by a crowd, and the screaming of rock singers can be played at a comfortable background level. Level now constructs imaginary relations, whether in acting, in singing or in public speech. In singing, the 'crooning' style of Bing Crosby pioneered an 'intimate, personal relationship with fans that worked best with domestic listeners' (Frith 1988: 19). When the movies acquired sound tracks, actors had to wean themselves away from the projected voices of 1930s box office plays and adopt more intimate, close-up styles. At the same time, politicians began to replace oratory with conversational speech, as in President Roosevelt's 1930s 'fireside chats', which addressed listeners in 'calm, measured statements … as though he were actually sitting on the front porch or in the parlour with them' (Barnouw 1968: 8), and radio speakers, too, learned to adopt low-key conversational manner (Cardiff 1981), so as to 'sound like the listener's best friend' (Leitner 1980).

# roughness and breathiness.

In rough voices we can hear other things beside the tone of the voice itself: hoarseness, harshness, rasp. The opposite of the rough voice is the clean, smooth, 'well-oiled' voice from which all noisiness is eliminated. Much of the effect of 'roughness' comes from the a-periodic vibration of the vocal cords which causes noise in the spectrum (Laver 1980: 128). As this is more audible in the lower pitches, it is more easily heard in male voices and in lower female voices. Perhaps this is why rough voices are especially common in male singing and highly valued in cultural contexts that encourage assertiveness and enterprise (Lomax 1968: 192). Again, the meaning of roughness lies in what it is: rough. Our experience tells us that roughness comes from wear and tear, whether as a result of smoking and drinking, hardship and adversity, or old age. The rough voice is the vocal equivalent of the weatherbeaten face, the roughly plastered wall, the faded jeans, the battered leather jacket. The smooth voice is the vocal equivalent of unblemished young skin, polished surfaces, designer plastic, immaculate tuxedos. How this is valued depends on the context. In Western classical music perfection and polish is highly valued, in Afro-American music roughness:

> In most traditional singing there is no apparent striving for the 'smooth' and 'sweet' qualities that are so highly regarded in the Western tradition. Some outstanding blues, gospel and jazz singers have voices that may be described as foggy, hoarse, rough or sandy. (Courlander, quoted in Williams-Jones 1975: 377)

In the breathy voice, another sound mixes in with the tone of the voice itself—breath. Its metaphor potential derives from our experience of what can make our voice breathy: exertion of some kind, excitement, sexual arousal. Breathiness often combines with a soft voice, suggesting intimacy. Advertisers use it to give their message a sensual, erotic appeal, and singers use it for the same reason.

## resonance.

Shepherd (1991) has discussed the voices of different kinds of rock singers. 'Hard rock' voices are rough, loud and high. Their timbre reminds of shouting, or even screaming. Resonance is produced almost entirely in the throat and the mouth. According to Shepherd (1991: 167), this 'reproduces tension and experiential repression as males engage with the public world'. In a female rock singing style that Shepherd describes as the style of 'woman as emotional nurturer', the voice is soft and warm, relatively low and with an open throat. It uses the resonating chambers of the chest, says Shepherd, so that the voice literally comes from the region of the heart or the breast. Softer male singers such as Paul McCartney tend to use the head as resonator and therefore sound 'lighter and thinner':

> The typical sound of the woman-as-sex-object involves a similar comparison. The softer, warmer, hollower tones of the woman singer as emotional nurturer become closed off with a certain edge, a certain vocal sheen that is quite different from the male-appropriated, hard core timbre typical of 'cock' rock. Tones such as that produced by Shirley Bassey in 'Big Spender', for instance, are essentially head tones,

and it could in this sense be argued that the transition from woman the nurturer to woman the sex object represents a shift, physiologically coded, from the 'feminine heart' to the 'masculine head'. (Shepherd 1991: 167–8)

Shepherd's discussion shows that singing styles are always a combination of features: 'soft' *and* 'warm' *and* 'hollow' *and* 'low and open' *and* 'coming from the heart or breast', and that meanings such as 'woman-as-nurturer' result from the way in which these features are combined. The famous voice of Marlon Brando in *The Godfather* (1972) is another example. It is a comparatively high voice, and we have seen that men tend to use high voices to dominate. It is also hoarse and rough, signalling the Godfather's harsh and unforgiving side. And it is articulated with a stiff jaw and an almost closed mouth, suggesting an unwillingness to 'give' that keeps us guessing as to what he might be keeping from us. Yet it is also soft and breathy, at times almost a whisper, making the Godfather's menacing presence disturbingly intimate and attractive.

# connotation.

So far I have sketched a 'physiologically coded' semiotics of the voice, to use John Shepherd's term, a semiotics in which the voice is what it means and means what it is, and in which meaning is made with the body, and understood on the basis of bodily experience. Such experiential semiotics comes to the fore in times of semiotic change, and the 20th century, with its new communication technologies, has certainly been a period of such change.

For a time voices had been disciplined towards uniform standards of educated propriety, and actors and singers had been schooled in singular aesthetic ideals. This had never meant complete uniformity. On the contrary, it had allowed for subtle forms of individuality and distinction, more or less in the same way that the cut of apparently almost identical grey business suits can signal subtle degrees of sartorial elegance and finesse. But amplification changed all this, allowing actors and singers to develop their own, immediately recognisable timbres. Voices such as those of Lauren Bacall, Marilyn Monroe, Jimmy Stewart, Marlon Brando and others built a new semiotic resource, a new language of the voice, as did the singing voices of Ray Charles, Bob Dylan, Nina Simone and Astrid Gilberto, to name just a few.

Dialects and accents were part of this as well. In the era of semiotic uniformity, their meaning had been indexical, signalling people's class, gender, age. Often they had stigmatised the speaker. To upper-middle class city dwellers, country dialects were backward, working-class dialects inferior and foreign accents either suspect or funny. They carried the kind of connotations **Barthes** (1973) called 'myths' and denoted with terms such as 'Italian-ness' to indicate that they condensed everything the 'bourgeoisie' 'knew' about Italians as well as the value judgments they attached to it into a single, diffuse concept. Much of this still lingers. The story of *Pygmalion* is still understood. Yet much has changed. In the early 1930s MGM worried about Greta Garbo's accent, but her voice was to become another key icon in the new semiotics of voices. Soon Hollywood scriptwriters would recommend the use of accents and dialects: 'Dialect ... is as revelatory as make-up, as picturesque as costume, as characteristic as gestures, as identifiable as physical disabilities, and as dramatically effective as facial expressions' (Herman 1952: 198). As a result, a wide range of dialects and accents would soon be familiar to movie audiences the world over, their meanings as easily understood as those of the clichés of classic Hollywood musical scores.

Once dialects, accents and vocal styles are no longer seen as a kind of fingerprint, an indelible social marker, they lose their ties with specific places or social groups and develop into a medium of expression. Speaking 'broad Australian', for instance, is no longer a matter of destiny, indexing the milieu in which you happen to be born, but a choice of how much to associate yourself with 'Aussie' lifestyle and values. And 'cool' young people everywhere pick up token elements of the speech of Afro-American rappers. The same goes for vocal styles. As Michel Chion has noted, actors' abilities as actors go beyond the mastery of accents:

> There is timbre, the way of creating a voice that is hoarser, more metallic, more full-throated, more sonorous, or less harmonically rich. Compare two roughly contemporaneous Dustin Hoffman movies. In Barry Levinson's *Rain Man*, he has a metallic and nasal voice and in Stephen Frears' *Hero* it is coarser. If you listen to both films without the picture, it is quite difficult to identify both voices as coming from the same actor. (Chion 1999: 173)

Marlon Brando's hoarse whisper is now part of the repertoire of many American actors, to be deployed whenever a sense of brooding yet sensuously attractive menace is required. And unlike Lauren Bacall or Marilyn Monroe, a singer like Gwen Stefani (and others like her) no longer cultivates a single style, but can alternate between vulnerable 'feminine' timbres, low, sensual timbres, hard, tough timbres, and much more, using her repertoire to convey contradictions and complexities, as for instance in 'What Are You Waiting For?', a song in which she alternates between excitement about her success ('You're still a superhot female') and insecurity about whether she can sustain it ('a scary conversation shut my eyes can't find the brake').

In a famous article on the singing voice called 'The Grain of the Voice', Roland Barthes made a radical contrast between language and voice quality. On the one hand, he said, there are 'the features which belong to the structure of the language being sung, the rules of the genre, the coded form of the composer's idiolect, the style of the interpretation: in short, everything in the performance which is in the service of communication, representation, expression'. On the other hand there is 'the grain of the voice', 'the materiality of the body speaking its mother tongue', 'something which is directly brought to your ears in one and the same movement from deep down in the cavities, the muscles, the membranes, the cartilages'. The 'grain of the voice', he argued, affects the listener in a deeply personal, almost erotic way, escaping the semiotic and the social (Barthes 1977: 179ff). Kaja Silverman (1988: 44), similarly, called the voice 'the site of perhaps the most radical of all subjective divisions—the division between meaning and materiality'.

As we have seen, the voice does engage the body—all of it—'the cavities, the muscles, the membranes, the cartilages'. But I do not think that this is opposed to 'communication, representation, expression'. On the contrary, the voice and its meanings can only be fully understood on the basis of paying close attention to the physicalities of articulation, as I have tried to do in this chapter. Speech is material and experiential as well as semiotic and social.

On the other hand, as a new 'language' of voice quality emerged, the voice gradually ceased to be 'the body speaking its mother tongue'. Although its meanings still derive from bodily experience, this became less foregrounded and voice qualities began to be understood on the basis of cultural connotation, on the basis of familiarity with the movie roles and songs in which they had been used. Another socially and culturally coded semiotic regime took over from the physiologically coded regime that gave birth to it. As speech synthesis proceeds, this new language of the voice may well harden into much more bony-structured and binary technological codes. Sound engineers can already enhance recorded voices, turning up the tension a little, or adding a touch of synthetic breathiness. Nevertheless, it is always possible to go back to the source, always possible to reconnect with the body, with the physicality of voice production, and to explore the many possible voices and the many possible meanings that have not yet entered into the mainstream of cultural production.

key readings

Barthes, Roland 1977. *Image-Music-Text*. London: Fontana, pp. 179–90.
Shepherd, John 1991. *Music as Social Text*. Cambridge: Polity, pp. 164–73.
Van Leeuwen, Theo 1999. *Speech, Music, Sound*. London: Macmillan, pp. 125–55.

CHAPTER TWENTY

# 'botanising on the asphalt': benjamin and practices of flanerie.

AUTHOR: tara forrest

## INTRODUCTION

> For two hours I walked the streets in solitude. Never again have I seen them so.
> From every gate a flame darted; each cornerstone sprayed sparks and every tram
> came toward me like a fire engine.
>
> (Walter Benjamin 1997a: 89–90)

I like to imagine that **Benjamin** is writing about the experience of walking
through the city after attending a film. Not just any movie, but an experimental
city film like Walter Ruttman's 1927 *Berlin: Symphony of a Great City*—a montage-
driven movie that hurtles (like flashing neon or a speeding train) towards the
body of the viewer. I picture him leaving the cinema and being taken aback by the
commotion of the city, its familiar goings on rendered magically strange by the
jarring configuration of the urban environs of *Berlin*, where slippery wet neon, the
hubbub of a station, the facade of a building reflected in the pavement flash up
and disappear again like the fast-moving train that surges across the screen in the
opening minutes of the film.

But Benjamin isn't writing about the experience of walking through the city after attending the cinema. The passage is taken from 'Ordnance', a fragment in 'One-Way Street' describing his arrival in Riga in 1925 to visit his friend Asja Lacis. Benjamin (1997a: 68) writes: 'Her house, the town, the language were unfamiliar to me. Nobody was expecting me, no one knew me'. So for two hours he wanders around the city in a state of solitude, his lack of familiarity with Riga affording him a sensitive, proximate relationship to the goings-on of the city. Trams scream across his path like fire engines and lights shoot towards him with the power of ordnance.

And yet, as Benjamin points out later in 'One-Way Street', this close, tactile relationship to an environment with which one has not yet become habituated is always short-lived. As soon as you begin to find your bearings in a place, as soon as those streets or trams become paths to home or means for getting you to work on time, the palpability of their initial impression—of colours and details which *impress* themselves on the body of the spectator—seems to dissipate. As the routes between home and the station, work and a café, the bus stop and a friend's house become well-travelled paths, that close, tactile relationship to stimuli (so palpably captured in Benjamin's snapshot of his arrival in Riga) grows into an insensitivity to, a spacing out from, that environment. Once habit, Benjamin (1997a: 78) writes, has begun to do its work, 'that earliest picture can never be restored'.

Underpinning Benjamin's analysis of the desensitised, habitual manner in which big-city dwellers (both in Benjamin's time and our own) frequently engage with their everyday environment is a broader concern about the decline in the capacity for perception and experience that he associates with life in the city. A key text in this regard is Georg Simmel's 1903 essay 'The Metropolis and Mental Life', which had an important impact on Benjamin's understanding of the perceptual and experiential effects generated by urban environments (Simmel 1997). In this influential essay, Simmel (1997: 175) claims that the 'psychological conditions' created by big-city environments differ significantly from those characteristic of life in the country. He argues that, in stark contrast to the slow, steady pace of rural environments, the big-city dweller is constantly bombarded by a broad range of stimuli (from crowds, traffic, flashing lights) and that over time, and as a way of coping with this bombardment, we become anaesthetised to stimuli. We space out from our environment, and engage with our surroundings in a 'blasé', one might even say absent or mechanised fashion (1997: 178). Employing terms discussed by Susan Buck-Morss in a different, albeit related, context: within this schema, our 'synaesthetic system' (that cognitive faculty which synthesises perception with memory and bodily sensation) is transformed into an 'anaesthetic' that numbs us from the excess energies characteristic of life in the city (Buck-Morss 1993: 130–2; see note 53).

What is interesting about Benjamin's writing, in this context, is the degree to which he explores the role that certain practices could play in prompting the habituated urban dweller to experience his or her environment and, as a consequence, him or herself, in a radically different manner. Foremost among these writings are Benjamin's reflections on the flaneur: a figure who takes delight in wandering around the city in a highly reflective, unhurried fashion. For Benjamin and, indeed, for Charles Baudelaire (whose writings acquainted Benjamin with practices of flanerie) the flaneur's journey is not motivated by a desire to get from A to B, but rather by a fascination with the various stimuli characteristic of urban environments. 'The street', Benjamin writes,

> becomes a dwelling for the flaneur; he is as much at home among the facades of houses as a citizen in his four walls. To him the shiny, enamelled signs of businesses are at least as good a wall ornament as an oil painting is to a bourgeois in his salon. (Benjamin 1997b: 37)

As Benjamin makes clear, the flaneur is not drawn to the kind of attractions that are earmarked in tourist guidebooks. The sites and structures that appeal to him are not famous buildings, statues, towers or monuments to the past. Rather, the flaneur finds himself irresistibly drawn to the minutiae of everyday environments. He is, as Benjamin points out, 'happy to trade all his knowledge of artists' quarters, birth places, and princely palaces for the scent of a single weathered threshold or the touch of a single tile' (1999: 263). Benjamin describes this practice as 'botanising on the asphalt' (1997: 36), a phrase that evokes the gentle, inquisitive manner in which the flaneur engages with his environment: homing in on samples, so to speak, placing them under the microscope of his gaze and, in the process, rendering strange (and sometimes magical) those everyday aspects of his environment that are ordinarily traversed in a habitual, absentminded fashion.

In his 1938 essay 'The Paris of the Second Empire in Baudelaire', Benjamin's analysis of the significance of the flaneur's practice emerges in the context of his delineation of an activity that originated in Paris in the first part of the 19th century. 'Around 1840', Benjamin writes,

> it was briefly fashionable to take turtles for a walk in the Arcades. The flaneurs liked to have the turtles set the pace for them. If they had had their way, progress would have been obliged to accommodate itself to this pace. But this attitude did not prevail; Taylor, who popularised the watchword, 'Down with dawdling!' carried the day. (Benjamin 1997: 54)

The reference to Frederick Taylor is important in this context because it demonstrates the degree to which Benjamin viewed the activities of the flaneur as a form of protest against the increasingly regimented nature of life associated with the development of big cities and modern industrialisation. Taylor was an American engineer who, in his 1911 study *The Principles of Scientific Management* (1967), developed a model via which industrial labour could be rendered more efficient. Following the practices outlined in this model (which subsequently became known as 'Taylorism'), managers observe and measure the amount of time and energy required to complete a particular task and then carefully calibrate the movements and activities of their workers in order to maximise profit and efficiency. Within this schema, a production line worker, for example, may be given one and a half seconds to screw a bolt into a panel—a task that he or she must repeat for hours on end in a highly mechanised, automated fashion. As illustrated to great comic effect in Charlie Chaplin's 1936 film *Modern Times*, people labouring under Taylorist conditions are only able to express themselves through reflex actions, because they are not in a position to set the pace for themselves.

If Benjamin, quoting Georges Friedman, notes that 'Taylor's obsession … is the "war on flanerie"' (Benjamin 1999: 436), then it is because the flaneur described by Benjamin is someone who set his own pace or, indeed, someone who, in some cases, allowed a turtle to set the pace for him. In stark contrast to the worker labouring under Taylorist conditions, the flaneur's activities are not organised around, or temporally geared towards, the production of a particular outcome. Rather, the flaneur is much more interested in exploring the degree to which his slow, relaxed pace enables him to reflect upon the world around him. Time, in this sense, is thus figured as a luxury that only some people can afford, and certainly, the image of the flaneur described in Benjamin's writings is often a wealthy figure—'a gentleman of leisure' (1997: 54)—who could afford to spend his time as he wished.

In the context of discussions of flanerie in the 1800s, the flaneur is almost always referred to as a male figure, mainly because, when it came to wandering the streets alone, women weren't afforded the same luxuries as men. In fact, if a woman walked alone in the city (and at night, in particular), she became known as a 'street-walker', a title that was synonymous with being a prostitute. As Buck-Morss (1986: 119) has pointed out, 'the flaneur was simply the name of a man who loitered; but all women who loitered risked being seen as whores, as the term "street-walker" or "tramp" applied to women makes clear'. Indeed, as Anne Friedberg (1993: 34) has argued, it wasn't until the development of the department store (a space in which it was publicly acceptable for women to wander around alone 'just looking') that the female flaneur or 'flaneuse' was born. According to Benjamin (1997: 54), the shopping arcade also served as one of the last refuges for the activities of the 19th-century flaneur, who discovered that, with the advent of big-city traffic, it was simply no longer safe to wander around town—at a turtle's pace—absorbed in one's thoughts.

If the practice of walking turtles was a short-lived affair, the rejuvenation in the capacity for perception and imagination associated with the flaneur's practice nonetheless exerted a significant influence on Benjamin's writings and, more specifically, his exploration of the various means by which we could put ourselves back in touch with our everyday environment. For Benjamin argued that it was only by undoing our perceptual habits and, by extension, our habits of thinking, that we could open up a space in which the possibilities of life could be reimagined outside the highly circumscribed, regimented mode of existence characteristic not only of Taylorist working environments, but of life in the city more generally.

In order to demonstrate the degree to which Benjamin's interest in, and reflections on, flanerie are imbricated with his writings on a diverse range of topics, the remaining sections of the chapter will provide an overview of three of the avenues that Benjamin himself explored in his attempts to conceive of the extent to which our capacity for perception and imagination could be rejuvenated by a range of different practices, each of which bears an interesting connection to the activities of the flaneur, but which encourages us to think about flanerie beyond the image of the flaneur as a 19th-century, well-to-do male figure.

# hashish.

In the notes on flanerie contained in *The Arcades Project*, Benjamin (1999: 417) writes that an 'intoxication comes over the man who walks long and aimlessly through the city'. In his description of his arrival in Riga and indeed in his reflections on foreign travel more generally, this state of intoxication is manifested in the heightened perceptual acuity that he experiences upon arrival in a foreign city. In the 1920s, however, Benjamin became interested in the effects of drug intoxication more specifically and, in 1927, he took part in a series of experiments with hashish that were to take place sporadically over the next seven years. As per his interest in flanerie, Benjamin's research into the perceptual effects generated by hashish intoxication was inspired, in part, by Baudelaire's writings on the topic in *Artificial Paradise*, and his delineation of the role that the 'magnifying mirror' (Baudelaire 1971: 43) of hashish could play in fostering a different kind of relationship to habitually traversed environments.

As Benjamin notes in 'Myslovice-Braunschweig-Marseille', his experiments with the drug are not fuelled by an escapist desire to immerse himself in a realm apart from his environment. Rather, in keeping with his analysis of the flaneur's practice, he is much more interested in the way in which hashish estranges him from, and thereby resituates him in a relationship of proximity to, aspects of his environment that are ordinarily traversed in a desensitised, absentminded manner. He writes:

> I do not believe that what induced me to take some hashish at around seven o'clock in the evening, upstairs in my room, was the unworthy desire to escape my depressed mood. It is more likely that this was an attempt to yield entirely to the magic hand with which the city had gently taken hold of me by the scruff of the neck. (Benjamin 1999: 389)

In his notes on the effects of the drug in 'Hashish in Marseille', Benjamin describes an encounter with this 'magical hand' (or 'magic wand' as he otherwise refers to it) in his delineation of the extent to which his experiments with the drug rejuvenate his perceptual and experiential relationship to his environment (1999: 678). The drug places him in a kind of trance, and yet it is a very different state to the absentminded, automated state that he associates with habit. If the latter condition is characterised by a distance from and insensitivity to environmental stimuli, hashish induces in Benjamin a close, tactile relationship to his environment. For example, in 'Hashish in Marseille', Benjamin describes the extraordinary tenderness to his environment induced by the drug: 'It was not far from the first café of the evening, in which, suddenly, the amorous joy dispensed by the contemplation of some fringes blown by the wind had convinced me that the hashish had begun its work' (1999: 678). In *Artificial Paradise*, Baudelaire expresses a similar sentiment: '[A] new sharpness—a greater keenness—becomes apparent in all the senses. The senses of smell, sight, hearing and touch alike participate in this development' (1971: 54).

However, as Hermann Schweppenhäuser (1995: 35) has pointed out, this 'increase in sensitivity' induced by the drug is, for Benjamin, 'not an end in itself but a medium' through which a different spatio-temporal relationship to his environment arises. In his preliminary remark to 'Hashish in Marseille', Benjamin writes:

> One of the first signs that hashish is beginning to take effect is a dull feeling of foreboding; something strange, ineluctable is approaching … Images and chains of images, long-submerged memories appear … All this does not occur in a continuous development; rather, it is typified by a continual alternation of dreaming and waking states, a constant and finally exhausting oscillation between totally different states of consciousness. (Benjamin 1999d: 673)

Crucial here is that these 'states of consciousness' are not dependent for their existence on the attention or concentration of the **subject**. 'This process', Benjamin writes, 'may result in the production of images that are so extraordinary, so fleeting, and so rapidly generated that we can do nothing but gaze at them' (1999e: 329). In 'Hashish in Marseille', these images (a fringe blowing in the wind, the contour of the pavement, the glow of a light) shoot from Benjamin's path and ignite in him traces of other moments, and memories of different, strangely familiar, environments.

# film.

In a similar vein to his writings on hashish intoxication, Benjamin argues in his highly influential essay 'The Work of Art in the Age of its Technological Reproducibility' (2003) that the significance of film lies not in its capacity to immerse us in a realm removed from our environment (such as out of space, or a period of history with which we are unfamiliar) but in its ability to re-sensitise the audience to aspects of their environment that are ordinarily traversed in a disengaged, absentminded manner. He writes:

> To put it in a nutshell, film is the prism in which the spaces of the immediate environment—the spaces in which people live, pursue their avocations, and enjoy their leisure—are laid open before their eyes in a comprehensible, meaningful, and passionate way. In themselves these offices, furnished rooms, saloons, big-city streets, stations, and factories are ugly, incomprehensible, and hopelessly sad. Or rather, they were and seemed to be, until the advent of film. The cinema then exploded this entire prison-world with the dynamite of its fractions of a second, so that we can take extended journeys of adventure between their widely scattered ruins. (Benjamin 1999f: 265)[1]

The fragmentary film practice outlined by Benjamin in this passage performs a similar function to his analysis of the perceptual effects induced by hashish. By placing a 'prism' between the spectator and his or her environment, the spectator is able to gaze anew at that which 'had previously floated unnoticed on the broad stream of perception' (Benjamin 2003: 265). 'Clearly', Benjamin writes, 'it is another nature which speaks to the camera as compared to the eye. "Other" above all in the sense that a space informed by consciousness gives way to a space informed by the unconscious' (2003: 266). Employing examples reminiscent of those sketched out in the observations he wrote while under the influence of hashish, Benjamin notes that although we are

> familiar with the movement of picking up a cigarette lighter or a spoon, [we] know almost nothing of what really goes on between hand and metal, and still less how this varies with different moods. This is where the camera comes into play, with all its resources for swooping and rising, disrupting and isolating, stretching or compressing a sequence, enlarging or reducing an object. It is through the camera that we first discover the optical unconscious, just as we discover the instinctual unconscious through psychoanalysis. (Benjamin 2003: 266)

Such a film practice could be said to achieve what Benjamin's contemporary Siegfried Kracauer describes as 'the redemption of physical reality'. Like Benjamin, Kracauer is interested not in dialogue-driven films that are organised around complicated narratives, but in films that reveal to the audience 'hidden aspects of the world around us' (Kracauer 1997: 49). In a passage reminiscent of Benjamin's reflections on the plant photographs of Karl Blossfeldt (1999g), Kracauer claims that '[i]n magnifying the small, the camera exposes to view fantastic shapes too tiny to be normally noticed'. These close-ups, he writes, 'cast their spell over the spectator, impressing upon him the magic of a leaf or the energies which lie dormant in a piece of cloth' (1997: 280).

For both Kracauer and Benjamin, the significance of such images lies not only in the degree to which they disclose (albeit in a larger format) familiar aspects of our everyday environment but, rather, the extent to which they fundamentally challenge our previously held conceptions about the material world. Paraphrasing Benjamin, Kracauer states that the significance of such images lies in the extent to which they 'blow up our environment in a double sense: they enlarge it literally; and in doing so, they blast the prison of conventional reality, opening up expanses which we have explored at best in dreams before' (Kracauer 1997: 48).[2]

# travel.

Throughout the 1920s and 1930s, Benjamin spent long periods travelling outside Germany, partly because he was an avid traveller and partly because he was forced to secure an existence for himself at a safe distance from **Nazi** Germany. Throughout the 1930s, in particular, Benjamin spent extended periods living in France, Spain, Russia and Denmark, and he frequently kept diaries and notebooks in which he recorded his impressions and experiences.[3]

As discussed earlier in relation to Benjamin's account of his arrival in Riga, one of the broad observations that can be made in regard to these writings is that what interested Benjamin about the experience of travel, in particular, was the degree to which the lack of familiarity that one experiences upon arrival in a foreign city affords the traveller a sensitive, proximate relationship to the goings-on of the city. As per his snapshot of Riga, what is fascinating about Benjamin's city portraits—including 'Naples' (1997c) (which was written with Asja Lacis), 'Moscow' (1997d) and 'Marseille' (1997e) in particular—is his interest in the degree to which the sensitivity to detail that a foreigner experiences upon arrival in an unfamiliar city can shed a different light on aspects of his/her environment to which he/she has become habituated. As Peter Szondi has pointed out, 'the picturesque and exotic' do not 'lure' Benjamin into a state of 'self-forgetfulness', but rather enable him to reflect upon his own environment, and himself, 'with an estranged vision' (Szondi 1995: 21).

What is particularly interesting about Benjamin's cityscapes, and his 1928 portrait of Marseille in particular, is the way in which he attempts to re-present the city in a manner that both resonates with, and reproduces for the reader, the sense of estrangement that Szondi is referring to here, effects which anticipate the possibilities that Benjamin attributes to film. If 'Marseille' is particularly interesting in this regard, it is because both its fragmentary structure and its subject matter resonate strongly with the kind of film practice outlined in Benjamin's 'The Work of Art in the Age of its Technological Reproducibility'.

Constructed out of ten image fragments (the titles of which include 'Walls', 'The Light', 'Cathedral', 'Noise', 'Shellfish and Oyster Stalls') Benjamin's portrait of Marseille cuts between images of steps, arches, turrets and bridges, the glow from a street lamp, the facade of a building, a ship in the harbour, a mountain of shellfish. Demonstrating a capacity for perception that resonates with the flaneur's practice, Benjamin's eyes pan across walls strewn with *Chocolat Mernier* and the latest aperitif, to the down-and-out at nightfall and a beggar in the street, to rue de Jamaïque and Bar Facultatif. Cut cut cut between a kiosk and a railway station, a café and 'Les Bricks', a weather-beaten doorframe and the sound of flapping linen (Benjamin 1997e: 209–14).

In contrast to 'Marseille', 'Moscow' is not strictly organised around a series of image fragments. And yet, despite this, a number of passages in 'Moscow' read, and feel, like a fragmentary sequence from a city film:

> Beams of excessive brilliance from the car headlights race through the darkness. The horses of the cavalry, who have a large drill around the Kremlin, shy in their light. Pedestrians force their way between cars and unruly horses. Long rows of sleighs transport snow away. Single horsemen. Silent swarms of ravens have settled in the snow. The eye is infinitely busier than the ear. The colours do their utmost against the white. The smallest coloured rag glows out of doors. Picture books lie in the snow; Chinese sell artfully made paper fans, and still more frequently, paper kites in the form of exotic deep-sea fish. (Benjamin 1997d: 180)

Although the sensitive, proximate relationship to the city captured, and rendered palpable, here is predicated on the traveller's experience of an unfamiliar place before habituation has taken place, the fragmentary (one could argue *filmic*) structure of Benjamin's writing encourages us to reflect on the way in which an experimental city film like *Berlin: Symphony of a Great City* (with its close-ups of street signs and oncoming trains, bustling crowds and neon-soaked pavements) could be said to resensitise the audience—and thereby foster a different spatio-temporal relationship—to aspects of urban environments that are ordinarily traversed in a desensitised, absentminded state.

While the perceptual and experiential effects generated by such a film practice are neither causally nor experientially the same as Benjamin's description of the rejuvenation in the capacity for perception and imagination facilitated by hashish and foreign travel, by drawing these practices into a constellation we can begin to get a sense of what fascinated Benjamin about the flaneur's practice of 'botanising on the asphalt', the curious, tactile dimensions of which are encapsulated in his reflections on the experience of growing up as a child in Berlin:

> Not to find one's way in a city may well be uninteresting and banal. It requires ignorance—nothing more. But to lose oneself in a city—as one loses oneself in a forest—that calls for quite a different schooling. Then, signboards and street names, passers-by, roofs, kiosks, and bars must speak to the wanderer like a cracking twig under his feet in the forest. (Benjamin 1999h: 598)

## key readings

Benjamin, Walter 1999. 'Convolute M (The Flaneur).' In *The Arcades Project*, trans. Howard Eiland and Kevin McLaughlin. Cambridge, Mass.: Harvard University Press.

Gleber, Anke 1999. *The Art of Taking a Walk: Flanerie, Literature and Film in Weimar Germany*. Princeton University Press.

Tester, Keith (ed.) 1994. *The Flaneur*. London and New York: Routledge.

## notes

[1] This passage also appears, in an altered format, in Benjamin 2003: 265.

[2] See also Benjamin 2003: 265.

[3] See, for example, Benjamin 1986.

CHAPTER TWENTY-ONE

# momentum.

AUTHOR stephen muecke

figure 21.1: Melbourne tram decorated in *chamak patti* style

stephen muecke

How much momentum can a thing have, to drive itself through the mere prose of the world, scattering myths and misconceptions? Can a *thing* really have the force to make us *think*? Maybe thinking is not a very self-generated activity at all. Maybe we should think again about the interiorising metaphors of mind, and, indeed, about the Judaeo-Christian asceticism that would make thought the reward of monastic seclusion. I prefer to think that thought runs on surfaces and turns itself always outwards towards things, so we wonder at the world, so present to us in all its strangeness. 'It is', says anthropologist Michael Taussig,

> more like having the reality depicted turn back on the writing, rather than on the writer, and ask for a fair shake. 'What have you learned?' the reality asks of the writing. 'What remains as an excess that can't be assimilated and what are you going to do with the gift that I bestow, I who am such strange stuff?' (Taussig 2006: vii–viii)

We are shocked when birds fall out of the sky over the town of Esperance in Western Australia. This happened over the summer, in 2007. In asking why, we gaze at these sad, dead, beautiful things and let their symptoms speak to us. We gather them, along with our tools, our microbiology labs, with all their chemicals and machines. All these things are assembled to make an argument. This argument is no longer your private thought; it has become a political position because it is a collective response to a serious matter of concern. And let us admit, with the philosopher Bruno Latour (2004), that this collectivity is not just a human one, but an assemblage of humans and non-humans, dead birds, chemicals, scientists, mass spectrometers, news reporters. It seems in the end that these birds were 'fallout' from the Western Australian resources boom that is giving us our tax cuts. They died from lead poisoning at this ore-exporting port, named in 'hope' by late 18th-century French explorers.

I was excited when Mick Douglas emailed and asked if I wanted to go on a tram ride in Melbourne. As soon as I saw the tram, on his website, I was enchanted by the beauty of the object. It is a standard Melbourne tram, but every inch of it, inside and out, is decorated in the beautiful *chamak patti* style of appliquéd multicoloured plastic. The special decoration of the tram was created by Mick, an artist and RMIT University academic who brought the team of decorators out from Pakistan. He writes on the TRAMTACTIC website:

> Lead chamak patti wallah (decorator) for the W-11 TRAM Nusrat Iqbal marks the other-worldly connections of his work with a simple sign on his Alli Walli workshop: W-11 Karachi 2 Melbourne. He displays no images of his work on vehicles though, as he thinks showing examples only limits his clients' willingness to take a risk with the decoration for a new job. He wants to be invested with his clients' trust. (www.tramtactic.net/)

In order to do his work, Mick Douglas had to assemble the elements, all of the things: the tram, of course, the support of the Melbourne City Council, the funding, the artists, the talent, and, not least, the *trust*. I want to dwell on this abstract concept in this essay, because, when it comes to Pakistan, Mick had to work against a deficit of trust. When he arranged for the team of *chamak patti* wallahs to come from Karachi, it was during the Commonwealth Games, and the immigration controls were very very stringent. After all, given the immense desirability of Australia as a place to live, can these guys be trusted not to slip the cordon and then claim refugee status? Can Pakistan, and by extension, Pakistanis, be trusted when that country, as we all know, *harbours terrorists*?

Trust is one of those 'more than human things' (combining a concept, a word, an **intersubjective** practice) that binds us socially, but it can split and break when pressed too hard, the fissures in trust becoming the rigid divisions of hatred. You cannot bring trust into being with a simple pronouncement. A few days ago, before I came to write this, a Centre-Right president was elected in France. Nicholas Sarkozy addressed a jubilant crowd of supporters at the Place de la Concorde in Paris, and his first words were, 'Je ne vous trahirai pas', I will not betray you, as if to solicit a trust that was already lacking in his connection with the whole nation to which he is bound in responsibility by virtue of his office, by virtue of his placement at the 'head' of this social 'body'.

So trust, like hatred, like hope and fear, is distributed around the social body, and we are always curious to trace the contours of that human geography: *my mother said/I never should/play with the gypsies in the wood*: *Those* ones, over *there* are not to be trusted, and fear creeps in. But close to home, we trust our loved ones instinctively, those with whom we share *protection, comfort* and *truth* (all in the etymology of the Nordic word at the origin of 'trust'). There, in our intimate relationships, the ties that bind are wound with the threads of trust, but not of belief. Because if I *believe* you, it is because you have convinced me this time. Belief is induced by knowledge, as the philosopher **Alphonso Lingis** says. But trust is induced through the intuitions that come of experience and time spent together; it is 'built up'; as an artwork is constructed by assembling forces that are aligned and work well together, trust depends on alliances. So I can trust you without believing you, and that is why trust is a very handy thing for politicians. Lingis further explains his vision of trust:

> Trust is a break, a cut made in the extending map of certainties and probabilities. It adheres to something or someone with a force that is not that of knowledge and conviction. This force, which breaks with the cohesion of doubts and deliberations, is an upsurge, a birth, a recommencement. It has its own momentum, and builds on itself. How one feels this force! Before these strangers in whom one's suspicious and anxious mind elaborates so many scheming motivations, abruptly one fixes on this one, at random, and one feels trust, like a river released from a lock, swelling one's mind and launching one on the way. The initial act of trust maintains itself only in extending itself, only in yet more acts of trust. (Lingis 2002: 99)

On the flight to Melbourne I am still excited about the invitation to participate in a 'Tram Overheard' event. I have spoken with Mick on the phone about the stranger he is lining me up to meet. The idea is for us to go to Federation Square, climb aboard, be given wireless mikes, and just talk, about anything. We will be having a random conversation as passengers get on and off randomly, and we will travel on a circuit around the city. Then we will relax as music is played on another circuit, and then there will be a performance, 'Tram Overboard', with live musicians or others kinds of performers.

On the plane I think about what I know about trams with a view to being spontaneous in conversation, always a slightly terrifying thing to do. In Sydney, of course, we are tramless, having decommissioned in the 1950s what was the largest tram system in Australia, second only to London in the Commonwealth. There were 1600 cars in service at its peak in the 1930s, while Melbourne has only about 500 in service today. When anyone thinks of Sydney trams, they think of the expression 'shoot through like a Bondi tram', and I always imagine a tram going too fast down the Bondi Road hill and then taking the corner into Campbell Parade on a dangerous lean before reaching the beach.

Sydney had high-capacity trams taking huge numbers of guys wearing grey felt hats to the Cricket Ground or the racecourses on Saturday afternoons. These were called toast-rack trams, because they had cross-bench seats, with a number of doors on each side and no corridor. Because he couldn't walk through, the conductor would collect the fares by moving down the footboards on the outside (www.abc.net.au/rn/rearvision/stories/2006/1755249.htm).

And I also think about going to Melbourne once, coming back to the place I was brought up, standing somewhere in Carlton and suddenly feeling a wave of nostalgia, a visceral feeling, not knowing where it came from. Then I realised I was looking at a tram. Its bell said *ding ding* and it rattled off in a friendly way.

Raimond Gaita, in an essay called *Breach of Trust*, goes straight to the heart of my political discussion of trust. 'George W. Bush has been re-elected decisively', he wrote in 2004,

> and we are still enlisted in his war on terror. He asked the American voters to trust him. Tony Blair has asked the same of the British voters. John Howard did it first, I believe. To him, it appears, the world owes the novel idea that, in politics at least, one might distract attention from mounting evidence that one has been systematically mendacious, perhaps even a liar, by laying claim to the people's trust. (Gaita 2004: 1)

I could add that only the other day, Gordon Brown was announced as replacement for Blair. And the headline on BBC news? 'Brown promises to "build trust"'. John Howard's slogan 'It is a matter of trust' came out just before he was returned to office in 2003. Thus we don't have to believe him, as long as we trust him; he has been with us for a long time, just like, (gulp!) like family. And so the political leader metaphorises himself into trustful patriarch. But as he does so, might not the responsibility for governing the *whole* social body weaken, because the appeal of trust is to each of us as individuals, and especially to those with whom we feel more kinship? Trust, like those other human concepts such as hope and fear, is unevenly distributed around the social body. Howard's trust is not the trust of social justice we might expect to be smoothly and indifferently spread around. Shouldn't all of us be able to trust government, not just family figures? Trust needs to exist also in the disinterested social domain, where we can be confident we will not be discriminated against. Where we can trust any stranger whose language we don't even speak, who might even come from a country like Pakistan that 'harbours terrorists'. This, then, is Mick Douglas' artful politics. It is an act of diplomacy, but not on a grand nation-to-nation scale. It is minor diplomacy between cities, between Karachi and Melbourne, as well as between Melbourne and Kolkata, where they also have trams. This cultural diplomacy, performed publicly, uses a very Melbourne object, the tram, coupled with a very Karachi style, the *chamak patti*. And the hybrid creation takes to the streets with the blessing of the Melbourne City Council.

While we are waiting at Federation Square, on a blisteringly hot Melbourne day, I meet Roberto D'Andrea, an activist and ex-tram conductor, back in a specially created uniform again for these tram performances. He hands out his cards, little snippets of local history, and I want to show you here the one nicely illustrated by Shamana of Wathaurong Women, and the text of the William Buckley one because of the Indian connection. Buckley came to Australia on the HMAS *Calcutta*: the history of Australia–India relations is a very long one, and after all, we are neighbours. Roberto is a lively conductor, he is *wired*. As we yarn, I mention my memory of the French tram conductor on the No 8, who had this trick of twirling his cap, spinning it in the air and it landing on his bald head. He would kiss the ladies, and then turn conspiratorially to a callow, dumbfounded, Melbourne High kid like me, doffing his cap, 'You see, no 'airs. *A toutes les femmes*, for every woman I love, I give one 'air.'

'Oh, yeah, Frenchie! He's still alive you know, he comes out with us sometimes when we do our performances. He came from a circus family in France, that's how he knew those tricks.'

And of course there are no 'connies' on the trams these days, automated out of a job, except when they are performers or cultural activists like Roberto and his mates. *Wa ji wa*, Good on you, as another card says, with the Arabic script, the tickets they hand out to passengers for the free inner-circle trip.

The website summarises the encounter that Mark Minchington and I had together:

> Two strangers have never met before yet they find out their paths are linked across lines of indigenous and non-indigenous Australia. With a palpable sense of goodwill, the conversation explores and enacts the experience of people sharing the same movement and rhythm going the same way together. How is it that

travelling fosters a desire to put trust in someone else? A diverse range of hues in relation between indigenous and non-indigenous Australians weave through an exchange of stories between Mark and Stephen, with references along the way to sheep, dingo, mice and the black family that moved around for years by getting their car towed by white family cars, only to reveal that their car had no engine.

Mick Douglas conducts his beautiful musical tram, directing it through the xenophobic myths whipped up by politicians and the media. The tram is **fictocritical**, in the sense that it tells a story and makes an argument at the same time. Would that our writing could also travel with such beauty, such weight and such momentum! Ursula Le Guin writes:

> In recent centuries we speakers of this lovely language have reduced the English verb almost entirely to the indicative mood. But beneath that specious and arrogant assumption of certainty all the ancient, cloudy, moody powers and options of the subjunctive remain in force. The indicative points its bony finger at primary experiences, at the Things; but it is the subjunctive that joins them, with the bonds of analogy, possibility, probability, contingency, contiguity, memory, desire, fear and hope: the narrative connection. (Le Guin 1990: 44)

This is true, the subjunctive mood is the one exploited by fictionalists, the indicative by the lawmakers. But what if, instead of pointing our 'bony finger' at the world, from the outside as it were, judging it, we wrote from the inside of things, from our necessary assembly or convocation with those non-human things that have always helped us to think. We think with telescopes, apples, tortoises and hares. With these prostheses we are always, were always, more than human. We tend to forget our modesty and are too quick to congratulate ourselves on our Grand Achievements (stunned like rabbits in the lights of the prize-giving ceremony), as if we, the master-species, had done it all by ourselves. Soon as we consider a 'thing' an achievement, we forget just how active things are in our lives, and how strange they continue to be. This 'strange stuff' that Mick Taussig says talks to the writing, not the writer, asking it for a fair shake.

I had pulled out my copy of *Walter Benjamin's Grave* and had just shown that quotation to Hamish Morgan, anthropologist and fictocritical writer, as we were sitting having a beer in Federation Square and waiting for the tram to come around again so I could board it for a last trip. It was supposed to come at 5. I looked at my watch.

'Five to, I'd better get down there,' I say to Hamish. But when I look, there's the bloody tram going through the Swanson Street lights!

'If I run, do you think I can catch it?' Hamish is diplomatic in his assessment of my age and fitness.

*Catching* a tram. It has, on its side, all that weight and momentum, plus all that mechanical and electrical advantage. It has more allies than me. I am light and bipedal, but I have to dodge traffic, wait at lights, pause to catch my breath.

I get close, then I hear the bell, and it takes off again, indifferent to my desire to close the gap between subject and object. Almost at Spencer Street, I give up. I had promised Mick Douglas I would be back for the second tour. This time, I guess, I have missed the tram. It turns out that for the moment we are all missing it. Deborah Kelly has posted her comment on the website, and I will leave it to her to carry the momentum that the gathering of allies to a good cause implies:

> I can't believe there are plans to retire this exquisite project, so beautiful, generous, funny and hospitable.
>
> It's one of those superdistinctive things that makes Melbourne so intricately detailed.
>
> And while it seems to me that it's partly an observation of cosmopolitanism, I'd also suggest that it is a self-fulfilling prophecy: it actually creates the sense of a city with its heart wide open.
>
> Please find a way to keep this project going.

# writing fictocriticism.

Fictocritical language challenges any firm distinction between description and fictionalisation and it introduces a queer defamiliarisation into the heart of the most familiar experiences. 'Momentum' tries to activate a language that will carry on on its own, without the motor of authorial intention, the constant effort of creation or pushing something into a style. It can do this, I think, because the material is conducive, it is friendly to the ideas I want to express. So I set up the 'machinery', with the help of friends like Mick Taussig and Alphonso Lingis (operating from afar), my own experiences and memories from the past, and then the singular experience that was the challenge of 'Tram Overheard'. I set it up and off it goes; it's like playing with toy trains.

'"What have you learned?" the reality asks of the writing …' Taussig's question is *quite* different from the old adage that truth is stranger than fiction because he is not going along with the old representational arrangement of *subject–text–object* whereby the conscious individual creates a representation that more or less 'reflects' a reality 'out there'. Our challenge is to do something a little more tricky: let the tram talk to the writing. Let's look, therefore, at the interrelationships of things as if they are all on the same level, all part of the same democracy: electricity, rails, memories, *chamak patti*, a feeling of trust, spoken and written words, work visas, music. This is a more than human vision of the world; it does not have that conceit, so common in phenomenology, that reality comes into being through human interpretation of it. You know how the argument goes: sure, trams exist, but the significance of the tram only emerges as someone comes along to create a representation in some sort of a text, then representations in other sorts of texts compete with this one and each other. In this process, could the singularity of the tram, in all its strangeness, get lost among these generic textual forms locked in a war of representation? The point is not to adjudicate representations, it is to create momentum.

And what of criticism in fictocriticism? This is not about moral agendas, like, I can do a *critique* of this or that because I am equipped with some kind of incisive intellectual tool. Far from it, that kind of critic is always right, and we should steer clear of them for that reason. But when we couple criticism to fiction, to the imaginative, we seek rather to perform a kind of ethics by asking, *what can that thing do that it couldn't do before? what can that sentence say?* and in consideration of these things, *how has my place in the world shifted?* So we find out that a tram can do much more than transport the public, that it can entertain and inform (you are so engaged, you forget to get off at Flinders Street!), and then that the relationship between Pakistanis and Australians need not be defined by the Bush war-on-terror political agenda. And it is not because 'we are all human'; it is because a tram has artfully brought us together.

Then the challenge goes on, for it can't stop there, as if satisfied now that it has achieved the status of completed text. An artful tram will feel let down by some dull text talking about it. So much contemporary fiction is blocked because, being hemmed in by two major constraints, it loses the critical edge needed to keep thought on the move. It is hemmed in by commodification on the one hand and its 'human scale' on the other; it keeps finishing itself off as products and relegating non-human things to the status of mere backdrop to human dramas. What is lost in this process is any real matter of concern. Sure, moral concerns are often expressed ('Isn't it terrible that …'), but concern might go a bit further if a practice can meet another one and they can learn from each other. *Chamak patti* meets Aboriginal prankster, say.

Fictocriticism is, of course, a capacious category, as it must be if it is inspired by the materials and situation at hand. One might urge the interested writer not to feel that their practice has to conform to one of another model, but to have the confidence that the problem characterising the situation before them will surprise them into *changing* their practices. Like all literature, fictocriticism experiments with ways of being in the world, with forms of **subjectivity** if you like. Isn't the lure of the literary the constantly posed question: can someone *really be like that*? This form of subjectivity is not just in the image and style of a fully formed character, it is also in a process of thought or a way of knowing. This is why the essays of **Walter Benjamin**, Joan Didion, **Roland Barthes** and **Meaghan Morris**, or the fiction of Don DeLillo, Tom Pynchon, Michael Ondaatje, Robert Musil or W.G. Sebald, are just a few of the diverse writers whose practice might be gathered under the banner of the fictocritical. A philosopher like Alphonso Lingis or an anthropologist like Kathleen Stewart, a film critic like Sam Rohdie or an archaeologist like Denis Byrne might all turn fictocritical in order to think their material differently. Students at school or university are sometimes, though not always, encouraged to be self-reflective. This is not the same as expressing their opinion (one reason why their teachers might *discourage* them from using the first person singular pronoun), for the challenge is not to express the opinion, but at the very least explain where the opinion came from. This can take the form of an interesting fictocritical journey, where the writer reveals what is at stake for him or her as they take the reader gently but firmly on a journey whose signposts sometime express feelings, sometimes ways of knowing. So that's how you got there, the reader sighs at the end. I never thought you'd make it!

## key readings

Kerr, Heather, and Amanda Nettelbeck 1998. *The Space Between: Australian Women Writing Fictocriticism*. Perth: University of Western Australia Press.
Lindqvist, Sven 1997. *Exterminate all the Brutes*, trans. Joan Tate. London: Granta Publications.
Muecke, Stephen 2002. 'The Fall: Fictocritical Writing.' *parallax* 25, October–December: 108–12.

# glossapedia.

**Acculturated:** Within cultural studies it is generally accepted than many ideas and qualities that are commonly described as 'natural' are actually produced by a nexus of social and cultural ideas and practices, that is, they are acculturated. For example, attitudes to (male and female) beauty are often described as acculturated because they change from one society to another and from one time within a society to another (and even from one group or subculture within a society to another).

**Adorno, Theodor (1903–69):** Philosopher, sociologist and musician, Adorno was involved with the Frankfurt School (see the Horkheimer entry). Adorno is famous for the comment 'to still write a poem after Auschwitz is barbaric'; what he meant was that the extraordinary horror of the Holocaust had rendered beauty in words unthinkable. His contribution to Marxism reflected his early musical interests, in that he became concerned about the emergence of a culture industry that would render people passive and easily pleased.

**Affective Genre:** Texts (such as film, music, television and books) that produce meanings and identities associated with emotions, moods, attitudes and feelings. These texts are also made sense of through emotions, moods, attitudes and feelings that circulate in public culture.

**Althusser, Louis (1918–90):** Born in Algiers, Louis Althusser was a professor of philosophy at École Normal Supérieure in Paris. He is best known for his Marxist philosophy, which attempted to bring toether or reconcile Marxism with structuralism. He was also famous for his theory of ideology (articulated in his essay 'Ideology and Ideological State Apparatuses: Notes towards an Investigation'), which is based on Gramsci's theory of hegemony. For Althusser, society makes an individual in its own image. That is, many of our roles and activities are given to us by social practice: for example, the production of steel workers is part of economic practice, while the production of lawyers is part of politico-legal practice. Thus our values, desires and preferences are inculcated in us by ideological practice, which is the sphere which has the defining property of constituting individuals as subjects through the process of interpellation. Interpellation means the process by which ideology addresses the individual subject, and which produces the subject as an effect. Ideological practices, then, consist of an assortment of institutions called Ideological State Apparatuses, which include the family, the media, religious organisations and the education system, where we learn to be an individual subject, that is, what it is to be a daughter, a schoolchild, black, a steel worker, a councillor, for instance. Althusser's ideas had an influence on not only Marxist but also poststructuralist philosophers. For example, the idea of interpellation was adapted by Judith Butler, Ideological State Apparatuses have been picked up by Slavoj Zizek, and the notion of structure and agency has been developed by Anthony Giddens, and so on.

**Barthes, Roland (1915–80):** French literary theorist Roland Barthes explored cultural phenomena through semiotics or semiological analysis, which was based on the theory of structuralism. His famous books *Image, Music, Text* and *S/Z* argue that there is no overarching meaning in the intentions of the author. He concluded that since meaning does not and cannot come from the author alone, it must be actively created by the reader through a process of textual analysis.

**Baudrillard, Jean (1929– ):** Baudrillard supports Jean-Francois Lyotard's contention that postmodernism can be characterised by the collapse of certainty and the metanarratives that underpin that certainty. Baudrillard goes further, however, when he argues that postmodern society (roughly the late capitalist era, particularly from the 1960s onwards), is now characterised by 'hyper-reality': the notion that reality and imagination collapse into each other. This collapse brings about 'simulacrum/simulation', meaning that the distinction between the original (the real) and copy is destroyed so that what we are left with is just copies of copies, so that there is no 'real' behind, beyond or beneath the appearance. The consequence of this 'hyper-reality' or 'simulation' is a culture of repetition. Baudrillard's famous book *Simulations* made a fleeting appearance in the first *Matrix* film, which paid homage to the ideas in that book.

**Being:** Being is most easily defined as what it is not. Being is not defineable, transcends most categories of understanding and yet is self-evident! As a shared common term we understand that being is related to 'the nature of existence'. However, Heidegger takes an entire book, *Being and Time*, to really answer what being could be.

**Benjamin, Walter (1892–1940):** Walter Benjamin was born into a Jewish family in Berlin in 1892. At university in Freiburg and Berlin he studied philosophy and literature, and he became a leading Marxist literary critic and philosopher and influenced by some members of the Frankfurt School such as Theodor Adorno and Max Horkheimer. Later in his life he moved to Paris and associated with, and was influenced by, the surrealists. Benjamin wrote on a wide variety of topics, from drama, literature, art, history and language to philosophy and film. Consequently his writings are difficult to classify into any particular genre associated with a particular discipline, because they moved between all these genres. With the outbreak of World War II Horkheimer and Adorno persuaded Benjamin to flee the Nazis by going to America via Spain. However, the border guards refused him a pass into Spain, so rather than risk being caught by the Gestapo, he committed suicide in 1940. Some of his many works include 'Theories of German Fascism', *Illuminations* and 'The Work of Art in the Age of Mechanical Reproduction' (1936).

**Binary Oppositions:** A pair of contrasted terms where one term in the opposition is privileged over the other. The privileging of one term is not universal; rather, one term is privileged over another by particular cultures or in certain historical eras. However, each term depends on the other for its meaning, no matter which term in the opposition is privileged. For example, take the binary opposition inside/outside: there would be no concept of an 'inside' without reference to and understanding of the 'outside'. So binary oppositions are governed by an either/or distinction, which operates to organise and classify events, objects and relationships and the way human beings think.

**Biopower:** A concept developed by Michel Foucault, most clearly in his *History of Sexuality*, vol. 1. It has been understood as how we can think of the relations between power, knowledge and bodies. Foucault wants us to think about the ways in which bodies are ordered by institutions (schools, hospitals, families, etc.) but also by ourselves (our emotions, our desires, our behaviours, etc.) to create a field of power through our body rather than against it or simply over it.

**Body-politic:** The society and political state or culture in which the subject lives.

**Bourdieu, Pierre (1930–2002):** Pierre Bourdieu was a famous French sociologist whose work traversed philosophy, anthropology and sociology. He coined the terms 'cultural capital', 'social capital' and 'symbolic capital' and created the concepts 'habitus', 'field' and 'symbolic violence'. Building on Maurice Merleau-Ponty's work, Bourdieu's work emphasised the role of embodiment in social dynamics. Bourdieu was an avid political activist, and a staunch opposer of modern forms of globalisation. He saw sociology as a weapon against social oppression and injustice. He became director of studies at L'École Pratique Des Hautes Études in Paris around 1963, before founding the Centre de Sociologie Européenne in 1968. In 1981 Bourdieu was made a professor at the Collège de France.

**Bricoleur:** refers to someone who engages in bricolage. In Cultural Studies bricolage is not just someone putting things together from diverse places but refers particularly to the way in which new cultural identities are produced by combining objects and languages from other places, contexts and times. This is particularly evident in subcultures. Examples of this include the uses of crosses in goth groups, and the way in which the safety pin was combined with torn shirts and boots to create a punk style.

**Butler, Judith (1956– ):** Judith Butler is an American feminist philosopher best known for her poststructuralist critique of the fundamental organising principles of second-wave feminism(s). Butler's book *Gender Trouble*, which outlines her theory of gender as performative—that is, as the performative effect of repeated acts and gestures, which produce the illusion of an interior core gender—has come to be regarded as one of the most influential feminist texts of the late 20th century. The ideas explored in *Gender Trouble* are further elaborated in *Bodies That Matter* (1993), *Excitable Speech: A Politics of the Performative* (1997) and *Undoing Gender* (2004). Butler's critique of identity politics and of the essentialist notions of identity that are central to such politics has made an important contribution to corporeal feminism(s) and to queer theory.

**Camp:** Notoriously resistant to simple definition, camp is perhaps best characterised as an aesthetic discourse that seeks to produce denaturalising effects through disruptive representational strategies such as irony, parody, pastiche and mimicry. Closely associated with Western homosexual subcultures of the early and mid-20th century, camp has been widely cast as an aesthetic sensibility informed by queer experiences.

**Cixous, Hélèn (1937– ):** Cixous is a French academic who is best known for her textual experimentation and feminist writings. Along with Luce Irigaray and Julia Kristeva she began poststructuralist feminist theory. Her key books include *The Laugh of the Medusa* (1975), *Reading with Clarice Lispector* (1990) and *Reveries of the Wild Woman* (2000).

**Colonialism:** The practice whereby one nation state appropriates land and people outside its own borders, usually for either economic gain or strategic military advantage. This practice is supported ideologically by an assumption on the part of the colonisers that their society and culture is superior to that of the colonised, who need either to be converted to the ways of the coloniser or eradicated (to 'die out' or to be killed). In Australia the English occupation of the country in the late 18th century was part of the colonial expansion of the British Empire, in this case to appropriate the land to solve England's domestic problems with civil disorder and poverty.

**Connotation:** Meanings that derive from the cultural associations of specific signs in semiotics. For example the word 'pig' has a secondary meaning or signifying sign, 'greedy'. In the world of sound we associate the voice of Marilyn Monroe (and her many imitators) with the kind of femininity she portrayed in her films, or an Italian accent with popular culture stereotypes of Italy and Italianness.

**Cosmopolitanism:** As in common parlance, the word refers to sophistication, worldliness, and the ability to represent oneself and be heard in different cultural contexts. This concept of cosmopolitanism appears to have evolved from the 18th-century *Weltburger* or world citizen, which was a key term of the Enlightenment. It is now also used in relation to ideas of postcolonial subjectivity.

**Counter-cultural:** This is an expression used to describe the values, actions and style of a cultural group or subculture, which run counter to, or are organised in opposition to, the mainstream (as opposed to normative). Counter-culture movements have included the Romantics and the Beatniks.

**Daly, Mary (1928– ):** Mary Daly is a controversial radical feminist theologian who has been publishing critiques of patriarchy since the late 1960s. Her best-known publication, *Gyn/Ecology: The Metaethics of Radical Feminism* (1978), could be thought of as an existential/quasi-spiritual quest to discover Woman's true self, an essential and powerful self that has been systematically eroded by patriarchy. This theologico-political quest involves women reclaiming the names that patriarchy has used to degrade them (hag, spinster, harpie etc.), and naming men for what, Daly believes, they essentially are, that is, necrophilic beings who 'deeply identify with unwanted fetal tissue'.

**de Beauvoir, Simone (1908–86):** While de Beauvoir was influenced by the theories of her lover, famous French existentialist Jean-Paul Sartre, she became famous for her book *The Second Sex* (1949), which analysed how social customs and institutions allocated women a secondary role in society. This book, along with her other essays and novels, is what began the modern feminist movement.

**de Certeau, Michel (1925–86):** Born and educated in Paris, Michel de Certeau is one of the most eclectic thinkers of our time. He was a Jesuit and scholar who combined psychoanalysis, philosophy and social sciences in his work. He became famous in the English-speaking world with the publication, and translation into English, of his book *The Practices of Everyday Life* (1974). For de Certeau everyday life does not mean pop culture, but instead the ways in which individuals unconsciously navigate everything around them: city streets, shopping, literary texts, eating, and so on.

**de Saussure, Ferdinand (1857–1913):** A Swiss linguist and founder of structuralism, Saussure argued that linguistic signs and their meanings come from their relationship to other signs in the language, and from their position within the system. His work was published after his death from his lecture notes, and other notes taken from his students.

**Deconstruction:** The term 'deconstruction' was first coined by French philosopher Jacques Derrida in his book *Of Grammatology*. The term is built on German philosopher Martin Heidegger's word '*destruktion*' (Ger.), which he used to challenge metaphysics (the primary principles and causes of things). However, Derrida considered *destruktion* to be too negative because it implied annihilation and demolition, and Derrida does not want to demolish metaphysics; instead he wants to reveal and disrupt its assumptions, so he reformulates *destruktion* into 'deconstruction'. For Derrida, deconstruction is a double movement: it is a disordering and disruption and also a rearranging. To rearrange is not to replace one system with another but to reveal how systems of metaphysical thought constantly undermine themselves and transgress their cultural, social and historical boundaries and limits and reveal themselves to be contextual and contingent. Since Derrida's coining of this term there have developed a number of different uses and schools of deconstruction. Not all of these uses or schools follow Derrida's understanding and use of the term.

**Denaturalise:** To interrogate and expose the operations that make culture and history familiar and natural, thereby creating critical awareness of the processes of naturalisation.

**Derrida, Jacques (1930–2004):** Derrida was a French philosopher whose work is controversial but also enormously influential across various disciplines around the world. His work is significant for the way in which he employed various strategies and tactics to challenge and undermine traditional concepts, philosophy and metaphysics. These strategies and tactics have involved undermining traditional notions about communication and language; contaminating the boundaries between philosophy and other disciplines; and destabilising political, social, cultural and individual conceptions of identity and subjectivity. These strategies and tactics have been named 'deconstruction', which his writing style often performs. Derrida is therefore considered the father of deconstruction. He has published over forty books and 250 articles, essays and interviews. Some of his books include *Of Grammatology*, *Speech and Phenomena*, *Glas*, *The Post Card*, *Margins of Philosophy* and *Of Hospitality*. Derrida's work in general, along with his notion of deconstruction, is employed in cultural studies as a tactic of reading political, ethical, social and cultural texts.

**Descartes, René (1596–1650):** René Descartes, often referred to as the father of modern philosophy, was also a physicist, physiologist and mathematician. These interests are clear in Descartes' rejection of religious authority and his quest for scientific and philosophical knowledge. The best-known example of Descartes' search for absolute certainty can be found in the method of hyperbolic doubt he employs when asking 'how do I know I exist?'—a question that led to the proposition *cogito ergo sum* (I think, therefore I am). Hence for Descartes the foundation of philosophy is the mind's capacity to know the material world in and through mathematically based scientific (rational) thought.

**Diachronic:** Adjective (from the Greek for 'across time') used to refer to the historical evolution of a given phenomenon and its development over an extended period of time. It is generally opposed to synchronic, which refers to something at a specific historical point in time.

**Diaspora:** The movement of people from particular communities or societies away from a traditional homeland or nation state, usually as a result of some form of catastrophic event—social, military, environmental, economic. For example, the African diaspora refers to the taking of African people from their home continent to be slaves in what is now the United States of America, and their subsequent movement to many different countries.

**Différance:** The word 'différance' is made up of the term 'to defer' (a form of spacing which enables words to differ from each other) and 'to differ' (where a word's meaning is constantly defined in relation to other words—synonyms and antonyms—and thus where their meaning is constantly postponed, and never permanently fixed) This neologism is a means by which Derrida could expose and challenge metaphysics, which relies for its foundation on fixed meaning, produced in and through binary oppositions.

**Discourse:** A widely used term in the humanities and social sciences, with competing meanings. In cultural theory it is closely associated with the work of Michel Foucault and defines a network of institutionalised beliefs and statements that cohere around a given topic or idea. Discourse constructs the ways we think, act and feel through the configurations of power.

**Discursive construct:** A text or portion of a text in which a particular discourse is described or elaborated. We might describe a section of written text or the composition of a particular image as a discursive construction because it describes or elaborates a particular set of ideas about gender or race or class or ability.

**Dworkin, Andrea (1946–2005):** Andrea Dworkin was an American radical feminist best known for her uncompromising work on pornography. In her third book, *Pornography: Men Possessing Women* (1981), Dworkin argued that pornography plays an integral role in the rape and abuse of women and ultimately is implicated in the patriarchal control of women's bodies, their sexuality, their movements and their psyches. In the mid-1970s she was involved in the formation of an activist group later known as Women Against Porn, and in 1986, along with Catherine MacKinnon, she played an integral role in the Meeks Commission's decision to remove popular porn magazines from convenience stores. This decision (since overturned) was premised on the claim that 'Pornography is a Civil Rights Issue'. In 1987 Dworkin published *Intercourse*, in which she extended her analysis of pornography to heterosexual intercourse itself. Dworkin was married to the gay male feminist activist and writer John Stoltenberg.

**Embodiment:** Embodiment means learning sets of knowledges (social rules and conventions), discourses and techniques (how to operate a computer or cross a road, for instance) that are habitually reproduced (in and through the body) so that they seem instinctual or 'natural'. They appear natural because they are 'unconsciously' reproduced through bodily habit. Identity is produced through embodiment.

**Enlightenment:** Usually a reference to an 18th-century movement in Western philosophy that claimed rationality as the basis of all knowledge; its proponents included David Hume, John Locke, Jean-Jacques Rousseau and Immanuel Kant. Enlightenment philosophy can be seen as a response to the religious wars that had erupted in Europe in the 16th and 17th centuries, attempting to establish principles for the peaceful ordering of human society (hence its influence on thinkers such as Edmund Burke, Thomas Jefferson, Thomas Paine). Enlightenment philosophers were influenced by the work of natural philosophers and scientists such as Isaac Newton, who founded his theories on observations of the world around him. This combination of axiomatic thought (associated earlier with the work of Spinoza) and scientific observation (as in Galileo's work) was the basis of Enlightenment rationality, which has continued to characterise Western philosophy. It came increasingly under attack in the 20th century because of the way its proponents assumed the inherent superiority of their way of thinking and ordering the world, which 20th-century thinkers such as Michel Foucault saw as leading to the construction of boundaries and borders, locating those who think differently as 'irrational', 'mad' and 'illogical' (or 'primitive') with associated social and cultural sanctions.

**Episteme:** Foucault described this in *Archaeology of Knowledge* (1969: 121) as: 'The total set of (i.e. economic, political, imaginary, individual, etc.) relations that unite at a given period the discursive practices that give rise to epistemological figures, science, and possibly formalised systems'. In other words, the set of relations that arise in a particular cultural period to make sense of that period as a particular period different from others.

**Epistemological:** Referring to theories of knowledge or ways of knowing.

**Essentialism:** Unlike theories which suggest that objects and humans should be studied in relation to the context in which they are situated or born, essentialism is the belief that humans have inherent qualities that exist outside or beyond their historical, cultural and social context. That is, essentialism argues that a person has an essential character, identity or personality.

**Experiential metaphor:** This phrase refers to the notion of sound in theories of linguistics and semiotics. It refers to the idea that our experience of what we physically have to do to produce a particular sound creates a potential for meaning. For instance, we know that we can create tense sounds by tensing our articulatory musculature. We also know that we tend to do this in situations where we are tense or 'charged up', or want to appear that way. Hence tense sound quality can come to be associated with meanings such as aggression, repression, nervousness, excitement, and so on.

**Fictocriticism:** According to Stephen Muecke fictocriticism is 'A mischievous little intellectual genre, pitches an argument to a situation, leavening the text with a little fictionalisation'. In a different language fictocriticism can be described as various styles of writing that combine elements of different writing practices into a single text which usually tells a story while making an argument. This writing has been called experimental, postmodern and feminist. It is distinguished from 'creative non-fiction' and other genre-bending works by fictocriticism's desire to be a critical intervention into a genre or discipline in a way that is recognisably of that form but seeks to challenge and transform that genre or discipline.

**Foucault, Michel (1926–84):** French philosopher and historian Michel Foucault was professor of the 'history of systems of thought' at the Collège de France from 1970 until his death from AIDS in 1984. His work questioned how people become constrained by history to think in particular ways. To explore this question, Foucault's work focused on

- the ways in which knowledge and thought historically and culturally emerged. This was outlined in his books *The Order of Things* and *The Archaeology of Knowledge*.
- how science and reason have been used as instruments of power to discipline human beings. Foucault argues that disciplinarity occurs in and through institutions such as medicine and psychology, which use particular techniques for controlling human beings. One of those techniques is to form people into 'types' of individuals by bringing them into accord with institutional and social norms (see his book *Discipline and Punish*).
- the ways in which disciplinarity and knowledge and power become carried out by people on themselves at an individual level. He called this self-governance or self-surveillance. (See Foucault's *History of Sexuality*, vols 1–3.)

**Freudian/Freud, Sigmund (1856–1939):** Born in Friedburg and educated in Vienna, Freud was the founder of psychoanalysis. He is famous for his notion that there is an active process of repression. For Freud, repression occurs when the balance between the seeking of pleasure and the avoidance of un-pleasure is tipped towards un-pleasure, thereby creating imbalance in the psyche. He was also famous for his notion of the psyche as an ego (conscious self), id (the part of the self alienated from the conscious self) and the super-ego (the conscience).

**Gatens, Moira (1954– ):** Gatens is an Australian philosopher whose early work radically questioned the distinction between sex and gender and retheorised the significance of the body. Her key texts include *Imaginary Bodies: Ethics, Power and Corporeality* (1996) and *Feminism and Philosophy: Perspectives on Difference and Equality* (1991). She has also made a major contribution to the scholarship on Spinoza.

**Genealogy:** a key term in Michel Foucault's thinking about history. Genealogy challenges presumptions of truth, origins or linearity in history. This is done by showing the ways in which the ordinary and contingent, rather than any key government directive or monarchical pronouncement, have produced new systems of thought. His key text which explores this is *Discipline and Punish*, in which he shows how the convergence of things as diverse as institutions, style of spectatorship and bodily comportment, and many other things, created a new form of disciplinary power.

**Giard, Luce:** An eminent French researcher within the history and philosophy of science. During the 1970s and early 1980s, Giard, together with Pierre Mayol, worked with Michel de Certeau on his government-commissioned project examining everyday rituals and practices. The result was the two-volume publication *The Practice of Everyday Life*.

**Globalisation:** Globalisation can be defined as the processes, such as capital, images and communication networks, that connect people and communities around the world so that they become incorporated into a single world society.

**Glocal:** This term emerged as a way of describing people and groups that might 'think globally and act locally'. But it now also refers to local effects and productions of globalization, acknowledging that we usually only know globalisation through its local manifestations. This might take the form of very local and specific celebrations of global phenomenon (such as the idea of cargo cults) or global circulation of very local moments (such as global news circulation of a highly local event like a particular car crash or local disaster).

**'Goods to think with':** A phrase borrowed from the anthropologist Claude Lévi-Strauss, who used it to refer to totemic categories among tribal peoples. It refers to material objects used in everyday life to enable the elaboration and exchange of social meaning among people; symbolic objects that mediate between us and the broader life-world from which we make meaning.

**Greer, Germaine (1939– ):** One of the most (in)famous of second-wave feminists, Germaine Greer was born in Australia but moved to the UK in 1964. Her first and perhaps best-known book, *The Female Eunuch* (1970), was concerned with the ways in which patriarchal institutions, in particular the nuclear family, had alienated women from their desire, their sexuality, their true selves. Consequently, like many feminists of the time, Greer called on women to find ways to get to know themselves and their bodies, and to reject their subordination and the practices that enabled it. Greer's vision was revolutionary rather than reformist. Over the last three decades Greer has published ten other books on subjects such as women artists, fertility, menopause, contemporary feminism and art history.

**Grosz, Elizabeth (1952– ):** Elizabeth Grosz is an Australian feminist philosopher whose work could loosely be described as poststructuralist. Like Moira Gatens, Grosz played an integral role in the formation of what has come to be known as 'sexual difference feminism' or 'corporeal feminism'. Grosz has published a number of books, including *Volatile Bodies: Toward a Corporeal Feminism* in which she articulates the main tenets of corporeal feminism.

**Haraway, Donna (1944– ):** Donna Haraway is a US-based feminist philosopher and author of the landmark essay 'A Cyborg Manifesto: Science, Technology and Socialist Feminism in the Late Twentieth Century' in which she develops an (anti-humanist) ontology centred on the figure of the cyborg, a hybrid creature of social reality and fiction whose very existence undermines the distinction between nature and culture, the natural and the technological, the human and the non-human, and so on. Like Michel Foucault and other poststructuralist thinkers, Haraway 'exercises a hermeneutics of suspicion towards the axiomatic boundaries and categories by which modernity is ordered' (Graham 2002: 202–3) and (modern) selves are constituted.

**Hebdige, Dick (1951– ):** Hebdige has taught at various universities around the world: Western Europe, the USA, Britain, Australia. He is currently director of the interdisciplinary Humanities Centre at the University of California in Santa Barbara, where he also teaches film studies. He has written extensively on contemporary art and design and music, media and critical theory, but he is most famous for his book *Subculture: The Meaning of Style*, where he discusses the notion and development of 'subculture'. Hebdige was one of the founders, along with Stuart Hall, in 1964 of the Birmingham Centre for Contemporary Cultural Studies.

**Hegel Georg (1770–1831):** Hegel was a German philosopher whose work on the teleological or progressive theory of history was reinterpreted by Marx to propose the inevitability of communism as the culmination of 'history'. Since the decline in popularity of Marxism, Hegel's other works on spirit, phenomenology, the logics of science and subjectivity are being re-explored by contemporary thinkers such as Butler and Zizek.

**Hegemony:** The power of one group (or culture or society) to enforce its views over others, either with or without having to resort to force. This is fundamentally a coercive power which means that one group is able to enforce its views and demands on others.

**Heidegger, Martin (1889–1976):** Heidegger was a German philosopher educated in Freiburg, Germany in the phenomenological tradition of Edmund Husserl. He became professor at the universities of Marburg (1923–28) and Freiburg (1928–51). His most important work is *Sein und Zeit* (1927), translated as

*Being and Time* in 1962. This work has made him famous for his theories of being and human nature and for his interpretation and critique of traditional Western metaphysics. He is acknowledged as a central figure to many continental and American philosophers and theorists in a wide variety of disciplines. For example, his works have had great influence on Jean-Paul Sartre (existentialism), Rudolf Bultmann (theology), Hans-Georg Gadamer (contemporary hermeneutics) and Jacques Derrida (literary theory, deconstruction and continental philosophy), to name only a few.

**Hermeneutics:** Originally derived from theology, where it was used to refer to the science of biblical interpretation, hermeneutics is used more broadly in contemporary cultural studies to refer to the theory and/or practice of any form of textual interpretation or decoding.

**Heteronormative:** Many feminists and gender theorists have used this term to describe, and to critique, the general and dominant belief that the sexual and marital practices between people of different genders (male and female) are 'normal' and 'right'. Heterosexuality, therefore, is considered the norm, because it is believed to be the only 'normal' sexual orientation. Heterosexuality is 'heteronormative'. This belief is perpetuated and reinforced through social institutions and social policy. Heteronormativity is often associated with patriarchy because while patriarchy transcends gender binaries, it privileges the male gender (by putting males in positions of social power). Therefore, patriarchy is reinforced by heteronormative relations, precisely because those relations are considered to be dominated by the male gender.

**Hobbes, Thomas (1588–1679):** During his time the philosopher Thomas Hobbes was outspokenly in favour of strong government, which is reflected in his book *Leviathan*. This book influenced and contributed to the establishment of philosophical anthropology. While he supported the power of the monarchy, it is his theories of how we come to have knowledge of the objects in the material world (that is, through the senses) and human nature, as self-interested cooperation, for which he is famous.

**hooks, bell (1952– ):** One of America's best-known contemporary Black intellectuals. She describes herself as a 'Black woman intellectual, revolutionary activist' because her work focuses on the various forms of racism and sexism in the USA. She is currently professor of English at the City College of New York.

**Horkheimer, Max (1895–1973):** German philosopher and director of the Frankfurt Institute for Social Research from 1930 to 1958, now famously known as the Frankfurt School, Horkheimer argued that theory itself would be the scene of the liberation of the working class. His most famous books are *Dialectic of Enlightenment* (with Theodor Adorno), and *Critique of Instrumental Reason*.

**Humanist/humanism:** Humanism began in the Renaissance, known in England as the Elizabethan Age (roughly the period from 1485 to 1603). Humanism was a system of learning, interpretation and meaning that focused on the rational abilities of humans to determine their own fates, to know about the world and to construct their own understanding of truth and falsity. In other words, reason is the fundamental capacity of human beings (or more precisely of 'Man') because it is what enables us not only to think, but to act, correctly. It is through 'Man's' use of reason that humanity as a whole can progress to a state of perfection. Humanism was a break with the thought, beliefs and doctrines of the Middle Ages (5th to early 15th centuries), which basically saw a belief in God as pivotal for understanding the world and attaining knowledge.

**Hybridity:** Generally this refers to the invention of new cultural forms that arise from contact between difference (e.g. in times of colonial 'contact' through global circulation). This term has a racist history that assumed a mixing of racial and cultural purities. But it also looks towards a hopeful future where hybridity becomes a way of moving beyond the racial and cultural binaries used to rule people under colonialism.

**Hypersensory:** A mode of perception that engages the individual in reflecting on perception itself by focusing on the nature of one or more particular perceptual practices (e.g. verbal, visual, aural, tactile, olfactory, gustatory) and challenging the individual to determine how that perception (or perceptions) affects her/his embodied subjectivity.

**Identity:** In Cultural Studies we use identity mostly to discuss the allegiances formed by individuals with particular groups and cultures, though identity also refers to the allegiances assumed of individuals. For example, it is assumed that people who reach powerful positions within institutions and organisations are middle-class; that is, their class identity is assumed to be middle-class. However, as we have seen in Australia, it is quite possible to have a prime minister—Paul Keating—who is working-class, in that his family background, education and early life experience took place within that class culture. The problem of situating Paul Keating (and the frequent use of his class identity as a slur against him) points also to the problems with notions of identity, in that they can be too rigid to describe the complexity of a person's life experience. This can also lead to a stereotyping of identity categories (of class, gender, sexuality, age, ability, race, ethnicity) that can be used to disempower individuals. For example, Keating's predilection for antiques and smart suits was used by his opponents to characterise him as a 'class traitor' because a stereotype of working-class identity identifies these tastes as not working-class. On the other hand, identity can also be used to form allegiances with others in order to argue a particular position or share life experiences and so can be empowering and life-affirming. A major 20th century example was the 'Gay Pride' movement and the positive construction of gay identity.

Ideology: A set of ideas characterising a text, organisation, institution, subculture or society. We can also think of ideology as a particular configuration of discourses that characterises—and so reveals the fundamental tenets and associated practices—of a text, organisation, institution, subculture or society. So we might argue that the ideology of most Western state education departments is liberal humanist, since the basic principles and the practices by which it operates are liberal humanist. This does not mean, however, that every teacher and administrator, and every teaching practice, is liberal humanist; simply that the overall tenor of the institution is liberal humanist. Influential theorists of ideology include Karl Marx and Louis Althusser.

(Inter)corporeal: Corporeal feminism rejects the traditional distinction between body and mind and the focus on the latter as the locus of the self (and thus of political intervention). Instead, corporeal feminism articulates a postmodern notion of subjectivity as always already (inter)corporeal (meaning not autonomous, but materially affected/effected). This kind of conceptual shift constitutes a radical and complex questioning of dominant forms of knowledge and the common-sense assumptions to which they give rise.

Intersubjectivity: Intersubjectivity is an interdisciplinary, and therefore complex, term. In a nutshell, it is the relationship between the self (subject) and other and the social and cultural world in which we are situated. Theories of intersubjectivity have been developed by philosophers such as Georg Hegel, Edmund Husserl and Martin Buber.

Irigaray, Luce (1932– ): A French philosopher known for her work in French feminism and continental philosophy, she is particularly concerned with the ways in which women have been excluded or constrained within psychoanalytic thinking. She has developed an embodied notion of female subjectivity. Irigaray's most famous works include *Speculum of the Other Women* (1974) and *This Sex Which Is Not One* (1977).

Jameson, Fredric (1934– ): Philosopher and famous theorist of post-modernism, Jameson is Professor of Comparative Literature and Director of the Duke Centre for Critical Theory at Duke University in the USA. He has published widely on Marxism, literary theory, poststructuralism and postmodernism. His book *Postmodernism, or The Cultural Logic of Late Capitalism* (1991) was highly influential. In it he argues that postmodernism, as the cultural logic of late capitalism, finds expression in practices of artistic and literary pastiche and nostalgia.

Kant, Immanuel (1724–1804): German philosopher Immanuel Kant is considered one of the most influential philosophers over the past three centuries. Today his influence is marked by the way continental philosophers such as Foucault, Levinas, Derrida and Heidegger critique, reference and engage with Kant's theories. In particular, epistemology, metaphysics, phenomenology, philosophy and ethics continue to feel the effects of Kant's thought. Kant's best-known writings are his three Critiques, which include the *Critique of Pure Reason* (1787), where he argues that it is impossible to know anything *a priori* about the world independently of our cognition, and he uses his method of 'transcendental deduction' to prove this. In the second Critique, the *Critique of Practical Reason* (1788), Kant agues for a universal ethics: a single overarching rational moral principle that guides our passions. And finally the *Critique of Judgement* (1790) deals with aesthetic questions and the problems involved in aesthetic judgment.

**Kristeva, Julia (1941– ):** One of the most influential French feminists, her work has engaged with philosophy, literature and Marxism and she has used semiotics and linguistics to reshape psychoanalysis. Using semiotics, she coined the phrase 'semanalysis', which focuses on the poetic or materiality of language: the pre-Oedipal sensual order. Poetic language disrupts conventional meaning and leads to new understanding. Semanalysis also reveals how the subject is not static or stable but is always in process, always heterogeneous, and thus never entirely analysable. Her work has had lasting significance for Cultural Studies and in particular her notion of the subject. Major writings include: *Revolution in Poetic Language* (1974) and *Powers of Horror: An Essay on Abjection* (1980).

**Kruger, Barbara (1945– ):** An American collage artist best known for her use of 'found photographs', usually of women, taken from fashion magazines and overlaid with anti-corporate, anti-consumerist messages, such as 'I shop therefore I am' and 'Your body is a battleground'.

**Lacan, Jacques (1901–81):** Jacques Lacan was a French psychoanalyst and intellectual. His work influenced intellectual thought at the time, and the famous series of lectures he gave at the University of Paris from 1953 was attended by other famous intellectuals, such as Michel Foucault, Jacques Derrida, Louis Althusser, Jacques-Alain Miller, Luce Irigaray, Jean Laplanche and Claude Lévi-Strauss. One of Lacan's seminars was published in English as *The Four Fundamental Concepts of Psychoanalysis*. His work is essentially a reinterpretation of Sigmund Freud in and through Saussure's structural approach to linguistics.

**Leiris, Michel (1901–90):** Leiris was a French surrealist (although he later broke with them), poet and ethnographer. He combined ethnography and autobiography and the best example of this is is his book *L'Age d'homme* (1939).

**Levinas, Emmanuel (1905–95):** A European philosopher well known for his work in the field of ethics and phenomenology, whose key works include *Totality and Infinity* and *Other Than Being*. Thinkers such as Jacques Derrida engaged with his thinking on moral philosophy.

**Lingis, Alphonso (1933– ):** Alphonso Lingis is an influential American philosopher, who has written numerous books and translated a number of texts from other languages. He is currently an Emeritus Professor of Philosophy at Pennsylvania State University. Lingis is most interested in phenomenology and ethics, and his work is often marked by his wide-ranging world travel. Lingis wrote his first book, *Excesses*, in 1982, combining anthropological scenes with references to the history of philosophy. In this way he gained a reputation for his compelling and lyrical writing style.

**Lyotard, Jean-François (1924–98):** Lyotard was a French philosopher and Professor of Philosophy at the University of Paris VIII until 1989. Lyotard began his intellectual career as a political activist of Marxism, but in later years became disillusioned with the totalitarian thought of Marxism. It was at this stage that Lyotard attributed to modernity (to which Marxism belonged) the attempt to answer and solve humanity's problems through coherent, universalising and totalising theories. Lyotard called this attempt the perpetuation of 'grand narratives' or 'metanarratives'. He outlined his suspicions of metanarratives in his book *The Postmodern Condition* (1979), where he argues that the postmodern era can be characterised by this rejection of metanarratives: the major systems of political, cultural and religious ideas that have underpinned our social and political institutions and practices. The publication of *The Postmodern Condition* brought Lyotard worldwide fame, and in the 1980s and 1990s he lectured widely outside France and became professor at the University of California, Irvine and Emory universities, and a founding member and sometime president of the Collège International de Philosophie. Lyotard was a visiting professor at numerous universities, including Johns Hopkins, the University of California, Berkeley and San Diego, the University of Minnesota, the Université de Montréal, Canada, the Universität Siegen, West Germany, and the University of Saõ Paulo, Brazil. In 1998 Lyotard died of leukaemia.

**MacKinnon, Catharine (1946– ):** Catharine MacKinnon is a US-born feminist and legal scholar who as early as 1979 published a paper in which she argued that sexual harassment in the workplace is a violation of civil rights statutes. MacKinnon has also long been an ardent critic of pornography and, in the 1980s, in conjunction with Andrea Dworkin, she drafted an anti-pornography civil rights ordinance that, if passed, would allow women who could prove they had been harmed by pornography to sue those responsible for its production and distribution. MacKinnon has also written about and been involved in cases concerning rape, abortion and genocide. MacKinnon's many books include *Feminism Unmodified: Discourses on Life and Law* (1987), *Pornography and Civil Rights: A New Day for Women's Equality* (1988) and *Women's Lives, Men's Laws* (2005).

**Marx, Karl (1818–83):** Marx argued against the traditional notion of his day that inequality was natural, and instead argued that inequality was a social creation perpetuated through class distinctions and hierarchies that are produced by economic processes. He claimed that the oppressed classes (the proletariat or working class) would one day revolt against the wealthy classes to overcome capitalism and constitute a new state, communism. Communism is a state where all property is in common ownership and not just owned by the aristocracy. This new state was to come about when the capitalist system collapsed in self-destruction.

**Mauss, Marcel (1872–1950):** Mauss was a French sociologist who, from 1901, was chair of the 'history of religion and uncivilized peoples' at the École Pratique des Hautes Études. It was during his time at this university that Mauss' work, drawing on ethnography, started to incorporate anthropology into his sociological methodologies. In 1931 he became chair of Sociology at the Collège de France. His famous work *The Gift* (about the origins of cultural anthropological studies of 'reciprocity', especially in relation to non-market economic exchange, and where Mauss famously argues that there is never a 'free gift', only reciprocal exchange), influenced other famous theorists and philosophers, such as Claude Lévi-Strauss and Jacques Derrida.

**Merleau-Ponty, Maurice (1908–61):** Merleau-Ponty was a philosopher of phenomenology and the corporeality of perception. Referred to as a phenomenologist, Merleau-Ponty published *Phenomenology of Perception* in 1945; it sought to develop an idea of the body-subject which opposed the Cartesian notion that the world was merely an extension and invention of our minds. Through his extended idea of perception as being a 'primordial openness' rather than a simple set of sensations, Merleau-Ponty challenged the mind/body divide and gave language a psychological and embodied dimension.

**Metaphysics:** Metaphysics is that which grounds the questions of God, Being, reality, morality, truth, and so on, in absolute and fundamental principles.

**Mimesis:** Mimesis is the Greek word for imitation or representation and was first used by Plato and then Aristotle. For Plato in particular, mimesis meant the imitation of nature. That is, God's creation is an imitation of the truth and essence of nature. So, according to this definition, there are things that exist (roses, clouds, dogs, children, tables, and so on) and these things are an imitation of some sort of essence or true meaning. Mimesis, then, is simply a reflection or imitation of something else.

**Mimetic realism:** a mode of realism that is based on physically lifelike appearance rather than, for example, expressive or psychological realism that may be fantastic in appearance; for example, the portrayal of the horrors of the Holocaust is mimetic realism in *Schindler's List* (1993) but psychological realism in *Pan's Labyrinth* (2006).

**Mimetic representation**: a representation of a person, object or event that attains a physically lifelike appearance.

**Modernism**: Modernism is a large and rather loose term used to refer to both a cultural movement and a (somewhat heterogeneous) system of meaning-making. It has been claimed by many that modernism emerged in France in the mid-19th century, and it is often associated with figures such as Baudelaire (literature), Manet (painting), Schoenberg (music), and Le Corbusier (architecture), and with revolutionary changes such as industrialisation and the rise of technology, the birth of the social sciences, the theory of relativity, and so on. In short, modernism is concerned, in a wide range of ways, with the rejection of traditional idea(l)s, in particular those associated with the Classical world. Modernists, then, attempted to radically undermine longstanding notions of form, order, the importance of hierarchies, and so on, and emphasised the need for freedom of expression, experimentation and radical dissonance.

**Morris, Meaghan (1950– )**: Considered one of the founders of Australian Cultural Studies, due to her contributions to cultural feminist and film theory, Morris is indelibly connected to the New England town of Tenterfield following her seminal essay 'At Henry Parkes Motel'. She famously brought together style and content in this essay as it ranged across spatial poetics and localism. With John Frow she edited the foundational *Australian Cultural Studies: A Reader*, and continues to publish in histories of popular culture, film and global cultures.

**Nancy, Jean-Luc (1940– )**: Nancy is a French philosopher who is interested in ideas of community or a collective 'we', and is most famous for *The Inoperative Community* (1982) and *Being Singular Plural* (2000). In what ways is 'community' possible without an idea of exclusivity or even identity? What is 'community' in a globalised world? How we can speak of a plurality of a 'we' without making the 'we' a singular identity? These are some of the issues and questions he raises in his writing. He has been  influenced by Derrida, Lyotard and Lacoue-Labarthe, among others.

**Nazi**: In English, Nazi stands for the National Socialist German Workers Party, which was founded in 1919 in Germany. In 1933 when Hitler came to power he appropriated the term Nazi, transforming it into the Fascist Party of the German Government (Third Reich). Members of the Nazi Party were required to offer the utmost devotion and loyalty and practise its policies, which included forming an Aryan master race that would rule the world, control ethnic groups and divest Germany of these ethnic groups and their property. This led to Jews and others being exterminated in concentration camps (and which is now known as the Holocaust).

**Nietzsche, Friedrich (1844–1900):** Nietzsche was a German philosopher whose idea of 'life-affirmation' challenged Christian tradition and established morality. He is sometimes referred to as the first existential philosopher and his work has influenced countless other philosophers including Foucault, Derrida, Sartre and Heidegger, and movements including existentialism, postmodernism and poststructuralism.

**Normative:** To make normal and usual within a culture and society where institutions produce behaviours and actions that conform to the status quo.

**Oedipal/Oedipus complex:** According to Freud, there are five stages in the psychosexual development of children (from birth to puberty). These are: 1. Oral Stage (birth to 1 year) where the infant's pleasurable activities centre on the activities of the mouth (feeding, sucking thumb, etc.). 2. Anal Stage (2–3 years) where pleasure is produced by control over the retention and expulsion of faeces. 3. Phallic Stage (3–5 years), the Oedipal and Electra complexes, the development of emotional tensions and resolutions. 4. Latency Stage (6–8 years) where a child's sexual interest lies dormant until puberty. 5. Genital Stage (adolescence onwards), adult sexuality, and according to Freud, interest in the 'opposite' sex. It is during the Phallic Stage that there arises the Oedipus complex (and in girls, the Electra complex). The Oedipal stage is the emotional climax in sexual development, where the male child focuses his pleasure-seeking activities on the mother, and views his siblings and his father as hostile rivals. The boy's Oedipus complex is resolved by the real or imagined threat of castration.

**Ontology:** Derived form the Greek word for 'being', ontology is the enquiry into, or the study of, 'being': that which exists, or the question of what there is. Ontology is a branch of metaphysical or theoretical philosophy.

**Orientalism:** Orientalism is the term coined by Edward Said to describe the ways in which the West objectifies and claims to know the East.

**Other:** The term 'Other' or 'other' is a contentious one and has different implications depending on who uses it and how it is used. The Other is a term commonly used in Cultural Studies to explain how some people or groups are marginalised by their difference from the norm. These people are placed outside the norm or convention and as a result are perceived as irrelevant and sometimes inhuman. In some continental philosophy, the term 'other' is used to refer to 'alterity', meaning that which is infinite and irreducibly different. This other is not a reference to people or material beings.

**Patriarchy:** An oppressive political and cultural system founded on the biologically determinist assumption that women are inferior to men. According to radical feminists, patriarchy ensures the continued systematic oppression of women, and the naturalisation of gender inequality. This term is associated with second-wave feminisms and is rarely used by postmodern feminists.

**Phenomenological tradition:** Phenomenology is a term that began with Johann Heinrich Lambert and Immanuel Kant in the 18th century to describe consciousness apart from consideration of its intentional content, that is, its directedness towards things in the world. In the 20th century, the term became associated with the work of Edmund Husserl and his attempts to describe consciousness independently of the causal explanations given by historians, psychologists and sociologists. Modern philosophers such as Heidegger, Sartre and Merleau-Ponty pursued and refined Husserl's phenomenological method: the method of attempting to separate consciousness from causal experience. This method involved 'bracketing' the content of experience in order to discover the 'subject-matter' that remains.

**Plato (429–347BC):** Plato was an ancient Greek philosopher who is known for his thinking around distinction, particularly between what appears beautiful or good and what is true beauty such as goodness, justice or unity. Reality is therefore split between what the soul should recall as the proper forms and a world that shows us corrupt versions of those ideal forms.

**Postcolonialism:** This refers to theories that span philosophy, film and literature that address the effects of colonial rule. It can be thought of as a critical tool to examine countries and societies that are, or were once, colonies of other countries. Postcolonialism also looks at literature written by members of colonised societies, or that was written in colonised countries. The key figure in the rise of postcolonial theory was Edward Said, whose book *Orientalism* continues to be the guiding reference for scholarship in this area. Postcolonialism aims to address the various problems caused by the process of colonialism, such as the difficulty of establishing a national identity after colonial rule, reclaiming cultural identities from colonisers, the perpetuation of the notion of colonised people as inferior, and the ways in which the knowledge of subordinate people is taken up and used by colonial powers.

**Postmodernism:** A notoriously complex and slippery term used to refer to the distinctive conditions and forms of contemporary post-industrialised cultures. In this context, postmodernism is defined variously as: a) an aesthetic style or movement characterised by overt stylisation, irony and pastiche, genre blurring, citation and intertextuality; b) a critical tradition that refutes the modernist belief in metanarratives and universal truths; or c) the contemporary historical epoch after modernity.

**Power/knowledge:** This is the relationship between power and knowledge. Foucault looks at how knowledge or human thought and action are produced through discourse and ideology. In other words, the discourses in texts produce knowledge about certain issues or topics, such as race, sexuality, identity or class, which we then internalise and act upon. Foucault argues that this production of knowledge is tied to forms of power where one entity or institution (the government, media, etc.) manipulates another to think and act in certain ways.

**Queer:** An umbrella term used to denominate a range of minority and/or non-mainstream sexualities such as gay, lesbian, bisexual, transgendered and intersex. It can also be used more abstractly in cultural theory to refer to discourses that resist and subvert social and sexual orthodoxies.

**Queer diaspora:** The term refers to the migrant gays, lesbians, bisexuals and transsexuals living away from their countries of birth, origin or 'homeland'. Conceptually, the term also refers to a theoretical position that challenges the colonial, patriarchal and heterosexual norms of a dominant culture. More recently, the term has also been used to invoke the marginal communities created by gays, lesbians, bisexuals and transsexuals who do not 'fit into' a dominant culture's mainstream queer communities.

**Representation:** To 'represent', in the sense cultural theorists use the word, means to stand for or to symbolise, or it can mean to speak or act on behalf of; it can also mean to make something that is absent, present (as in to present what is absent). What these definitions have in common is a system of producing and communicating meaning. However, there are various ways in which meaning is represented. For example, there is the 'mimetic model' of representation, an intentional model, and a constructionist model. It is the last model of representation—that which does not simply reflect but constructs reality or meaning—that is adopted by cultural studies and is reflected in its methodologies.

**Rouch, Jean (1917–2004):** Rouch was a French ethnographic filmmaker of mainly African societies. The particular poetry of his films is well explored in his 'biography' by Stoller titled: *The Cinematic Griot: The Ethnography of Jean Rouch*.

**Rubin, Gayle (1949– ):** An activist and trained as an anthropologist, Gayle is best known for her influential theories of sex and gender politics. She is currently Assistant Professor of Comparative Literature at the University of Michigan. Gayle first came to prominence with her essay 'The Traffic in Women: Notes on the "Political Economy" of Sex', which was published in 1975. It is in this essay that she coined the term 'sex/gender system', which has been taken up and used by various feminist philosophers and cultural theorists worldwide.

**Said, Edward (1935–2003):** Edward Said was the first to introduce the notion of 'Orientalism', which means the way in which Western images conceived of and constructed the non-West. He argues that Western representation of the non-West shaped the ideology of colonial capitalism. So Orientalism is a Western narrative that is tied to Western imperialism and knowledge. Following the work of Michel Foucault, Said's notion of Orientalism as a Western form of representation led to a whole set of writings known as post-colonial theory.

**Schmitt, Carl (1888–1985):** Schmitt was a German theorist known for his involvement with Nazism and his work on the idea of the political and political theology. In the West he has been taken up by thinkers such as Giorgio Agamben and Chantel Mouffe, most clearly through his work on sovereignty. Two of his best-known works are *War/Non-War: A Dilemma* and *The Tyranny of Values*.

**Scopic power:** The word 'scopic' is derived from the Greek *skopeo*, which means 'I look at'. Scopic power refers to the way in which the act of looking (the scopic) is inscribed with relations of power according to the particular positions that subjects occupy. For example, a soldier photographing a prisoner occupies a superior position of scopic power over the prisoner because he/she can exercise both physical and symbolic acts of violence over the captive subject. The soldier can thus, because of his/her superior position of power, command the prisoner to strip naked and perform sexual acts for the scopic gratification of fellow soldiers or other spectators.

**Sedgwick, Eve (1950– ):** An American philosopher and critic, Sedgwick's work on homosocial desire led to her being one of the founders of gay and lesbian studies in America. Her work revolves around queer politics, and Queer Studies as a formal academic discipline is largely due to her theoretical writings, her most famous being *Epistemology of the Closet*. She is currently Newman Ivy White Professor of English at Duke University.

**Semiotics:** Sometimes called 'the science (or study) of signs', semiotics is an analytical practice that consists of reading the direct and implicit meanings of texts in all media, based on an essentially historical and/or intertextual study of their component elements. Developed from the work of Ferdinand de Saussure (1857–1913), C.S. Pierce (1839–1914) and Louis Hjelmslev (1899–1965), semiotics influenced poststructuralist linguists and theorists such as Roland Barthes and Umberto Eco. Semiotics identifies texts as active social practices, as ways of intervening in the world, not simply as reflections or expressions of a person or institution or organisation.

**Speech-act theory:** 'Speech act theory' was pioneered by the linguist-philosopher J.L. Austin, who classified the performative aspect of speech acts into locutionary acts, illocutionary acts and perlocutionary acts. Locutionary acts can be defined as the meaningful phonetic, grammatical forms produced when we speak. Illocutionary acts indicate what is actually 'performed' when uttering words or a sentence, such as promising, demanding or accusing. The perlocutionary acts are those that directly affect their hearer(s); for instance, frightening or embarrassing someone.

**Stolen Generations:** The Stolen Generations is the name given to Australian Aboriginal children who were forcibly removed from their parents between the 1900s and the 1970s by the Australian government and the churches and placed in foster care with white Australians or in church missions. A government inquiry estimates that around 30 per cent of all Aboriginal children during this period were removed (about 100 000 children).

**Subculture:** A term from sociology that refers to a social group that holds and/or exhibits distinctive practices, beliefs or behaviours different from those of the wider or 'parent' culture to which they belong.

**Subject/Subjectivity:** In Cultural Studies the 'I' or 'self' is not something pre-given, that is, something that exists outside an historical context or society and culture. However, the terms 'self' or 'I' have traditionally been designated to describe this pre-given essentialist notion. Because of this, cultural studies uses the term 'subject' or 'subjectivity' to convey the self as that which is situated and constructed in relations of power: that is, to others, to culture and society, as well as to gender, language, and political and ethnic contexts. Philosophers and theorists who have influenced this general view of subjectivity that has been taken up by Cultural Studies include Friedrich Nietzsche, Michel Foucault, Julia Kristeva, Gilles Deleuze, Felix Guattari and Jacques Derrida.

**Whiteness:** whiteness theory explores 1) the racial sense of national belonging in European and ex-colonial nations, where legal and political institutions and cultural representations have been shaped by the exclusion and exploitation of those not recognised as white; 2) the ways in which the state uses forms of property to protect citizens from state intervention and social discrimination based on the meanings attributed to racial 'difference'; and 3) how whiteness is an everyday experience of members of a group who enjoys relative privilege compared to those marked as racially 'different' in European and ex-settler colonial nations.

**Worlding:** The everyday activity of creating and sustaining subcommunities within the broader social collectivity, bringing together individuals who collectively enact shared interests, desires, identities and material practices.

# bibliography.

### introduction.

Booth, Wayne 2004. 'All Who Care about the Future of Criticism'. *Critical Inquiry* 30(2): 350–4.

Chandler, James 2004. 'Critical Disciplinarity'. *Critical Inquiry* 30(2): 355–60.

Eagleton, Terry 2003. *After Theory*. New York: Basic Books.

Galison, Peter 2004. 'Specific Theory'. *Critical Inquiry* 30(2): 379–83.

Harootunian, Harry 2004. 'Theory's Empire: Reflections on a Vocation for *Critical Inquiry*'. *Critical Inquiry* 30(2): 396–402.


## PART 1. bodies and embodiment.

Butler, Judith 1999. *Gender Trouble*. London: Routledge.

Cranny-Francis, Anne 1995. *The Body in the Text*. Melbourne University Press.

Crossley, Nick 1994. *The Politics of Subjectivity: Between Foucault and Merleau-Ponty*. Aldershot, UK: Ashgate.

Derrida, Jacques 1981. *Dissemination*. University of Chicago Press.

Descartes, René 1986. *Meditations on first philosophy*, trans. John Cottingham, introduced by Bernard Williams. Cambridge University Press.

Descartes, René 1989. *The Passions of the Soul*, trans. Stephen Voss. Indianapolis, Ind.: Hackett Pub. Co.

Descombes, Vincent 1991. 'A Propos of the "Critique of the Subject" and the Critique of this Critique.' In E. Cadava, P. Connor & J.-L. Nancy (eds) *Who Comes After the Subject?* New York and London: Routledge.

Deutscher, Penelope 1998. 'The Body.' In Barbara Caine et al. (eds) *Oxford Companion to Australian Feminism*. Oxford: Oxford University Press, pp. 11–19.

Foucault, Michel 1973. *Madness and civilization: a history of insanity in the Age of Reason*, trans. Richard Howard. New York: Vintage Books.

—— 1980. *Power/Knowledge: Selected Interviews and Other Writings 1972–1977*. New York: Pantheon Books.

—— 1991. *Discipline and Punish: The Birth of the Prison*. London: Penguin.

Grosz, Elizabeth 1994. *Volatile Bodies: Toward a Corporeal Feminism*. Sydney: Allen & Unwin.

Harvey, Irene 1983. 'Derrida and the Concept of Metaphysics.' *Research in Phenomenology* 13.

Merleau-Ponty, Maurice 1968. *The Visible and the Invisible*. Trans. Alphonso Lingis. Evanston, Ill.: Northwestern University Press.

—— 2002. *Phenomenology of Perception: An Introduction*, trans. Colin Smith. 2nd edn. New York: Routledge.

Plato 1964. *Meno*. R.S. Bluck (ed.). Cambridge: Cambridge University Press.

Rubin, Gayle 1975. 'The Traffic in Women: Notes on the "Political Economy" of Sex.' In Rayna Reiter (ed.) *Toward an Anthropology of Women*. New York: Monthly Review Press.

—— 1984. 'Thinking Sex: Notes for a Radical Theory of the Politics of Sexuality.' In C. Vance (ed.) *Pleasure and Danger: Exploring Female Sexuality*. London: Routledge & Kegan Paul.

Sullivan, Nikki 2002. 'Fleshly (Dis)Figuration, or How to Make the Body Matter.' *International Journal of Critical Psychology* 5: 12–29.

—— 2005. 'The Body'. *Macquarie Online Lecture*. Sydney: Macquarie University.

## 1. alternative therapies as disciplinary practices: the uses and limitations of a foucauldian approach.

Armstrong, David 1995. 'The Rise of Surveillance Medicine.' *Sociology of Health and Illness* 17(3): 393–404.

Barcan, Ruth, and Jay Johnston 2005. 'The Haunting: Cultural Studies, Religion and Alternative Therapies.' *Iowa Journal of Cultural Studies* 7: 63–81.

Bennett, Tony 1998. *Culture: A Reformer's Science*. Sydney: Allen & Unwin.

Bernauer, James W., and Michael Mahon 1994. 'The Ethics of Michel Foucault.' In G. Gutting (ed.) *The Cambridge Companion to Foucault*. Cambridge University Press, pp. 141–58.

Coward, Rosalind 1989. *The Whole Truth: The Myth of Alternative Health*. London: Faber.

Featherstone, Mike 1991. 'The Body in Consumer Culture.' In M. Featherstone, M. Hepworth and B. Turner (eds) *The Body: Social Process and Cultural Theory*. London: Sage, pp. 170–96.

Foucault, Michel 1979a. *Discipline and Punish: The Birth of the Prison*, trans. Alan Sheridan. London: Peregrine.

—— 1979b. *The History of Sexuality: An Introduction*, trans. Robert Hurley. London: Peregrine.

—— 1980. 'Truth and Power.' In C. Gordon (ed.) *Power/Knowledge: Selected Interviews and Other Writings 1972–1977*. New York: Harvester Wheatsheaf, pp. 109–33.

—— 1983. 'On the Genealogy of Ethics: An Overview of Work in Progress.' In H.L. Dreyfus and P. Rabinow, *Michel Foucault: Beyond Structuralism and Hermeneutics*, 2nd edn. Chicago University Press, pp. 229–52.

—— 1986. 'Kant on Enlightenment and Revolution.' *Economy and Society* 15(1): 88–9.

—— 1989. 'Subjectivité et vérité.' In *Résumé des cours 1970–1982*. Paris: Julliard, pp. 133–42.

Frow, John 1998. 'Is Elvis a God? Cult, Culture, Questions of Method.' *International Journal of Cultural Studies* 1(2): 197–210.

Gibbs, Anna 2002. 'Disaffected.' *Continuum: Journal of Media and Cultural Studies* 16(3): 335–41.

Hay, Louise L. 1987. *You Can Heal Your Life*. Sydney: Specialist Printing.

Heyes, Cressida J. 2007. *Self-Transformations: Foucault, Ethics, and Normalized Bodies*. Oxford: Oxford University Press.

Johnston, Jay 2007 forthcoming. *Angels of Desire: Esoteric Bodies, Aesthetics and Ethics*. London: Equinox.

Johnston, Jay, and Ruth Barcan 2006. 'Subtle Transformations: Imagining the Body in Alternative Health Practices.' *International Journal of Cultural Studies* 9(1): 25–44.

Morris, Meaghan 1990. 'Banality in Cultural Studies.' In P. Mellencamp (ed.), *Logics of Television: Essays in Cultural Criticism*. Bloomington, Ind.: Indiana University Press, pp. 14–43.

Probyn, Elspeth 2005. *Blush: Faces of Shame*. Sydney: University of NSW Press.

Rimke, Heidi Marie 2000. 'Governing Citizens through Self-Help Literature.' *Cultural Studies* 14(1): 61–78.

Rose, Nikolas 1996. *Inventing Ourselves: Psychology, Power, and Personhood*. Cambridge University Press.

—— 1999. *Governing the Soul: The Shaping of the Private Self*, 2nd edn. London: Free Association Books.

Sedgwick, Eve Kosofsky 2003. 'Paranoid Reading and Reparative Reading, Or, You're so Paranoid, You Probably Think This Essay is About You.' In *Touching Feeling: Affect, Pedagogy, Performativity*. Durham, N.C.: Duke University Press, pp. 123–51.

Shumsky, Susan G. 1996. *Divine Revelation*. New York: Fireside.

Stacey, Jackie 1997. *Teratologies: A Cultural Study of Cancer*. London: Routledge.

Turner, Bryan 1992. *Regulating Bodies: Essays in Medical Sociology*. London: Routledge.

Veyne, Paul 1993. 'The Final Foucault and his Ethics.' *Critical Inquiry* 20: 1–9.

Wilson, Elizabeth A. 2004. *Psychosomatic: Feminism and the Neurological Body*. Durham, N.C.: Duke University Press.

## 2. body, gender, *gurlesque*, intersex.

Agamben, Giorgio 1999. *Remnants of Auschwitz: The Witness and the Archive*. New York: Zone Books.

Bodies Like Ours 2005. <www.bodieslikeours.org/missionstatement.htm>, <www.bodieslikeours.org/missionstatement.htm> (accessed 23 June 2005).

Butler, Judith 1999. *Gender Trouble: Feminism and the Subversion of Identity*. New York: Routledge.

—— 1993. *Bodies That Matter: On the Discursive Limits of 'Sex'*. New York and London: Routledge.

—— 1997a. *The Psychic Life of Power: Theories of Subjection*. Stanford University Press.

—— 1997b. *Exciteable Speech: A Politics of the Performative*. New York: Routledge.

—— 2001. 'Doing Justice to Someone: Sex Reassignment and Allegories of Transexuality.' *GLQ* 7(4): 621–36.

—— 2004a. 'Beside Oneself: On the Limits of Sexual Autonomy.' In *Undoing Gender*. New York and London: Routledge, pp. 17–39.

—— 2004b. *Precarious Life*. London and New York: Verso.

—— 2004c. *Undoing Gender*. New York and London: Routledge.

—— 2005. *Giving an Account of Oneself*. New York: Fordham University Press.

Crowley, Vicki 2000. 'The Unforgiving Scalpel, Clinical Precision, and the Untold of Gender.' *Australia Education Researcher* 29(2): 145–59.

Dreger, Alice Domurat 1999. 'A History of Intersex: From the Age of Gonads to the Age of Consent.' In A. Dreger (ed.) *Intersex in the Age of Ethics*. Hagerstown, Md.: University Publishing Group, pp. 5–22.

Fiske, John 1992. 'Cultural Studies and the Culture of Everyday Life.' In L. Grossberg, C. Nelson and P. Treichler (eds) *Cultural Studies*. New York and London: Routledge, pp. 154–65.

Foucault, Michel 1973. *The Birth of the Clinic: An Archaeology of Medical Perception*, trans. A.M. Sheridan. New York: Vintage.

—— 1977. *Discipline and Punish: The Birth of the Prison*, trans. Alan Sheridan. London: Allen Lane.

—— 1978. *The History of Sexuality* vol. 1, trans. Robert Hurley. New York: Vintage Books.

—— 1984. 'Polemics, Politics, and Problematizations: An Interview with Michel Foucault.' In Paul Rabinow (ed.) *The Foucault Reader*. London: Penguin Books, pp. 381–90.

Gandhi, Leela 2006. *Affective Communities: Anticolonial Thought, Fin-de-Siècle Radicalism and the Politics of Friendship*. Durham, N.C. and London: Duke University Press.

Gatens, Moira 1996. *Imaginary Bodies: Ethics Power and Corporeality*. London and New York: Routledge.

Gopinath, Gayatri 2005. *Impossible Desires: Queer Diasporas and South Asian Public Culture*. Durham, N.C. and London: Duke University Press.

Gramsci, Antonio 1971. *Selections form the Prison Notebooks of Antonio Gramsci*, ed. and trans. Quintin Hoare and Geoffrey Nowell Smith. London: Lawrence & Wishart.

Grosz, Elizabeth 1994. *Volatile Bodies: Toward a Corporeal Feminism*. Sydney: Allen & Unwin.

Grosz, Elizabeth, and Elspeth Probyn (eds) 1995. *Sexy Bodies: The Strange Carnalities of Feminism*. London and New York: Routledge.

*Gurlesque Burlesque Lezzo Strip Club* 2007. Sydney. <www.gurlesque.com/>, accessed 3 April 2007.

Honig, Bonnie 2006. 'Another Cosmopolitanism? Law and Politics in the New Europe.' In S. Benhabib (ed.) *Another Cosmopolitanism*. Oxford and New York: Oxford University Press.

Intersex Society of North America (ISNA). <www.isna.org/>.

Long, Gothard, and Helen Brash 1997. *Forging Identities: Bodies, Gender and Feminist History*. Perth: University of Western Australia Press.

MacCannell, Juliet Flower and Laura Zakarin 1994. *Thinking Bodies*. Stanford University Press.

Mack, Phyllis 1997. 'Preface: Dostoevsky's Toothache: Body, Selfhood and the Historian.' In J. Long, J. Gothard and H. Brash, *Forging Identities: Bodies, Gender and Feminist History*. Perth: University of Western Australia Press, pp. i–xx.

Mercer, Kobena 1994. *Welcome to the Jungle: New Positions in Black Cultural Studies*. New York: Routledge.

Munoz, José Esteban 1999. *Disidentifications: Queers of Color and the Performance of Politics*. Minneapolis, Minn.: University of Minnesota Press.

Mussawir, Edward 2007. 'Intersex: Between Law and Nature.' In Anna Hickey-Moody and Peta Malins (eds) *Deleuzian Encounters: Studies in Contemporary Social Issues.* London: Palgrave Macmillan, pp. 50–61.

Nancy, Jean-Luc 1993. *The Birth to Presence.* Stanford University Press.

Probyn, Elspeth 1993. Sexing the Self: Gendered Positions in Cultural Studies. London and New York: Routledge.

Rich, Adrienne 1980/1994. 'Compulsory Heterosexuality and Lesbian Existence.' In *Blood Bread and Poetry.* New York: Norton Paperback.

Rubin, Gayle 1984. 'Thinking Sex: Notes for a Radical Theory of the Politics of Sexuality.' In C. Vance (ed.) *Pleasure and Danger.* New York: Routledge & Kegan Paul.

Salzman, Martha, Ira Matathia and Anne O'Reilly 2005. *The Future of Men.* London: Palgrave Macmillan.

Sappington, Rodney, and Tyler Stallings (eds) 1994. *Uncontrollable Bodies: Testimonies of Identity and Culture.* Seattle: Bay Press.

se Mbessakwini, Shorona 2002. *Intersex Exposition: Full Monty,* videocassette (VHS) 7 min. Editors, Inka Stafrace, Ainslee Hunter, Robert John Leggo. Performer, Shorona se Mbessakwini. Sydney.

*Urban Dictionary* 2007. <www.urbandictionary.com/define.php?term=ubersexual>, accessed 23 July 2007.

Wittig, Monique 1992. *The Straight Mind and Other Essays.* Boston: Beacon Press.

## 3. touching skin: embodiment and the senses in the work of ron mueck.

Bolland, Andrea 2000. '*Desiderio* and *Diletto*: Vision, Touch, and the Poetics of Bernini's *Apollo and Daphne.*' Art Bulletin 82(2): 309–30.

Greeves, Susanna 2003. 'Ron Mueck: a Redefinition of Realism.' In Heiner Bastian (ed.) *Ron Mueck.* Ostfildern-Ruit: Hatje Cantz, pp. 26–40.

Heidegger, Martin 1993. *Basic Writings from Being and Time (1927) to the Task of Thinking (1964),* ed. David Farrell Krell. London: Routledge.

Hopkins, Robert 2004. 'Painting, Sculpture, Sight, and Touch.' *British Journal of Aesthetics* 44(2): 149–66.

Howes, David 2006. 'Charting the Sensorial Revolution.' *Senses and Society* 1(1): 113–28.

Langer, Suzanne K. 1953. *Feeling and Form: A Theory of Art Developed from Philosophy in a New Key.* London: Routledge & Kegan Paul.

Latour, Bruno 2003. 'Do You Believe in Reality? News from the Trenches of the Science Wars?' In Robert C. Scharff and Val Dusek (eds) *Philosophy of Technology: The Technological Condition. An Anthology.* Oxford: Blackwell, pp. 126–37.

## PART 2. poststructuralism.

Benjamin, Andrew (ed.) 1988. *Post-structuralist Classics.* London and New York: Routledge.

Derrida, Jacques 1973. *Speech and Phenomena: and Other Essays on Husserl's Theory of Signs.* Trans. David B. Allison. Evanston: Northwestern University Press.

—— 1976. *Of Grammatology*, trans. G.C. Spivak. Baltimore: Johns Hopkins University Press.

—— 1981. *Dissemination*. University of Chicago Press.

—— 1982. *Positions*, trans. Alan Bass. University of Chicago Press.

—— 1986. *Margins of Philosophy*, trans. Alan Bass. University of Chicago Press.

—— 1995. *Writing and Difference*, trans. A. Bass. London: Routledge.

Foucault, Michel 1973. *The Order of Things: An Archaeology of the Human Sciences*. New York: Vintage Books.

—— 1980. *Power/Knowledge: selected interviews & other writings 1972-1977*. New York: Pantheon Books.

—— 1989. *The Archaeology of Knowledge*. New York: Routledge.

—— 1990. *The History of Sexuality: An Introduction, volume 1*, trans. Robert Hurley. New York: Vintage Books

—— 1991. *Discipline and Punish: The Birth of the Prison.*England: Penguin Books.

Hawthorn, Jeremy 1992. *A Concise Glossary of Contemporary Literary Theory*. London: Edward Arnold.

McHoul, Alec, and Wendy Grace 1993. *A Foucualt Primer: Discourse, Power and the Subject*. Melbourne University Press.

Saussure, Ferdinand de 1991. 'The object of study' and 'Nature of the linguistic sign'. In Devid Lodge (ed.) *Modern Criticism and Theroy: A Reader*. London and New York: Longman.

Storey, John 1993. *An Introductory Guide to Cultural Theory and Popular Culture*. UK: Harvester Wheatsheaf.

Thwaites, Tony, Lloyd Davis and Warwick Mules 1995. *Tools for Cultural Studies: An Introduction*. Melbourne: Macmillan Education Australia.

## 4. no peace without war, no war without peace: deconstructing war.

Derrida, Jacques 1997. *Politics of Friendship*, trans. George Collins. Verso: London.

—— 1999. *Adieu To Emmanuel Levinas*, trans. Pascale-Anne Brault and Michael Naas. Stanford University Press.

Levinas, Emmanuel 1969. *Totality and Infinity: An Essay on Exteriority*, trans. Alphonso Lingis. Pittsburgh: Duquesne University Press.

Schmitt, Carl 1996. *The Concept of the Political*, trans. George Schwab. University of Chicago Press.

Shaw, Martin 2005. *The New Western Way of War*. Cambridge: Polity.

## 5. eating the other: deconstructing the 'ethics' of cannibalism.

Anderson, Nicole 2003. 'The Ethical Possibilities of the Subject as Play: in Nietzsche and Derrida.' *Journal of Nietzsche Studies* 26: 79–90.

—— 2006a. 'Freeplay? Fairplay! Defending Derrida.' *Social Semiotics* 16(3): 407–20.

—— 2006b. 'Deconstructing Technologies of Subjectivity.' *SCAN: Journal of Media Arts Culture* 3(3).

Derrida, Jacques 1973. *Speech and Phenomena: and Other Essays on Husserl's Theory of Signs*, trans. David B. Allison. Evanston, Ill.: Northwestern University Press.

—— 1986. *Margins of Philosophy*, trans. Alan Bass. University of Chicago Press.

—— 1991. '"Eating Well", or the Calculation of the Subject: An Interview with Jacques Derrida.' In E. Cadava, P. Connor and J.-L. Nancy (eds) *Who Comes After the Subject?* New York and London: Routledge.

—— 1992. 'Force of Law: The "Mystical Foundation" of Authority.' In D. Cornell, M. Rosenfeld and D.G. Carlson (eds) *Deconstruction and the Possibility of Justice.* New York and London: Routledge.

—— 1999. *Adieu: To Emmanuel Levinas*, eds W. Hamacher and D.E. Wellbery, trans. Pascale-Anne Brault and Michael Naas. Stanford University Press.

—— 2000. *Of Hospitality*, eds Miele Bal and Hent de Vries, trans. Rachel Bowlby. Stanford University Press.

Deutscher, Penelope 1998. 'Mourning the Other: Cultural Cannibalism and the Politics of Friendship (Jacques Derrida and Luce Irigaray).' *differences: A Journal of Feminist Cultural Studies* 10(3): 159–84.

Diprose, Rosalyn 1994. *The Bodies of Women: Ethics, Embodiment and Sexual Difference.* London and New York: Routledge.

Foucault, Michel 1997. *Ethics: Subjectivity and Truth: The Essential Works 1*, ed. Paul Rabinow. London: Allen Lane.

Guyer, Sara 1995. 'Albeit Eating: Towards an Ethics of Cannibalism.' *Angelaki* 2(1): 63–81.

Levinas, Emmanuel 1996. *Totality and Infinity*. Philosophical Series no. 24, trans. Alfonso Lingis. Pittsburgh: Duquesne University Press.

## 6. tattooing: the bio-political inscription of bodies and selves.

Atkinson, Michael 2003. 'The Civilizing Resistance: Straightedge Tattooing.' *Deviant Behaviour: An Interdisciplinary Journal* 24: 197–220.

Baden, M. 1973. 'Symbols: Tattoos on Teenage Cadavers.' *Medical World News* August.

Bennahum, D.A. 1971. 'Tattoos of Heroin Addicts in New Mexico.' *Rocky Mountain Medical Journal* 68(9): 63–6.

Body Play … 1993. Online journal, <www.bodyplay.com/bodyplay/index.htm>.

Braithwaite, R., A. Robillard, T. Woodring et al. 2001. 'Tattooing and Body Piercing Among Adolescent Detainees: Relationship to Alcohol and Other Drug Use.' *Journal of Substance Abuse* 13: 5–16.

Braunberger, Christine 2000. 'Revolting Bodies: The Monster Beauty of Tattooed Women.' *NWSA Journal* 12(2): 1–20.

Brooks, Traci I., Elizabeth R. Woods, John R. Knight and Lydia A. Schrier 2003. 'Body Modification and Substance Abuse in Adolescents: Is There a Link?' *Journal of Adolescent Health* 32: 44–9.

Butler, Judith 2005. 'Bodies that Matter.' In M. Fraser and M. Greco (eds) *The Body: A Reader.* London: Routledge, pp. 62–5.

Caplan, Richard, Judith Komaromi and Mike Rhodes 1996. 'Obsessive-Compulsive Disorder, Tattooing and Bizarre Sexual Practices.' *British Journal of Psychiatry* 168: 379–80.

Claes, L., W. Vandereycken and H. Vertommen 2005. 'Self-care Versus Self-harm: Piercing, Tattooing, and Self-injury in Eating Disorders.' *European Eating Disorders Review* 13(1): 11–18.

Colman, Adrian 2001. 'Body Piercing.' *Youth Studies Australia* 20(3): 8.

Copes, J., and C.J. Forsyth 1993. 'The Tattoo: A Social Psychological Explanation.' *International Review of Modern Sociology* 23(2): 83–9.

Curry, David 1993. 'Decorating the Body Politic.' *New Formations* 19: 69–82.

Edgerton, R., and H. Dingman 1963. 'Tattooing and Identity.' *International Journal of Social Psychiatry* 9: 143–53.

Ferguson-Rayport, S.M., R.M. Griffith and E.W. Strauss 1955. 'The Psychiatric Significance of Tattoos.' *Psychiatric Quarterly* 29: 112–31.

Foucault, Michel 1979. *Discipline and Punish: The Birth of the Prison*, trans. A. Sheridan. London: Penguin.

—— 1980a. *The History of Sexuality* vol.1, trans. R. Hurley. New York: Vintage Books.

—— 1980b. *Power/Knowledge: Selected Interviews and Other Writings 1972–77*, ed. C. Gordon. Brighton, Sussex: Harvester Press.

—— 2004. *Society Must Be Defended: Lectures at the Collège de France, 1975–76*, trans. D. Macey. Harmondsworth: Penguin Books.

Gittleson, N., G. Wallen and K. Dawson-Butterworth 1969. 'The Tattooed Psychiatric Patient.' *British Journal of Psychiatry* 115: 1249–53.

Gladsjo, Leslie Asako 1991. *Stigmata: The Transfigured Body* (Videorecording). New York: Women Make Movies.

Goldstein, Norman 1979. 'Psychological Implications of Tattoos.' *Journal of Dermatology and Surgical Oncology* 5: 883–8.

Grosz, Elizabeth 1990. 'Inscriptions and Body-maps: Representations and the Corporeal.' In A. Cranny-Francis and T. Threadgold (eds) *Feminine, Masculine and Representation*. Sydney: Allen & Unwin, pp. 62–74.

Grumet, Gerald W. 1983. 'Psychodynamic Implications of Tattoos.' *American Journal of Orthopsychiatry* 53(3): 482–92.

Hall, Stuart 1997. *Representation: Cultural Representations and Signifying Practices*. London: Sage.

Hamburger, E. 1966. 'Tattooing as a Psychic Defense Mechanism.' *International Journal of Social Psychiatry* 12: 60–2.

Irigaray, Luce 1985. 'When Our Lips Speak Together.' In *This Sex Which Is Not One*, trans. C. Porter with Carolyn Burke. Ithaca, N.Y.: Cornell University Press.

Jeffreys, Sheila 1994. 'Sadomasochism, Art and the Lesbian Sexual Revolution.' *Artlink* 14(1): 19–21.

—— 2000. '"Body Art" and Social Status: Cutting, Tattooing and Piercing from a Feminist Perspective.' *Feminism and Psychology* 10(4): 409–29.

—— 2005. *Beauty and Misogyny: Harmful Cultural Practices in the West*. London: Routledge.

Jessor, R. 1991. 'Risk Behaviour in Adolescence: A Psychosocial Framework for Understanding and Action.' *Journal of Adolescent Health* 12: 597–605.

Juno, Andrea, and V. Vale 1989. *Modern Primitives*. London: Re/Search Publications.

Koch, J., Z. Zhu, J. Cannon, M. Armstrong and D. Owen 2005. 'College Students, Tattooing, and the Health Belief Model: Extending Social Psychological Perspectives on Youth Culture and Deviance.' *Sociological Spectrum* 25(1): 79–102.

Lander, J., and A. Kohn 1943. 'A Note on Tattooing among Selectees.' *American Journal of Psychiatry* 100: 326–7.

Loos, Adolf 1908. 'Ornamentation and Crime.' In *The Architecture of Adolf Loos*. New York: Arts Council, pp. 100–3.

Mifflin, Margot 1997. *Bodies of Subversion: A Secret History of Women and Tattoo*. New York: Juno Books.

Parry, Albert 1934. 'Tattooing Among Prostitutes and Perverts.' *Psychoanalytic Quarterly* 3: 476–82.

Pitts, Victoria 1999. 'Body Modification, Self-Mutilation and Agency in Media Accounts of a Subculture.' *Body and Society* 5: 2–3.

—— 2003. *In the Flesh: The Cultural Politics of Body Modification*. New York: Palgrave Macmillan.

Post, Richard S. 1968. 'The Relationship of Tattoos to Personality Disorders.' *Journal of Criminal Law, Criminology, and Police Science* 59: 516–24.

Roberts, T., P. Auinger and S. Ryan 2002. 'Gender Differences in the Association Between Body Piercing and Adolescent Risk Behaviour.' *Journal of Adolescent Health* 30: 103–4.

Roberts, T., and S. Ryan 2001. 'Tattooing and High Risk Behaviour in Adolescents.' *Paediatric Research* 32: 49–50.

Sanders, Clinton 1989. *Customizing the Body: The Art and Culture of Tattooing*. Philadelphia, Pa.: Temple University Press.

Skin & Ink Magazine 1994. April Issue. Magna Publishing Group.

Sullivan, Nikki 2001. *Tattooed Bodies: Subjectivity, Textuality, Ethics, and Pleasure*. Westport Conn.: Praeger.

—— 2002. 'Fleshly (Dis)Figuration, or How to Make the Body Matter.' *International Journal of Critical Psychology* 5: 12–29.

—— 2006. 'Transmogrification: (Un)Becoming Other(s).' In S. Stryker and S. Whittle (eds) *The Transgender Studies Reader*. London: Routledge, pp. 552–64.

—— 2007. 'Incisive Bodies: Lolo, Lyotard, and the "Exorbitant Law of Listening to the Inaudible".' In M. Grebowicz (ed.) *Gender After Lyotard*. Albany, N.Y.: State University of New York Press, pp. 47–66.

Terry, Jennifer, and Jacqueline Urla (eds) 1995. *Deviant Bodies: Critical Perspectives on Difference in Science and Popular Culture*. Indianapolis, Ind.: Indiana University Press.

Verbene, T. 1969. 'The Personality Traits of Tattooed Adolescent Offenders.' *British Journal of Criminology* 9: 172–5.

Wojcik, Daniel 1995. *Punk and Neo-Tribal Body Art*. Jackson, Miss.: University Press of Mississippi.

Yamamoto, J., W. Seeman and B.K. Lester 1963. 'The Tattooed Man.' *Journal of Nervous and Mental Disorders* 136: 365–7.

## PART 3. postmodernism.

Baudrillard, Jean 1983. *Simulations*. New York: Semiotext(e).

—— 1987. *The Evil Demon of Images*. Sydney: Power Institute Publications.

Docherty, Thomas (ed.) 1993. *Postmodernism: A Reader*. New York: Harvester Wheatsheaf.

Habermas, Jurgen 1987. *The Philosophical Discourse of Modernity*. Cambridge, Mass.: MIT Press.

Harvey, David 1989. *The Condition of Postmodernity*. Oxford: Blackwell.

Hassan, Ihab 1985. 'The Culture of Postmodernism.' *Theory, Culture and Society* 2(3): 121.

Hawthorn, Jeremy 1992. *A Concise Glossary of Contemporary Literary Theory*. London: Edward Arnold.

Hutcheon, Linda 1989. *The Politics of Postmodernism*. London: Routledge.

Huyssen, Andreas 1988. *After the Great Divide: Modernism, Mass Culture and Postmodernism*. London: Macmillan.

Jameson, Fredric 1991. *Postmodernism, or The Cultural Logic of Late Capitalism*. London: Verso and Duke University Press.

Lucy, Niall 1997. *Postmodern Literary Theory: An Introduction*. Oxford: Blackwell.

Lyotard, Jean-Francois 1979/1984. *The Postmodern Condition: A Report on Knowledge*. Manchester University Press.

Norris, Christopher 1990. *What's Wrong with Postmodernism*. New York: Harvester Wheatsheaf.

Rorty, Richard 1983. 'Postmodernist Bourgeois Liberalism.' *Journal of Philosophy* 80: 583–9.

—— 1984. 'Habermas and Lyotard on postmodernity.' *Praxis International* 4: 32–44.

Storey, John 1993. *An Introductory Guide to Cultural Theory and Popular Culture*. New York: Harvester Wheatsheaf.

Waugh, Patricia 1992. *Practicing Postmodernism, Reading Modernism*. London: Edward Arnold.

## 7. living with things: consumption, material culture and everyday life.

Adorno, T., and M. Horkheimer 1947/1973. *The Dialectic of Enlightenment*, trans. John Cumming. London: Allen Lane.

Arnold, M. 1869/1960. *Culture and Anarchy*. Cambridge University Press.

Baudrillard, J. 1996. *The System of Objects*, trans. J. Benedict. London: Verso.

Bayley, S. 1986. *Sex, Drink and Fast Cars: The Creation and Consumption of Images*. London: Faber & Faber.

Berking, H. 1999. *The Sociology of Giving*, trans. P. Camiller. London: Sage.

Bourdieu, P. 1984. *Distinction*, trans. R. Nice. Cambridge, Mass.: Harvard University Press.

Branzi, A. 1988. *Learning from Milan*. Cambridge, Mass.: MIT Press.

Carrier, J. 1993. 'The Rituals of Christmas Giving.' In D. Miller (ed.) *Unwrapping Christmas*. Oxford: Clarendon Press, pp. 55–64.

Csikszentmihalyi, M., and E. Rochberg-Halton 1981. *The Meaning of Things*. Cambridge University Press.

Dant, T. 1999. *Material Culture in the Social World*. Buckingham: Open University Press.

Diprose, R. 1996. 'The Gift, the Sexed Body and the Law.' In P. Chea, D. Fraser and J. Grbich (eds) *Thinking Through the Body of the Law*. Sydney: Allen & Unwin, pp. 120–35.

Douglas, M., and B. Isherwood 1980. *The World of Goods*. Harmondsworth: Penguin.

Dupuis, A., and D. Thorns 1998. 'Home, Home Ownership and the Search for Ontological Security.' *Sociological Review* 46(1): 24–47.

Gray, A. 1992. *Video Playtime: The Gendering of a Leisure Technology*. London: Routledge.

Hebdige, D. 1979. *Subculture: The Meaning of Style*. London: Methuen.

Hegel, G. 1807/1977. *The Phenomenology of Spirit*, trans. A.V. Miller. Oxford: Oxford University Press.

Hobsbawm, E. 1969. *Industry and Empire*. Harmondsworth: Pelican.

Klein, N. 2000. *No Logo*. London: Flamingo.

Kopytoff, I. 1986. 'The Cultural Biography of Things.' In A. Appadurai (ed.) *The Social Life of Things*. Cambridge University Press, pp. 64–91.

Langman, L. 1992. 'Neon Cages.' In R. Shield (ed.) *Lifestyle Shopping*. London: Routledge.

Livingstone, S. 1992. 'The Meaning of Domestic Technologies.' In R. Silverstone and E. Hirsch (eds) *Consuming Technologies*. London: Routledge, pp. 113–30.

McCracken, G. 1988, *Culture and Consumption*. Bloomington, Ind.: Indiana University Press.

Marx, K. 1869/1976. *Capital*, trans. Ben Fowkes. Harmondsworth: Penguin.

Mauss, M. 1925/1967. *The Gift*, trans. Ian Cunnison. New York: W.W. Norton & Co.

Miller, D. 1987. *Material Culture and Mass Consumption*. Oxford: Blackwell.

—— 1988. 'Appropriating the State on the Council Estate.' *Man* 23: 353–72.

—— 1998. *A Theory of Shopping*. Cambridge: Polity.

Noble, G. 1999. 'Domesticating Technology: Learning To Live With Your Computer.' *Australian Journal of Communication* 26(2): 55–74.

—— 2002. 'Comfortable and Relaxed: Furnishing the Home and Nation.' *Continuum* 16(1): 53–66.

—— 2004. 'Accumulating Being.' *International Journal of Cultural Studies* 7(2): 233–56.

Noble, G., and R. Baldwin 2001. 'Sly Chicks and Troublemakers: Car Stickers, Nonsense and the Allure of Strangeness.' *Social Semiotics* 11(1): 75–89.

Oakley, A. 1974. *The Sociology of Housework*. London: Martin Robertson.

Packard, V. 1962. *The Hidden Persuaders*. Harmondsworth: Penguin.

Silverstone, R. *et al.* 1992. 'Information and Communication Technologies and the Moral Economy of the Household.' In R. Silverstone and E. Hirsch (eds) *Consuming Technologies*. London: Routledge, pp. 15–31.

Veblen, T. 1899/1998. *Theory of the Leisure Class*. Amherst, N.Y.: Prometheus Books.

Wernick, A. 1991. *Promotional Culture*. London: Sage.

## 8. flesh machines: self-making and the postmodern body.

Baudrillard, Jean 1994. *Simulacra and simulation*, trans. Sheila Faria Glaser. Ann Arbor: University of Michigan Press.

Braidotti, Rosi 2002. *Metamorphoses: Towards a Materialist Theory of Becoming*. Malden: Blackwell Publishers.

Butler, Judith 2003. *Bodies that Matter: On the Discursive Limits of 'Sex'*. New York: Routledge.

Connor, Steven 1997. *Postmodernist Culture: An Introduction to Theories of the Contemporary*. Oxford UK and Cambridge, Mass.: Blackwell.

Critical Art Ensemble 2007. <www.critical-art.net>, accessed 26 September 2007.

—— 1998. *The Flesh Machine: Cyborgs, Designer Babies, Eugenic Conscousness*. Brooklyn, N.Y.: Autonomedia. <www.critical-art.net/books/flesh/index.html>.

Foucault, Michel 1977. *Discipline and Punish: The Birth of the Prison*, trans. Alan Sheridan. London: Penguin.

Grosz, Elizabeth 1994. *Volatile Bodies: Towards a Corporeal Feminism*. Sydney: Allen & Unwin.

Halberstam, Judith, and Ira Livingston (eds) 1995. *Posthuman Bodies*. Bloomington, Ind.: Indiana University Press.

Haraway, Donna 1991. 'A Cyborg Manifesto: Science, Technology, and Socialist-Feminism in the Late Twentieth Century.' In *Simians, Cyborgs and Women: The Reinvention of Nature*. New York: Routledge, pp. 149–81.

Kroker, Arthur and Marilouise 1988. *Body Invaders: Sexuality and the Postmodern Condition*. London: Macmillan Education.

Lyotard, Jean-Francois 1984. *The Postmodern Condition: A Report on Knowledge*, trans. Geoff Bennington and Brian Massumi, foreword Fedrick Jameson. Minneapolis: University of Minnesota Press.

## 9. rrapping irigaray: flesh, passion, world.

Alexander, George 2002. 'Sexing the Cyborg: Julie Rrap's Overstepping.' *Artlink* 22: 1.

Alexander, George, Catriona Moor, Terence Maloon and Sam Schoenbaum 1998. *Julie Rrap*. Australia: Piper Press.

Backhouse, Megan 2003. 'Flesh Taking Form.' *The Age*, 9 August.

Irigaray, Luce 1985(a). *This Sex Which is Not One*, trans. Catherine Porter. Ithaca, N.Y.: Cornell University Press.

—— 1985(b). *Speculum of the Other Woman*, trans. Gillian C. Gill. Ithaca, N.Y.: Cornell University Press.

—— 1993. *An Ethics of Sexual Difference*, trans. Carolyn Porter. Ithaca, N.Y.: Cornell University Press.

—— 1996. *I Love To You: Sketch of a Possible Felicity in History*, trans. Alison Martin. New York: Routledge.

Marr, David, and Marian Wilkinson 2003. *Dark Victory*. Sydney: Allen & Unwin.

Parr, Adrian 2003. 'Stone into Flesh.' *Artlink* 23(3): 58–9.

Plato 1988. *Republic*, trans. Robin Waterfield. Oxford: Oxford University Press.

Ziarek, Ewa Plonowska 1998. 'Toward a Radical Female Imaginary: Temporality and Embodiment in Irigaray's Ethics.' *Diacritics* 28(1): 60–75.

Ziarek, Krzysztof 2000. 'Proximities: Irigaray and Heidegger on Difference.' *Continental Philosophy Review* 33.

# PART 4. gender and sexuality.

Butler, Judith 1990. *Gender Trouble: Feminism and the Subversion of Identity*. New York: Routledge.

Deleuze, Gilles, and Felix Guattari 1983. *Anti-Oedipus:Capitalism and Schizophrenia*. Minneapolis, Miss.: University of Minnesota Press.

Gatens, Moira 1996. *Imaginary Bodies: Ethics, Power and Corporeality*. New York: Routledge.

Laqueur Thomas 1990. *Making Sex: Body and Gender from the Greeks to Freud*. Cambridge, Mass.: Harvard University Press

Rubin, Gayle 1984. 'Thinking Sex: Notes for a Radical Theory of the Politics of Sexuality.' In Carol Vance (ed.) *Pleasure and Danger*. New York: Routledge.

## 10. kung fu fighting: doing action and negotiating masculinity.

Arroyo, Jose (ed.) 2000. *Action/Spectacle Cinema*. London: British Film Institute.

Bordwell, David 1997. 'Aesthetics in Action: Kung Fu, Gunplay, and Cinematic Expressivity.' In *The 21st Hong Kong International Film Festival Retrospective: Fifty Years of Electric Shadows*, Hong Kong: Urban Council, pp. 81–8.

Bordwell, David 2000. *Planet Hong Kong: Popular Cinema and the Art of Entertainment*. Cambridge, Mass.: Harvard University Press.

Brown, Bill 1997. 'Global Bodies/Postnationalities: Charles Johnson's Consumer Culture.' *Representations* 58: 24–48.

Ching, Leo 2000. 'Globalizing the Regional, Regionalizing the Global: Mass Culture and Asianism in the Age of Late Capital.' *Public Culture* 12(1): 233–57.

Connell, Robert W. 1995. *Masculinities*. Sydney: Allen & Unwin.

Desser, David 2000. 'The Kung Fu Craze: Hong Kong Cinema's First American Reception.' In Poshek Fu and David Desser (eds) *The Cinema of Hong Kong: History, Arts, Identity*. Cambridge University Press, pp. 19–43.

Eldridge, Elizabeth 2003. 'History.' *King Victoria Online Drag Kingdom*. <www.kingvictoria.figasia.com/history.htm>, accessed 2 June 2003.

Foucault, Michel 1997. *Ethics: Essential Works of Foucault 1954–1984*, ed. Paul Rabinow, trans. Robert Hurley. London: Penguin.

Halberstam, Judith 1998. *Female Masculinity*. Durham, N.C.: Duke University Press.

Hunt, Leon 2003. *Kung Fu Cult Masters: From Bruce Lee to Crouching Tiger*. London: Wallflower Press.

Jeffords, Susan 1984. *Hard Bodies: Hollywood Masculinity in the Reagan Era*. New Brunswick, N.J.: Rutgers University Press.

—— 1989. *The Remasculinization of America: Gender and the Vietnam War*. Bloomington, Ind.: Indiana University Press.

Kaminsky, Stuart 1974. 'Kung Fu Film as Ghetto Myth.' *Journal of Popular Film* 3(2): 129–38.

Kenny, Simon B. 2001. *The Pocket Essential Bruce Lee.* UK: Harpendon: Pocket Essentials.

Kim, James 2004. 'The Legend of the White-and-Yellow Black Man: Global Containment and Triangulated Racial Desire in Romeo Must Die.' *Camera Obscura* 1(1): 151–80.

Li, Siu Leung 2001. 'Kung Fu: Negotiating Nationalism and Modernity.' *Cultural Studies* 15(3–4): 515–42.

Logan, Bey 1995. *Hong Kong Action Cinema.* London: Titan.

Louie, Kam 2002. *Theorising Chinese Masculinity: Society and Gender in China.* Cambridge University Press.

Marchetti, Gina 2001. 'Jackie Chan and the black connection.' In Matthew Tinkcom and Amy Villarejo (eds) *Keyframes: Popular Cinema and Cultural Studies.* London: Routledge, pp. 137–58.

Mintz, Marilyn 1978. *The Martial Arts Film.* South Brunswick and New York: A.S. Barnes.

Morris, Meaghan 2001. 'Learning from Bruce Lee: Pedagogy and Political Correctness in Martial Arts Cinema.' In Matthew Tinkcom and Amy Villarejo (eds) *Keyframes: Popular Cinema and Cultural Studies.* London: Routledge, pp. 171–86.

—— 2004. 'Transnational Imagination in Action Cinema: Hong Kong and the Making of a Global Popular Culture.' *Inter-Asia Cultural Studies* 5(2): 181–99.

Morris, Meaghan, Siu Leung Li and Stephen Ching-kiu Chan (eds) 2005. *Hong Kong Connections: Transnational Imagination in Action Cinema.* Durham, N.C.: Duke Uuniversity Press.

Pang, Laikwan 2006. *Cultural Control and Globalization in Asia.* London: Routledge.

Stringer, Julian 1997. 'Problems with the Treatment of Hong Kong Cinema as Camp.' *Asian Cinema* 8(2): 44–65.

Srinivas, S.V. 2003. 'Hong Kong Action Film in the Indian B Circuit.' *Inter-Asia Cultural Studies* 4(1): 40–62.

Tasker, Yvonne 1997. 'Fists of Fury: Discourses of Race and Masculinity in the Martial Arts Cinema.' In Harry Stecopoulos and Michael Uebel (eds) *Race and The Subject of Masculinities.* Durham, N.C.: Duke University Press, pp. 315–36.

Teo, Stephen 1997. *Hong Kong Cinema: The Extra Dimensions.* London: British Film Institute.

Williams, Linda 1995. 'Film Bodies: Gender, Genre and Excess.' In Barry K. Grant (ed.) *Film Genre Reader 11,* Austin, Texas: University of Texas, pp. 166–86.

Yue, Audrey 2008. 'King Victoria: Asian Drag Kings, Multicultural Sexuality and Postcolonial Female Masculinity in Australia.' In Peter Jackson, Mark McLelland, Fran Martin and Audrey Yue (eds) *AsiaPacifiQueer: Rethinking Gender and Sexuality.* University of Illinois Press, in press.

## 11. can't get you out of my head: consuming celebrity, producing sexual identity.

Amico, Stephen 2001. '"I Want Muscles": House Music, Homosexuality and Masculine Signification.' *Popular Music* 20(3): 359–78.

Baker, William, and Kylie Minogue 2003. *Kylie: La La La.* London: Hodder & Stoughton.

Beemyn, Brett (ed.) 1997. *Creating a Place for Ourselves: Lesbian, Gay, and Bisexual Community Histories*. New York: Routledge.

Chisholm, Dianne 2004. *Queer Constellations: Subcultural Space in the Wake of the City*. Minneapolis: University of Minnesota Press.

Cleto, Fabio (ed.) 1999. *Camp: Queer Aesthetics and the Performing Subject, A Reader*. Ann Arbor: University of Michigan Press.

Dubecki, Larissa 2006. 'The Mother of Reinvention.' *The Age* [Online], 4 November. Available at <www.theage.com.au/articles/2006/11/03/1162340051016.html>.

Dyer, Richard 1987. *Heavenly Bodies: Film Stars and Society*. Basingstoke, Hants.: Macmillan.

Farmer, Brett 2000. *Spectacular Passions: Cinema, Fantasy, Gay Male Spectatorships*. Durham, N.C.: Duke University Press.

Grahn, Judy 1984. *Another Mother Tongue: Gay Words, Gay Worlds*. Boston: Beacon Press.

Harris, Mary B. 1998. *School Experiences of Gay and Lesbian Youth: The Invisible Minority*. New York: Haworth Press.

Ives, Brian, and C. Bottomley 2004. 'Kylie Minogue: Disco's Thin White Dame.' *VH1. com.* [Online] Available at: <www.vh1.com/artists/interview/1485255/02232004/minogue_kylie.jhtml>.

Jenkins, Henry. 1992. *Textual Poachers: Television Fans and Participatory Culture*. London and New York: Routledge.

Koestenbaum, Wayne 1993. *The Queen's Throat: Opera, Homosexuality and the Mystery of Desire*. New York: Poseidon.

'Kylie's greatest gay icon ever.' *The Sun*, 6 January 2007, p. 1.

Sender, Katherine 2004. *Business, not Politics: The Making of the Gay Market*. New York: Columbia University Press.

Simon, William 1996. *Postmodern Sexualities*. London and New York: Routledge.

Sullivan, Michael 2006. *Sexual Minorities: Discrimination, Challenges and Development in America*. New York: Haworth Press.

Thornton, Sarah 1996. *Club Cultures: Music, Media and Subcultural Capital*. London: Hanover.

Wallace, Richard 1998. 'Kylie Chameleon.' *The Mirror*, 24 July, pp. 12–14.

White, Patricia 1999. *Uninvited: Classical Hollywood Cinema and Lesbian Representability*. Bloomington, Ind.: Indiana University Press.

## 12. comics as everyday theory: the counterpublic world of taiwanese women fans of japanese homoerotic manga.

Bacon-Smith, Camille 1992. 'Homoerotic Romance.' In *Enterprising Women: Television Fandom and the Creation of Popular Myth*. Philadelphia: University of Pennsylvania Press.

Brooker, Will 2003. 'Slash and Other Stories.' In *Using the Force: Creativity, Community and* Star Wars *Fans*. London: Continuum.

Cicioni, Mirna 1998. 'Male Pair-bonds and Female Desire in Fan Slash Writing.' In C. Harris and A. Alexander (eds) *Theorizing Fandom: Fans, Subculture and Identity*. Cresskill, N.J.: Hampton Press.

Fujimoto, Yukari 1991. Vol. 2 1991 'The Significance of *Shonen-ai*' in Shojo-manga' (unpublished translation by Taeko Yamada); available in Japanese at: <www.mattthorn.com/shoujo_manga/fujimoto.html>.

Green, Shoshanna, Cynthia Jenkins and Henry Jenkins 1998. 'Normal Female Interest in Men Bonking.' In C. Harris and A. Alexander (eds) *Theorizing Fandom: Fans, Subculture and Identity*. Cresskill. N.J.: Hampton Press.

Lent, John A. 1999. 'Local Comic Books and the Curse of Manga in Hong Kong, South Korea and Taiwan.' *Asian Journal of Communication* 9(1): 108–28.

McLelland, Mark 2000. 'The Love Between "Beautiful Boys" in Japanese Women's Comics.' *Journal of Gender Studies* 9(1): 13–25.

—— 2005. 'The World of Yaoi: The Internet, Censorship and the Global "Boys' Love" Fandom.' *Australian Feminist Law Journal* 23: 61–77.

McLelland, Mark, and Seunghyun Yoo 2007. 'The International Yaoi Boys' Love Fandom and the Regulation of Virtual Child Pornography: The Implications of Current Legislation.' *Sexuality, Research and Social Policy* 4(1): 93–104.

Orbaugh, Sharalyn (ed.) 2003. Special issue of *US-Japan Women's Journal* 25 on *manga*.

Penley, Constance 1991a. 'Feminism, Psychoanalysis and the Study of Popular Culture.' In L. Grossberg, C. Nelson and P. Triechler (eds) *Cultural Studies*. New York: Routledge.

—— 1991b. 'Brownian Motion: Women, Tactics and Technology.' In C. Penley and A. Ross (eds) *Technoculture*. Minneapolis: University of Minnesota Press.

—— 1997. *Nasa/Trek: Popular Science and Sex in America*. London: Verso.

Russ, Joanna 1985. 'Pornography by Women, for Women, with Love.' In *Magic Mommas, Trembling Sisters, Puritans and Perverts*. New York: Crossing Press.

Sedgwick, Eve Kosofsky 1990. *Epistemology of the Closet*. Berkeley: University of California Press.

Warner, Michael 2002. *Publics and Counterpublics*. New York: Zone Books.

Welker, James 2006. 'Beautiful, Borrowed, and Bent: Boys' Love as Girls' Love in *Shōjo* Manga.' *Signs: Journal of Women and Culture in Society* 31(3): 841–70.

—— (forthcoming a). 'Drawing Out Lesbians: Blurred Representations of Lesbian Desire in *Shōjo* Manga.' In Subhash Chandra (ed.) *Lesbian Voices, Canada and the World*. New Delhi: Allied Publishing.

—— (forthcoming b). 'Lilies of the Margin: Beautiful Boys and Lesbian Identities.' In Fran Martin, Peter Jackson, Mark McLelland and Audrey Yue (eds) *AsiaPacifiQueer: Rethinking Gender and Sexuality in the Asia-Pacific*. Urbana, Ill.: University of Illinois Press.

Zhong, Ruiping 1999. 'A Study of the Relationality between the Characteristics and Motivations of the Readers of Homosexual Manga'. MA thesis, Chinese Culture University.

## PART 5. empire and globalisation.

Appadurai, Arjun 2001. *Globalization*. Durham N.C.: Duke University Press.

Bauman, Zygmunt 1998. *Globalization: The Human Consequences*. New York: Columbia University Press.

Hall, Stuart 1996. 'When was the 'Post-colonial'? Thinking at the limit.' In *The Post-Colonial Question: Common Skies, Divided Horizons*. New York: Routledge.

Hardt, Michael, and Antonio Negri 2000. *Empire*. Cambridge, Mass.: Harvard University Press.

Marks, Susan 2003. 'Empires Law.' *Indiana Journal of Global Legal Studies* 10(1): 449–66.

Paula Rothenberg (ed.) 2002. *White Privilege: Essential Readings on the Other Side of Racism*. New York: Worth Publishers.

## 13. what's so funny about indian casinos? comparative notes on gambling, white possession and popular culture in australia and the usa.

Ahmed, Sara 2000. *Strange Encounters: Embodied Others in Postcoloniality*. New York and London: Routledge.

Anderson, Brian C. 2005. *South Park Conservatives: The Revolt Against Liberal Media Bias*. Washington, D.C.: Regnery Publishing.

Belanger, Yale D. 2006. *Gambling with the Future: The Evolution of Aboriginal Gaming in Canada*. Saskatoon: Purich Press.

Bonnett, Alastair 2000. *White Identities: Historical and International Perspectives*. Harlow: Prentice Hall.

Chaney, Michael A. 2004. 'Coloring Whiteness and Blackvoice Minstrelsy: Representations of Race and Place in *Static Shock, King of the Hill* and *South Park*.' *Journal of Popular Film and Television* 31(4): 167–75.

Churchill, Ward 1998. *Fantasies of the Master Race: Literature, Cinema and the Colonization of American Indians*. San Francisco: City Lights.

—— 2003. *'Indians "R" Us.' Acts of Rebellion*. New York: Routledge.

Cuillier, Davie, and Susan Dente Ross 2007. 'Gambling with Identity: Self-Representation of American Indians on Official Tribal Websites.' *Howard Journal of Communications* 18: 197–219.

Darian-Smith, Eve 2004. *New Capitalists: Law, Politics, and Identity Surrounding Casino Gaming on Native American Land*. Victoria, USA: Thomson Wadsworth.

Dyer, Richard 1997. *White*. New York and London: Routledge.

Fanon, Franz 1982. *Black Skin: White Masks*. New York: Grove Press.

Frankenberg, Ruth 1993. *White Women, Race Matters: The Social Construction of Whiteness*. Minneapolis, Minn.: University of Minnesota Press.

Goldberg, David Theo 2001. *The Racial State*. Malden, Mass.: Blackwell.

Hage, Ghassan 1998. *White Nation: Fantasies of White Supremacy in a Multicultural Society*. Sydney: Pluto Press.

Hall, Stuart 1997. 'The Spectacle of the Other.' In *Representations and Signifying Practices*. London: Sage.

Harris, Cheryl 1993. 'Whiteness as Property.' *Harvard Law Review* 106(8): 1707.

hooks, bell 1992. *Black Looks: Race and Representation*. Boston: South End Press.

Light, Steven, and Kathryn Rand 2005. *Indian Gaming and Tribal Sovereignty: The Casino Compromise*. University Press of Kansas.

Lipsitz, G. 1998. *The Possessive Investment in Whiteness: How White People Profit from Identity Politics*. Philadelphia: Temple University Press.

Mason, Dale 2000. *Indian Gaming: Tribal Sovereignty and American Politics*. Norman: University of Oklahoma Press.

Moreton-Robinson, Aileen 2000. *Talkin' Up to the White Woman*. Brisbane: University of Queensland Press.

—— 2003. 'I Still Call Australia Home: Indigenous Belonging and Place in a White Postcolonizing Society.' In Sara Ahmed (ed.) *Uprootings/Regroundings: Questions of Home and Migration*. New York: Berg Publishers.

—— 2004. 'The Possessive Logic of Patriarchal White Sovereignty: The High Court and the Yorta Yorta Decision.' *Borderlands eJournal* 3(2): para 5.

—— (ed.) 2007. *Sovereign Subjects: Indigenous Sovereignty Matters*. Sydney: Allen & Unwin.

Nicolacopoulos, Toula, and George Vassiliacopoulos 2004. 'Racism, Foreigner Communities and the Onto-Pathology of White Australian Subjectivity.' In Aileen Moreton-Robinson (ed.) *Whitening Race*. Canberra: Aboriginal Studies Press.

Nicoll, Fiona 2000. 'Indigenous Sovereignty and the Violence of Perspective: A White Woman's Coming-Out Story.' *Australian Feminist Studies* 15(33): 381–2.

Osuri, Goldie, and Subhabrata Bobby Banerjee 2004. 'White Diasporas: Media Representations of September 11 and the Unbearable Whiteness of Being in Australia.' *Social Semiotics* 14(2): 151–71.

Perera, Suvendrini 2004. 'Who Will I Become? The Multiple Formations of Australian Whiteness.' *Australian Critical Race and Whiteness Studies Association Journal* 1(1).

Riggs, Damien 2006. *Priscilla: (White) Queen of the Desert: Queer Rights/Race Privilege*. New York: Peter Berg.

Rothenberg, Paula (ed.) 2002. *White Privilege: Essential Readings on the Other Side of Racism*. New York: Worth Publishers.

Schech, Susanne, and Jane Haggis 2005. 'Terrains of Migrancy and Whiteness: How British Migrants Locate Themselves in Australia.' In Aileen Moreton-Robinson (ed.) *Whitening Race: Critical Contexts and Crucial Conversations*. Canberra: Aboriginal Studies Press.

Roediger, David 1991. *The Wages of Whiteness: Race and the Making of the American Working Class*. London: Verso.

Schlunke, Katrina 2005. *Bluff Rock: Autobiography of a Massacre*. Perth: Curtin University and Freemantle Arts Press.

Stratton, Jon 1998. *Race Daze: Australia in Identity Crisis*. Sydney: Pluto Press.

Ware, Vron, and Les Back 2002. *Out of Whiteness: Color, Politics and Culture*. University of Chicago Press.

## 14. beauty and the bollywood star: stories of skin colour and transnational circulations of whiteness.

Challapalli, Sravanthi 2002. 'All's fair in this market.' *The Hindu Business Line: Internet Edition*. <http://thehindubusinessline.com/catalyst/2002/09/05/stories/2002090500040300>, accessed 31 October 2006.

Gaonkar, Dilip Parameshwar, and Elizabeth Povinelli 2003. 'Technologies of Public Forms: Circulation, Transfiguration, Recognition.' *Public Culture* 15(3): 385–97.

Grewal, Inderpal 2005. *Transnational America: Feminisms, Diasporas, Neoliberalisms.* Durham, N.C. and London: Duke University Press.

Heneghan, Bridget T. 2003. *Whitewashing America: Material Culture and Race in the Antebellum Imagination.* Jackson: University Press of Mississippi.

*Hindustan Times.com* 2005. 'Whitewashing dark fantasies.' <http://in.news.yahoo.com/050430/32/5yd6c.html>, accessed 31 October 2006.

Lal, Priya 2003, 'Bollywood From Beyond: Beauty Queens and Fairness Creams.' *PopMatters.* <www.popmatters.com/columns/lal/031218.shtml>, accessed 31 October 2006.

Lee, Benjamin, and Edward Lipuma, 2002. 'Cultures of Circulation: The Imaginations of Modernity.' *Public Culture* 14(1): 191–213.

Niraj 2004, 'Aishwarya Rai in American TV AD.' 8 July 2004. *Blog: Nirajweb.* <www.nirajweb.net/mt/niraj/archives/002614.html>, accessed 31 October 2006.

Parameswaran, Radhika E. 2004. 'Spectacles of Gender and Globalization: Mapping Miss World's Media Event Space in the News.' *Communication Review* 7: 371–406.

Rai, Aishwarya 2005. 'The Bollywood Blog: Interview—Aishwarya Rai.' *Bollywood.com* <http://bollywood.com/archives/2005/05/interview_aisw_1.html>, accessed 31 October 2006.

Simon, Bob 2005. 'The World's Most Beautiful Woman?' *CBSNews.com.* <www.cbsnews.com/stories/2004/12/29/60minutes/printable663862.shtml>, accessed 31 October 2006.

Smith, Carrie 2006. 'The New Racism and the Changing Beauty Norm.' *Bad Subjects.* <http://bad.eserver.org/issues/2006/76/raceandbeauty.html>, accessed 31 October 2006.

t-hype 2006. 'Racist Lil' Rimi Sen.' *Blog: Beliefs, Blackness & Bollywood.* <http://t-hype.blogspot.com/2006/08/racist-lil-rimi-sen.html>, accessed 31 October 2006.

## 15. visual cultures of orientalism and empire: the abu ghraib images.

Allen, James, Hilton Als, John Lewis and Leon F. Litwack 2005. *Without Sanctuary: Lynching Photography in America.* Santa Fe: Twin Palms.

Alloula, Malek 1986. *The Colonial Harem.* Minneapolis: University of Minnesota Press.

Bacevich, Andrew J. 2006. 'What's an Iraqi Life Worth?' <www.washingtonpost.com/wpdyn/content/article/2006/07/07/AR20060701155.html>, accessed 12 October 2006.

Bersani, Leo 1987. 'Is the Rectum a Grave?' *October* 43: 197–222.

Bryson, Norman 1988. 'The Gaze in the Expanded Field.' In Hal Foster (ed.) *Vision and Visuality.* Seattle: Bay View Press.

Danner, Mark 2005. *Torture and Truth.* London: Granta.

Davis, Angela 2005. *Abolition Democracy.* New York: Seven Stories Press.

Democracy Now! 2007. 'Seymour Hersh Reveals Rumsfeld Misled Congress over Abu Ghraib; How General Taguba was Forced to Retire over his Critical Abu Ghraib Report'. <www.democracynow.org/article.pl?sid=07/06/19/1433252>, accessed 21 June 2007.

Edelman, Lee 1994. *Homographesis*. New York: Routledge.

Greenberg, Karen, and Joshua Dratel (eds) 2005. *The Torture Papers: The Road to Abu Ghraib*. Cambridge University Press.

Maxwell, Anne 1999. *Colonial Photography and Exhibitions*. London: Leicester University Press.

McCoy, Alfred 2006. *A Question of Torture*. New York: Metropolitan Books.

Mercer, Kobena 1996. 'Dialogue.' In Allan Reed (ed.), *The Fact of Blackness*. London and Seattle: Institute of Contemporary Arts, Institute of International Visual Arts and Bay Press.

Neale, Steve 1992. 'Masculinity as Spectacle.' In Mandy Merck (ed.) *The Sexual Subject: A Screen Reader in Sexuality*. New York: Routledge.

Pinar, William 2001. *The Gender of Racial Politics and Violence in America*. New York: Peter Lang.

Puar, Jasbir K. 2005. 'On Torture: Abu Ghraib.' *Radical History Review* 93: 13–38.

Pugliese, Joseph 2006. 'Asymmetries of Terror: Visual Regimes of Racial Profiling and the Shooting of Jean Charles de Menezes in the Context of the War in Iraq.' *Borderlands* 5. <www.borderlandsejournal.adelaide.edu.au/vol5no1_2006.html>, accessed 21 March 2007.

—— 2007a. 'The Event-Trauma of the Carceral Post-Human.' *Social Semiotics* 17: 63–86.

—— 2007b. 'Geocorpographies of Torture.' *Australian Critical Race and Whiteness Studies Journal* 3. <www.acrawsa.org.au/>, accessed 15 January 2008.

Said, Edward 1991. *Orientalism*. London: Penguin.

—— 1994. *Culture and Imperialism*. London: Vintage.

Scarry, Elaine 1987. *The Body in Pain*. New York and Oxford: Oxford University Press.

Semmerling, Tim Jon 2006. *'Evil' Arabs in American Popular Film*. Austin, Texas: University of Texas Press.

Shaheen, Jack G. 2001. *Reel Bad Arabs*. New York: Olive Branch Press.

Yegenoglu, Meyda 1998. *Colonial Fantasies*. Cambridge University Press.

# PART 6. ethnography.

Clifford, James 1988. *The Predicament of Culture: Twentieth Century Ethnography, Literature, Art*. Cambridge, Mass: Harvard University Press.

Clifford, James, and George E. Marcus, 1986. *Writing Culture: The Poetics and Politics of Ethnography: A School of American Research Advanced Seminar*. Berkeley: University of California Press.

Douglas, Mary 1991. *Purity and Danger: An Analysis of the Concepts of Pollution and Taboo*, London and New York: Routledge.

Grimshaw, Anna 2001. *The Ethnographer's Eye: Ways of Seeing in Modern Ethnography*. Cambridge University Press.

Malinowski, Bronislaw 1944. *A Scientific Theory of Culture and Other Essays*. Chapel Hill, N.C.: University of California Press.

Levi-Strauss, Claude 1944. *The Savage Mind*. London: Weidenfield & Nicolson.

Rouch, Jean 1955. *Les Maîtres Fous* (The Mad Masters). Film.

Stoller, Paul 1997. *Sensuous Scholarship*. Philadelphia: University of Pennsylvania.

Taussig, Michael 1986. *Shamanism, Colonialism and the Wild Man: A Study in Terror and Healing*. University of Chicago Press.

## 16. from other to self and back: the curious history of ethnography.

Bourdieu, Pierre 1977. *Outline of a Theory of Practice*. Cambridge University Press.

Geertz, Clifford 1973. *The Interpretation of Cultures*. London: Fontana.

Mead, Margaret 1943. *Coming of Age in Samoa*. Harmondsworth: Penguin.

Said, Edward 1978. *Orientalism*. Harmondsworth: Penguin.

## 17. talk table: doing-ethnography in the kitchen.

Abarca, Meredith E. 2006. *Voices in the Kitchen: Views of Food and the World from Working-Class Mexican and Mexican American Woman*. College Station, Texas: Texas A & M University Press.

Belk, Russell W. 1996. 'Studies in the New Consumer Behaviour.' In Daniel Miller (ed.) *Acknowledging Consumption: A Review of New Studies*. London: Routledge.

Bourdieu, Pierre 1984. *Distinction: A Social Critique of the Judgment of Taste*. London: Routledge & Kegan Paul.

Cook, Ian, Phil Crang and Mark Thorpe 1999. 'Eating into Britishness: Multicultural Imaginaries and the Identity Politics of Food.' In Sasha Roseneil and Julie Seymour (eds) *Practising Identities: Power and Resistance*. Basingstoke, Hants.: Macmillan.

de Certeau, Michel 1984. *The Practice of Everyday Life*. Berkeley: University of California Press, pp. xix–xx.

Derrida, Jacques 2001. *On Cosmopolitanism and Forgiveness*. London: Routledge.

Duruz, Jean 2001. 'Home Cooking, Nostalgia and the Purchase of Tradition.' *Traditional Dwellings and Settlements Review* 12(2): 23–4.

—— 2004. 'Haunted Kitchens: Cooking and Remembering', *Gastronomica* 4(1): 63–5.

Giard, Luce 1998a. 'The Nourishing Arts'. In Michel de Certeau, Luce Giard and Pierre Mayol, *The Practice of Everyday Life* vol. 2. Minneapolis, Minn.: University of Minnesota Press.

—— 1998b. '"When it Comes Down to it, Cooking Worries Me …"' In de Certeau et al., *The Practice of Everyday Life* vol. 2, pp. 225–6.

—— 1998c. 'Plat du Jour.' In de Certeau et al., *The Practice of Everyday Life* vol. 2, p. 183.

Heldke, Lisa 2003. *Exotic Appetites: Ruminations of a Food Adventurer*. New York: Routledge.

Highmore, Ben 2002. *Everyday Life and Cultural Theory: An Introduction*. London: Routledge.

hooks, bell 1992. 'Eating the Other.' In bell hooks (ed.) *Black Looks: Race and Representation*. Boston: South End.

Koval, Ramona 2001. *Jewish Cooking and Jewish Cooks*. Sydney: New Holland.

Lawson, Nigella 2000. *How to be a Domestic Goddess: Baking and the Art of Comfort Cooking*. London: Chatto & Windus.

Levinas, Emmanuel 1982. *Ethics and Infinity*. Pittsburgh: Duquesne University Press.

Lupton, Deborah 1996. *Food, the Body and the Self*. London: Sage.

Probyn, Elspeth 2000. *Carnal Appetites: FoodSexIdentities*. London: Routledge.

Reiden Juliet (ed.) 2000. *Time Out: Complete Sydney Guide*. Sydney: Time Out Australia.

Rista, Christine (ed.) 2000. *The Essential Guide to London's Best Food Shops*. London: New Holland.

Santich, Barbara 1996. *Looking for Flavour*. Adelaide: Wakefield Press.

Seton, Nora 2000. *The Kitchen Congregation*. London: Weidenfeld & Nicolson.

Sutton, David E. 2001. *Remembrance of Repasts: An Anthropology of Food and Memory*. Oxford: Berg.

Symons, Michael 1998. *The Pudding that Took a Thousand Cooks: The Story of Cooking in Civilisation and Daily Life*. Melbourne: Penguin.

Winterson, Jeanette 1988. *The Passion*. London: Penguin.

## 18. ethnografts.

Clifford, James 1986. 'On Ethnographic Allegory.' In *Writing Culture: The Poetics and Politics of Ethnography*. Berkeley: University of California Press.

Eipper, Chris 1998. 'Anthropology and Cultural Studies: Difference, Ethnography and Theory.' *Australian Journal of Anthropology* 9(3): 310–26.

Geyer-Ryan, Helga 1994. 'Counterfactual Artefacts: Walter Benjamin's Philosophy of History.' In *Fables of Desire*. Cambridge: Polity Press, pp. 11–25.

Kennedy, Barbara 2002. *Deleuze and Cinema: The Aesthetics of Sensation*. New York: Routledge.

McEachern, Charmaine 1998. 'A Mutual Interest? Ethnography in Anthropology and Cultural Studies.' *Australian Journal of Anthroplogy* 9(3): 251–64.

Muecke, Stephen 1992. *Textual Spaces: Aboriginality and Cultural Studies*. Sydney: University of NSW Press.

Sheridan, Susan (ed.) 1988. *Grafts: Feminist Cultural Criticism*. New York: Verso.

Wainburranga, Paddy, and Chips Mackinolty 1982. 'Too Many Captain Cooks.' *Aboriginal Australians and Christian Missions: Ethnographic and Historical Studies*, Special Studies in Religion, No. 6.

## PART 7. text, sensation and writing.

Barthes, Roland 1968. 'Death of the Author.' *In Image, Music, Text*. New York: Hill & Wang.

Threadgold, Terry 2005. 'Text.' In Tony Bennett, Lawrence Grossberg and Meaghan Morris (eds) *New Key Words: A Revised Vocabulary of Culture and Society*. Oxford: Blackwell.

# 19. metaphors of voice quality.

Aristotle 1954. *The Rhetoric and the Poetics*. New York: Random House.

Bacall, L. 1979. *Lauren Bacall By Myself*. London: Jonathan Cape.

Barnouw, E. 1968. *The Golden Web: A History of Broadcasting in the United States 1933–1953*. New York: Oxford University Press.

Barthes, R. 1973. *Mythologies*. London: Paladin.

—— 1977. *Image-Music-Text*. London: Fontana.

Cardiff. D. 1981. 'The Serious and the Popular: Aspects of the Evolution of Style in the Radio Talk 1928–1939.' *Media, Culture and Society* 2(1): 29–47.

Chion, M. 1999. *The Voice in Cinema*. New York: Columbia University Press.

Frith, S. 1988. *Music for Pleasure*. Cambridge: Polity.

Hall, E.T. 1964. 'Silent Assumptions in Social Communication.' In D. McK. Rioch and E.A. Weinstein (eds) *Disorders of Communication, Research Publications* 42: 41–55. Association for Research in Nervous and Mental Diseases.

—— 1966. *The Hidden Dimension*. New York: Doubleday.

Hawkes, T. 1972. *Metaphor*. London: Methuen.

Herman, L. 1952. *A Practical Manual for Screen Playwriting for Theater and Television Films*. New York: New American Library.

Lakoff, G., and M. Johnson 1980. *Metaphors We Live By*. University of Chicago Press.

Laver, J. 1980. *The Phonetic Description of Voice Quality*. Cambridge University Press.

Leitner, G. 1980. 'BBC English and Deutsche Rundfunksprache: A Comparative and Historical Analysis of the Language on the Radio.' *International Journal of the Sociology of Language* 26: 75–100.

Lévi-Strauss, C. 1962. *Structural Anthropology*. New York: Basic Books.

Lomax, A. 1968. *Folk Song Style and Culture*. New Brunswick, N.J.: Transaction Books.

Poynton, C. 1996. 'Giving Voice.' In E. McWilliam and P. Taylor (eds) *Pedagogy, Technology and the Body*. New York: Peter Lang.

Shepherd, J. 1991. *Music as Social Text*. Cambridge: Polity.

Silverman, K. 1988. *The Acoustic Mirror: The Female Voice in Psychoanalysis and Cinema*. Bloomington, Ind.: Indiana University Press.

Sontag, S. 1979. *Illness as Metaphor*. London: Allen Lane.

Van Leeuwen, T. 1983. 'Impartial Speech: Observations on the Intonation of Radio Announcers.' *Australian Journal of Cultural Studies* 2(1): 84–98.

—— 1999. *Speech, Music, Sound*. London: Macmillan.

Whorf, Benjamin Lee 1956/1998. *Language, Thought And Reality: Selected Writings of Benjamin Lee Whorf*, ed. with an introduction by John B. Carroll, foreword by Stuart Chase. Cambridge, Mass.: MIT Press.

Williams-Jones, P. 1975. 'Afro-American Gospel Music: A Crystallization of the Black Aesthetic.' *Ethnomusicology* September 1975: 373–85.

## 20. 'botanizing on the asphalt': benjamin and practices of flanerie.

Baudelaire, Charles 1971. *Artificial Paradise: On Hashish and Wine as Means of Expanding Individuality*, trans. Ellen Fox. New York: Herder & Herder.

Benjamin, Walter 1986. *Moscow Diary*, trans. Richard Sieburth. London and Cambridge, Mass.: Harvard University Press.

—— 1997a. 'One-Way Street.' In *One-Way Street and Other Writings*, trans. Edmund Jephcott and Kingsley Shorter. London and New York: Verso.

—— 1997b. 'The Paris of the Second Empire in Baudelaire.' In *Charles Baudelaire: A Lyric Poet in the Era of High Capitalism*, trans. Harry Zohn. London and New York: Verso.

—— 1997c. 'Naples.' In *One-Way Street and Other Writings*.

—— 1997d. 'Moscow.' In *One-Way Street and Other Writings*.

—— 1997e. 'Marseille.' In *One-Way Street and Other Writings*.

—— 1999a. 'The Return of the Flaneur.' In Michael W. Jennings, Howard Eiland and Gary Smith (eds) *Walter Benjamin: Selected Writings* vol. 2. Cambridge, Mass. and London: Harvard University Press.

—— 1999b. *The Arcades Project*, trans. Howard Eiland and Kevin McLaughlin. Cambridge, Mass. and London: Harvard University Press.

—— 1999c. 'Myslovice-Braunschweig-Marseill.' In Jennings et al., *Walter Benjamin: Selected Writings* vol. 2.

—— 1999d. 'Hashish in Marseille.' In Jennings et al., *Walter Benjamin: Selected Writings* vol. 2.

—— 1999e. 'Hashish, Beginning of March 1930.' In Jennings et al., *Walter Benjamin: Selected Writings* vol. 2.

—— 1999f. 'Reply to Oscar A. H. Schmitz.' In Jennings et al., *Walter Benjamin: Selected Writings* vol. 2.

—— 1999g. 'News about Flowers.' In Jennings et al., *Walter Benjamin: Selected Writings* vol. 2.

—— 1999h. 'A Berlin Chronicle.' In Jennings et al., *Walter Benjamin: Selected Writings* vol. 2.

—— 2003. 'The Work of Art in the Age of its Technological Reproducibility', 3rd edn. In Howard Eiland and Michael W. Jennings (eds) *Walter Benjamin: Selected Writings* vol. 4. Cambridge, Mass. and London: Harvard University Press.

Buck-Morss, Susan 1986. 'The Flaneur, the Sandwichman and the Whore: The Politics of Loitering.' *New German Critique* 39, Fall.

—— 1993. 'Aesthetics and Anaesthetics: Walter Benjamin's Artwork Essay Reconsidered.' *New Formations* 20, Summer.

Friedberg, Anne 1993. *Window Shopping: Cinema and the Postmodern*. University of California Press: Berkeley.

Kracauer, Siegfried 1997. *Theory of Film: The Redemption of Physical Reality*. New Jersey: Princeton University Press.

Schweppenhäuser, Hermann 1995. 'Propaedeutics of Profane Illumination', trans. Lloyd Spencer, Stephan Jost and Gary Smith. In Gary Smith (ed.) *On Walter Benjamin: Critical Essays and Recollections*. London and Cambridge, Mass.: MIT Press.

Simmel, Georg 1997. 'The Metropolis and Mental Life.' In David Frisby and Mike Featherstone (eds) *Simmel on Culture: Selected Writings*. London, Thousand Oaks, Calif., and New Delhi: Sage.

Szondi, Peter 1995. 'Walter Benjamin's City Portraits.' In Gary Smith (ed.) *On Walter Benjamin: Critical Essays and Recollections*. London and Cambridge, Mass.: MIT Press.

Taylor, Frederick Winslow 1967. *The Principles of Scientific Management*. New York: Norton.

## 21. momentum.

Byrne, Denis 2007. *Surface Collection: Archaeological Travels in Southeast Asia*. Lanham, Pa.: AltaMira Press.

DeLillo, Don 1986. *White Noise*. New York: Penguin Books.

Didion, Joan 1993. *The White Album*. London: Flamingo.

Gaita, Raimond 2004. *Breach of Trust: Truth, Morality and Politics*. Quarterly Essay 16, Melbourne: Black Inc.

Latour, Bruno 2004. *The Politics of Nature: How to Bring the Sciences into Democracy*, trans. Catherine Porter. Cambridge, Mass.: Harvard University Press.

Le Guin, Ursula K. 1990. *Dancing at the Edge of the World: Thoughts on Words, Women, Places*. New York: Perennial Library.

Lingis, Alphonso 1994. *Abuses*. Berkeley: University of California Press.

—— 2002. 'Typhoons.' *Cultural Studies Review* 8(1): 99.

Morris, Meaghan 1992. *Ecstasy and Economics: American Essays for John Forbes*. Sydney: Empress Publishing.

Musil, Robert 1995. *The Man without Qualities*, trans. Sophie Wilkins. London: Picador.

Ondaatje, Michael 1996. *Coming through Slaughter*. New York: Vintage International.

Pynchon, Thomas 2000. *The Crying of Lot 49*. London: Vintage.

Rohdie, Sam 2001. *Promised Lands: Cinema, Geography, Modernism*. London: BFI.

Sebald W.G. 1996. *The Emigrants*, trans. Michael Hulse. London: Vintage.

Stewart, Kathleen 1996. *A Space on the Side of the Road: Cultural Poetics in an 'Other' America*. Princeton University Press.

Taussig, Michael 1997. *The Magic of the State*. New York: Routledge.

—— 2006. *Walter Benjamin's Grave*. Chicago University Press.

# index.

Printed in Australia
17 Aug 2015
426815